RECORD OF
GRANCREST
WAR

7

Original Story by **Ryo Mizuno**
Story & Art by **Makoto Yotsuba**
Character Design by **Miyuu**

PREVIOUSLY...

Story

Previously...

In a world where chaos is the most powerful force, the people are terrified of the threat it poses. They live under the protection of lords, who are the only ones capable of wielding crests that can quell chaos.

However, the lords use their crests to fight each other in petty battles over territory, and the continent has been plunged into a war-torn era.

Theo, a noble-minded wandering lord, and Siluca Meletes, a talented mage, declare allegiance to the Fantasia Union and throw themselves into battle against the Alliance. With the help of many comrades and the aid of Count Villar of Altirk, they succeed in defeating the Waldlind Army, rumored to be the best on the continent.

The witch Jana, who controls Waldlind's Heavy Arms Knights, uses them to hunt down the werewolves.

Key

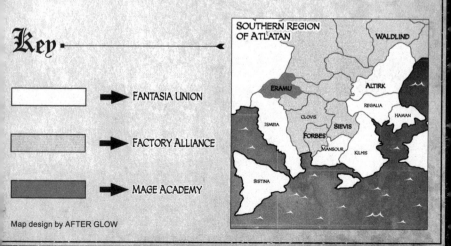

FANTASIA UNION

FACTORY ALLIANCE

MAGE ACADEMY

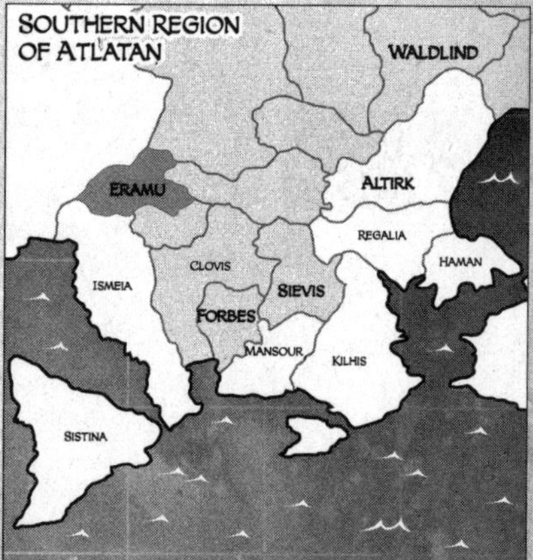

SOUTHERN REGION OF ATLATAN
WALDLIND
ERAMU
ALTIRK
REGALIA
HAMAN
CLOVIS
ISMEIA
SIEVIS
FORBES
MANSOUR
KILHIS
SISTINA

Map design by AFTER GLOW

Characters

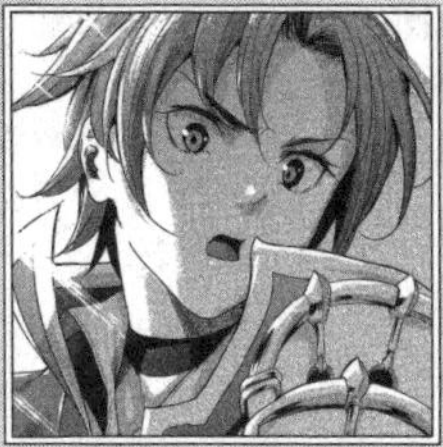

Theo

A wandering lord who hopes one day to free his homeland from tyranny. He enters into a contract with Siluca. He cares about his people and has great instincts.

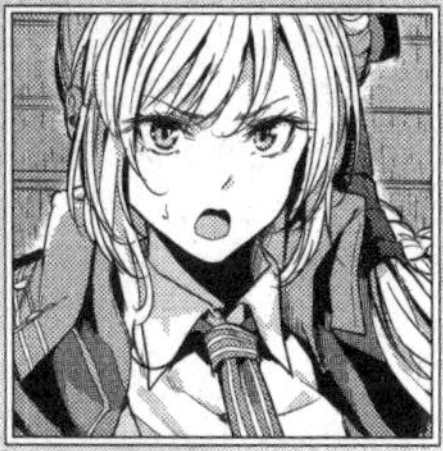

Siluca Meletes

A mage thought at school to be a genius. She believes that Theo could be an ideal lord and decides to serve him.

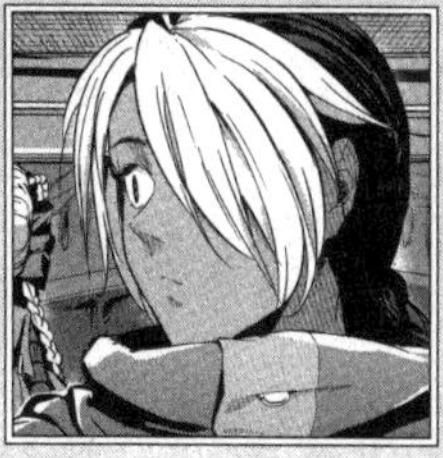

Irvin

A brilliant Artist who used to serve an Archduke. Seeing potential in Siluca due to her ability to "treat him roughly," he chooses to serve her.

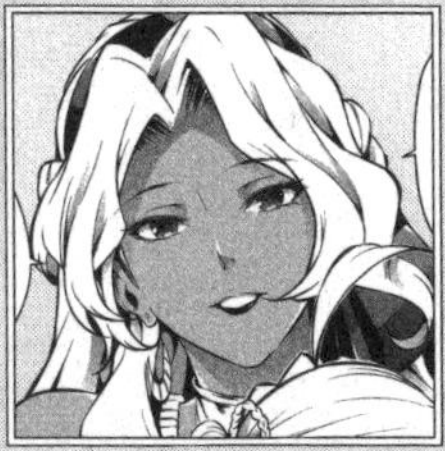

Clara

Queen of the werewolves. She is usually a kind mother, but is quick to rage and release her inner werewolf when a family member is hurt.

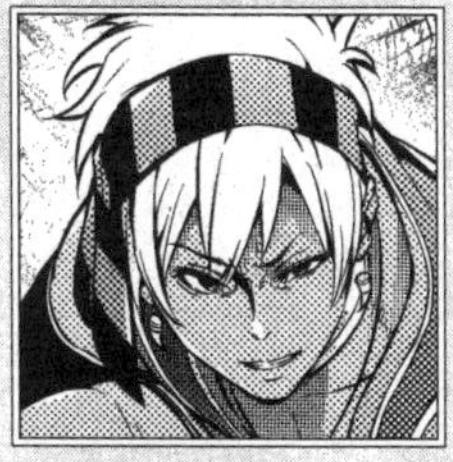

Aeon

Clara's son. He was wounded but managed to return with the news that Waldlind is hunting the werewolves.

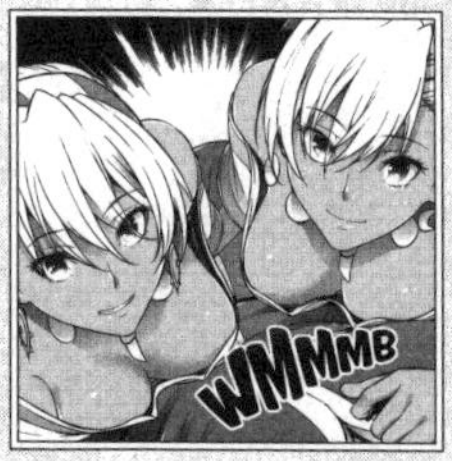
WMMMB

Emma & Luna

Clara's twin daughters. They are still young and are naive enough to ask Theo about "making babies with them."

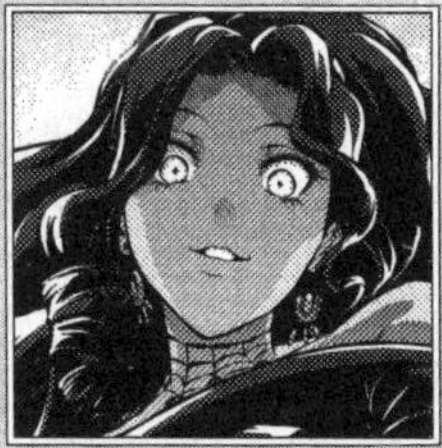

Jana

A descendant of the Dark Witch who has immense powers. She is hunting the werewolves and gathering their chaos cores for mysterious reasons.

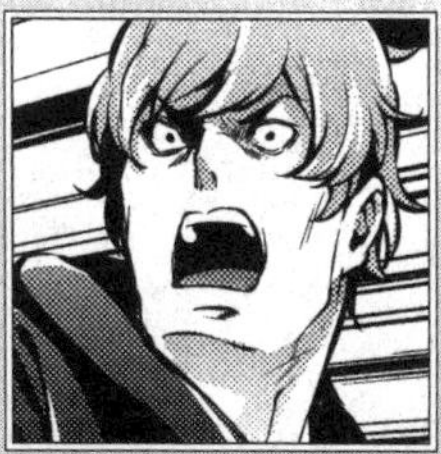

Elmer Zeals

An important member of the Heavy Arms Knights of Waldlind. He is currently hunting werewolves with his men.

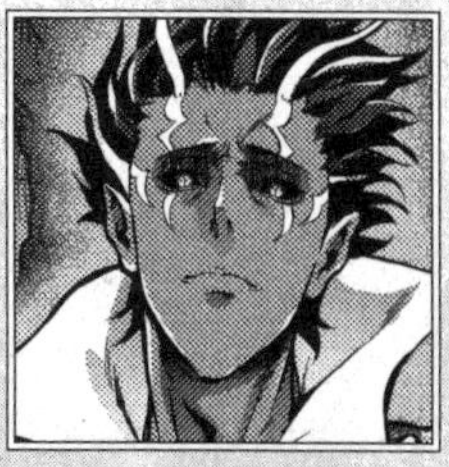

Dimitrie

The Lord of the Forest of Eternal Darkness and the King of the Vampires. He is cooperating with Jana in order to awaken Adele.

Contents

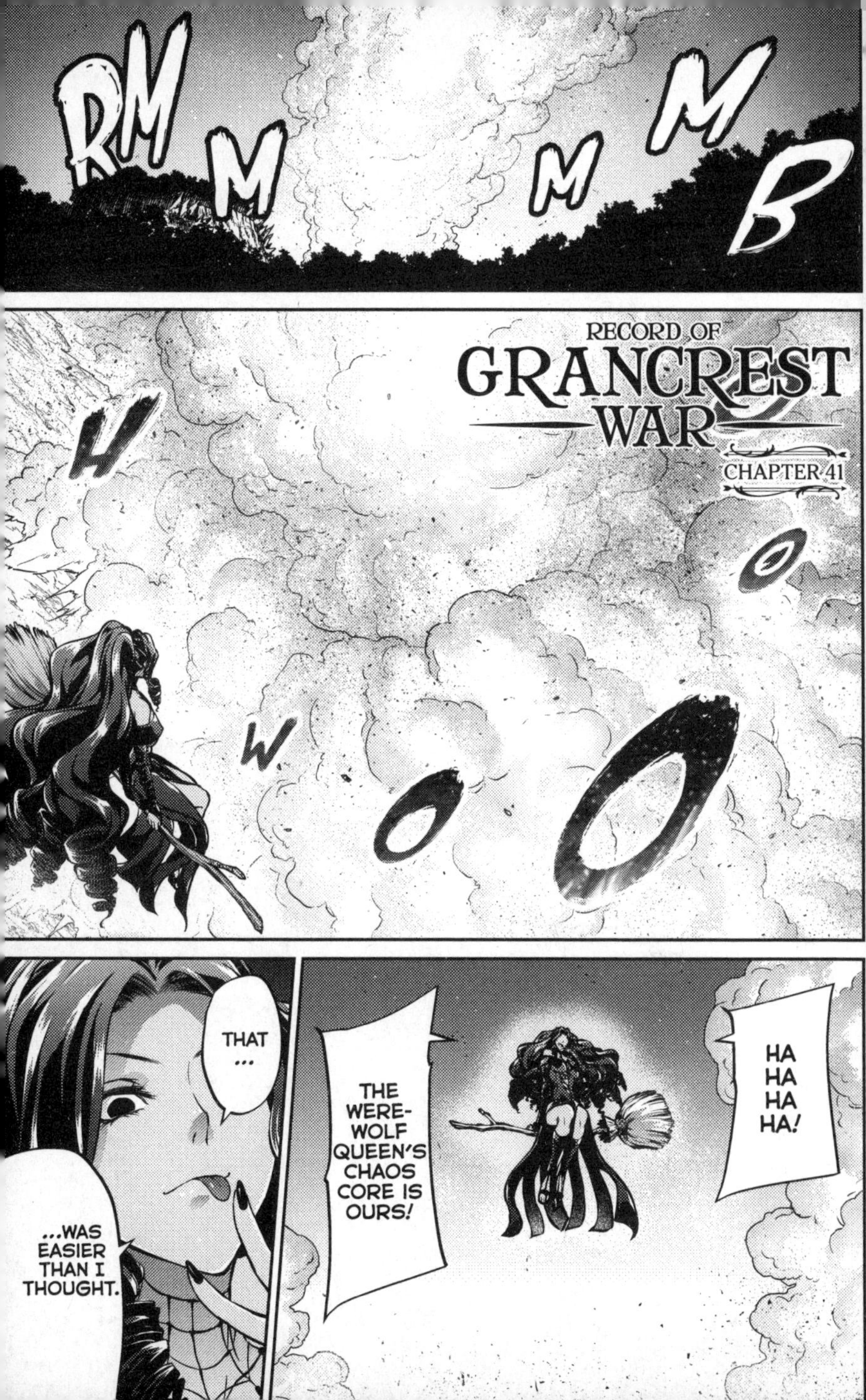

RMMMMB
RECORD OF GRANCREST WAR
CHAPTER 41
HWOOO
HA HA HA HA!
THE WERE-WOLF QUEEN'S CHAOS CORE IS OURS!
THAT...
...WAS EASIER THAN I THOUGHT.

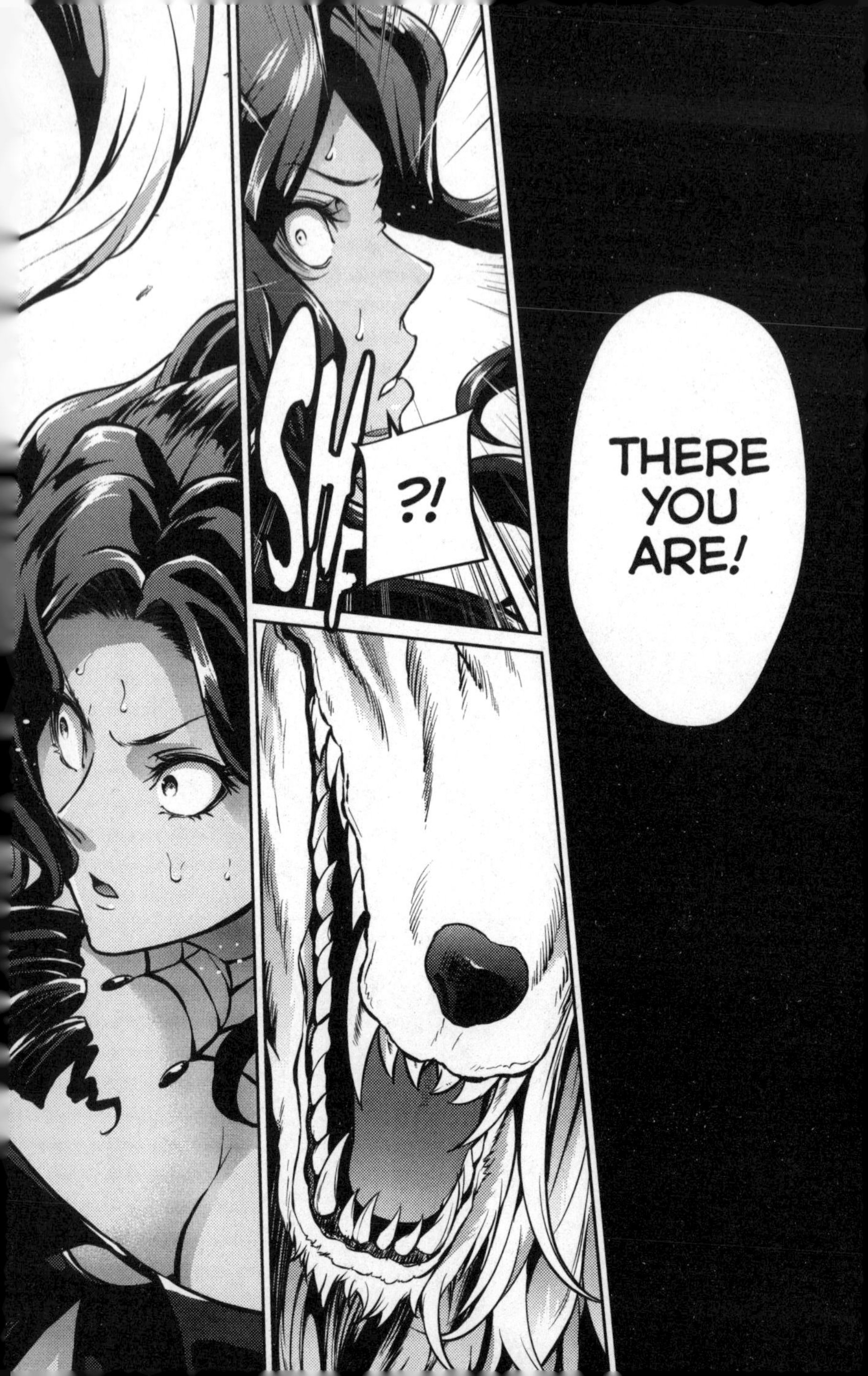
THERE YOU ARE!
?!

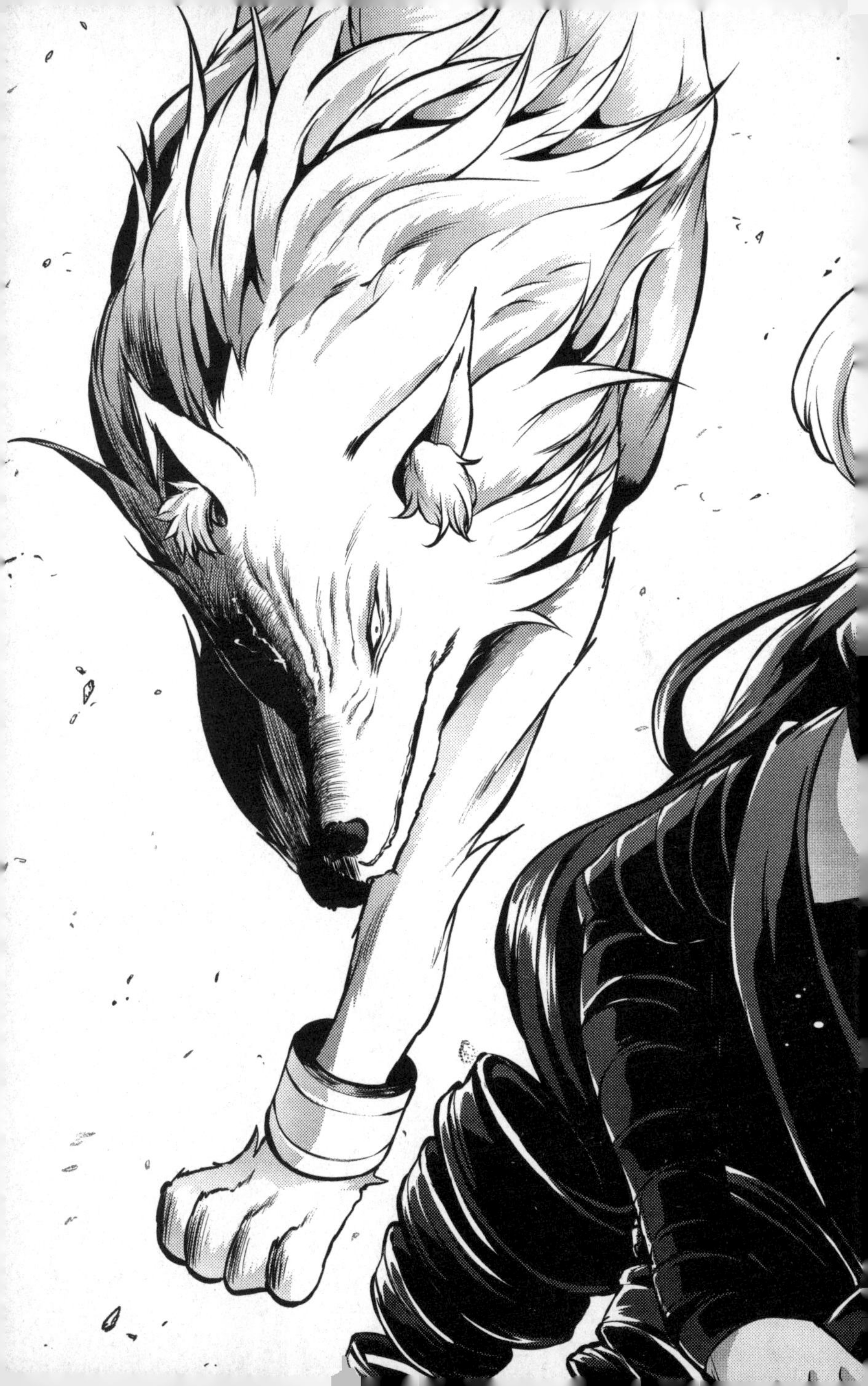

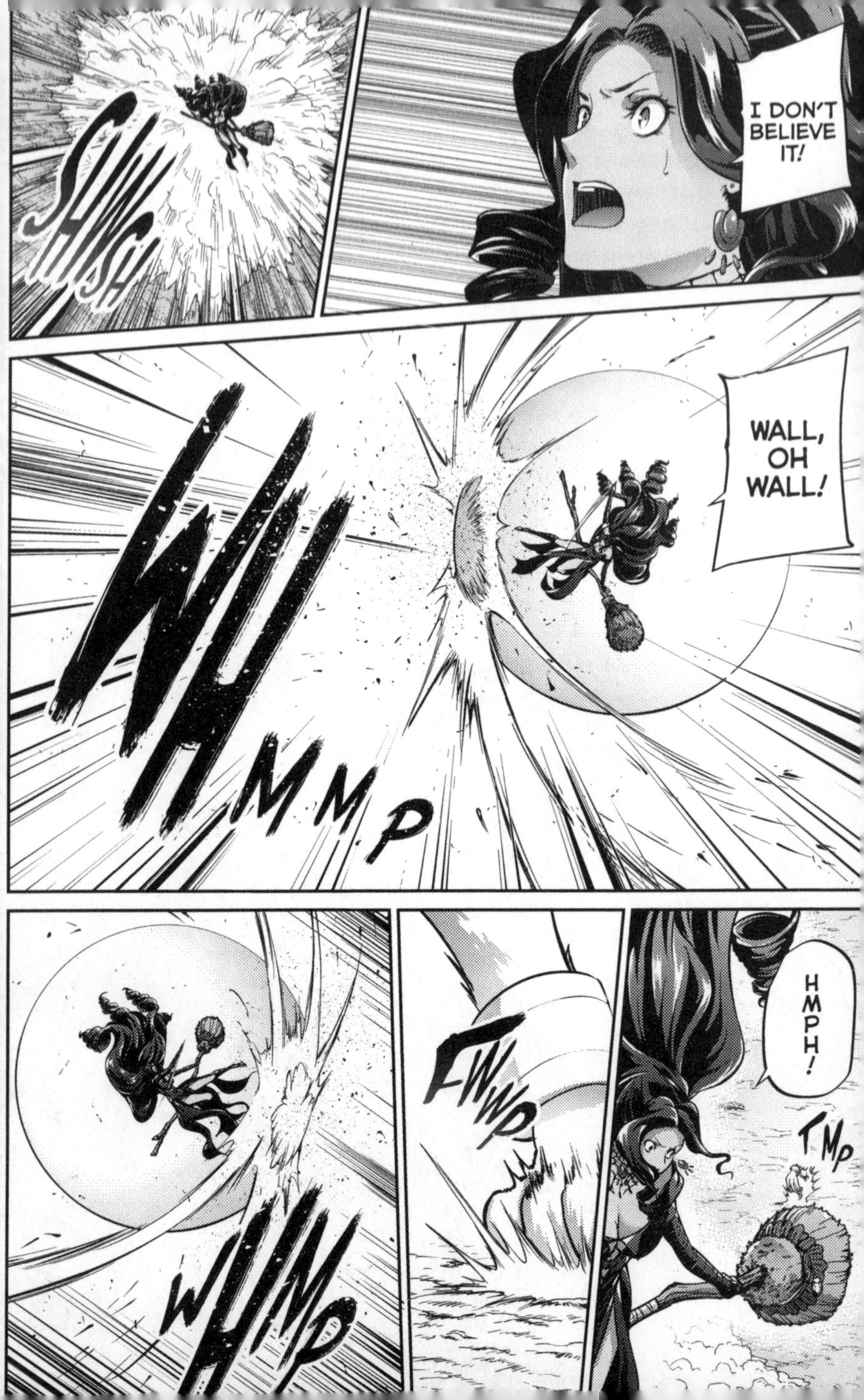
I DON'T BELIEVE IT!
SHASH
WALL, OH WALL!
WHMMMP
HMPH!
TMP
FWMP
WHMP

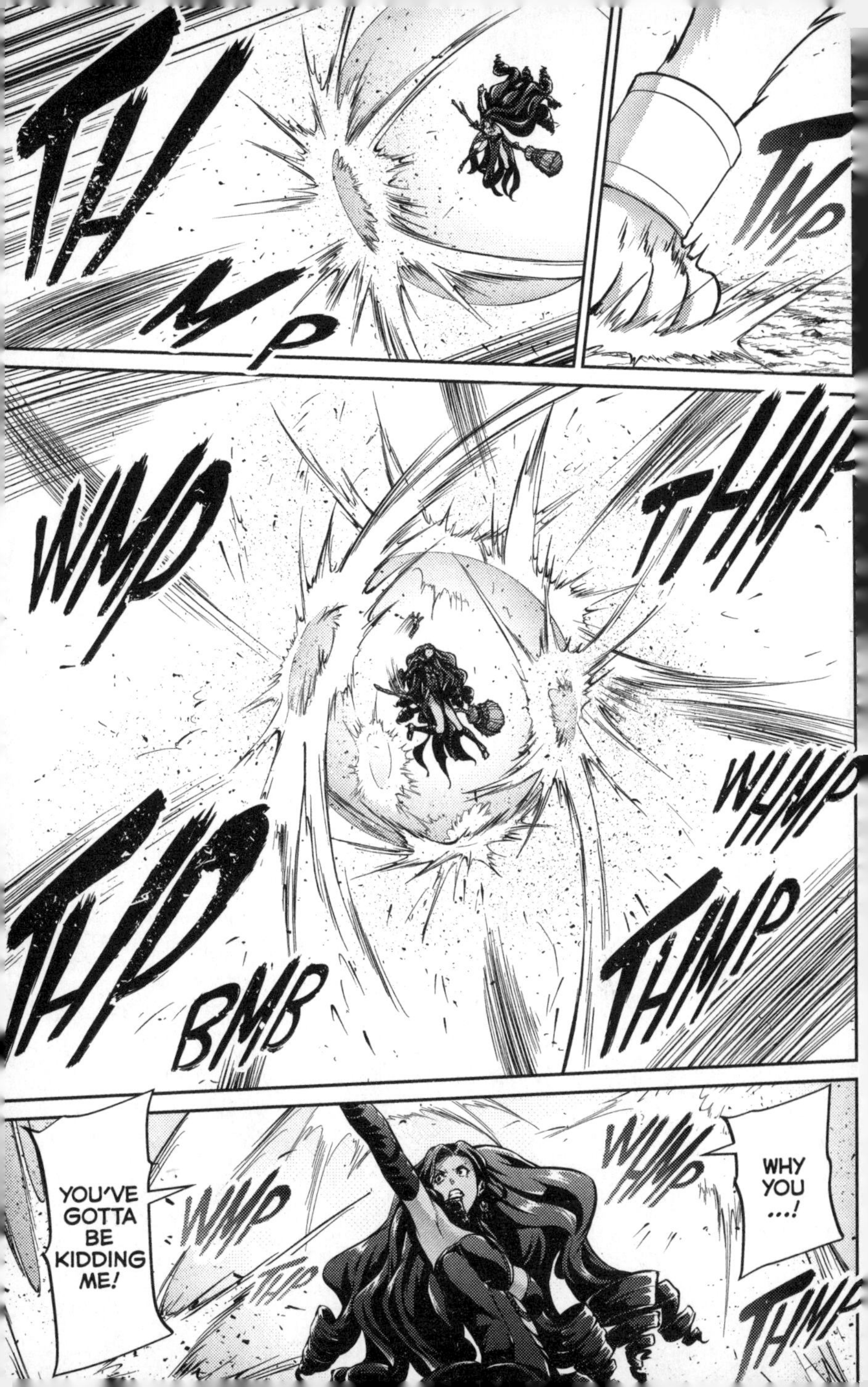
THMP
THUMP
THMP
WMP
WHMP
THMP
THP
BMB
WHY YOU ...!
WHMP
THMP
WMP
THP
YOU'VE GOTTA BE KIDDING ME!

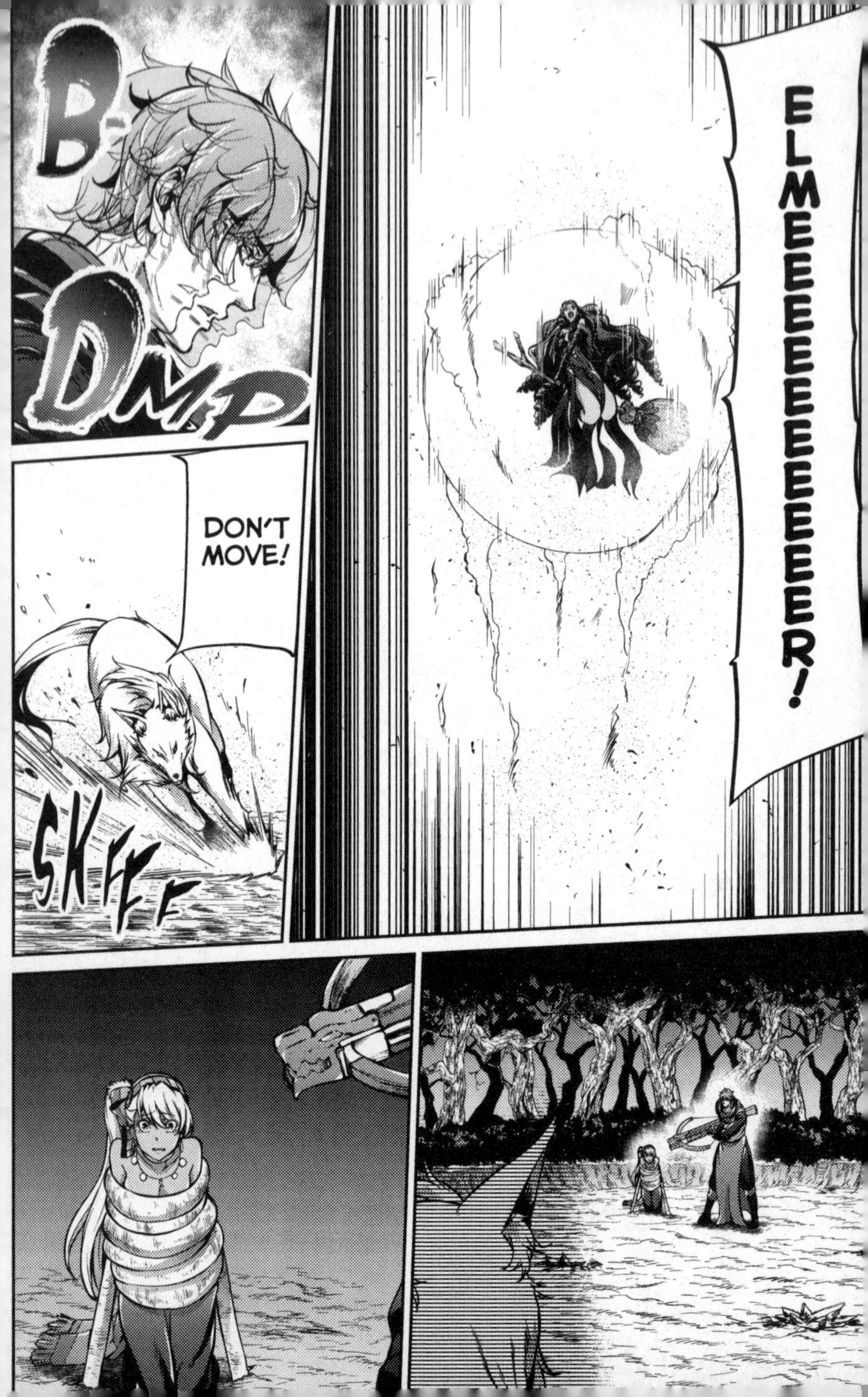
ELMEEEEEEEEEEEER!
B-DMP
DON'T MOVE!
SKRRR

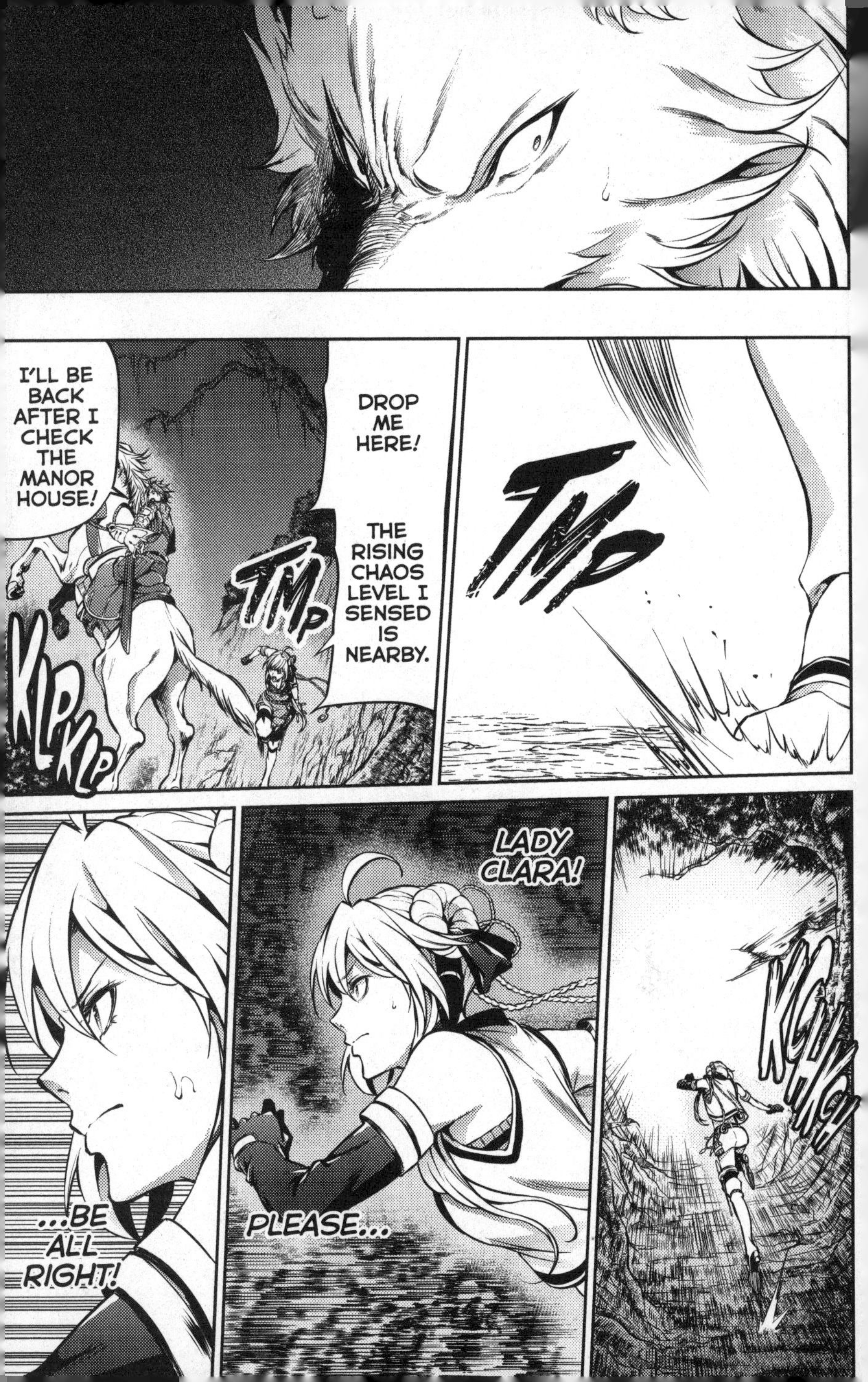
TMP
DROP ME HERE!
THE RISING CHAOS LEVEL I SENSED IS NEARBY.
I'LL BE BACK AFTER I CHECK THE MANOR HOUSE!
TMP
KLIP KLIP
KCHKCH!
LADY CLARA!
PLEASE...
...BE ALL RIGHT!

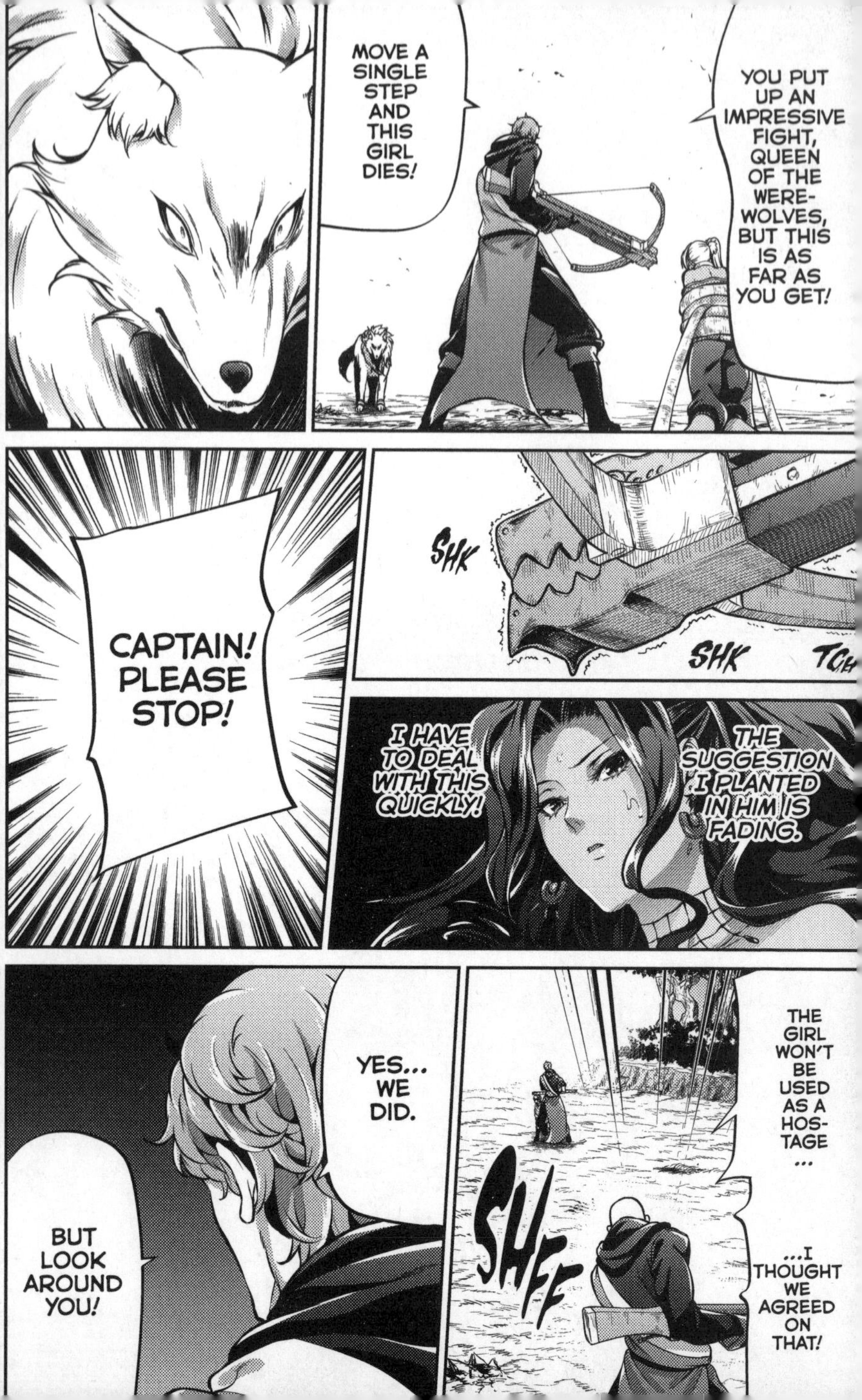
YOU PUT UP AN IMPRESSIVE FIGHT, QUEEN OF THE WERE-WOLVES, BUT THIS IS AS FAR AS YOU GET!
MOVE A SINGLE STEP AND THIS GIRL DIES!
SHK
SHK
TCH
THE SUGGESTION I PLANTED IN HIM IS FADING.
I HAVE TO DEAL WITH THIS QUICKLY!
CAPTAIN! PLEASE STOP!
THE GIRL WON'T BE USED AS A HOS-TAGE...
...I THOUGHT WE AGREED ON THAT!
SHFF
YES... WE DID.
BUT LOOK AROUND YOU!

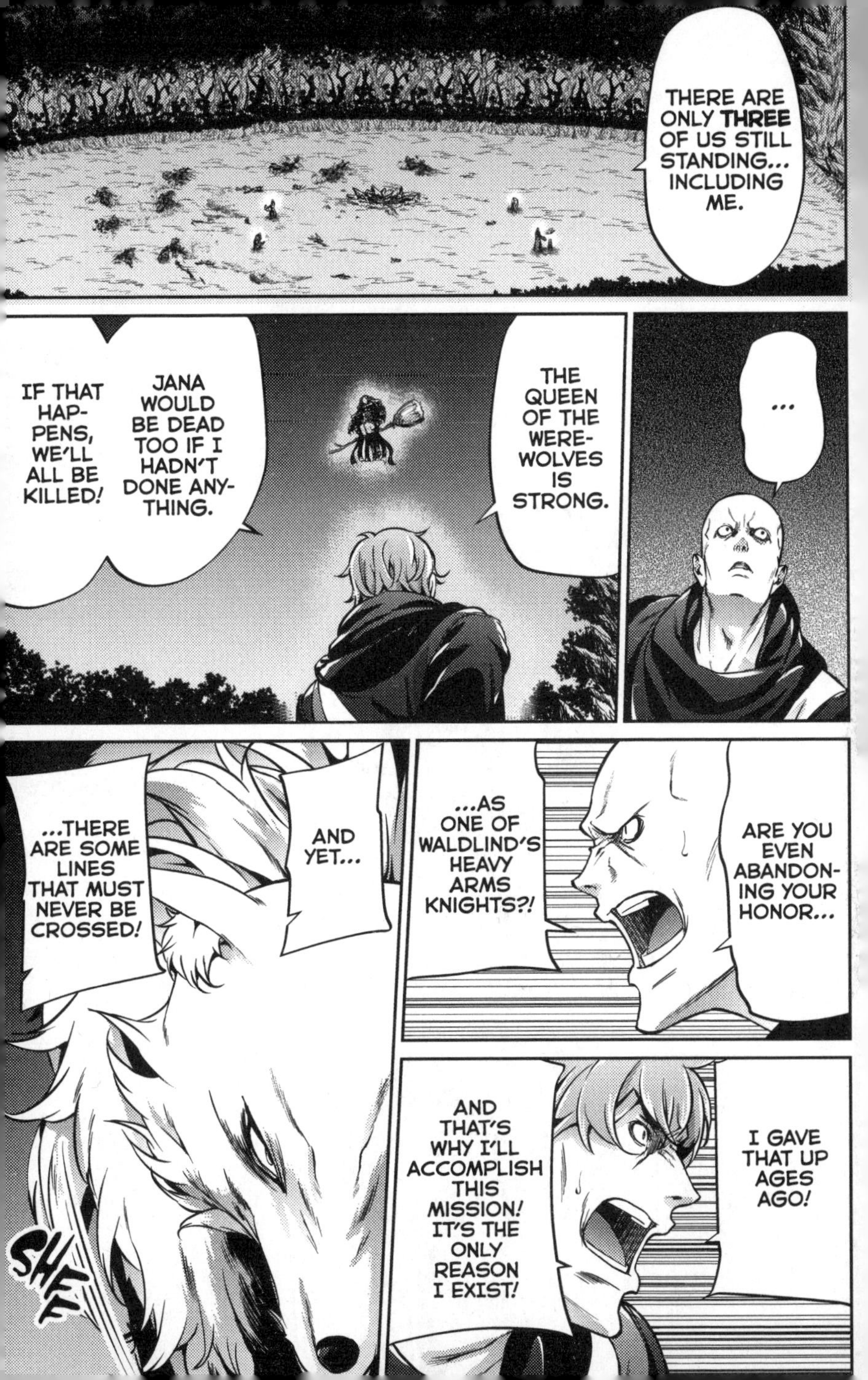
THERE ARE ONLY THREE OF US STILL STANDING... INCLUDING ME.
...
THE QUEEN OF THE WERE-WOLVES IS STRONG.
JANA WOULD BE DEAD TOO IF I HADN'T DONE ANY-THING.
IF THAT HAP-PENS, WE'LL ALL BE KILLED!
ARE YOU EVEN ABANDON-ING YOUR HONOR...
...AS ONE OF WALDLIND'S HEAVY ARMS KNIGHTS?!
I GAVE THAT UP AGES AGO!
AND THAT'S WHY I'LL ACCOMPLISH THIS MISSION! IT'S THE ONLY REASON I EXIST!
AND YET...
...THERE ARE SOME LINES THAT MUST NEVER BE CROSSED!
SHF

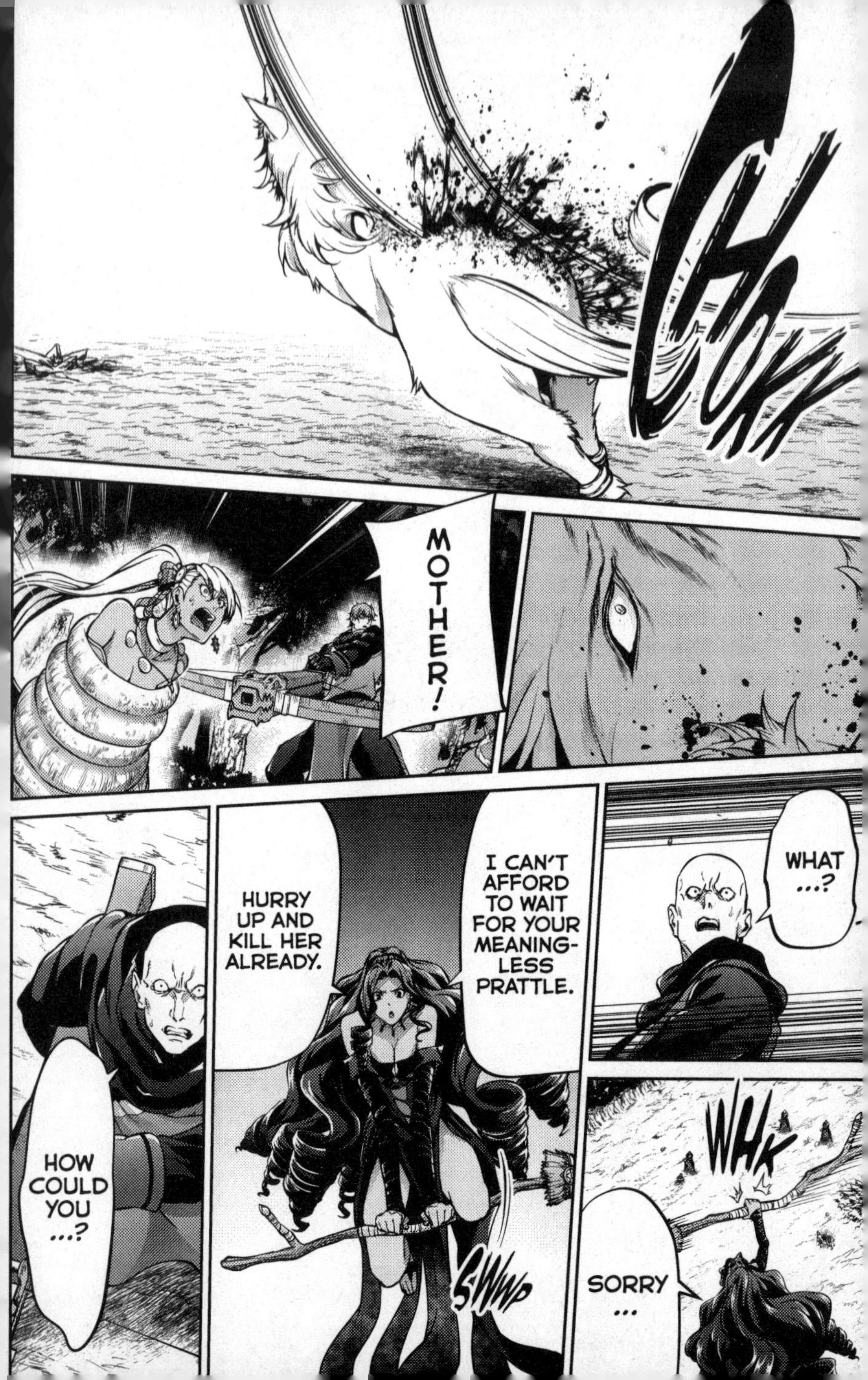
CHOMK
MOTHER!
WHAT ...?
WHK
SORRY ...
I CAN'T AFFORD TO WAIT FOR YOUR MEANING-LESS PRATTLE.
HURRY UP AND KILL HER ALREADY.
SWWP
HOW COULD YOU ...?

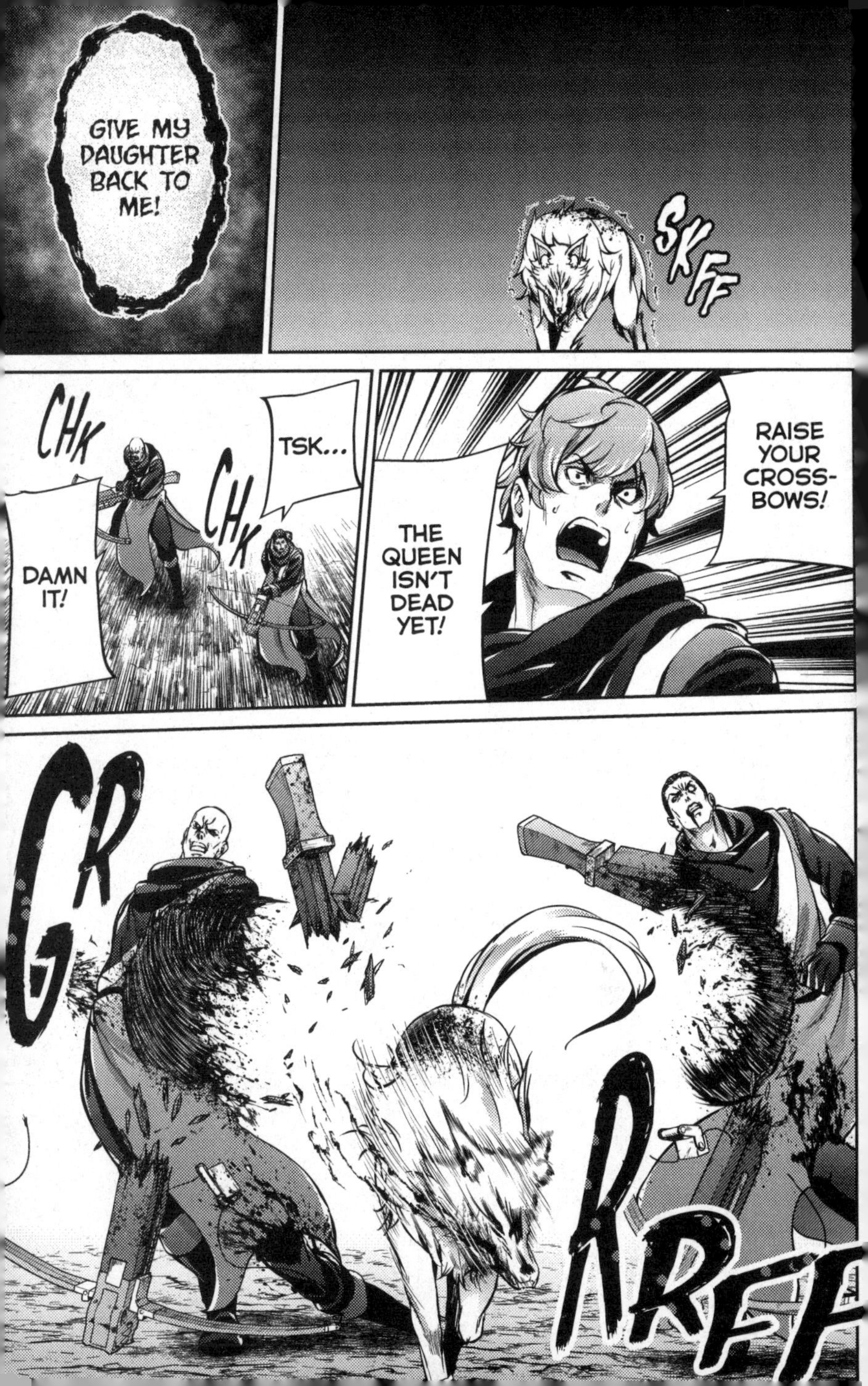
SKFF
GIVE MY DAUGHTER BACK TO ME!
RAISE YOUR CROSS-BOWS!
THE QUEEN ISN'T DEAD YET!
TSK...
CHK
CHK
DAMN IT!
GR
RRFF

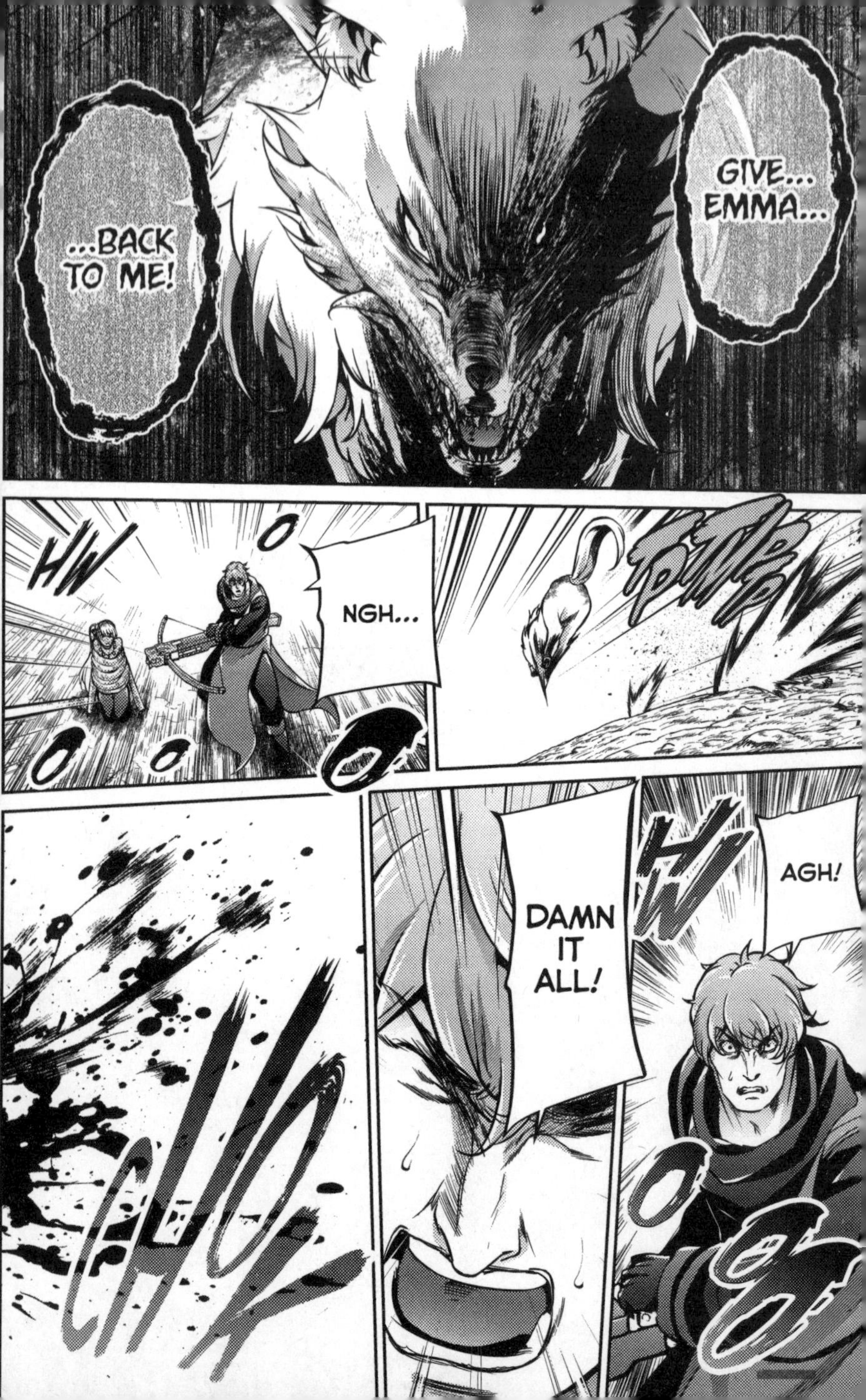
GIVE... EMMA...
...BACK TO ME!
NGH...
AGH!
DAMN IT ALL!

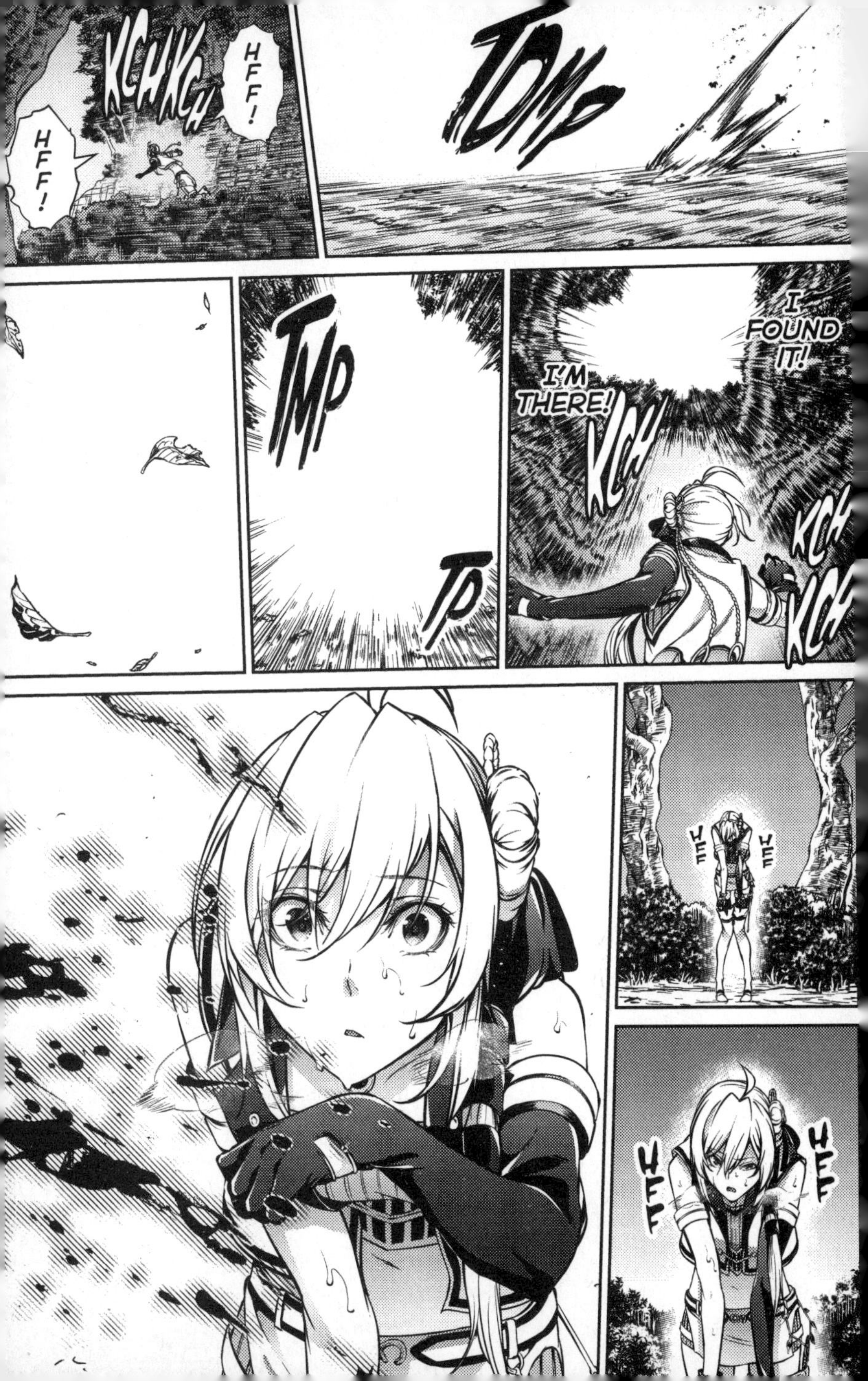
TDMP
HFF!
KCHKCH
HFF!
I FOUND IT!
I'M THERE!
KCH
KCH KCH
TMP
TP
HFF HFF
HFF HFF

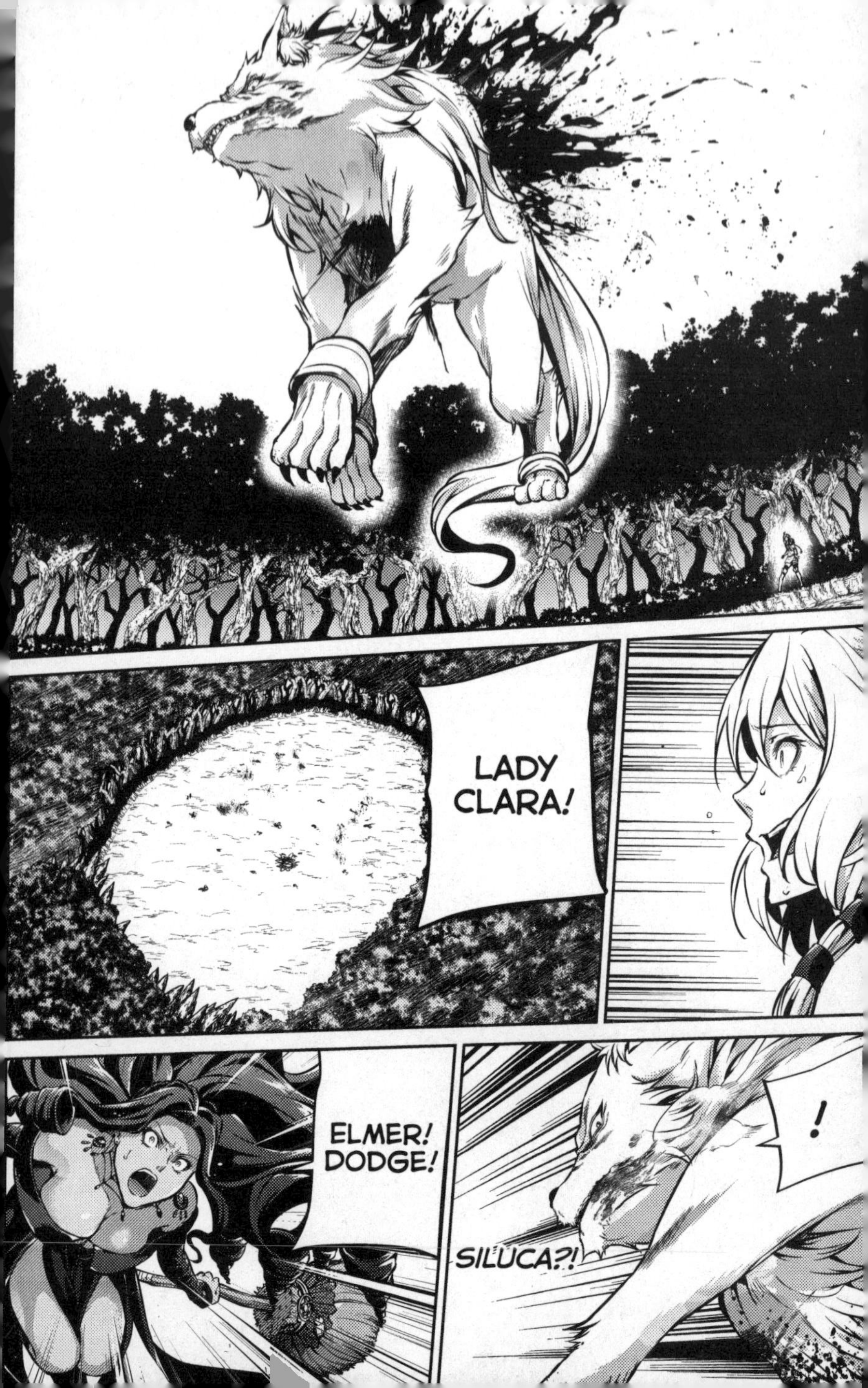
LADY CLARA!
!
SILUCA?!
ELMER! DODGE!

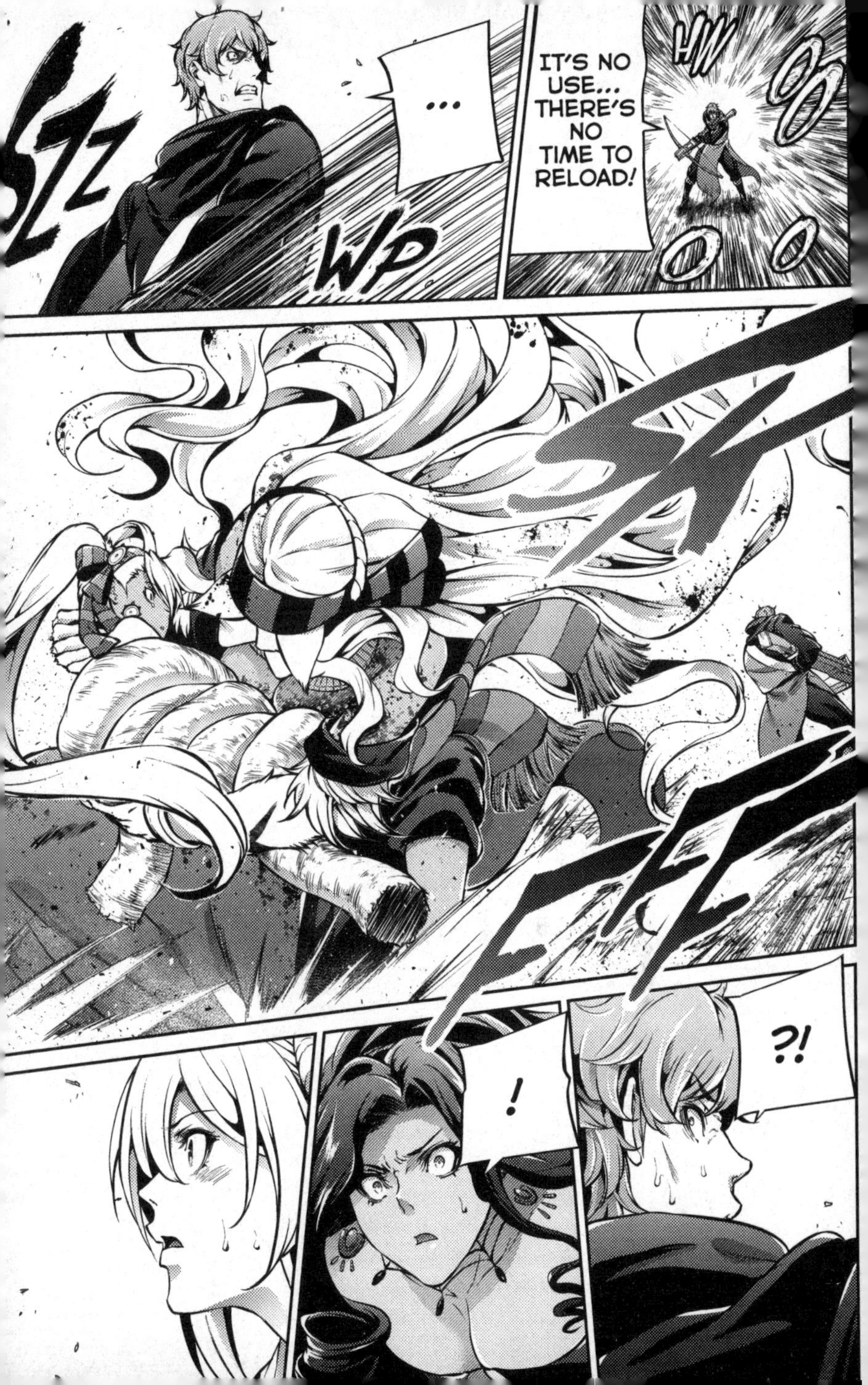
HW
IT'S NO USE... THERE'S NO TIME TO RELOAD!
...
SZZ
WP
?!
!

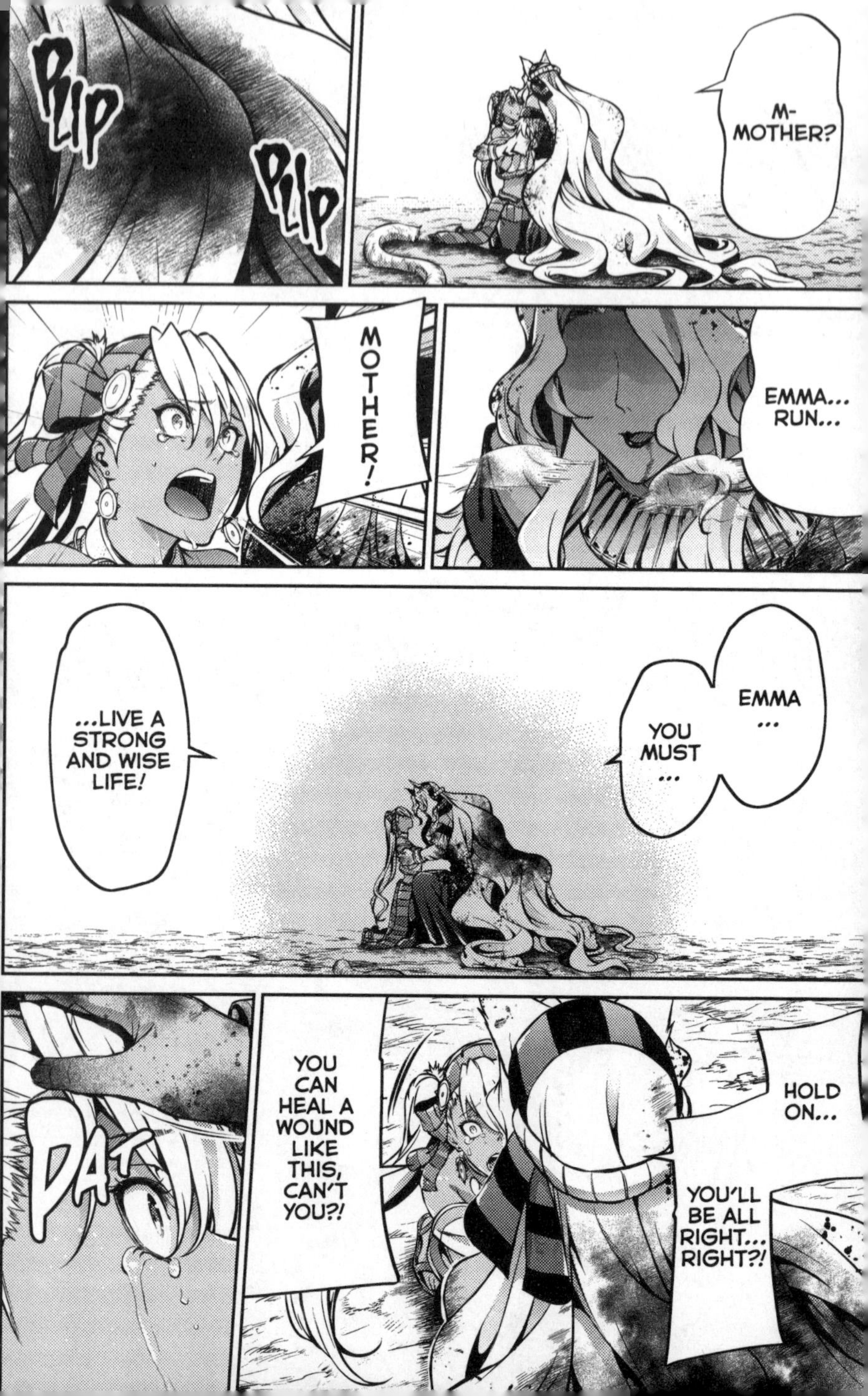
M-MOTHER?
PLIP
PLIP
EMMA... RUN...
MOTHER!
EMMA ...
YOU MUST ...
...LIVE A STRONG AND WISE LIFE!
HOLD ON...
YOU'LL BE ALL RIGHT... RIGHT?!
YOU CAN HEAL A WOUND LIKE THIS, CAN'T YOU?!
DAT

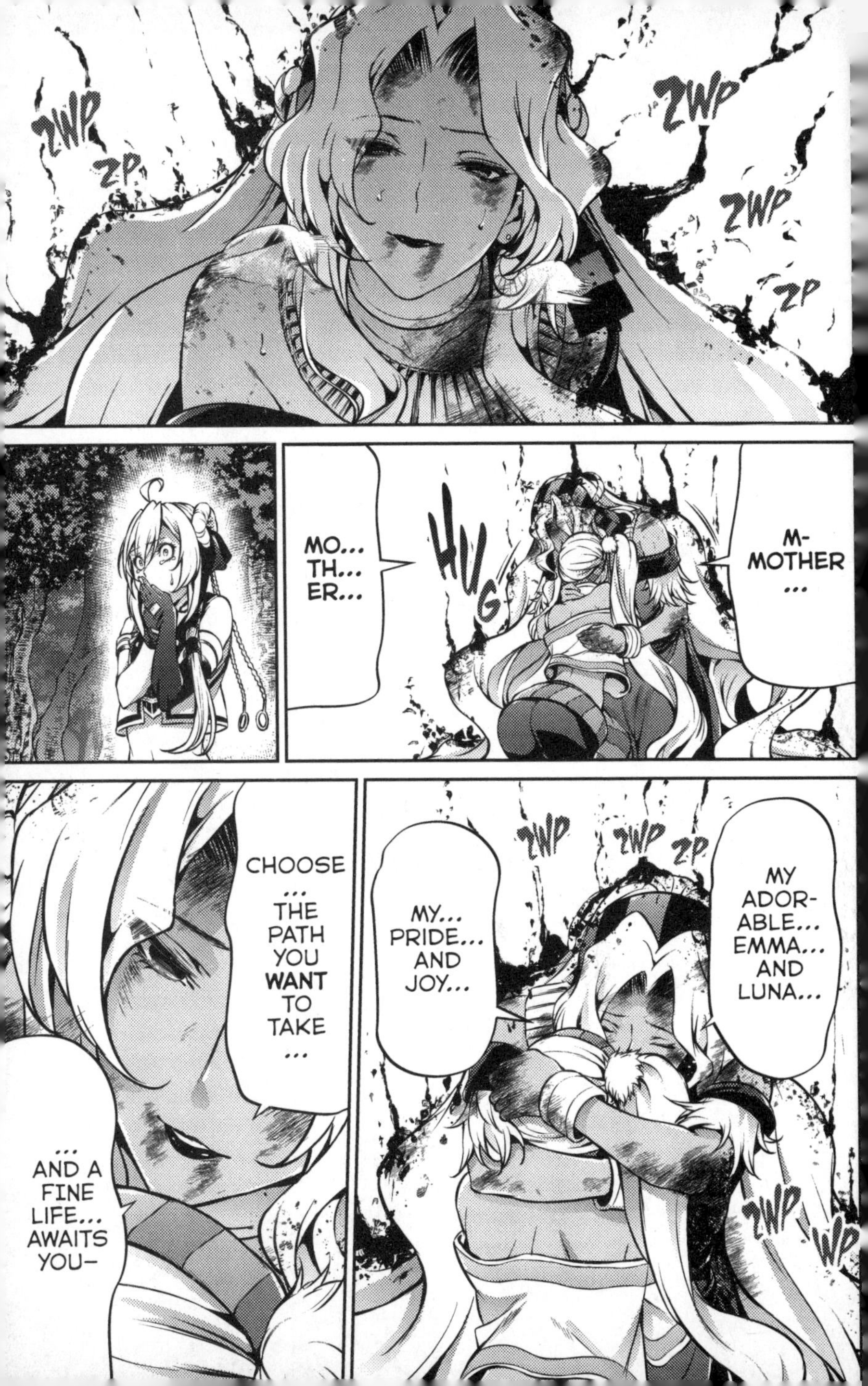
ZWP
ZWP
ZP
ZWP
ZP
M- MOTHER ...
HUG
MO... TH... ER...
MY ADORABLE... EMMA... AND LUNA...
ZWP
ZP
ZWP
MY... PRIDE... AND JOY...
ZWP
WP
CHOOSE ... THE PATH YOU **WANT** TO TAKE ...
... AND A FINE LIFE... AWAITS YOU—

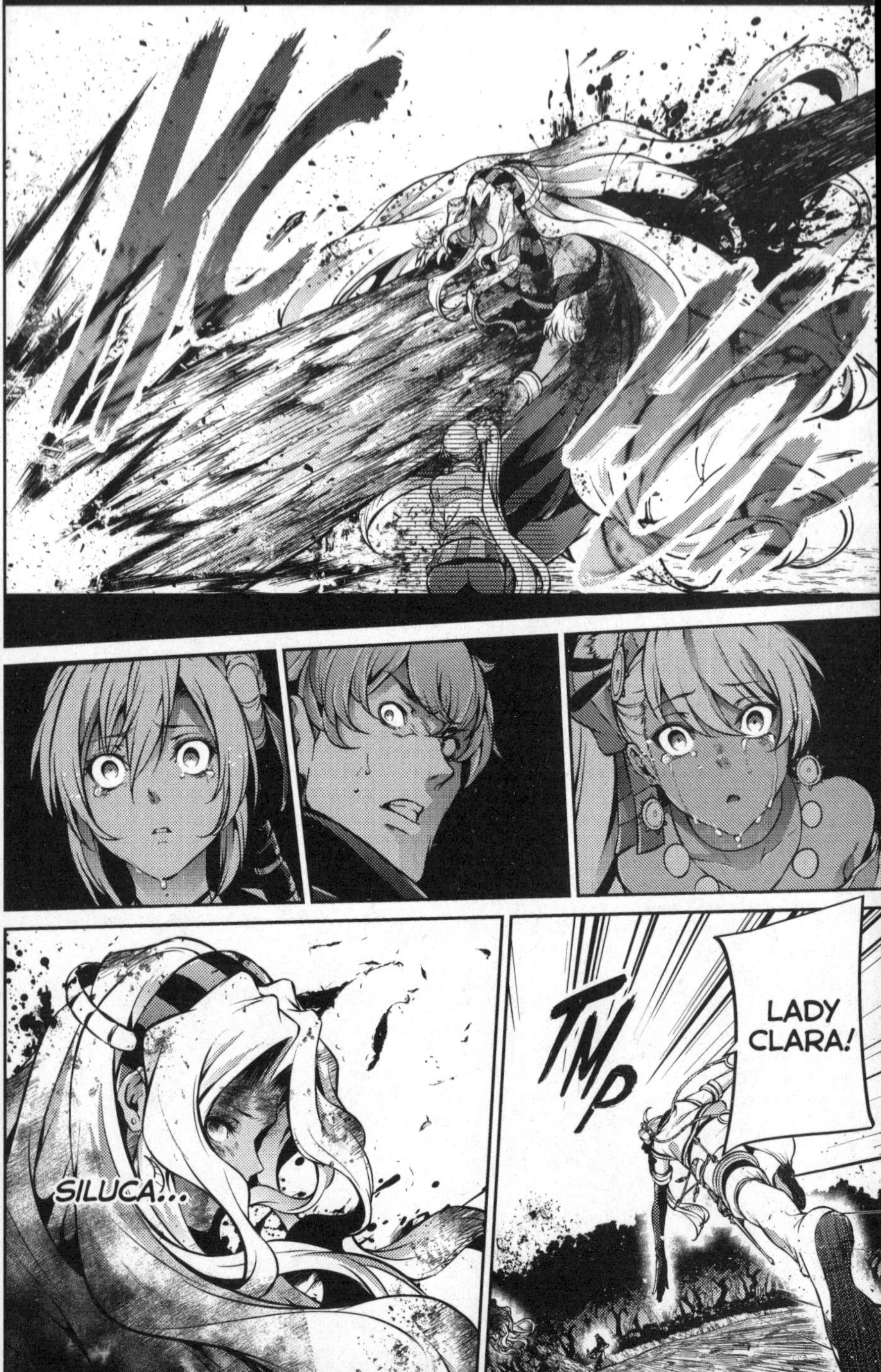
LADY CLARA!
TMP
SILUCA...

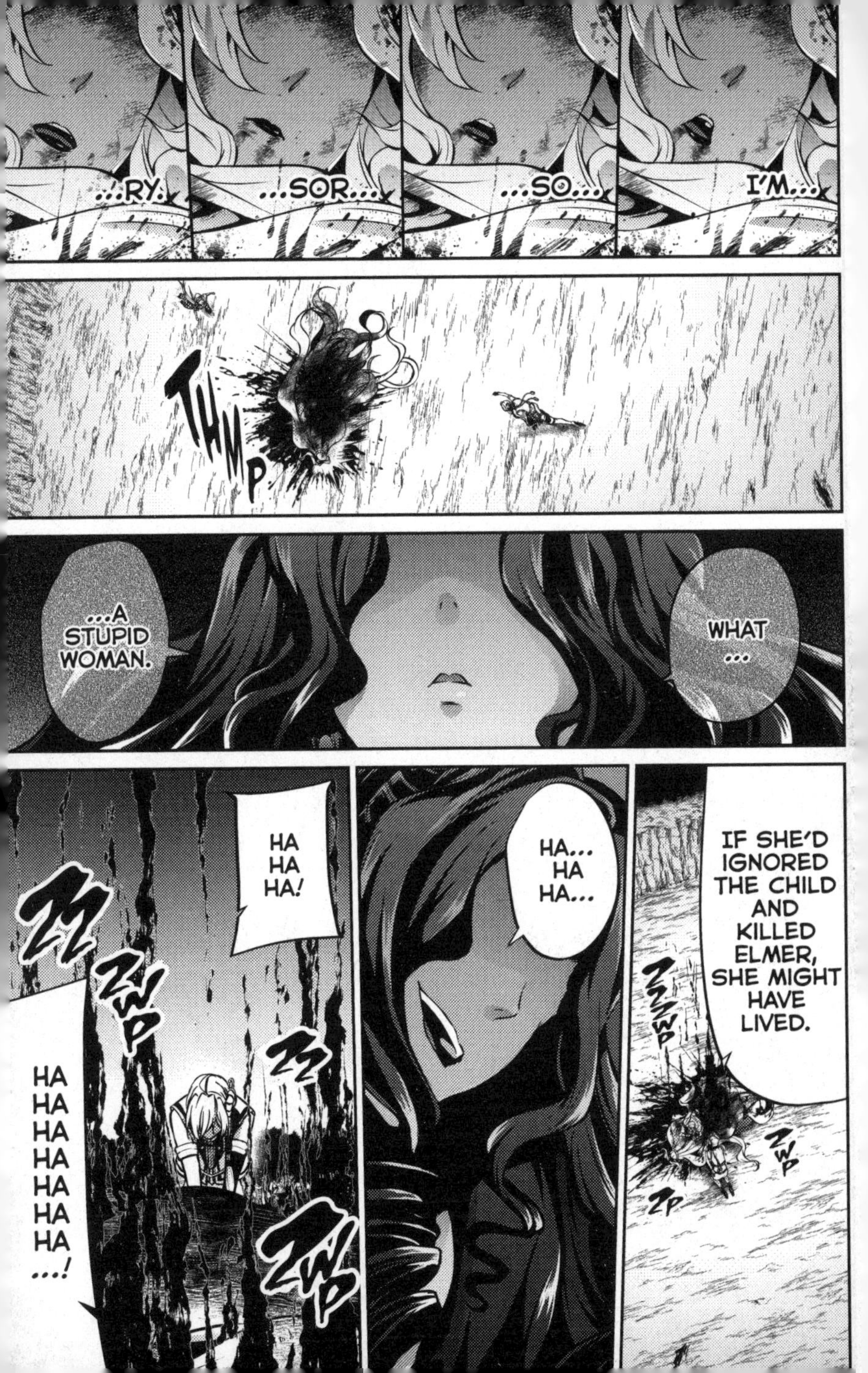
I'M...
...SO...
...SOR...
...RY.
THMP
WHAT ...
...A STUPID WOMAN.
IF SHE'D IGNORED THE CHILD AND KILLED ELMER, SHE MIGHT HAVE LIVED.
ZZZWP
ZWP
ZP
HA... HA HA...
HA HA HA!
ZZ
ZWP
ZZ
ZWP
HA HA HA HA HA HA HA ...!

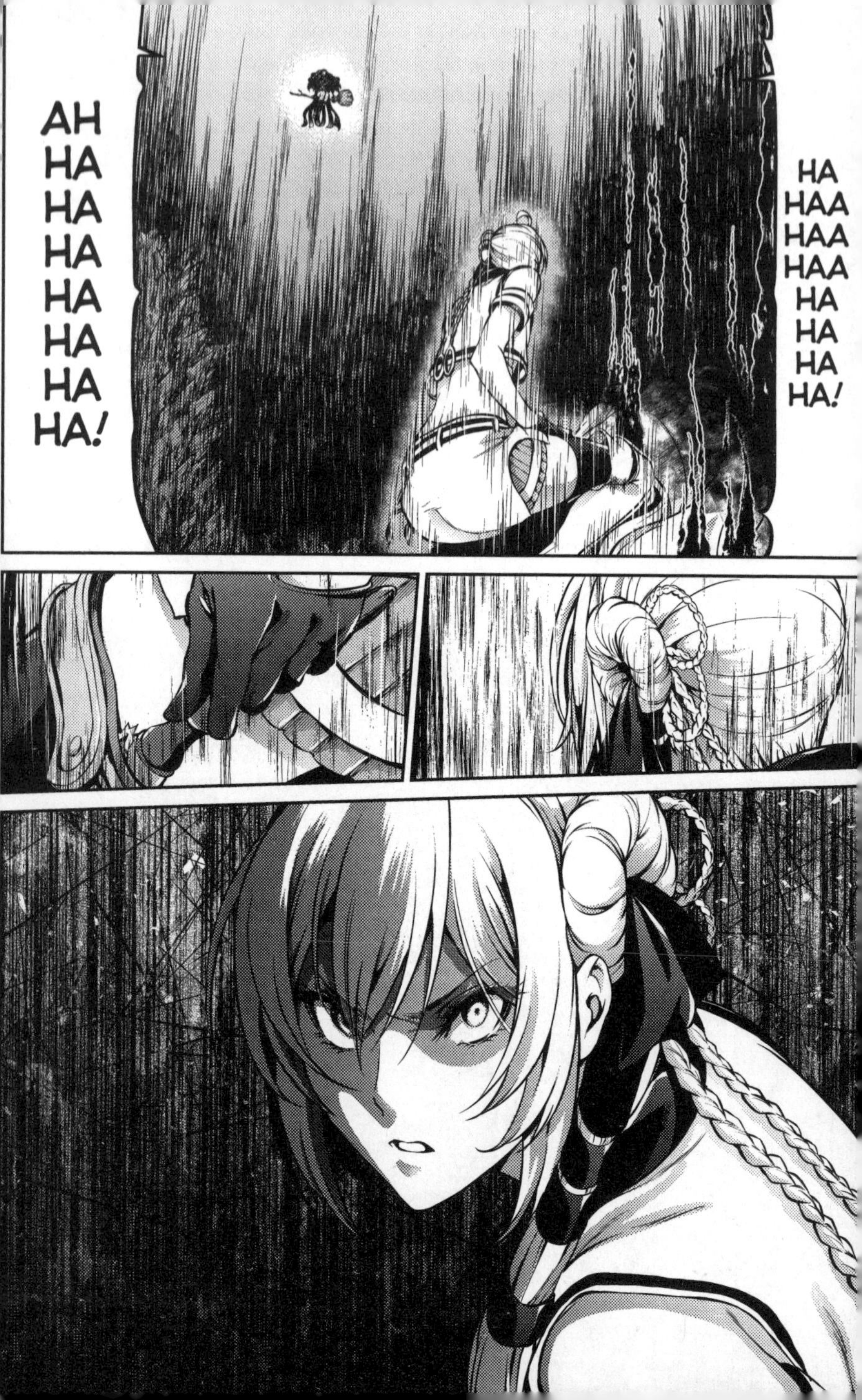
HA
HAA
HAA
HAA
HA
HA
HA
HA!
AH
HA
HA
HA
HA
HA
HA
HA!

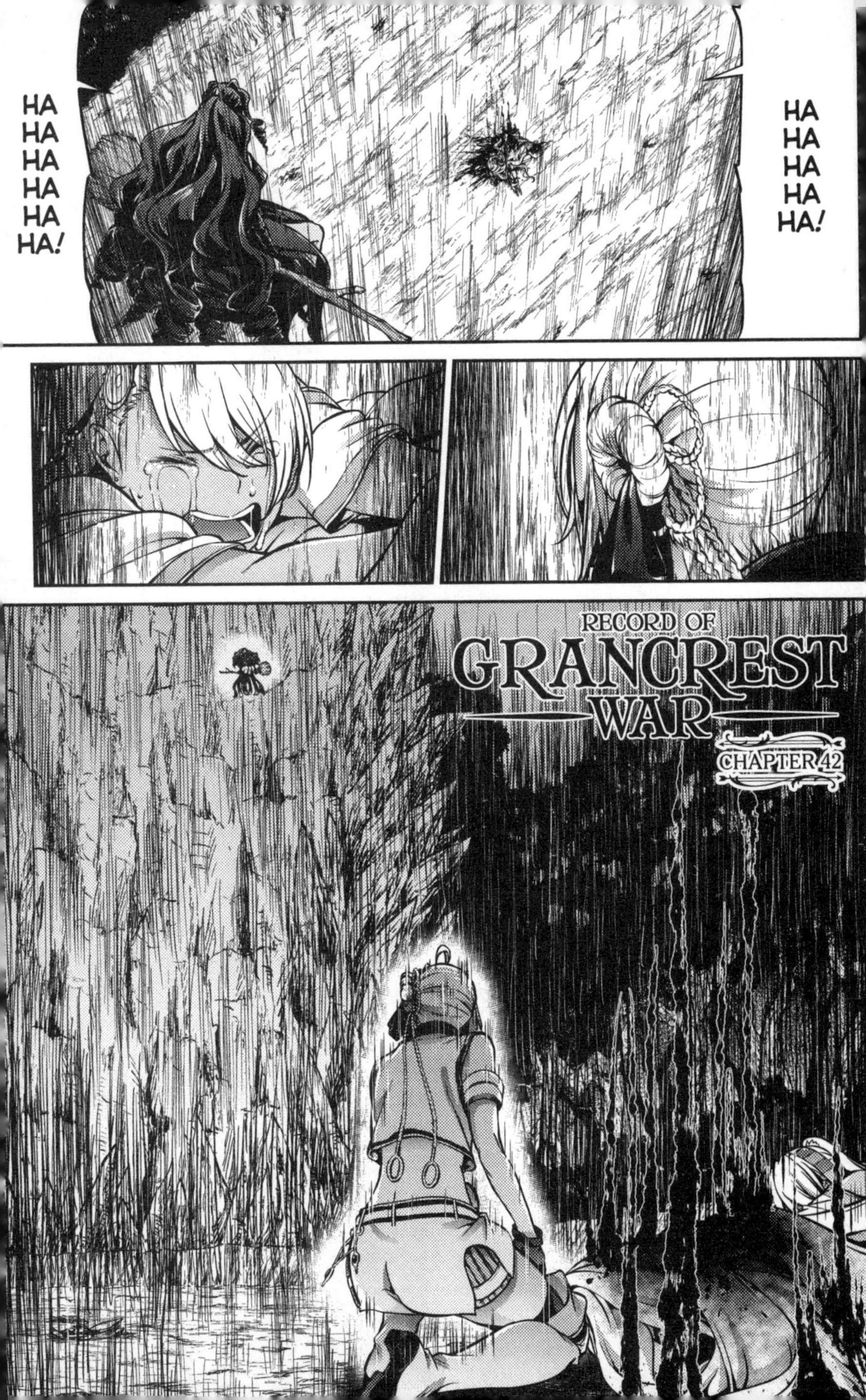
HA HA HA HA HA!
HA HA HA HA HA HA!
RECORD OF GRANCREST WAR
CHAPTER 42

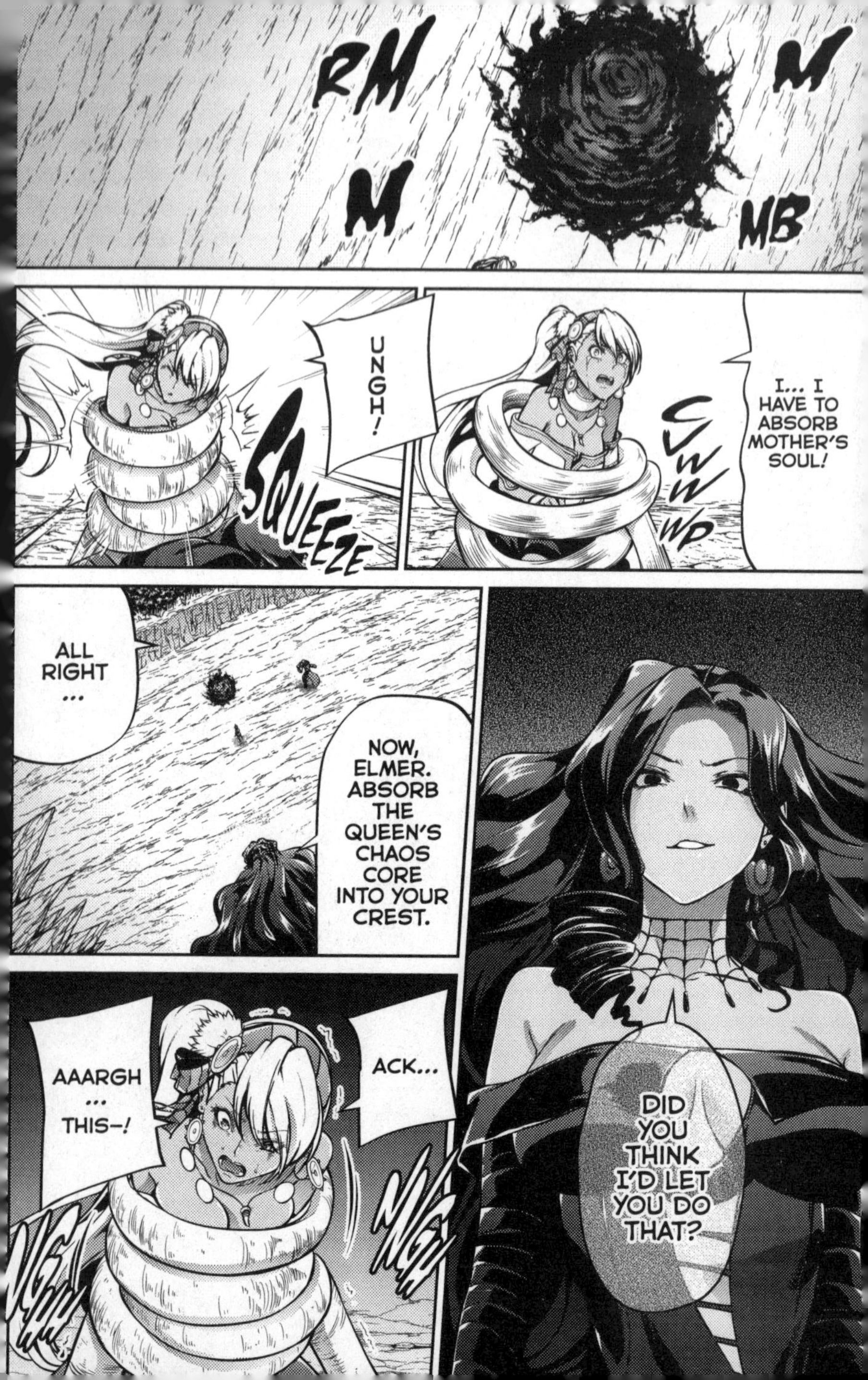
RM
M
M
MB
I... I HAVE TO ABSORB MOTHER'S SOUL!
CWWWP
UNGH!
SQUEEZE
DID YOU THINK I'D LET YOU DO THAT?
ALL RIGHT...
NOW, ELMER. ABSORB THE QUEEN'S CHAOS CORE INTO YOUR CREST.
ACK...
AAARGH... THIS-!

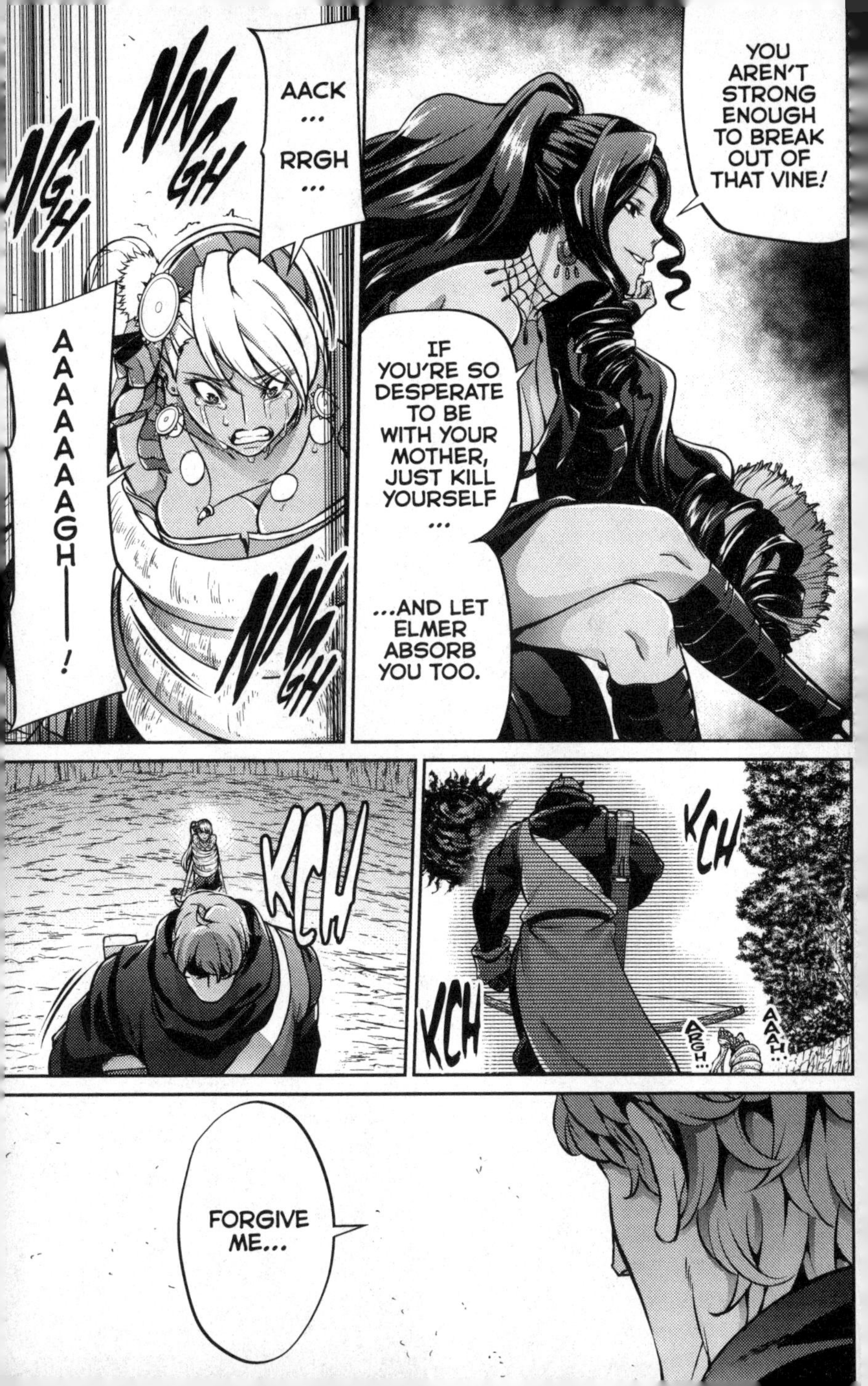
YOU AREN'T STRONG ENOUGH TO BREAK OUT OF THAT VINE!
IF YOU'RE SO DESPERATE TO BE WITH YOUR MOTHER, JUST KILL YOURSELF ...
...AND LET ELMER ABSORB YOU TOO.
NNAGH
AACK ... RRGH ...
NGH
AAAAAAAAGH—!
NNAGH
KCH
KCH
ARGH...
AAAH...
KCH
FORGIVE ME...

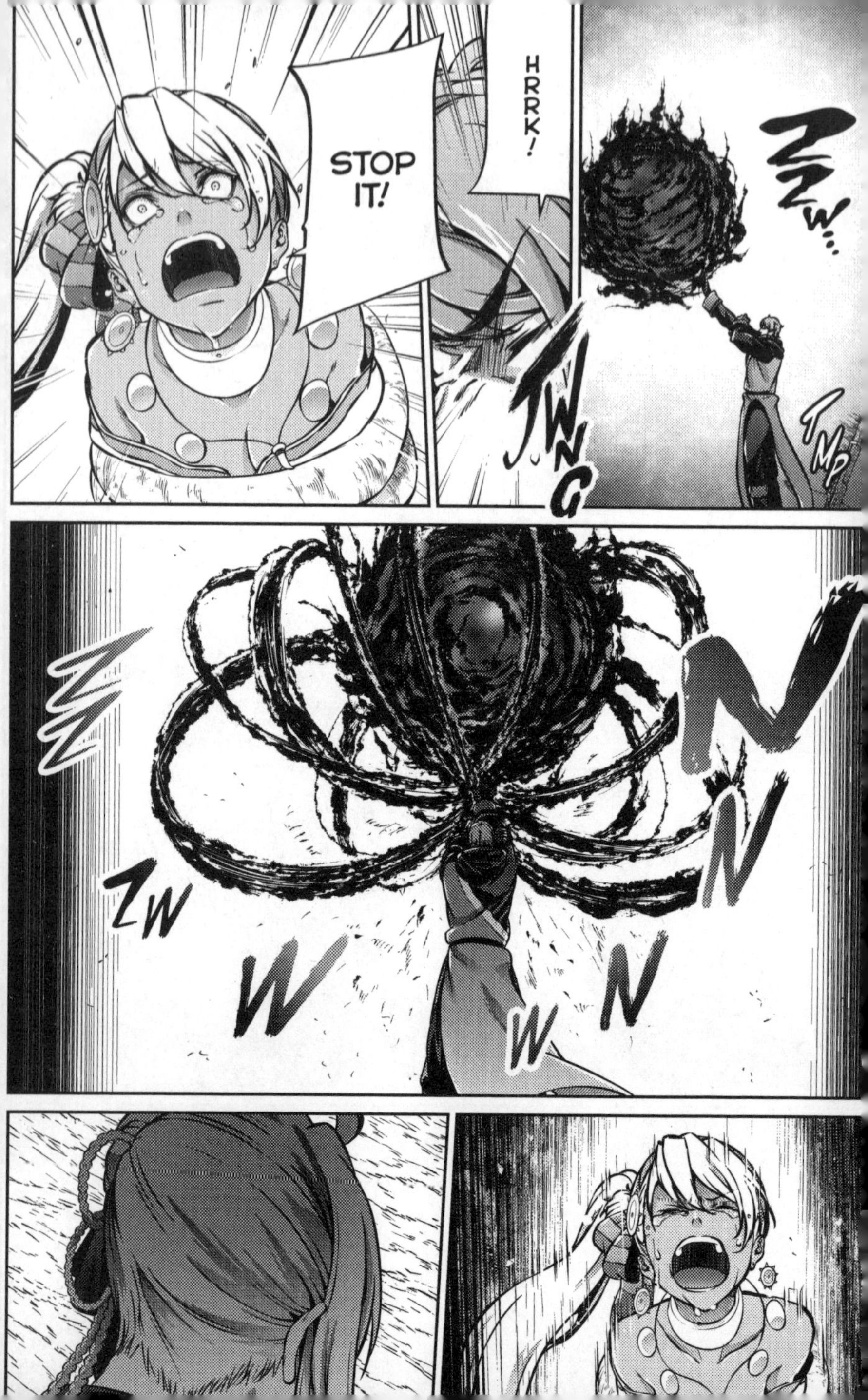
ZZZW...
TMP
HRRK!
TWNG
STOP IT!
NNN
ZZZ
ZW
W
W
N

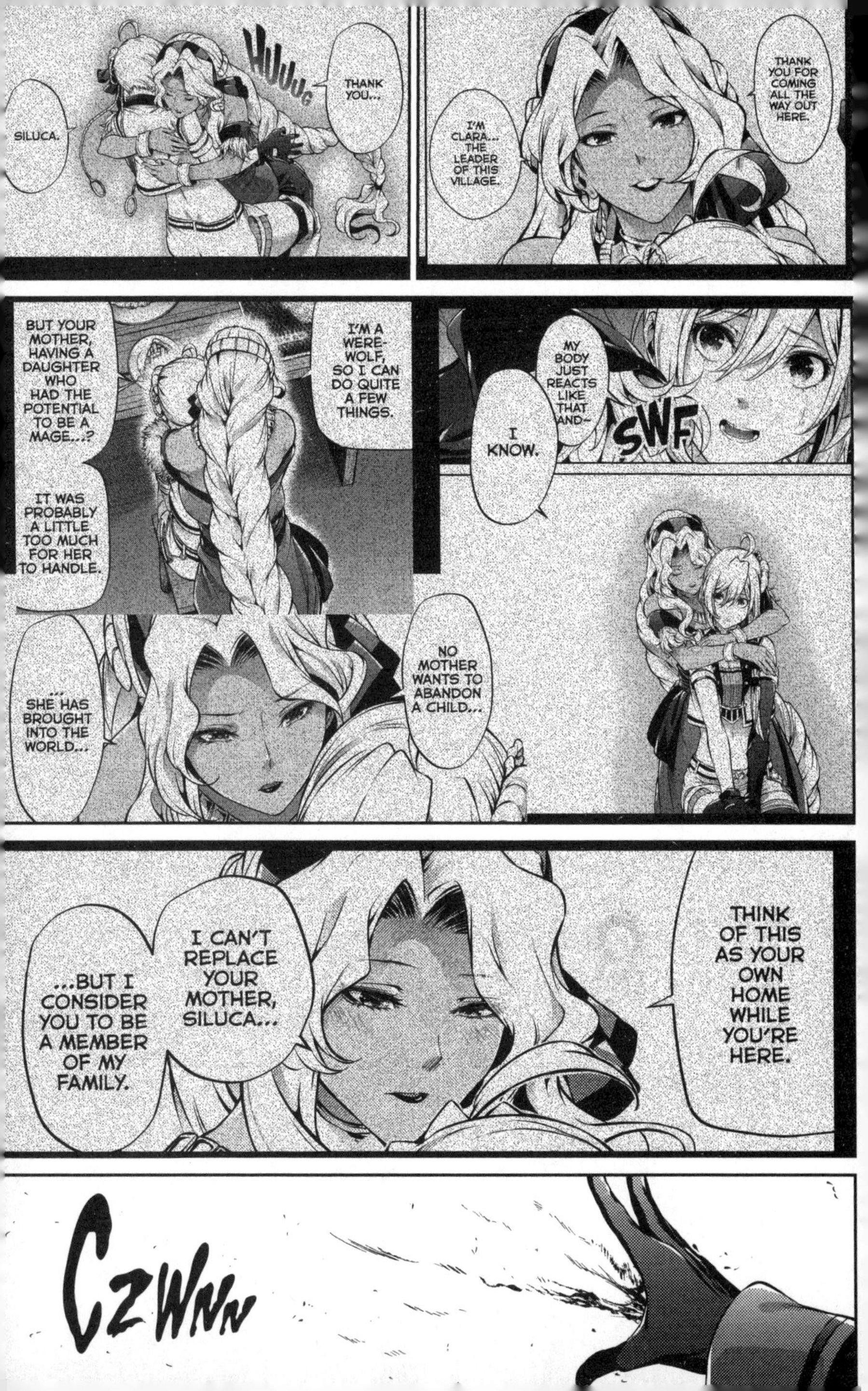
THANK YOU FOR COMING ALL THE WAY OUT HERE.
I'M CLARA... THE LEADER OF THIS VILLAGE.
HUUUUG
THANK YOU...
SILUCA.
MY BODY JUST REACTS LIKE THAT AND—
SWF
I KNOW.
I'M A WERE-WOLF, SO I CAN DO QUITE A FEW THINGS.
BUT YOUR MOTHER, HAVING A DAUGHTER WHO HAD THE POTENTIAL TO BE A MAGE...?
IT WAS PROBABLY A LITTLE TOO MUCH FOR HER TO HANDLE.
NO MOTHER WANTS TO ABANDON A CHILD...
...SHE HAS BROUGHT INTO THE WORLD...
THINK OF THIS AS YOUR OWN HOME WHILE YOU'RE HERE.
I CAN'T REPLACE YOUR MOTHER, SILUCA...
...BUT I CONSIDER YOU TO BE A MEMBER OF MY FAMILY.
CZWNN

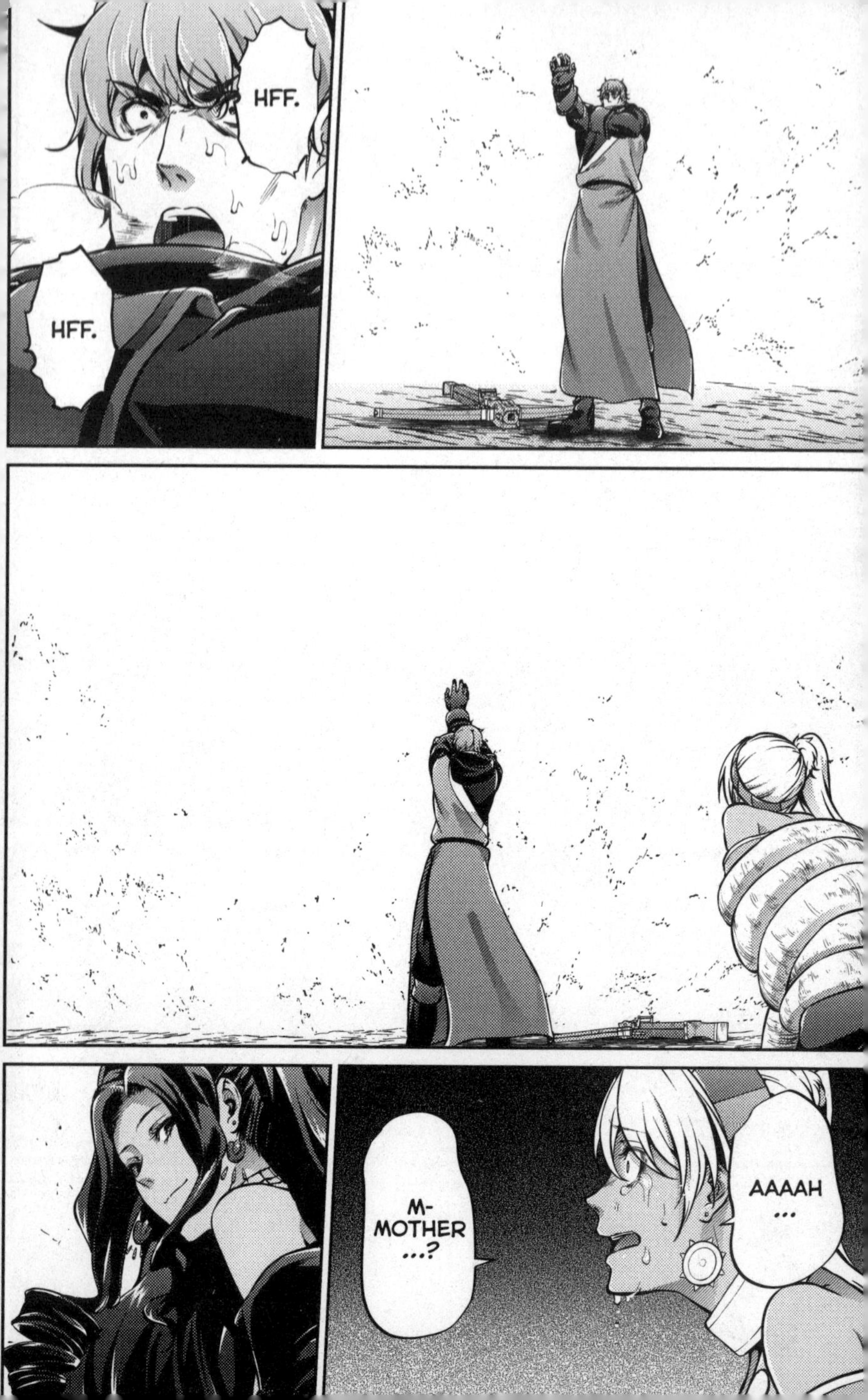
HFF.
HFF.
AAAAH ...
M-MOTHER ...?

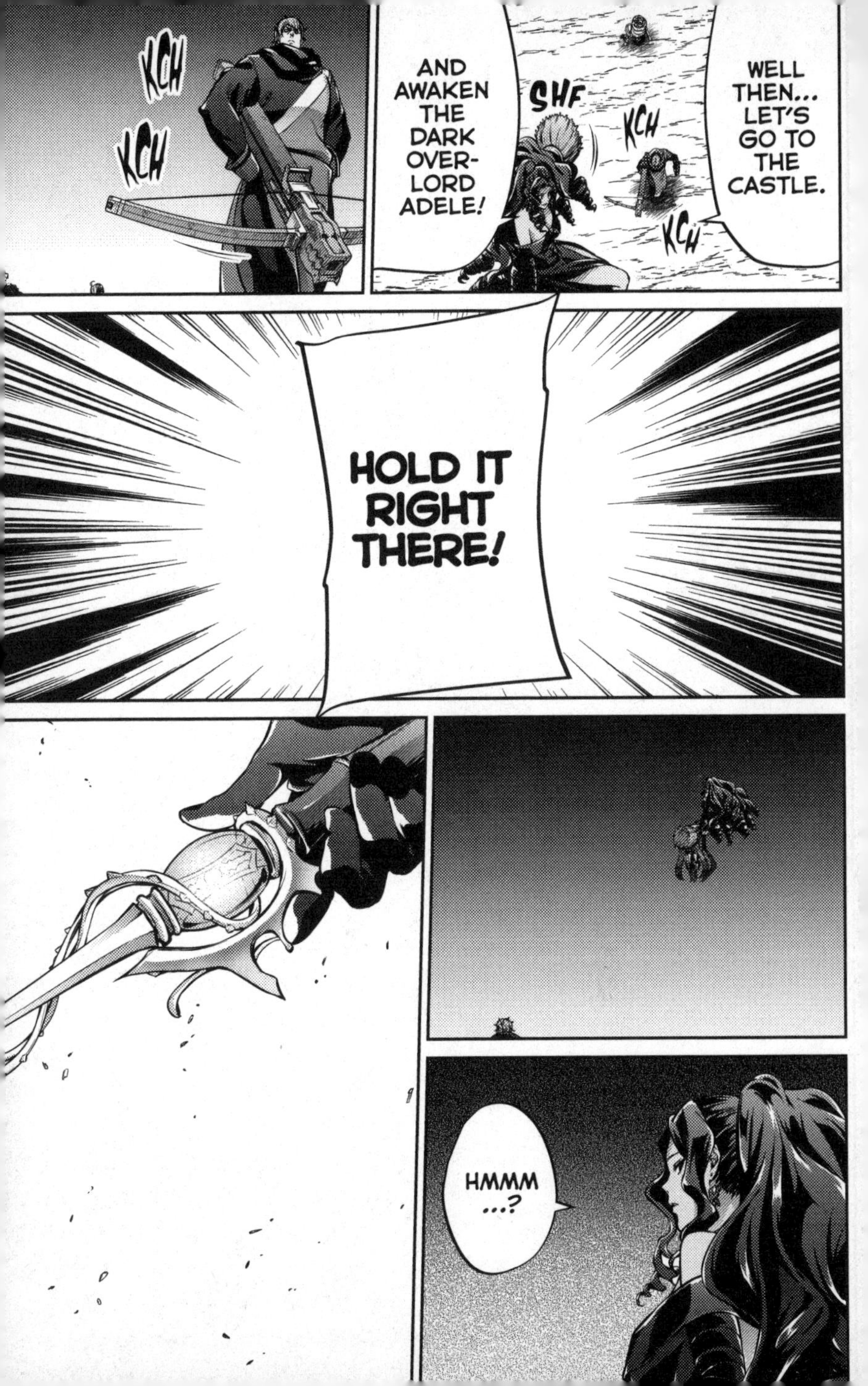
WELL THEN... LET'S GO TO THE CASTLE.
KCH
KCH
SHF
AND AWAKEN THE DARK OVER-LORD ADELE!
KCH
KCH
HOLD IT RIGHT THERE!
HMMM ...?

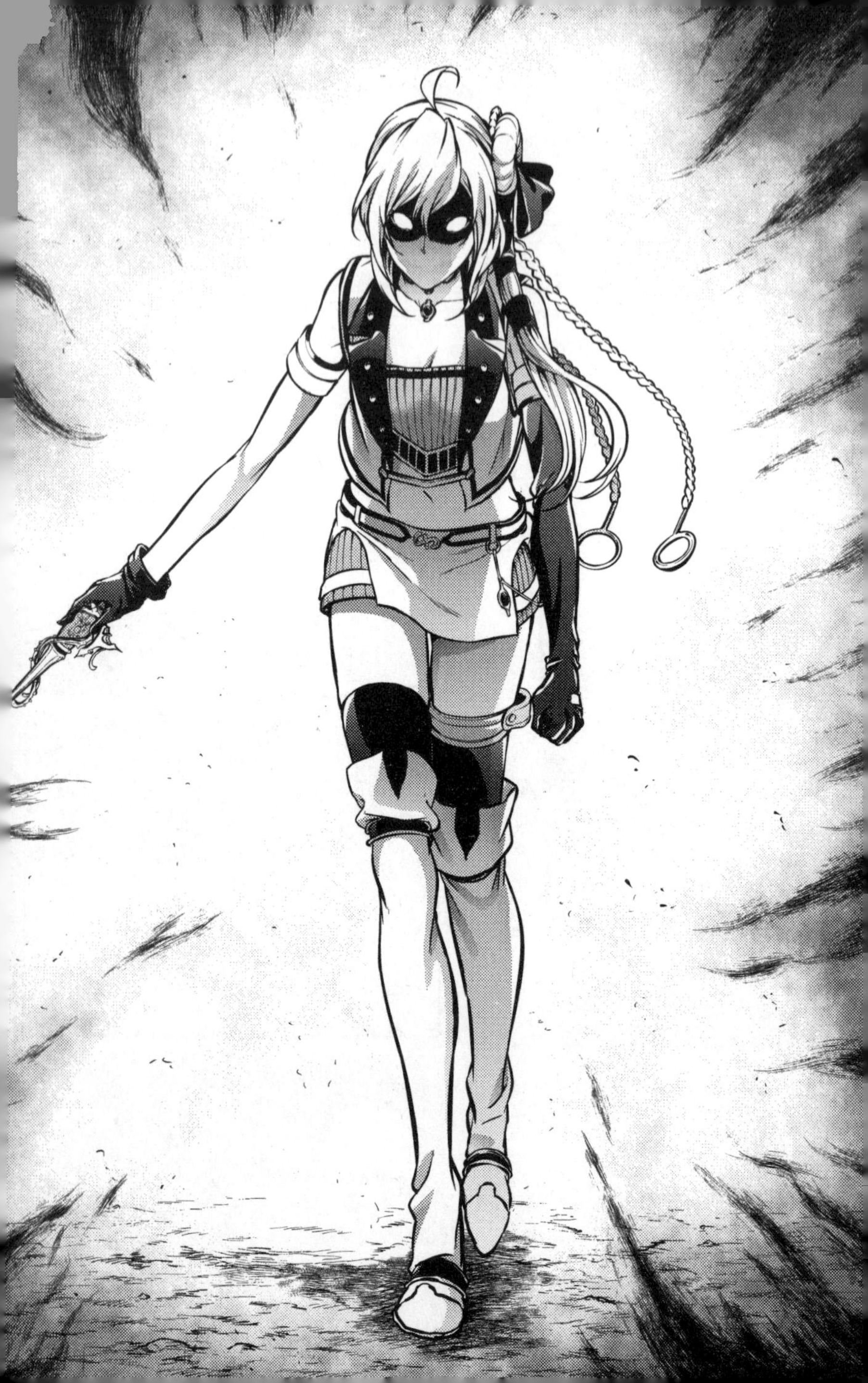

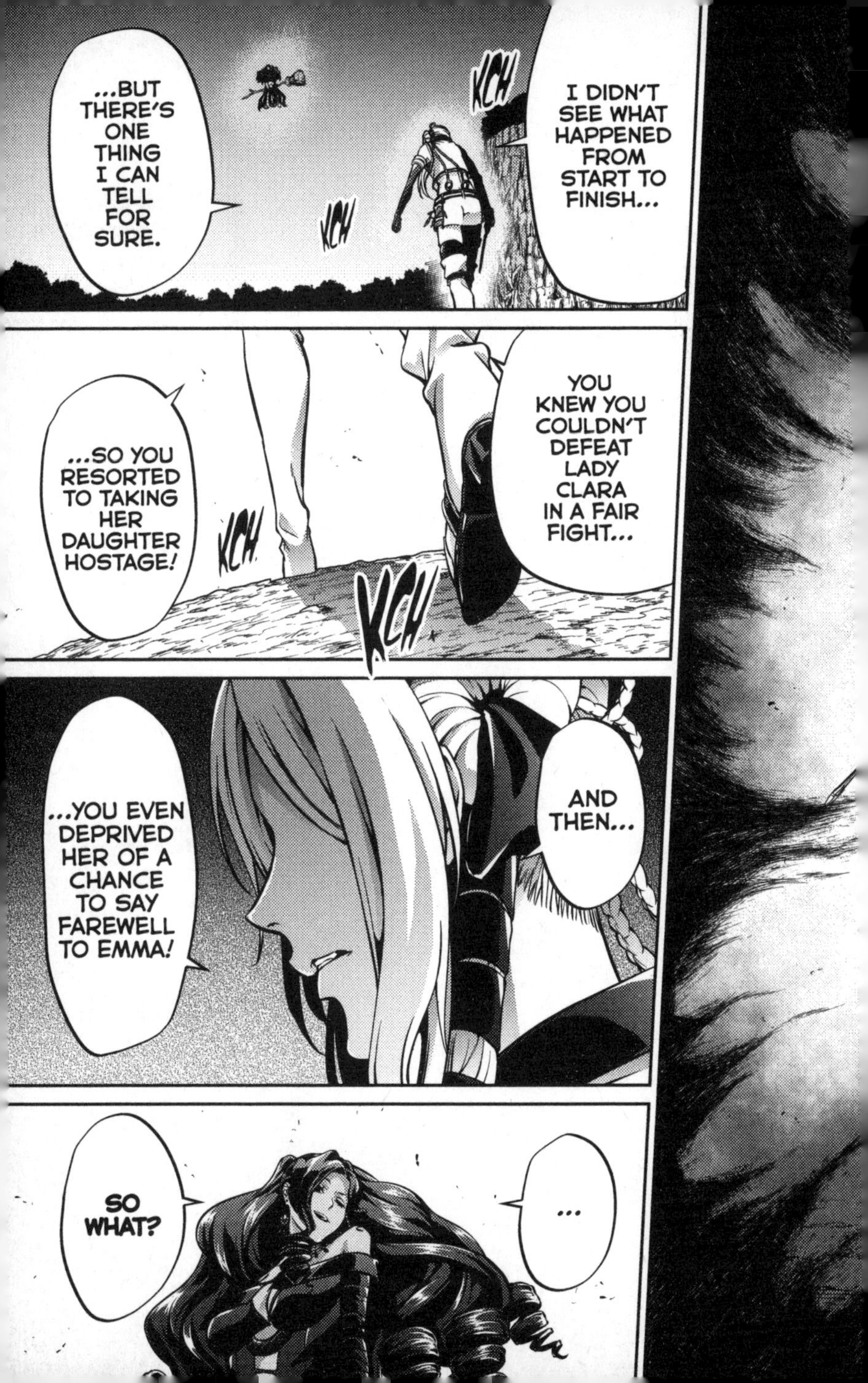
I DIDN'T SEE WHAT HAPPENED FROM START TO FINISH...
KCH
KCH
...BUT THERE'S ONE THING I CAN TELL FOR SURE.
YOU KNEW YOU COULDN'T DEFEAT LADY CLARA IN A FAIR FIGHT...
KCH
KCH
...SO YOU RESORTED TO TAKING HER DAUGHTER HOSTAGE!
AND THEN...
...YOU EVEN DEPRIVED HER OF A CHANCE TO SAY FAREWELL TO EMMA!
...
SO WHAT?

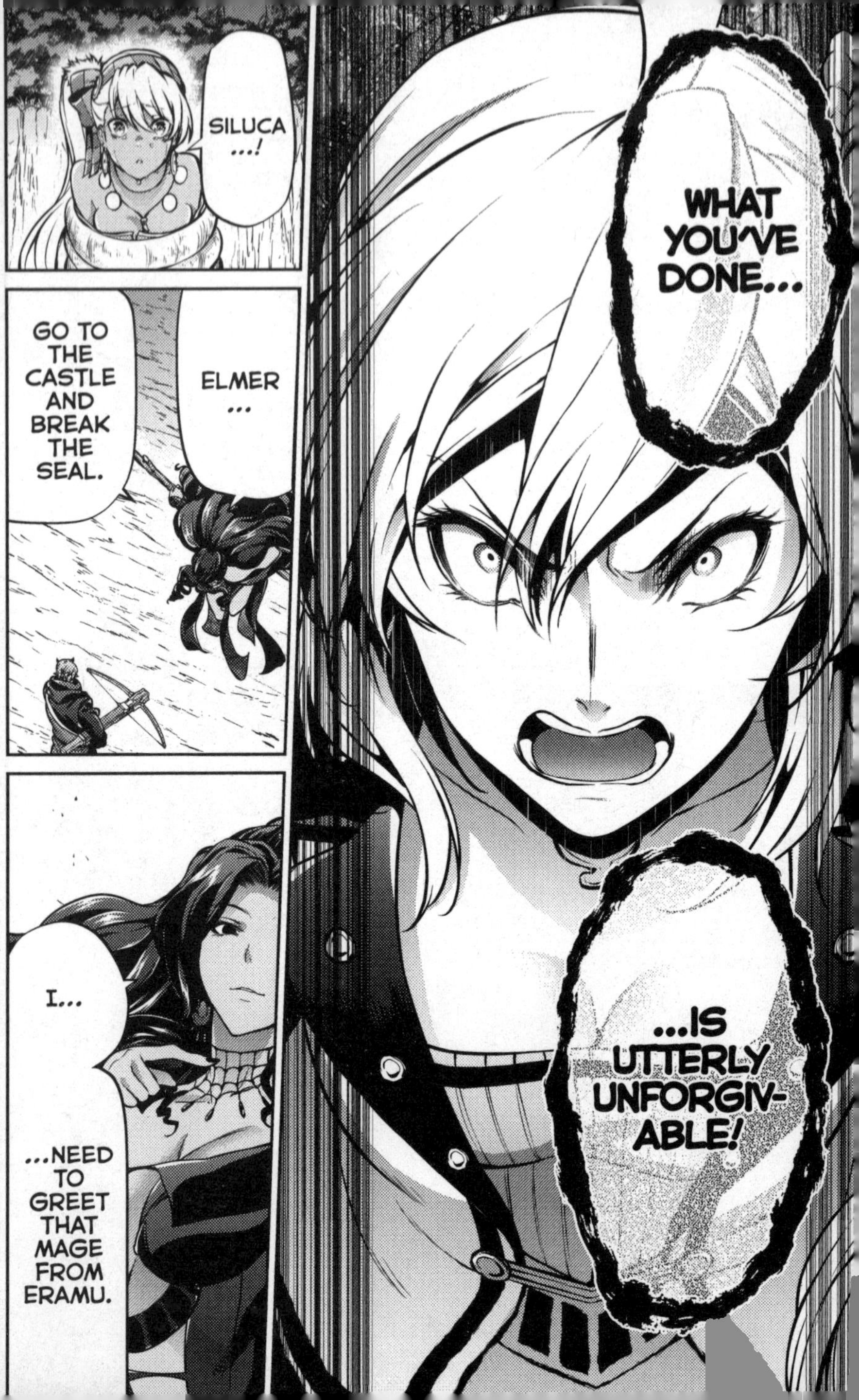
WHAT YOU'VE DONE...
...IS UTTERLY UNFORGIVABLE!
SILUCA ...!
ELMER ...
GO TO THE CASTLE AND BREAK THE SEAL.
I...
...NEED TO GREET THAT MAGE FROM ERAMU.

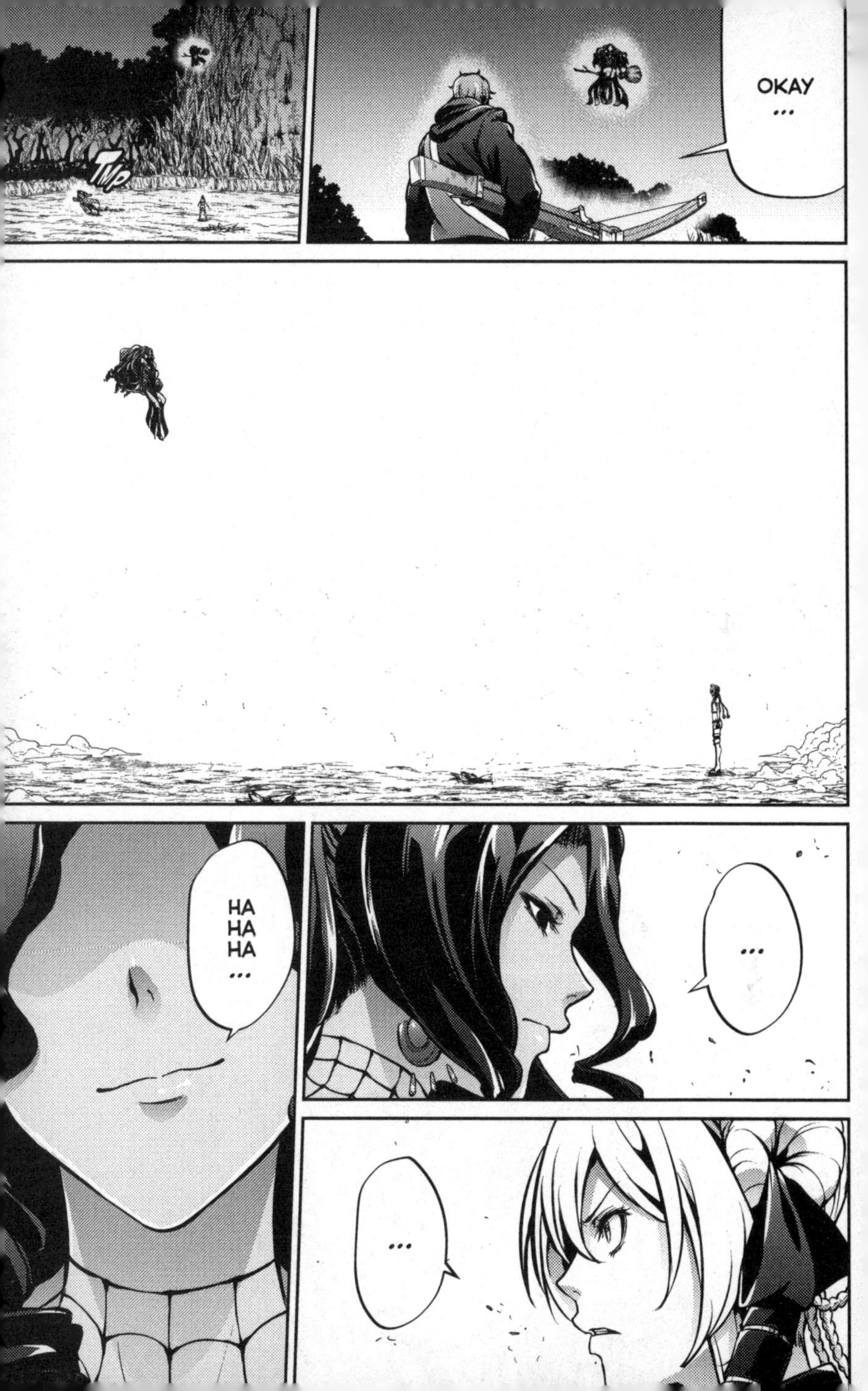
OKAY ...
TMP
...
...
HA HA HA ...

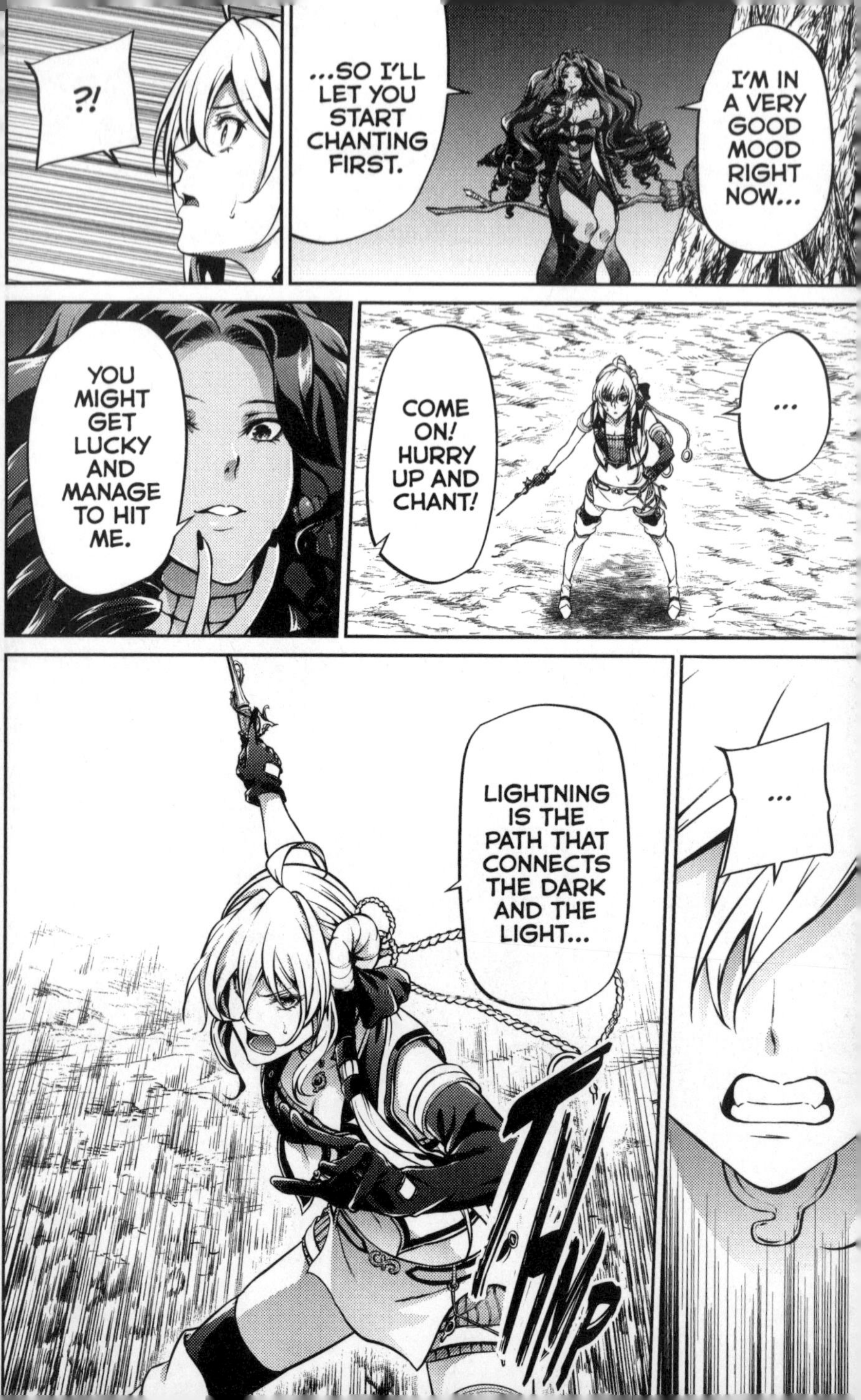
I'M IN A VERY GOOD MOOD RIGHT NOW...
...SO I'LL LET YOU START CHANTING FIRST.
?!
...
COME ON! HURRY UP AND CHANT!
YOU MIGHT GET LUCKY AND MANAGE TO HIT ME.
...
LIGHTNING IS THE PATH THAT CONNECTS THE DARK AND THE LIGHT...
THMP

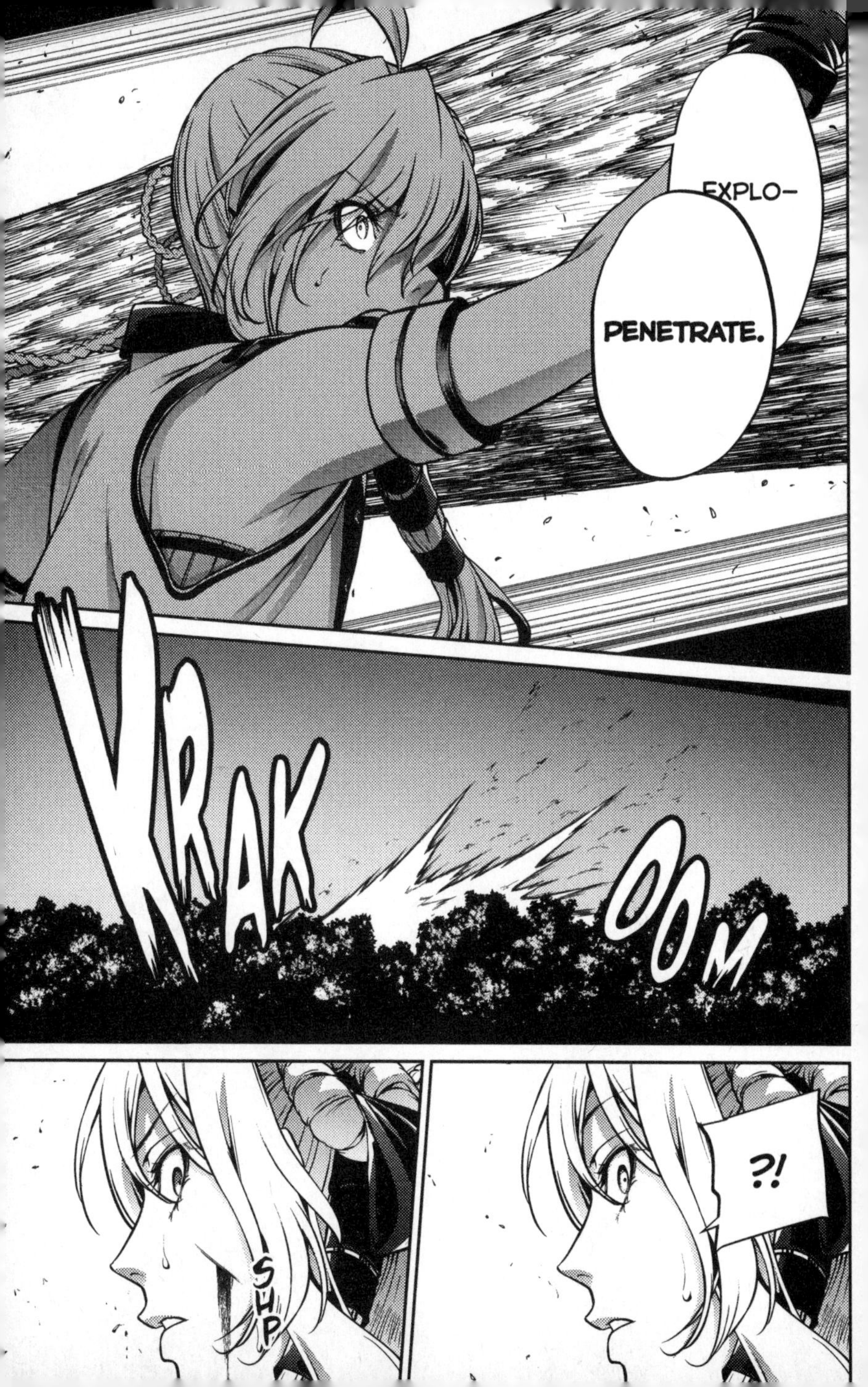
EXPLO—
PENETRATE.
VRAK
OOM
?!
SHP

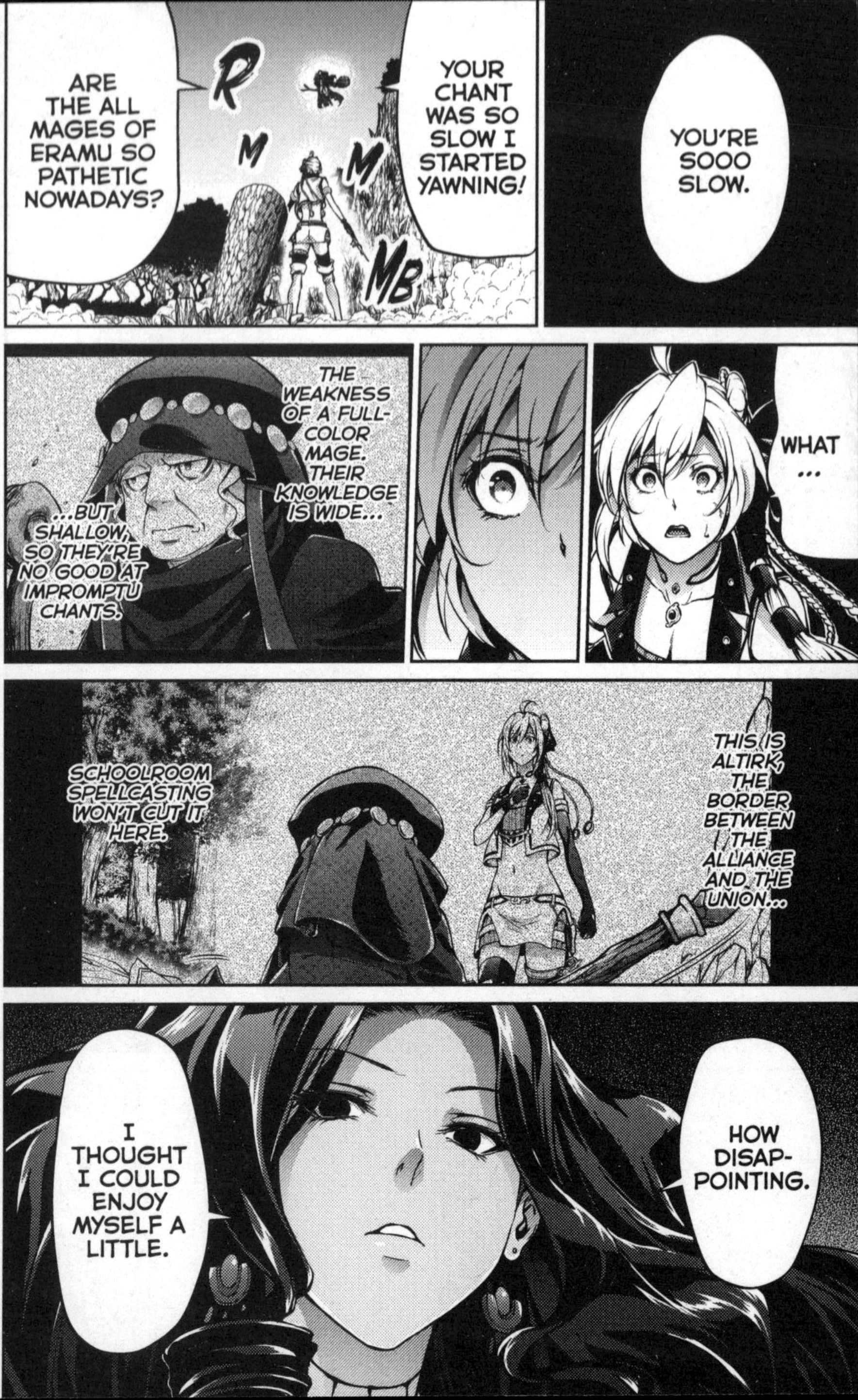

YOU'RE SOOO SLOW.
YOUR CHANT WAS SO SLOW I STARTED YAWNING!
RMMMB
ARE THE ALL MAGES OF ERAMU SO PATHETIC NOWADAYS?
WHAT ...
THE WEAKNESS OF A FULL-COLOR MAGE. THEIR KNOWLEDGE IS WIDE...
...BUT SHALLOW, SO THEY'RE NO GOOD AT IMPROMPTU CHANTS.
THIS IS ALTIRK, THE BORDER BETWEEN THE ALLIANCE AND THE UNION...
SCHOOLROOM SPELLCASTING WON'T CUT IT HERE.
HOW DISAP-POINTING.
I THOUGHT I COULD ENJOY MYSELF A LITTLE.

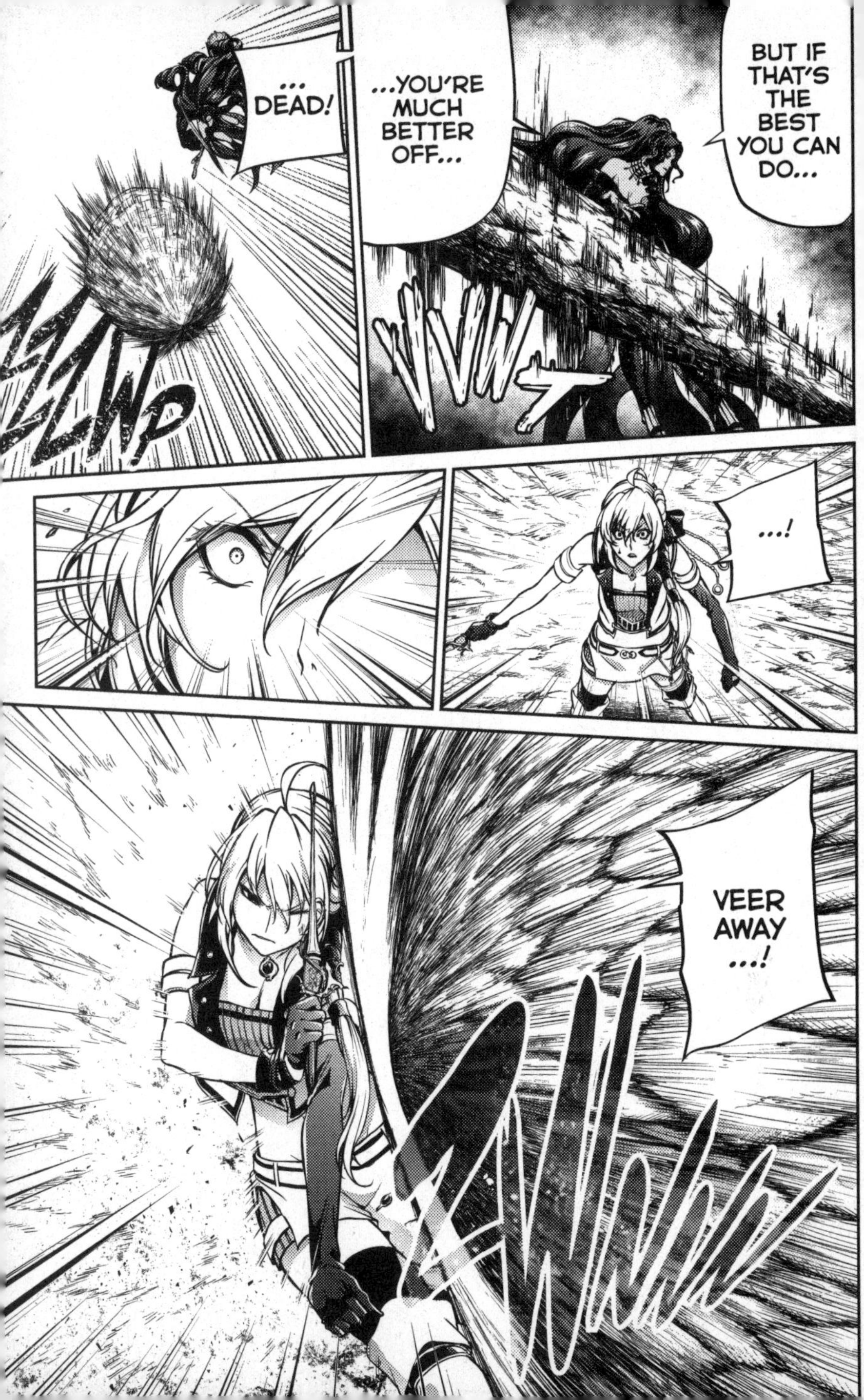
BUT IF THAT'S THE BEST YOU CAN DO...
...YOU'RE MUCH BETTER OFF...
... DEAD!
...!
VEER AWAY ...!

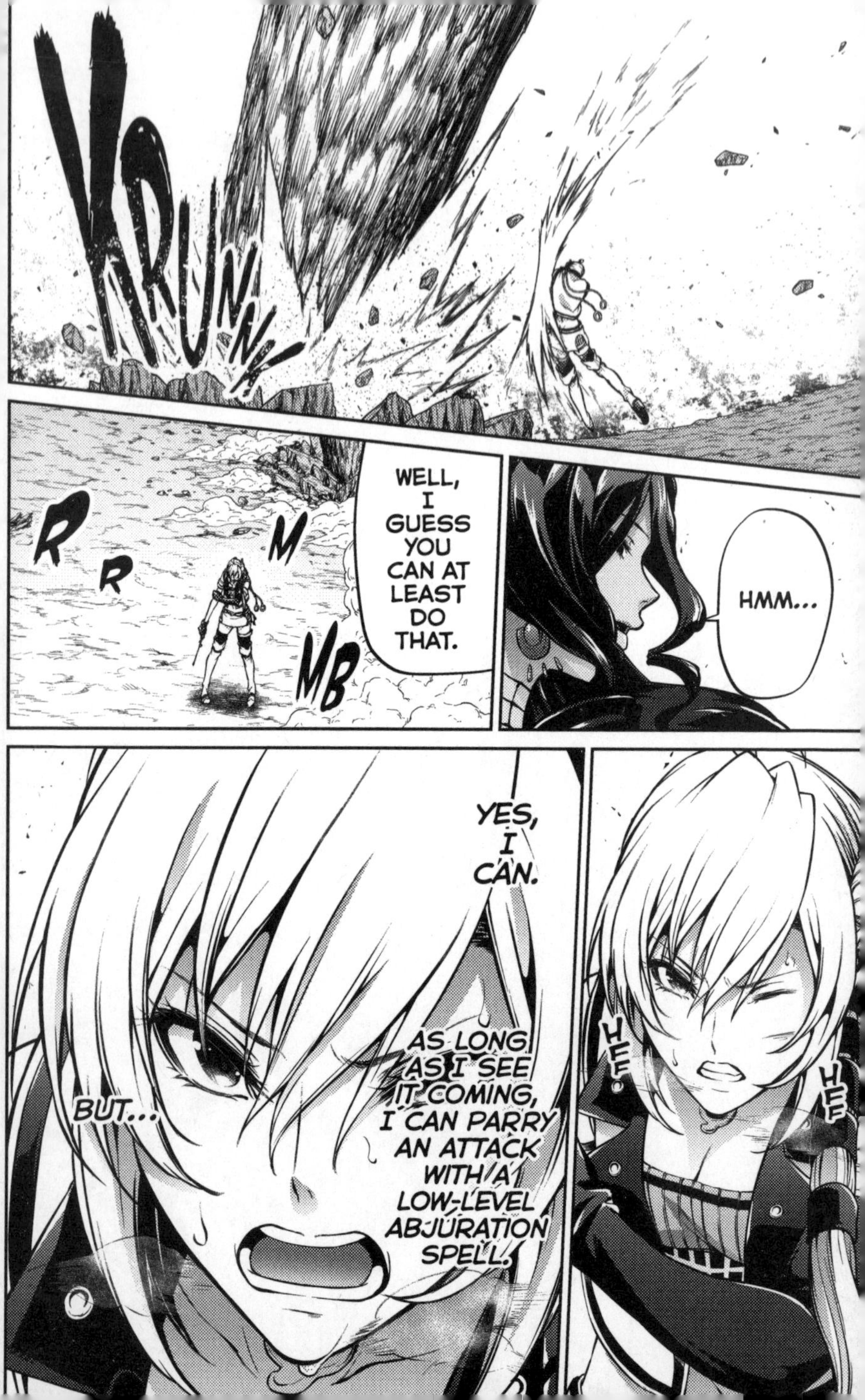
KRUNN
HMM...
WELL, I GUESS YOU CAN AT LEAST DO THAT.
RRMMB
HEF
HEF
YES, I CAN.
AS LONG AS I SEE IT COMING, I CAN PARRY AN ATTACK WITH A LOW-LEVEL ABJURATION SPELL.
BUT...

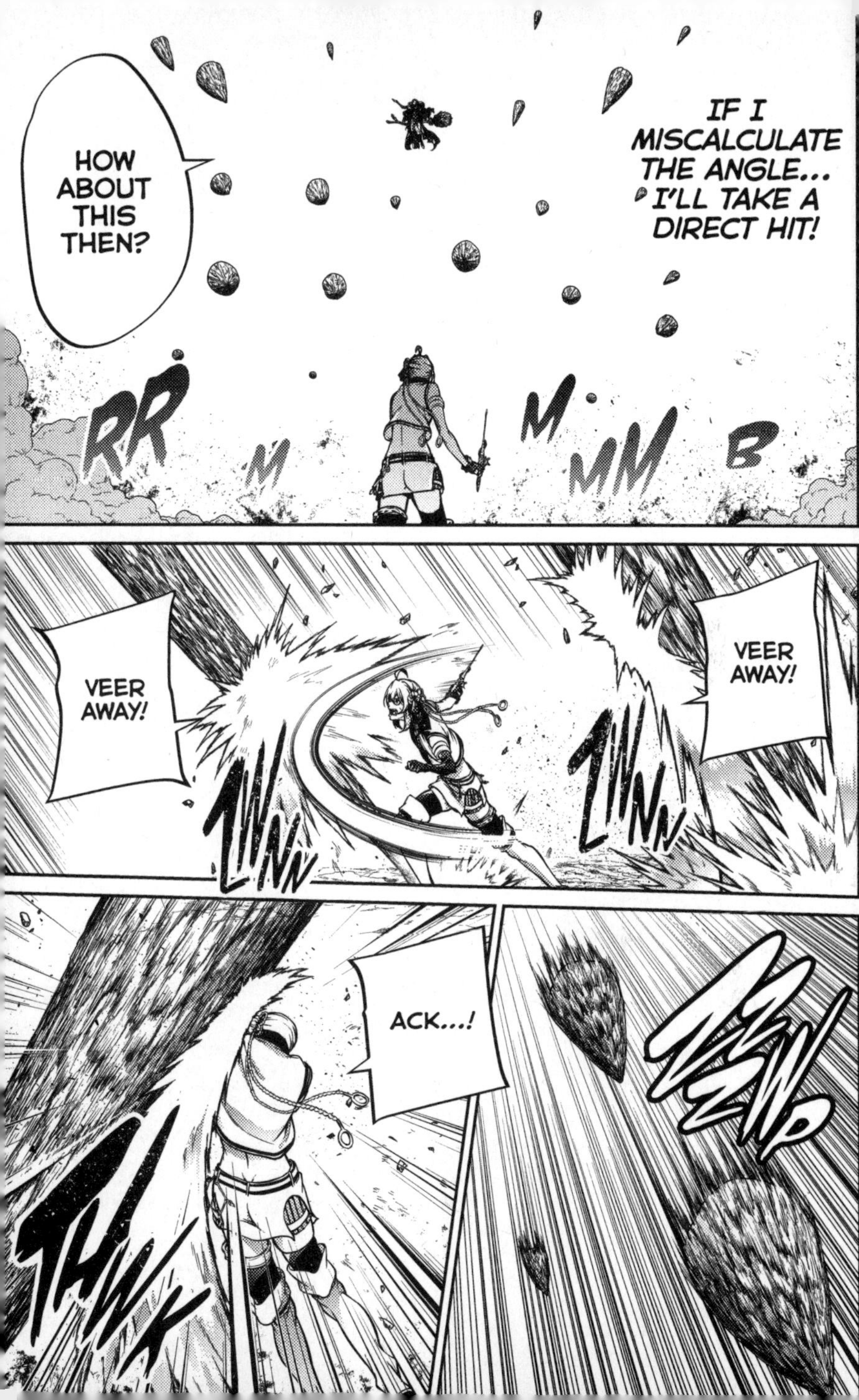
IF I MISCALCULATE THE ANGLE... I'LL TAKE A DIRECT HIT!
HOW ABOUT THIS THEN?
RRMMMMMB
VEER AWAY!
ZINNN
VEER AWAY!
ZINNN
ACK...!
THWK

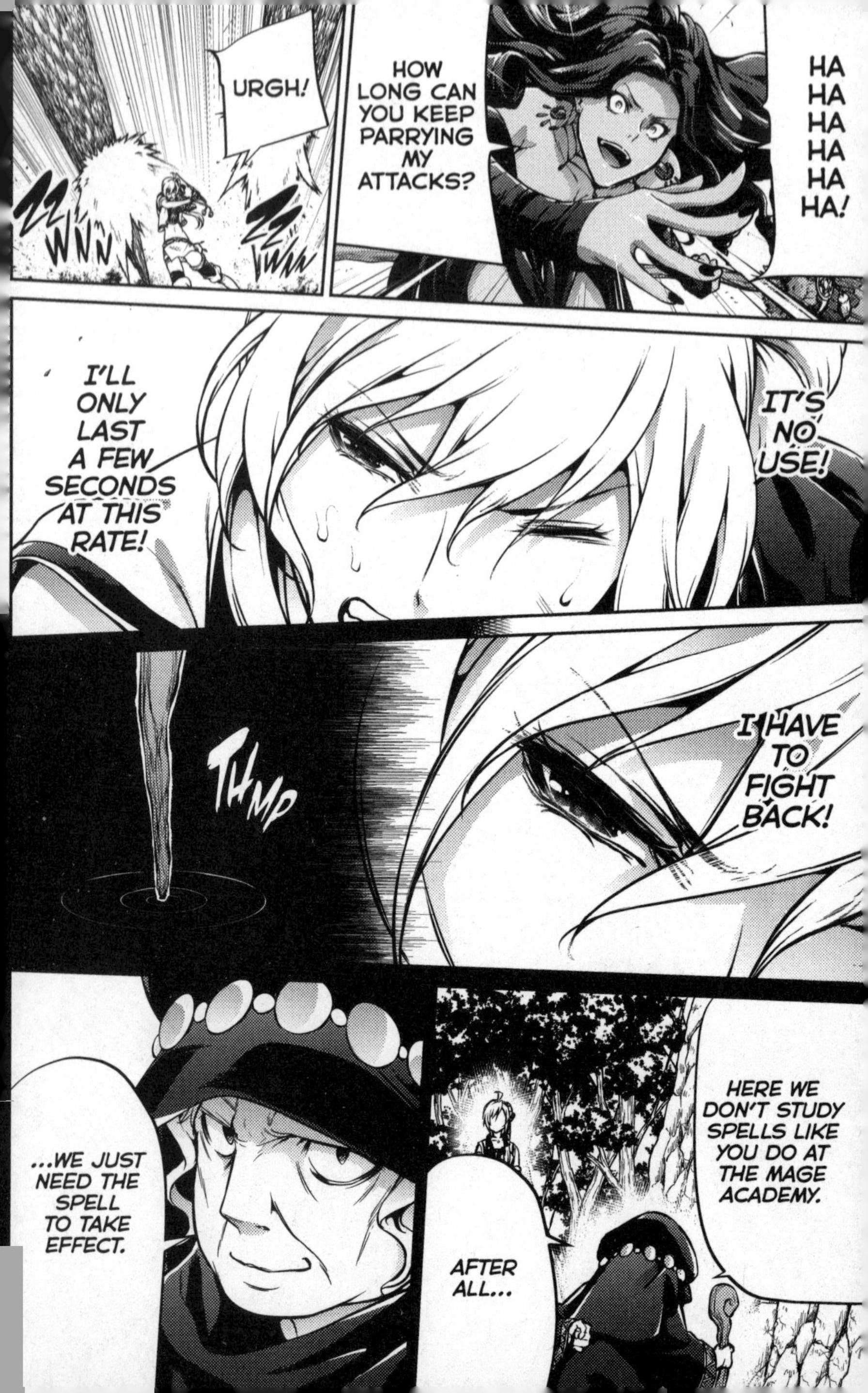

HA HA HA HA HA HA!
HOW LONG CAN YOU KEEP PARRYING MY ATTACKS?
URGH!
ZZWNN
ZZWNN
IT'S NO USE!
I'LL ONLY LAST A FEW SECONDS AT THIS RATE!
I HAVE TO FIGHT BACK!
THUMP
HERE WE DON'T STUDY SPELLS LIKE YOU DO AT THE MAGE ACADEMY.
AFTER ALL...
...WE JUST NEED THE SPELL TO TAKE EFFECT.

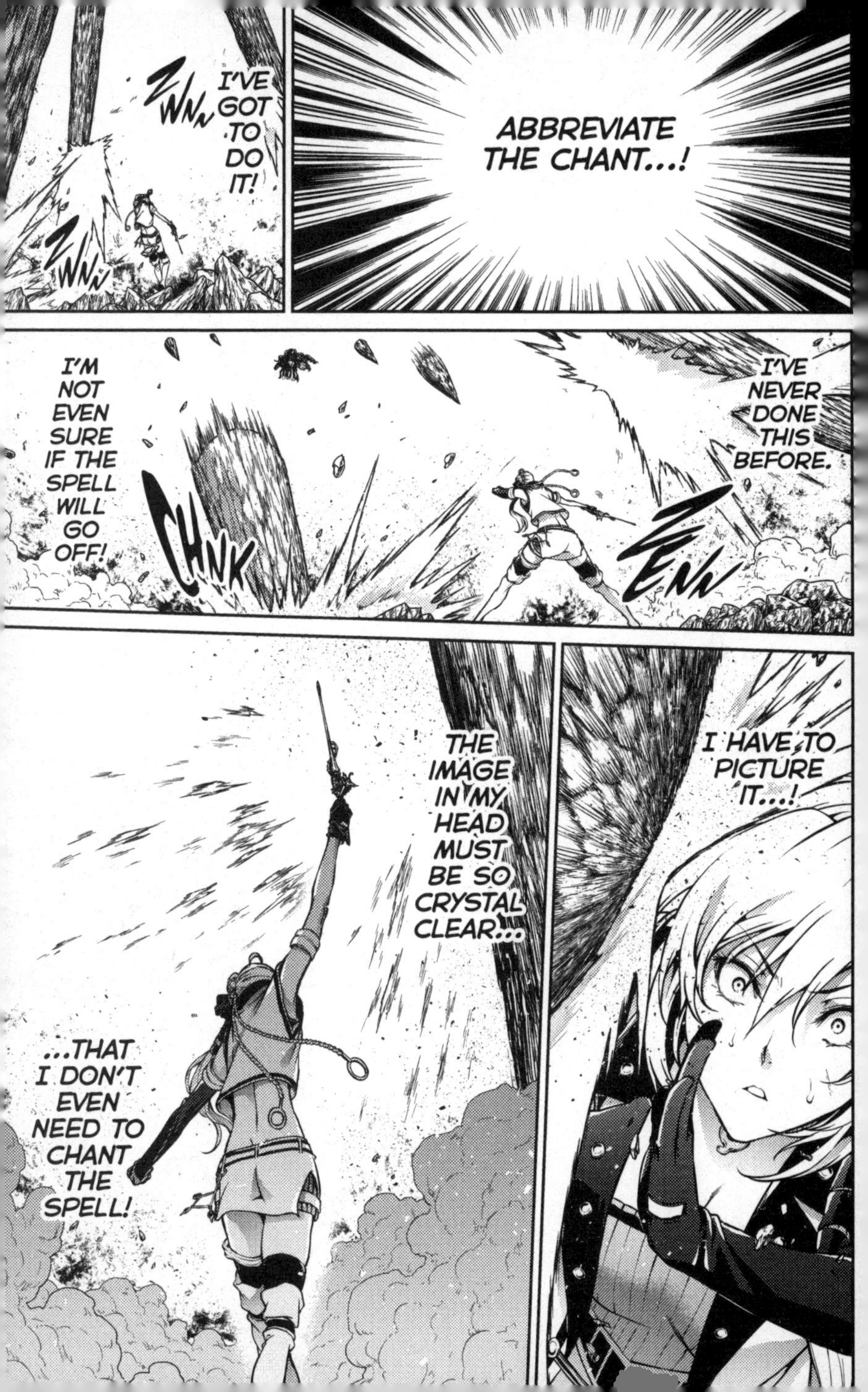
ABBREVIATE THE CHANT...!
I'VE GOT TO DO IT!
ZWNN
ZWNN
I'VE NEVER DONE THIS BEFORE.
ZENN
CHNK
I'M NOT EVEN SURE IF THE SPELL WILL GO OFF!
I HAVE TO PICTURE IT...!
THE IMAGE IN MY HEAD MUST BE SO CRYSTAL CLEAR...
...THAT I DON'T EVEN NEED TO CHANT THE SPELL!

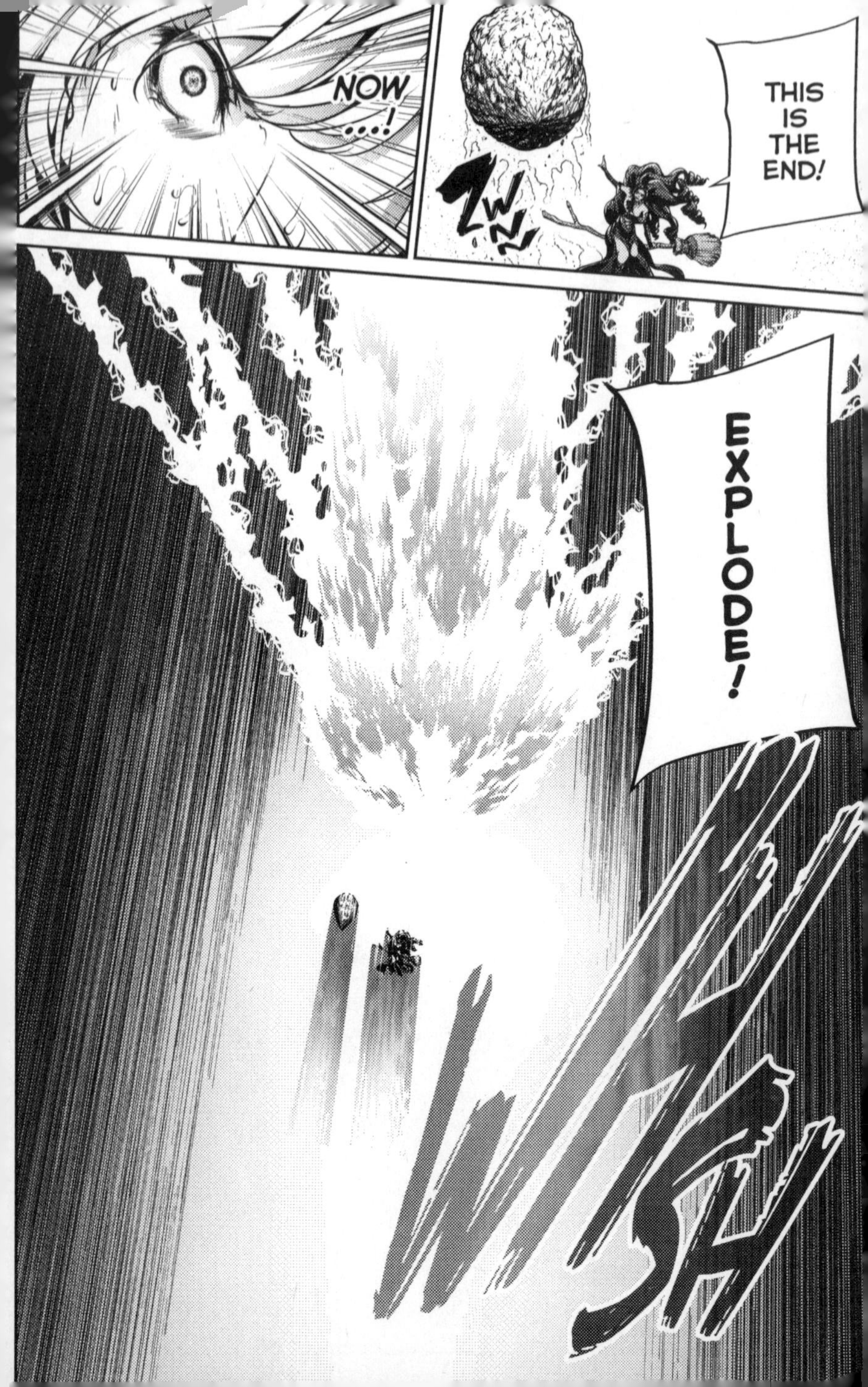
THIS IS THE END!
ZWNN
NOW ...!
EXPLODE!
WHSH

A CONVERSATION BETWEEN JANA AND ELMER THAT LED UP TO VOLUME 6 OF THE ORIGINAL NOVELS. IT WAS CUT OUT BECAUSE THE MANGA SERIES WAS COMING TO AN END.

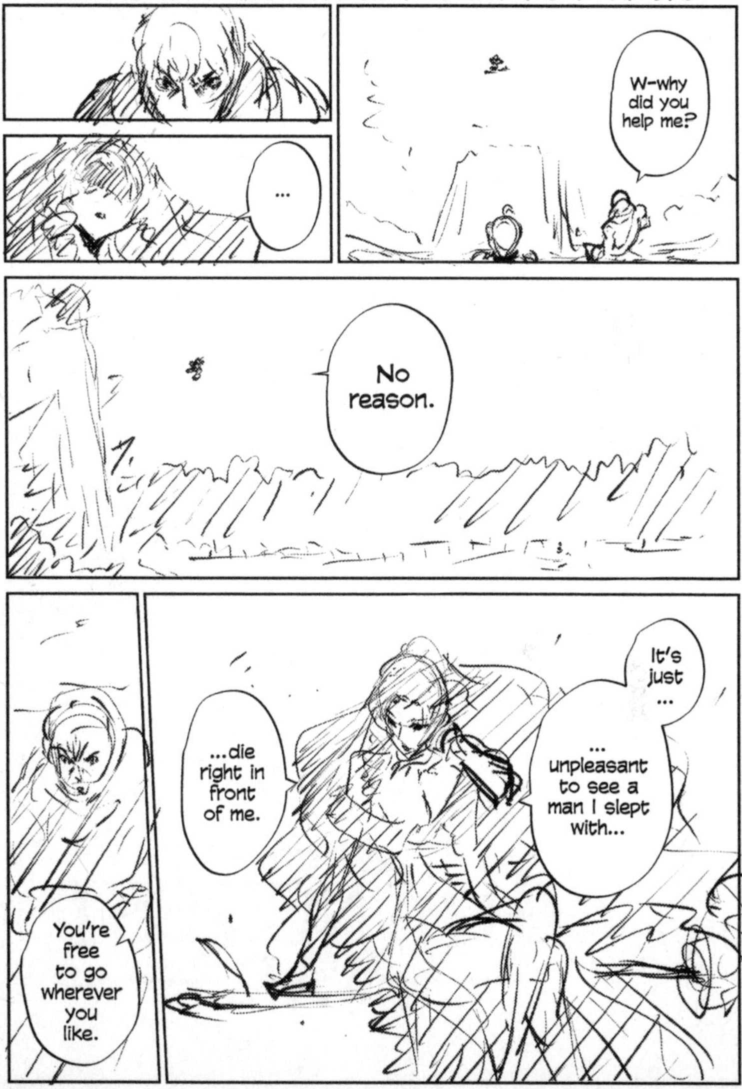
W-why did you help me?
...
No reason.
It's just...
...unpleasant to see a man I slept with...
...die right in front of me.
You're free to go wherever you like.

RECORD OF
GRANCREST
WAR

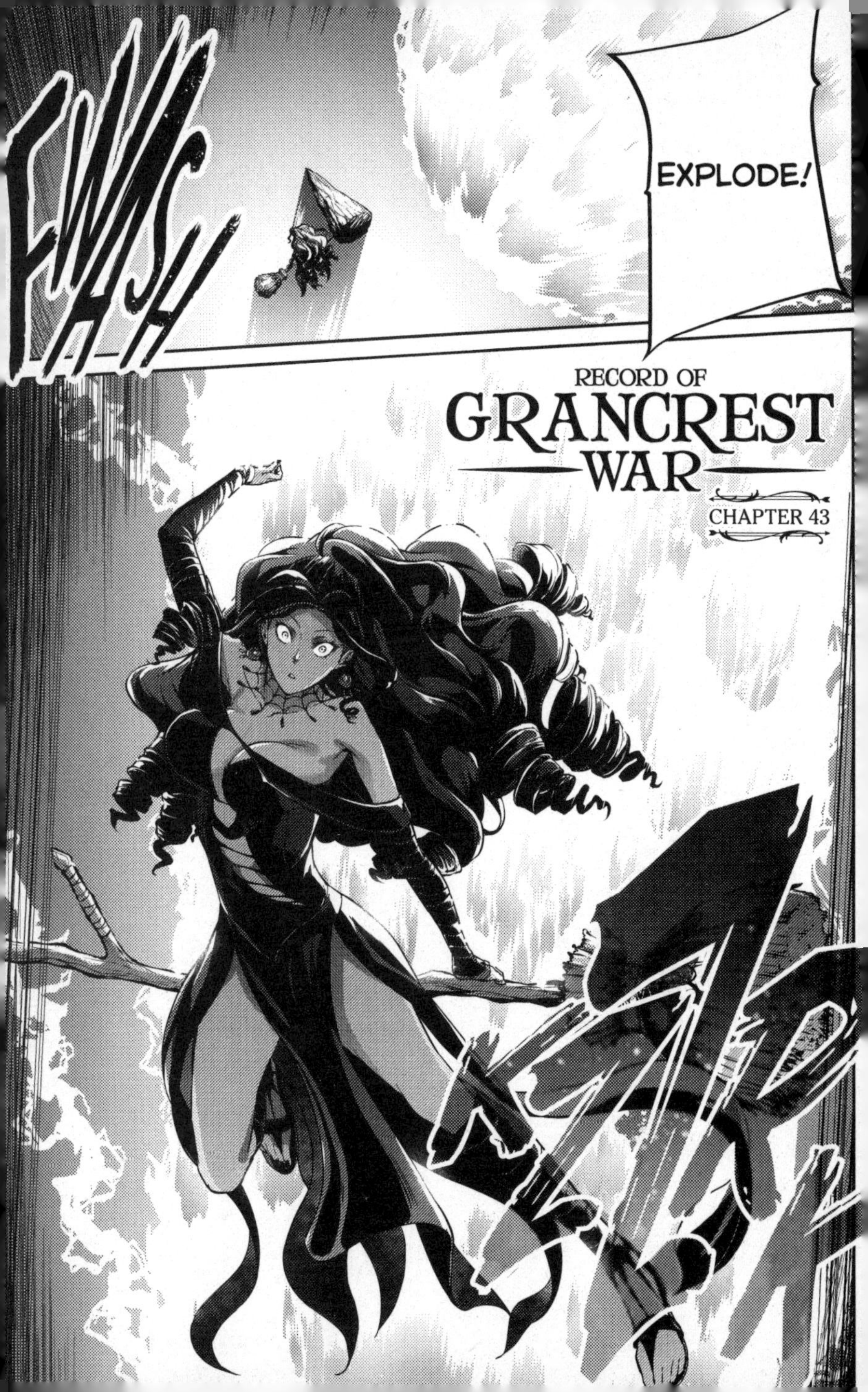
EXPLODE!
FWSH
RECORD OF
GRANCREST
WAR
CHAPTER 43

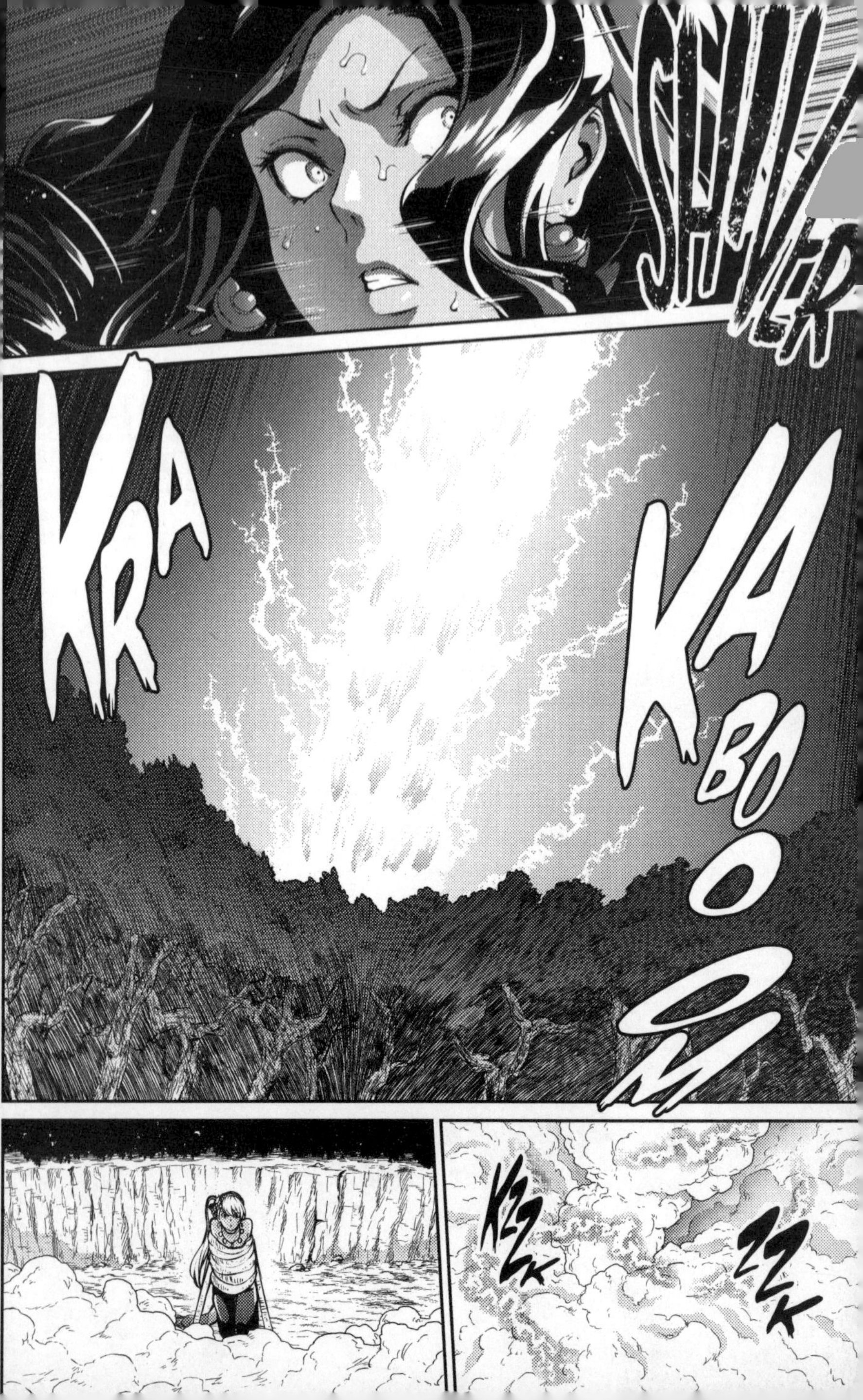
SHIVER
KRA
KABOOM
KZZZK
ZZZK

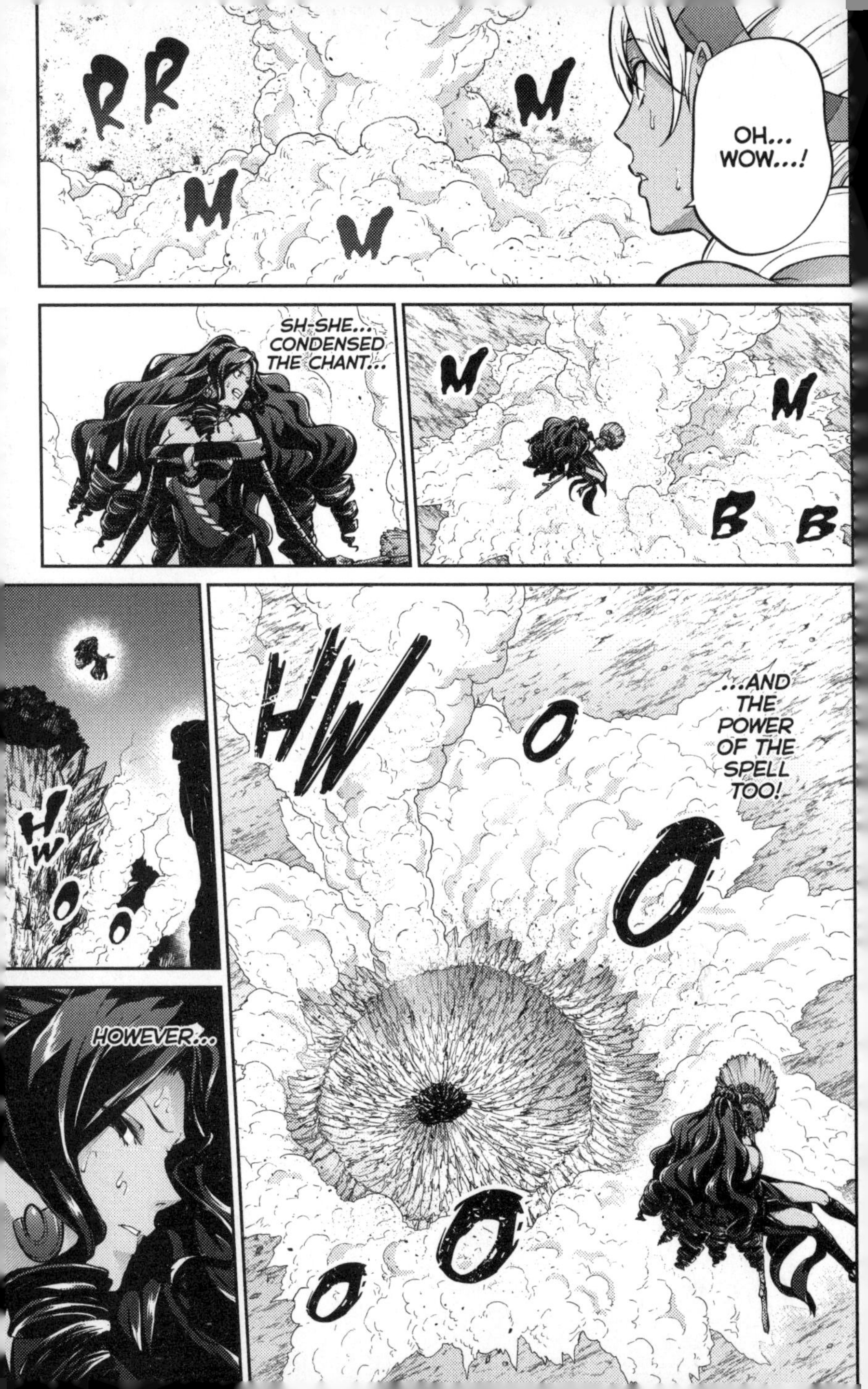
RRMMM
OH... WOW...!
MMBB
SH-SHE... CONDENSED THE CHANT...
HWOOOO
...AND THE POWER OF THE SPELL TOO!
HWOO
HOWEVER...

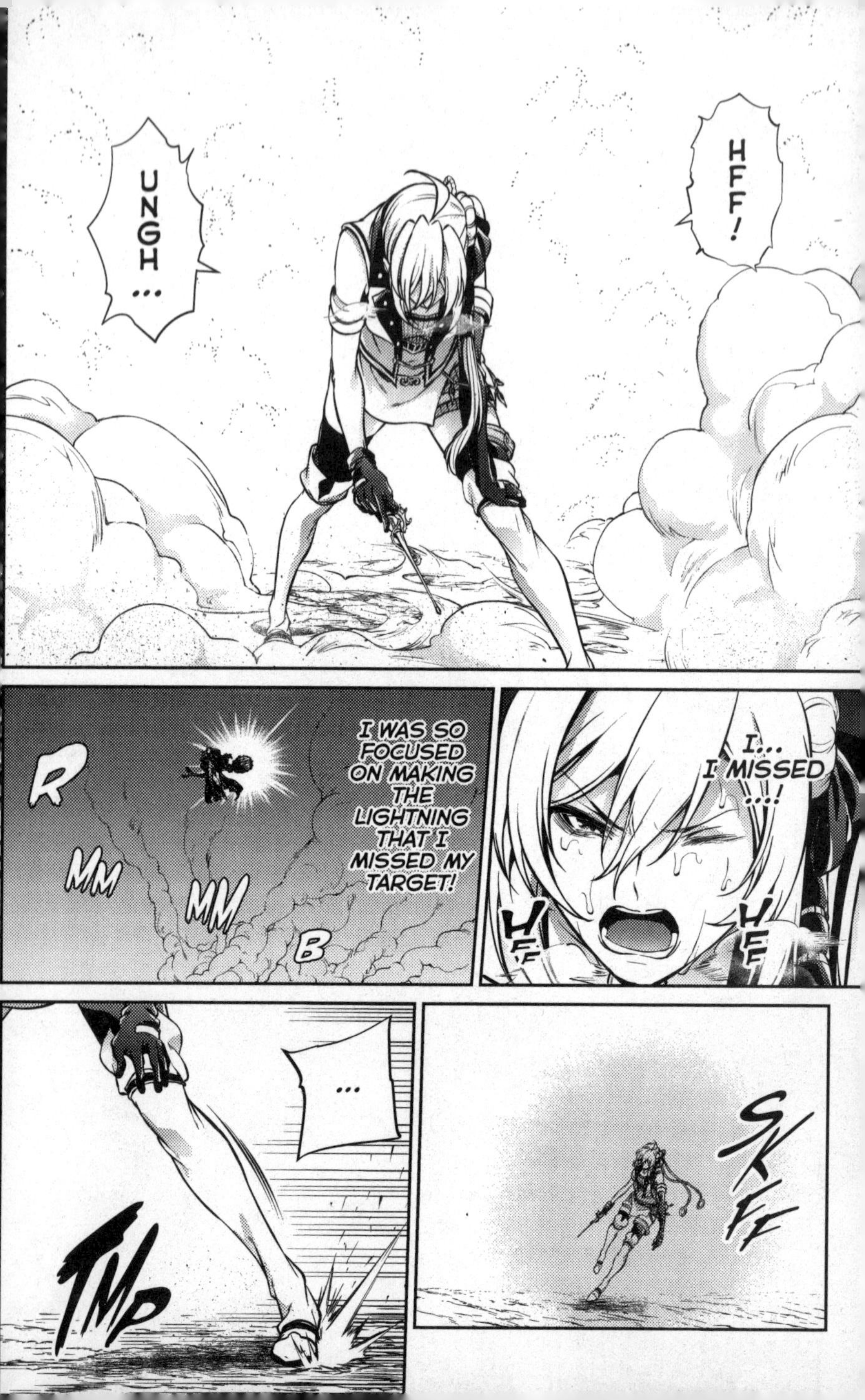
HFF!
UNGH...
I... I MISSED...!
HFF
HFF
I WAS SO FOCUSED ON MAKING THE LIGHTNING THAT I MISSED MY TARGET!
RMMMMB
SKFF
...
TMP

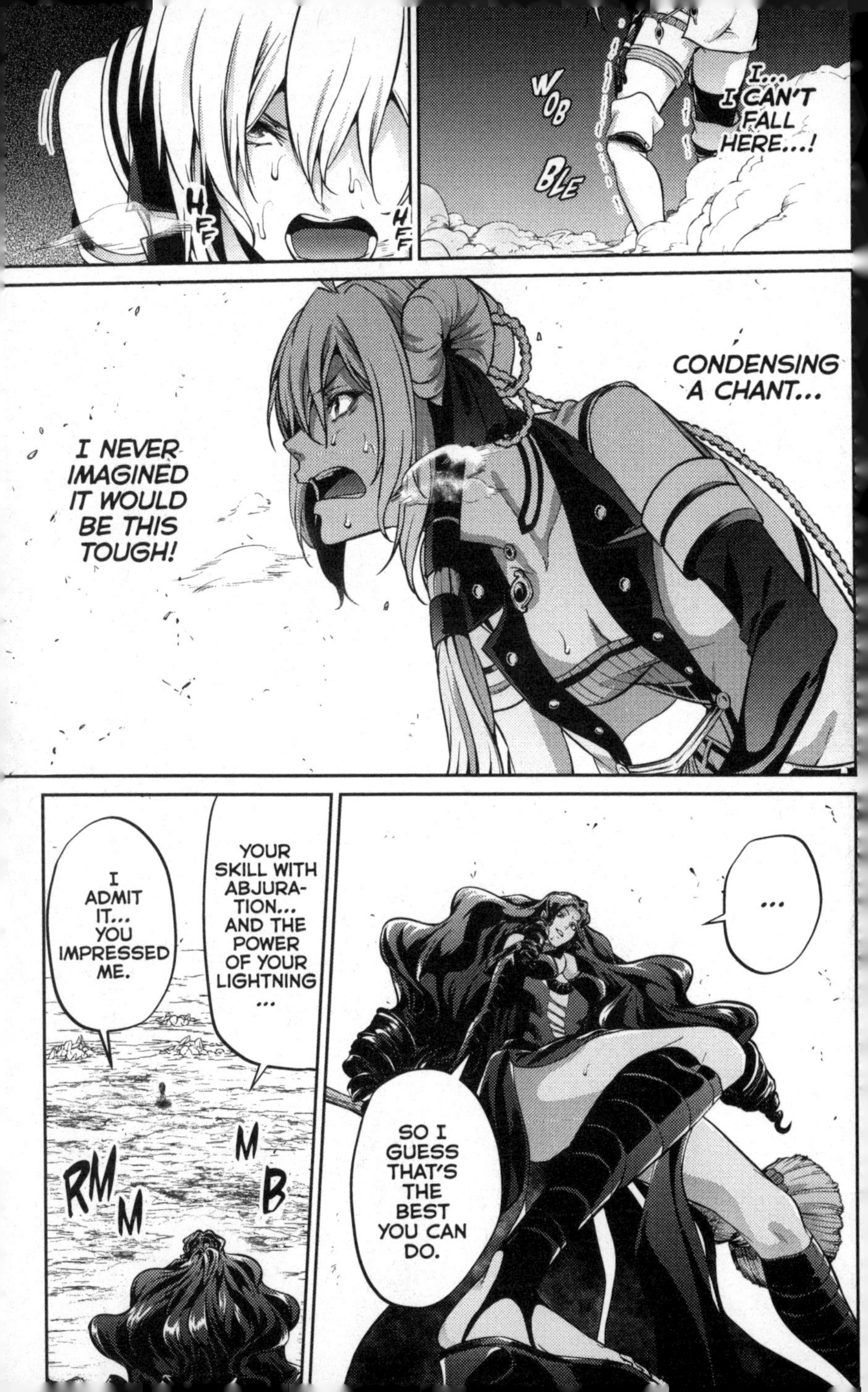
I... I CAN'T FALL HERE...!
WOBBLE
HFF HFF
CONDENSING A CHANT...
I NEVER IMAGINED IT WOULD BE THIS TOUGH!
...
YOUR SKILL WITH ABJURATION... AND THE POWER OF YOUR LIGHTNING...
I ADMIT IT... YOU IMPRESSED ME.
SO I GUESS THAT'S THE BEST YOU CAN DO.
RMMMB

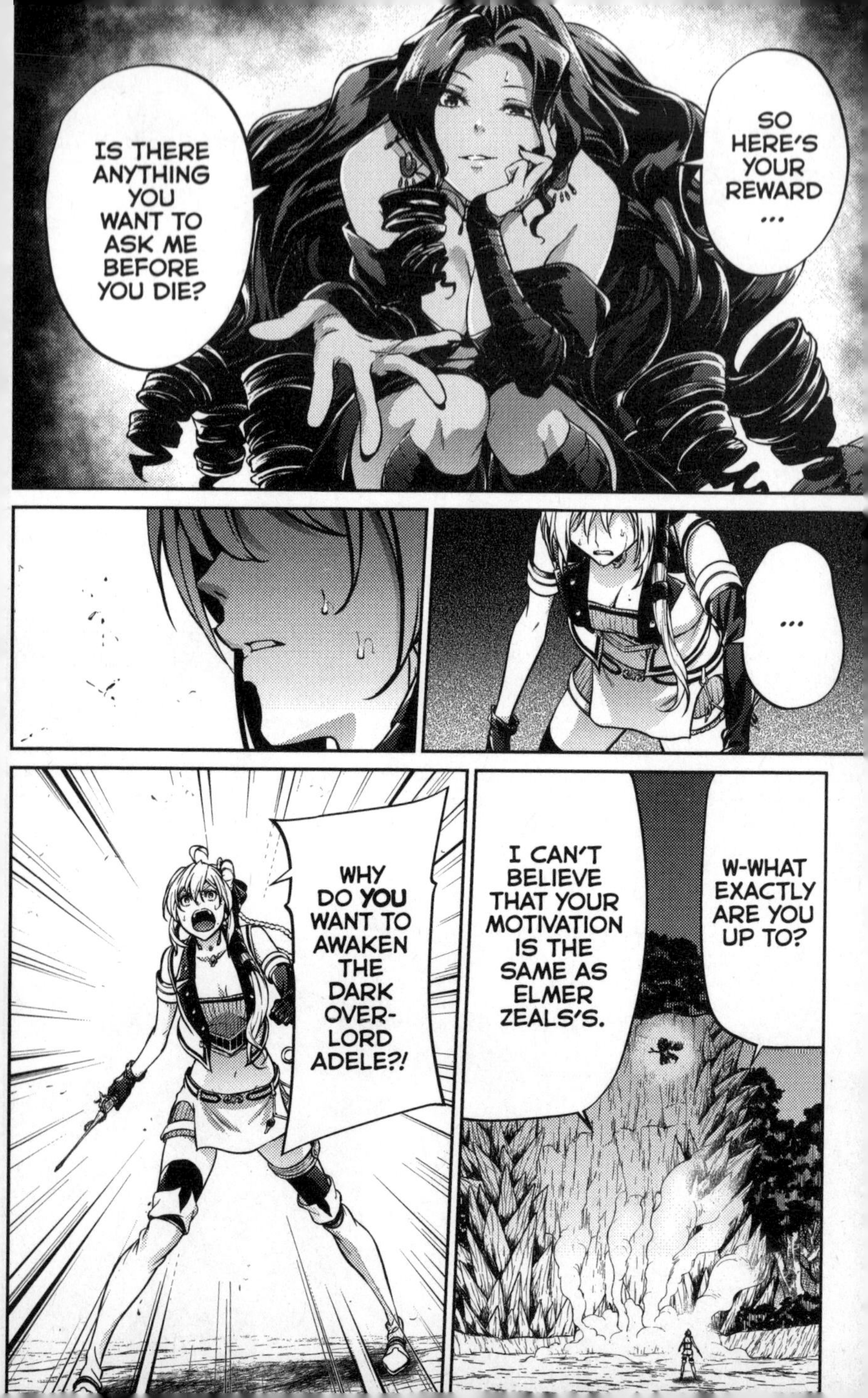
SO HERE'S YOUR REWARD...
IS THERE ANYTHING YOU WANT TO ASK ME BEFORE YOU DIE?
...
W-WHAT EXACTLY ARE YOU UP TO?
I CAN'T BELIEVE THAT YOUR MOTIVATION IS THE SAME AS ELMER ZEALS'S.
WHY DO YOU WANT TO AWAKEN THE DARK OVER-LORD ADELE?!

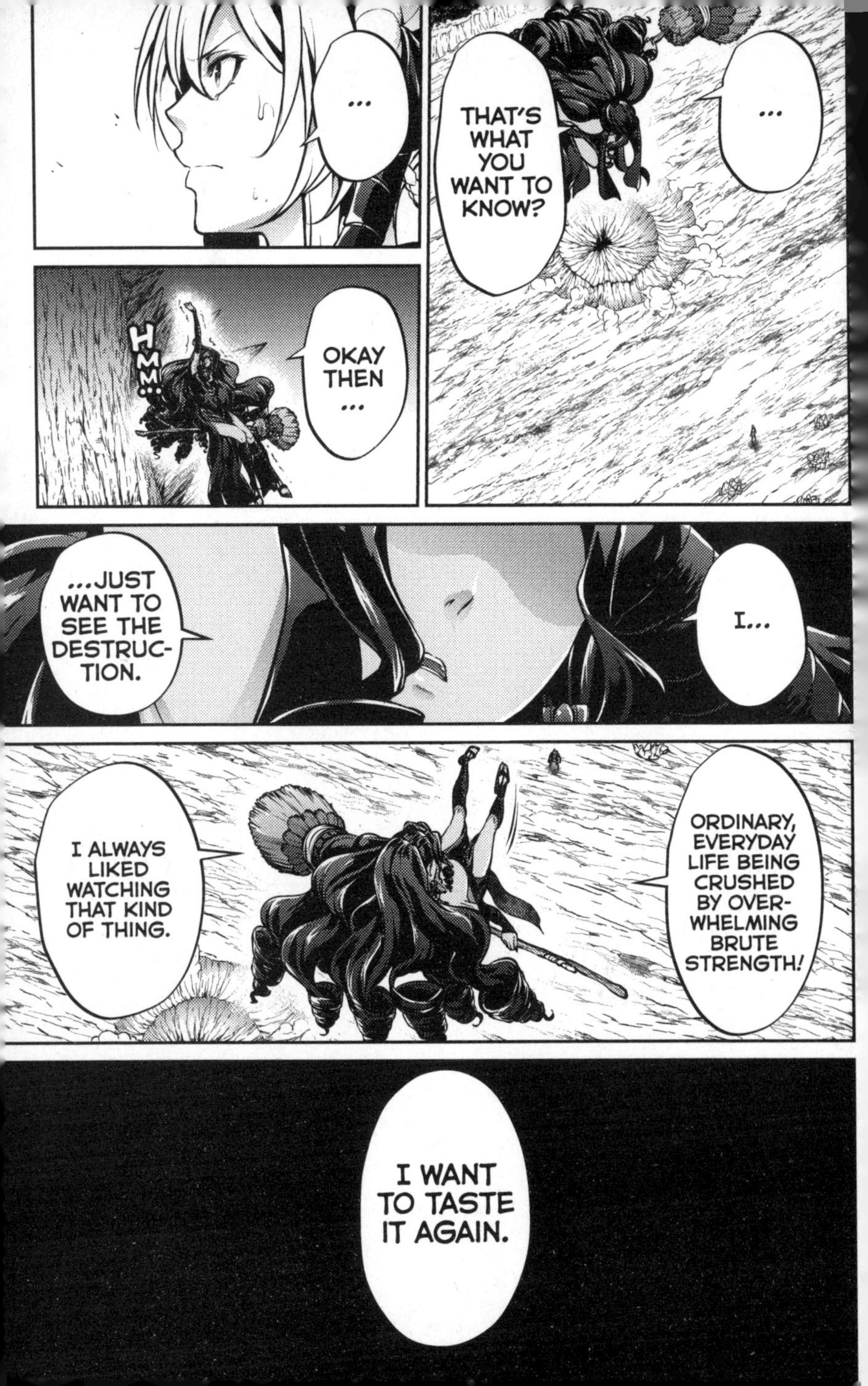
...
THAT'S WHAT YOU WANT TO KNOW?
...
OKAY THEN ...
HMM...
I...
...JUST WANT TO SEE THE DESTRUCTION.
ORDINARY, EVERYDAY LIFE BEING CRUSHED BY OVERWHELMING BRUTE STRENGTH!
I ALWAYS LIKED WATCHING THAT KIND OF THING.
I WANT TO TASTE IT AGAIN.

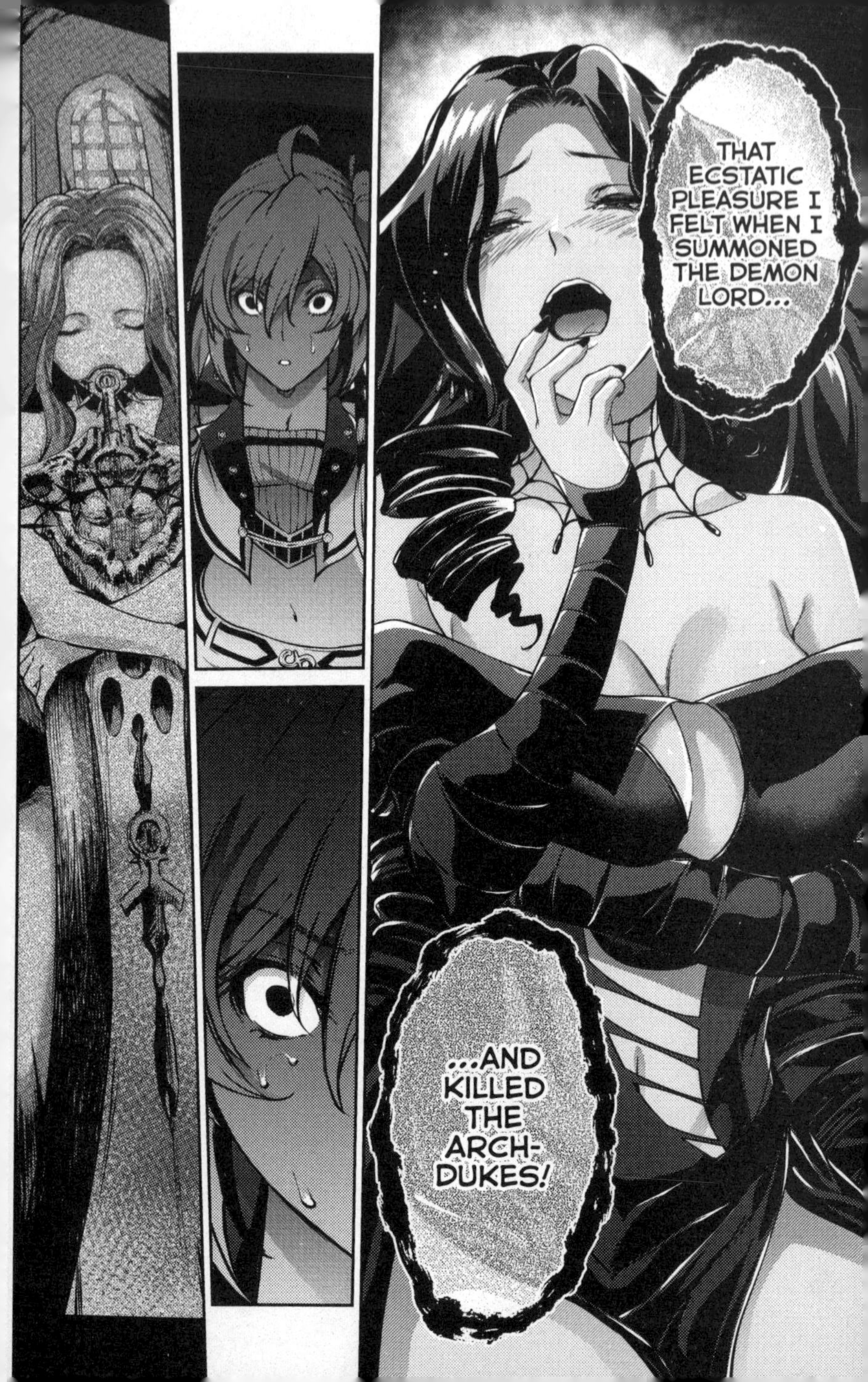
THAT ECSTATIC PLEASURE I FELT WHEN I SUMMONED THE DEMON LORD...
...AND KILLED THE ARCH-DUKES!

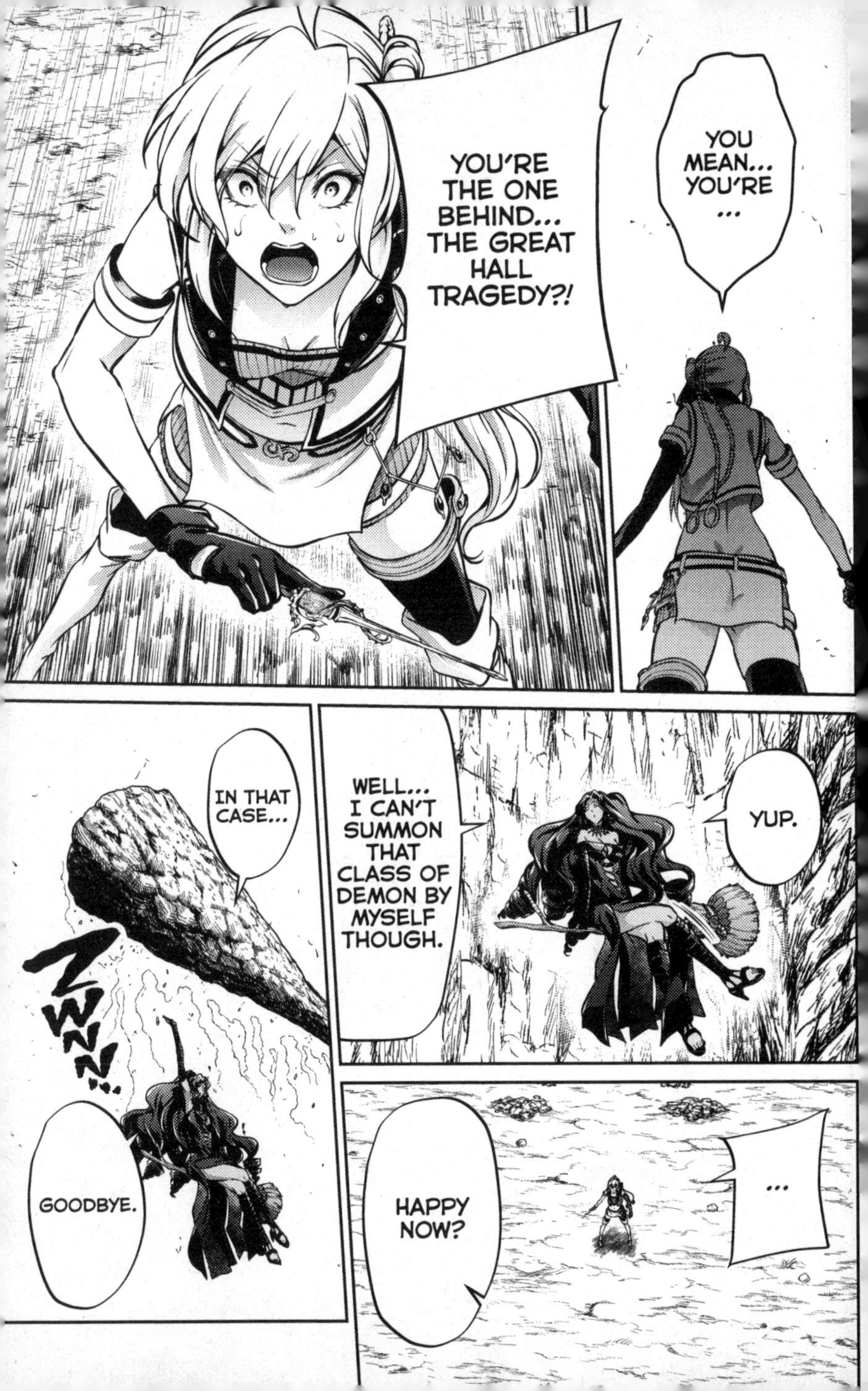
YOU MEAN... YOU'RE ...
YOU'RE THE ONE BEHIND... THE GREAT HALL TRAGEDY?!
YUP.
WELL... I CAN'T SUMMON THAT CLASS OF DEMON BY MYSELF THOUGH.
...
HAPPY NOW?
IN THAT CASE...
ZWNN..
GOODBYE.

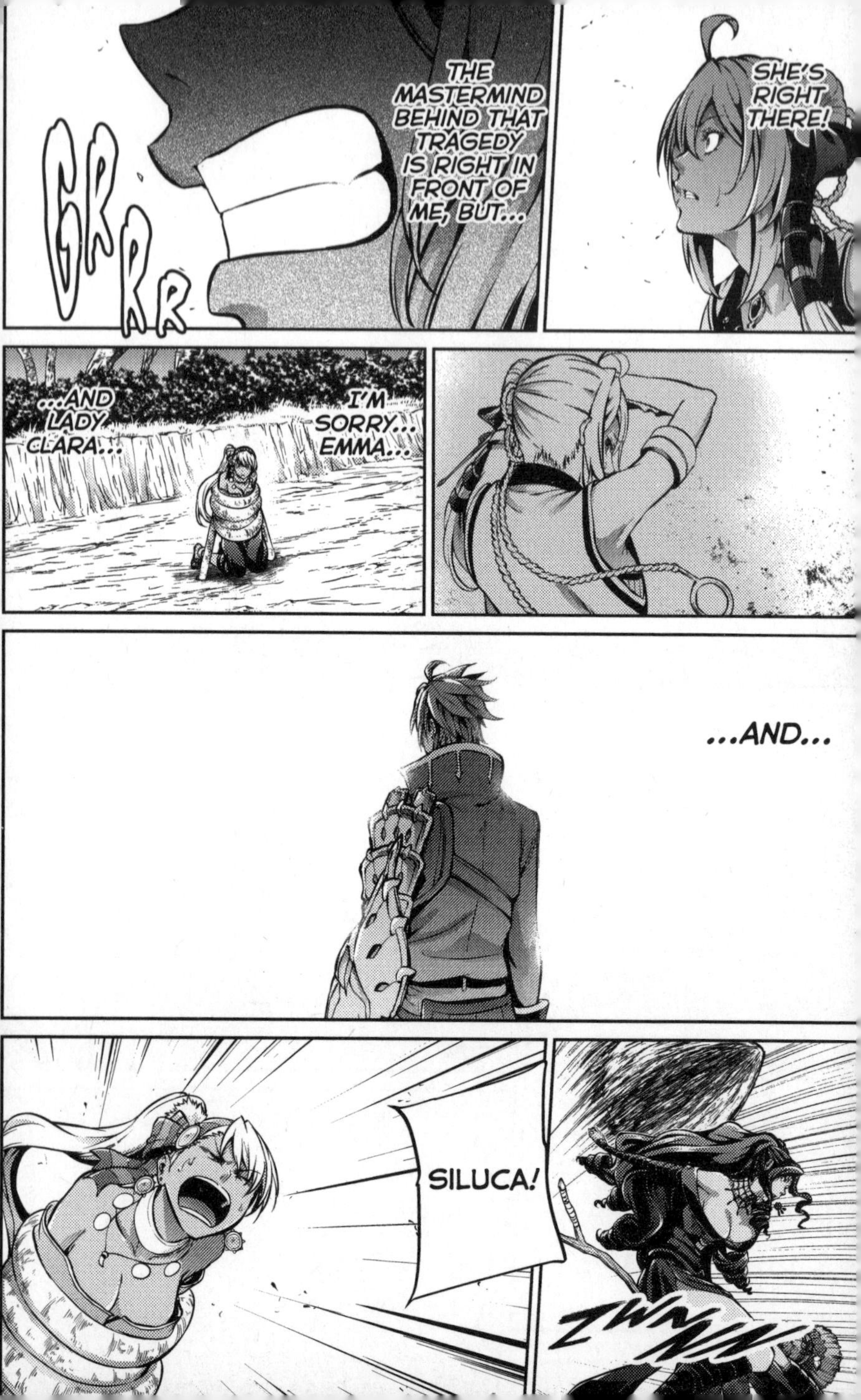
SHE'S RIGHT THERE!
THE MASTERMIND BEHIND THAT TRAGEDY IS RIGHT IN FRONT OF ME, BUT...
GRRR
I'M SORRY... EMMA...
...AND LADY CLARA...
...AND...
ZWNNN
SILUCA!

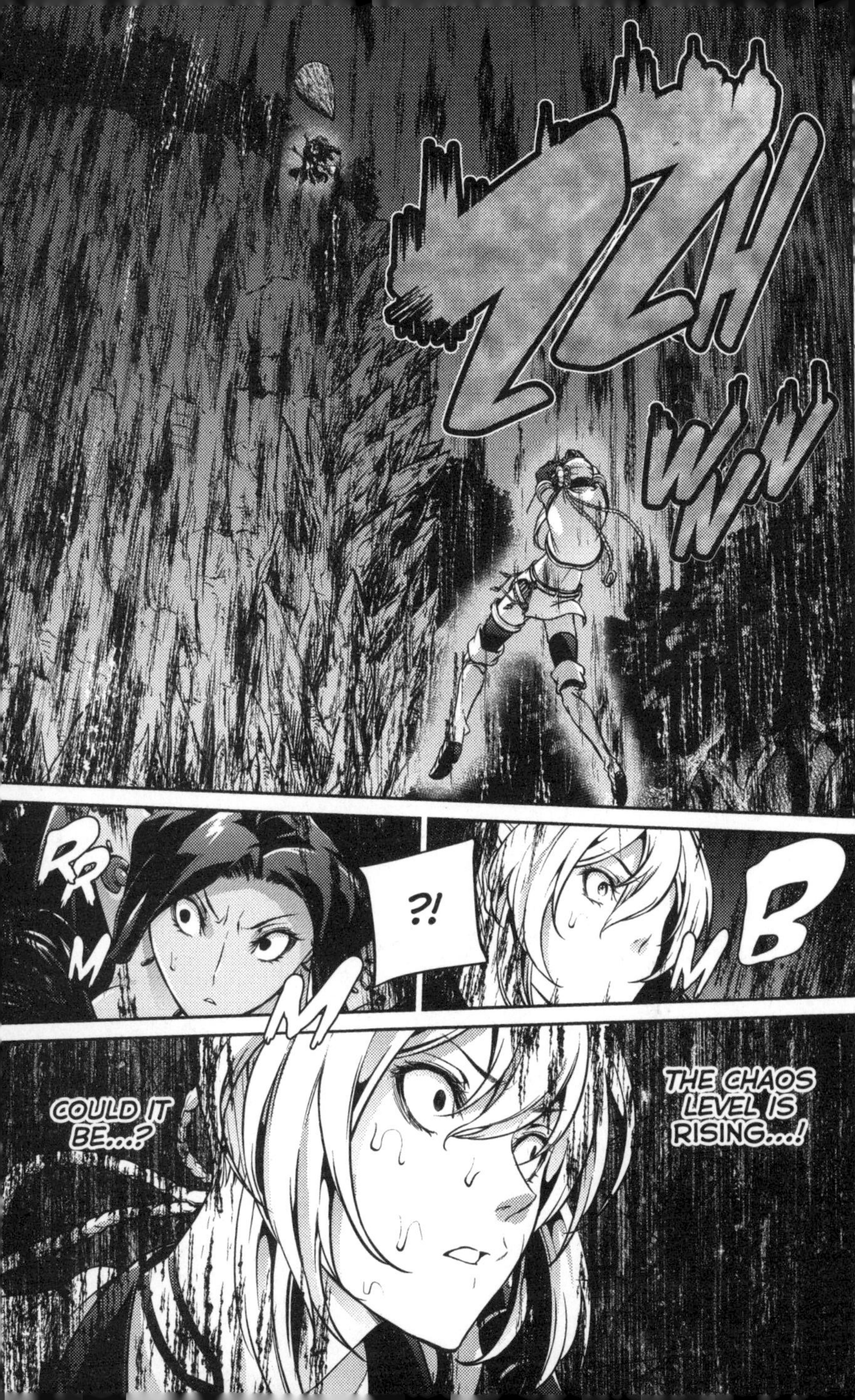
ZZAH
WNN
?!
THE CHAOS LEVEL IS RISING...!
COULD IT BE...?

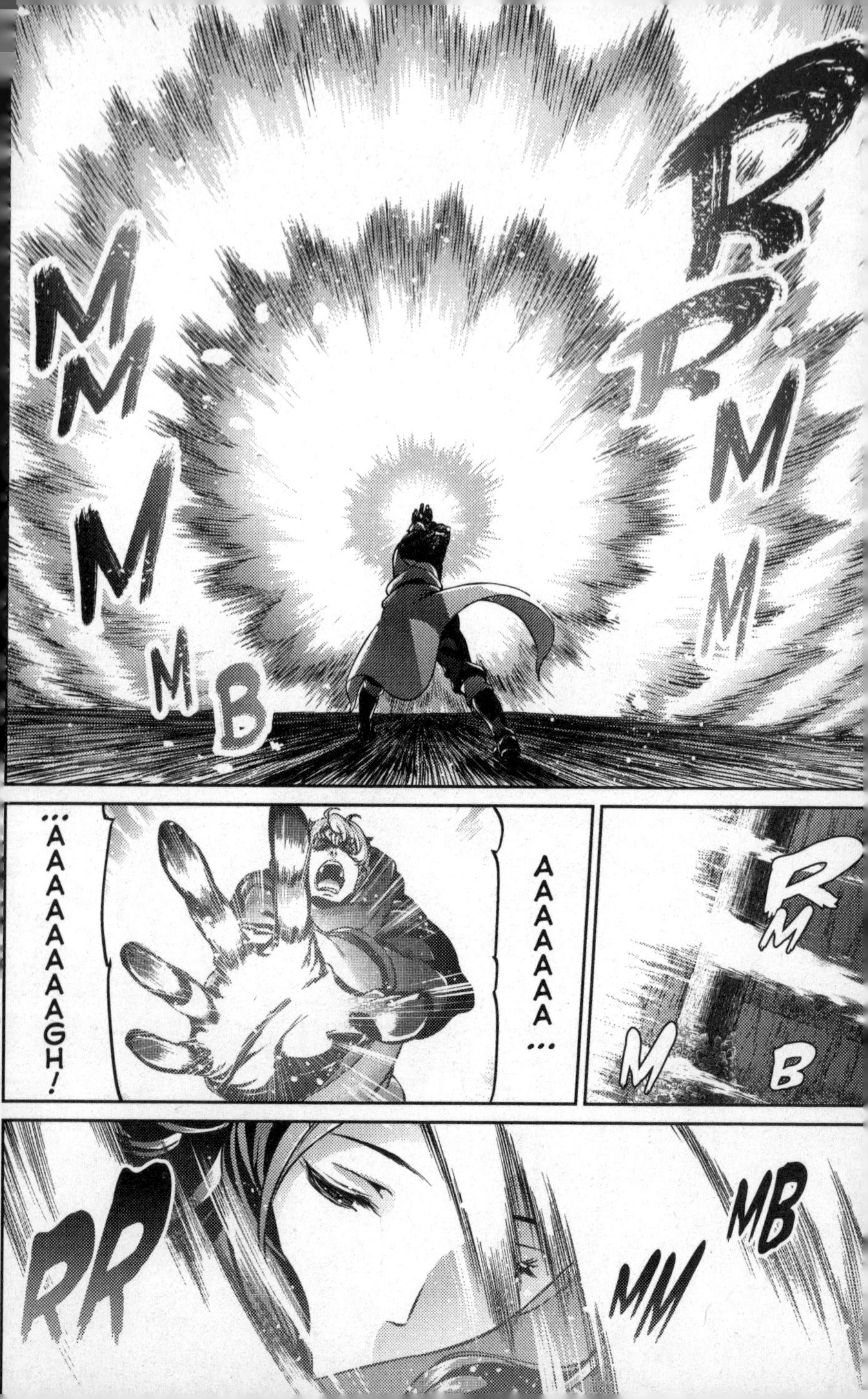

RRMMM
MMMMMB
RMMB
AAAAAAA...
...AAAAAAAAAAGH!
MB
MM
RR

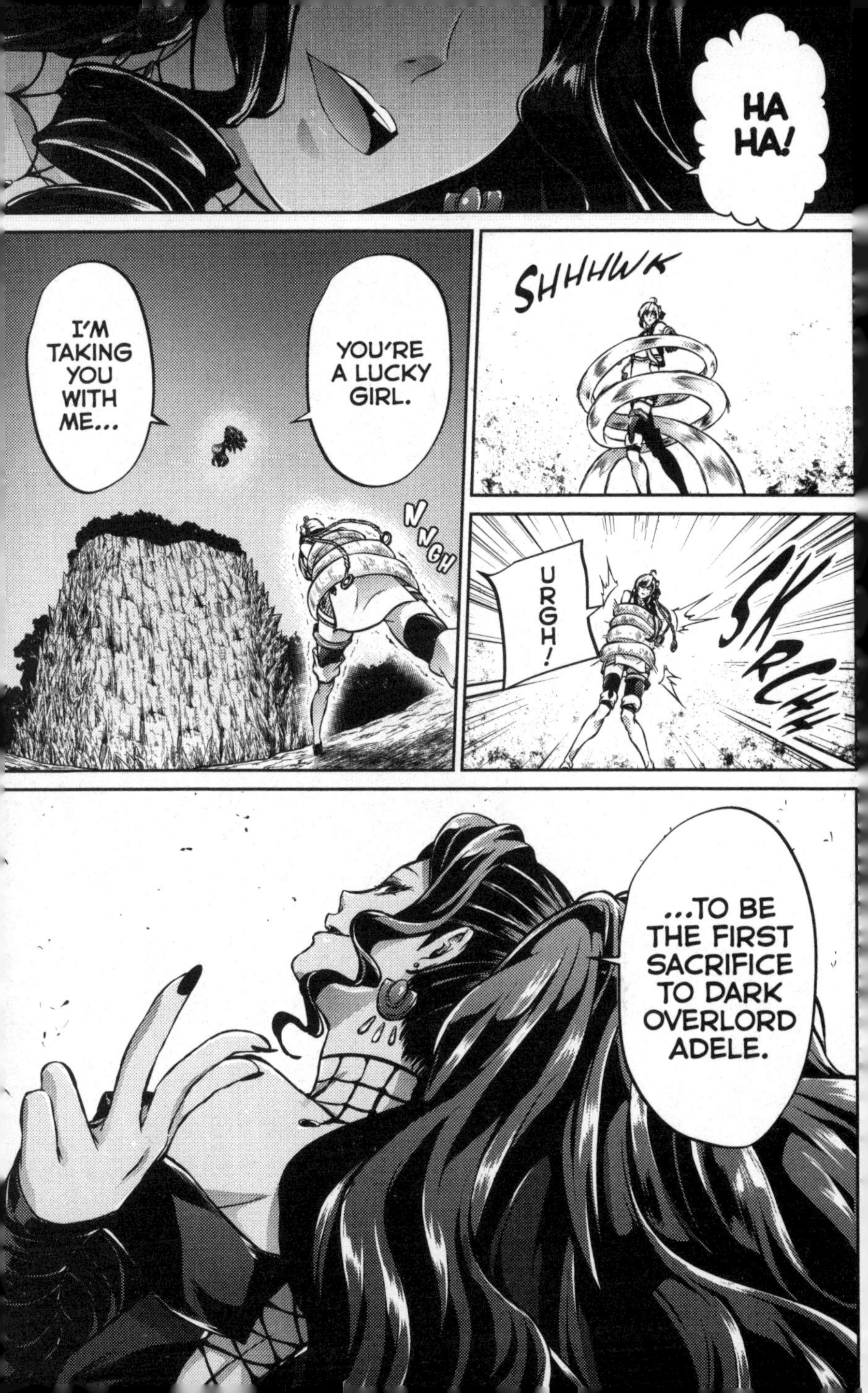
HA HA!
SHHHWK
URGH!
SKRCHH
YOU'RE A LUCKY GIRL.
I'M TAKING YOU WITH ME...
NNGH
...TO BE THE FIRST SACRIFICE TO DARK OVERLORD ADELE.

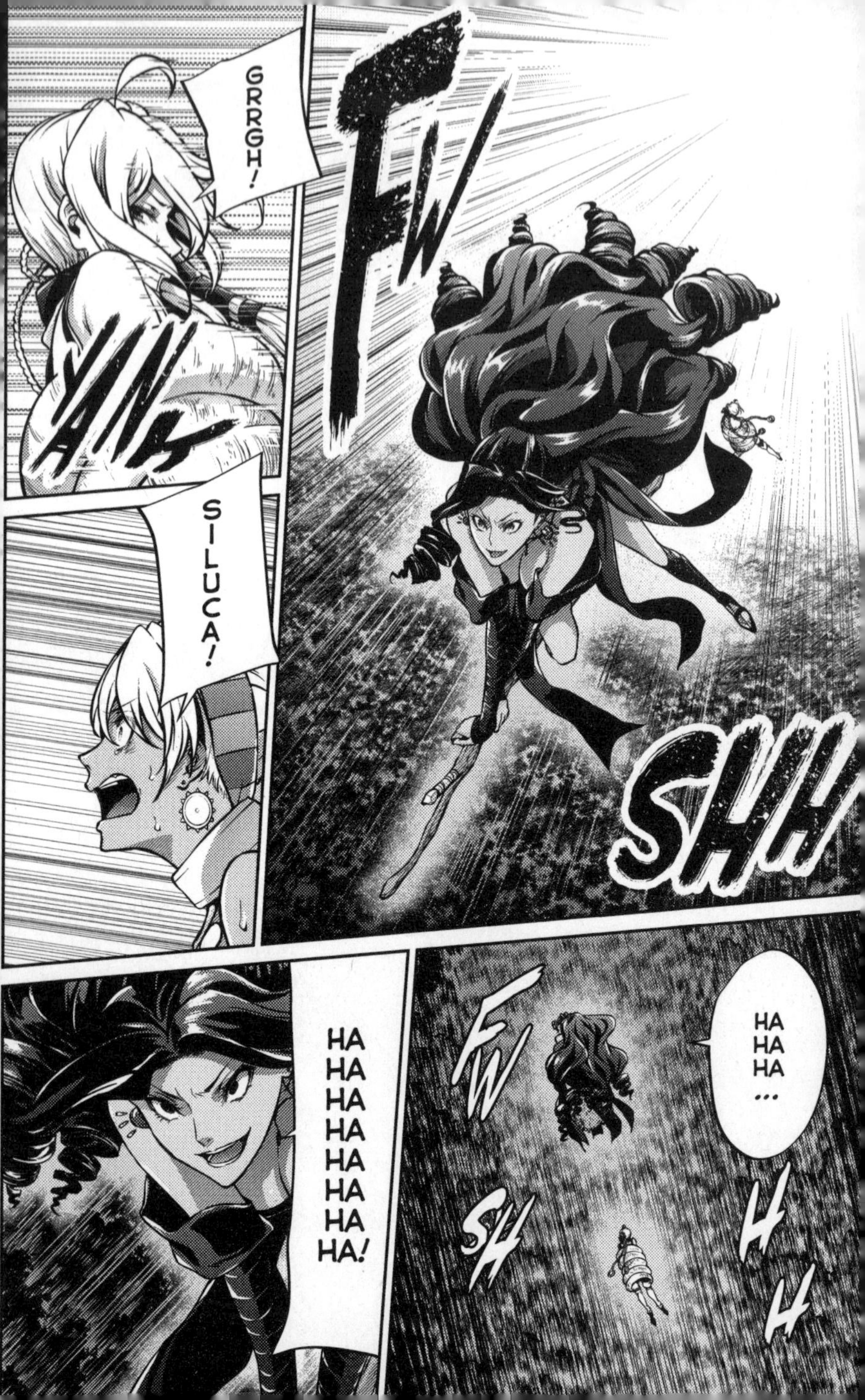
FW
SHH
GRRGH!
YANK
SILUCA!
HA HA HA...
FW
SH
H H
HA HA HA HA HA HA HA HA!

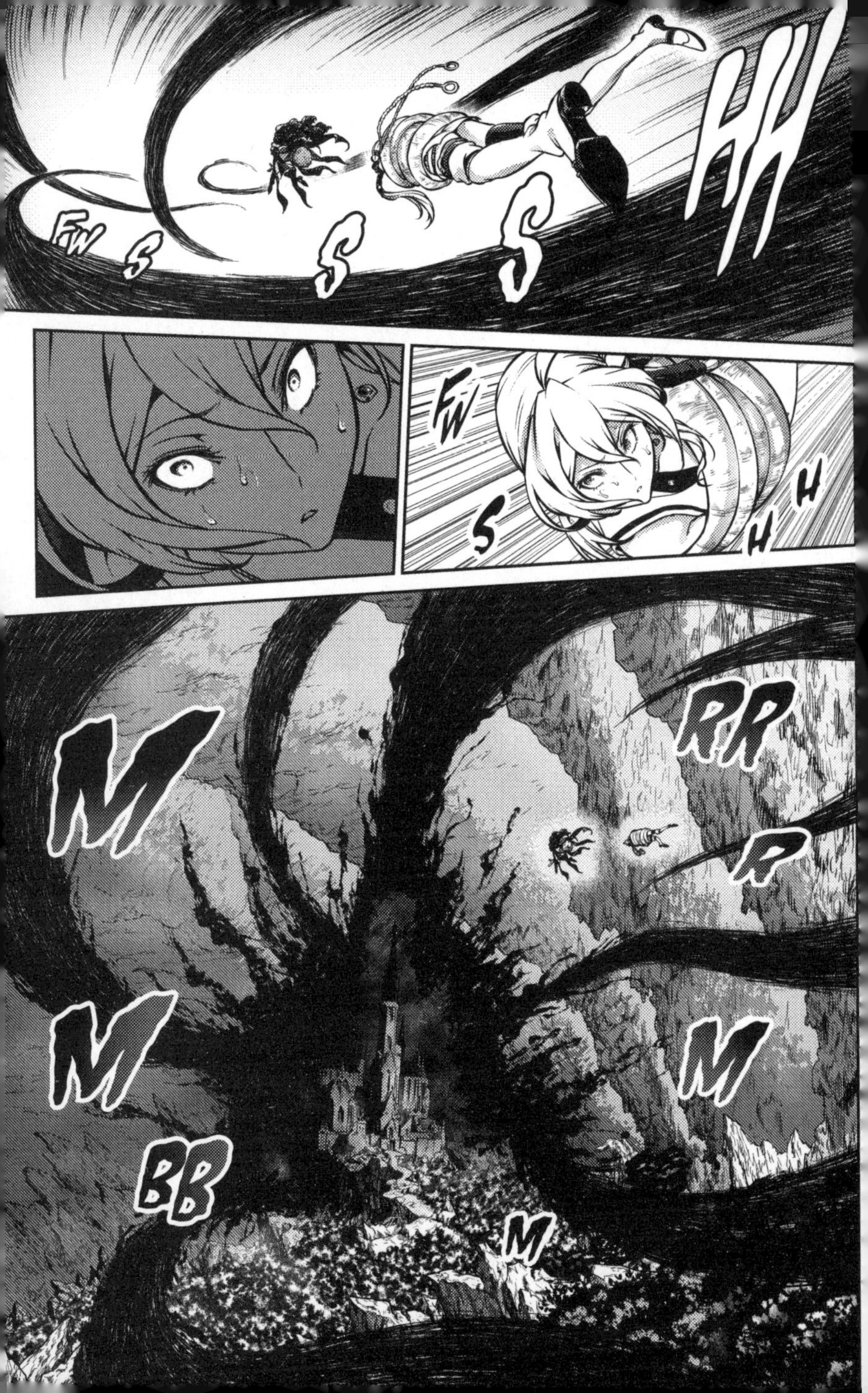

FW S S S HH
FW S H H H
RR R
M M
M
BB
M

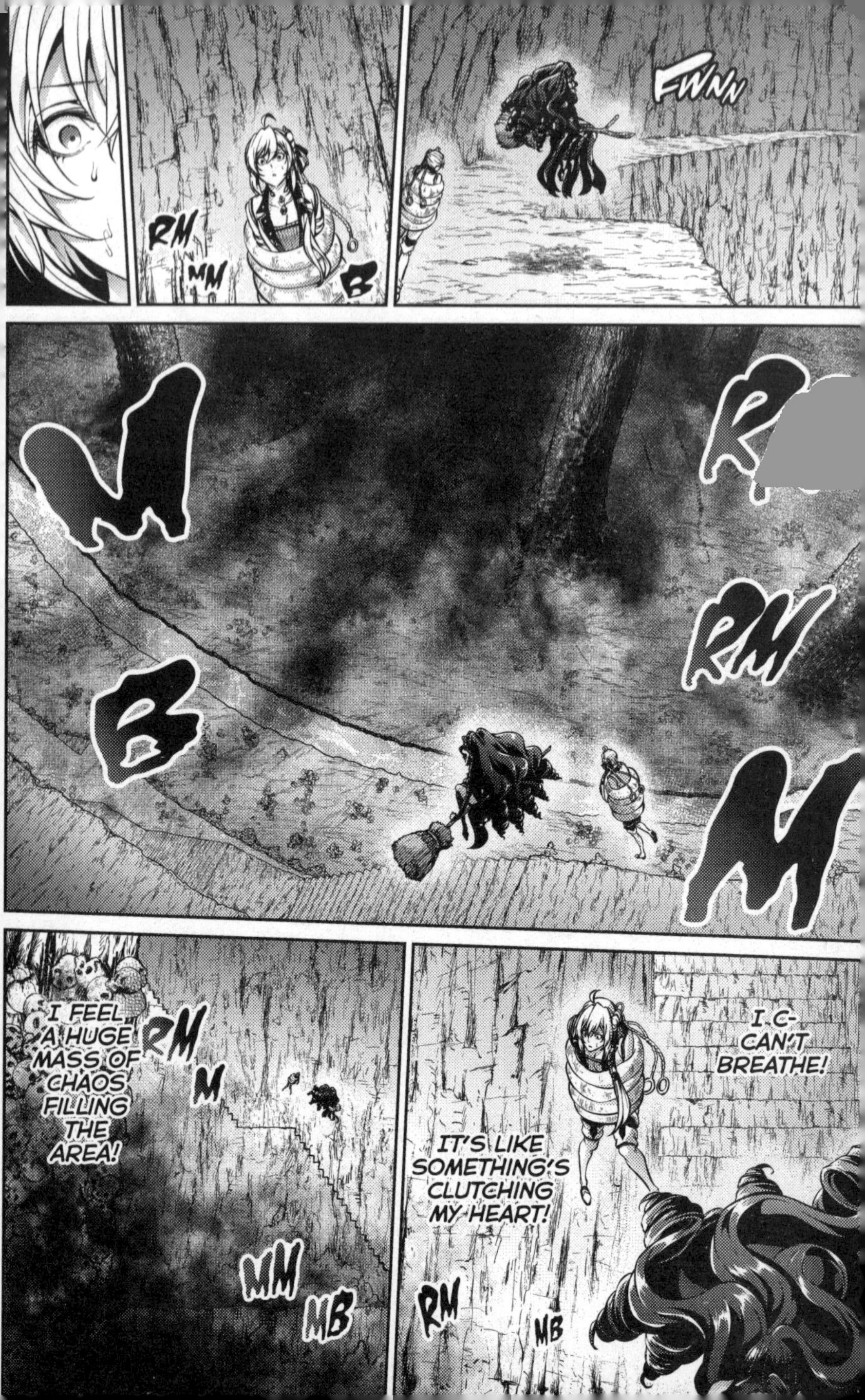
FWNN
RM
MM
B
R
RM
M
M
B
I C- CAN'T BREATHE!
IT'S LIKE SOMETHING'S CLUTCHING MY HEART!
RM
MB
I FEEL A HUGE MASS OF CHAOS FILLING THE AREA!
RM
M
MM
MB

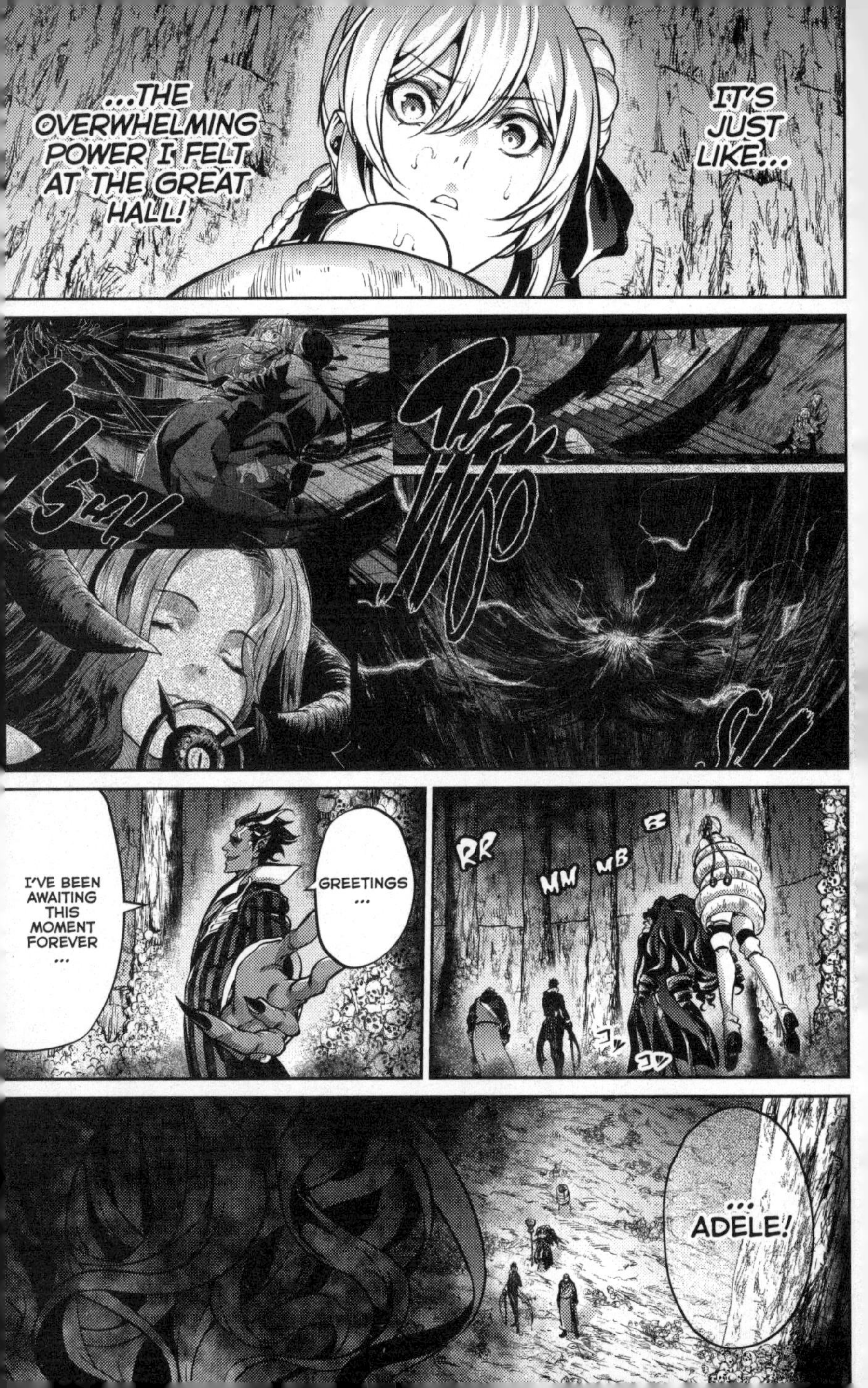
IT'S JUST LIKE...
...THE OVERWHELMING POWER I FELT AT THE GREAT HALL!
RR MM MB B
GREETINGS ...
I'VE BEEN AWAITING THIS MOMENT FOREVER ...
... ADELE!

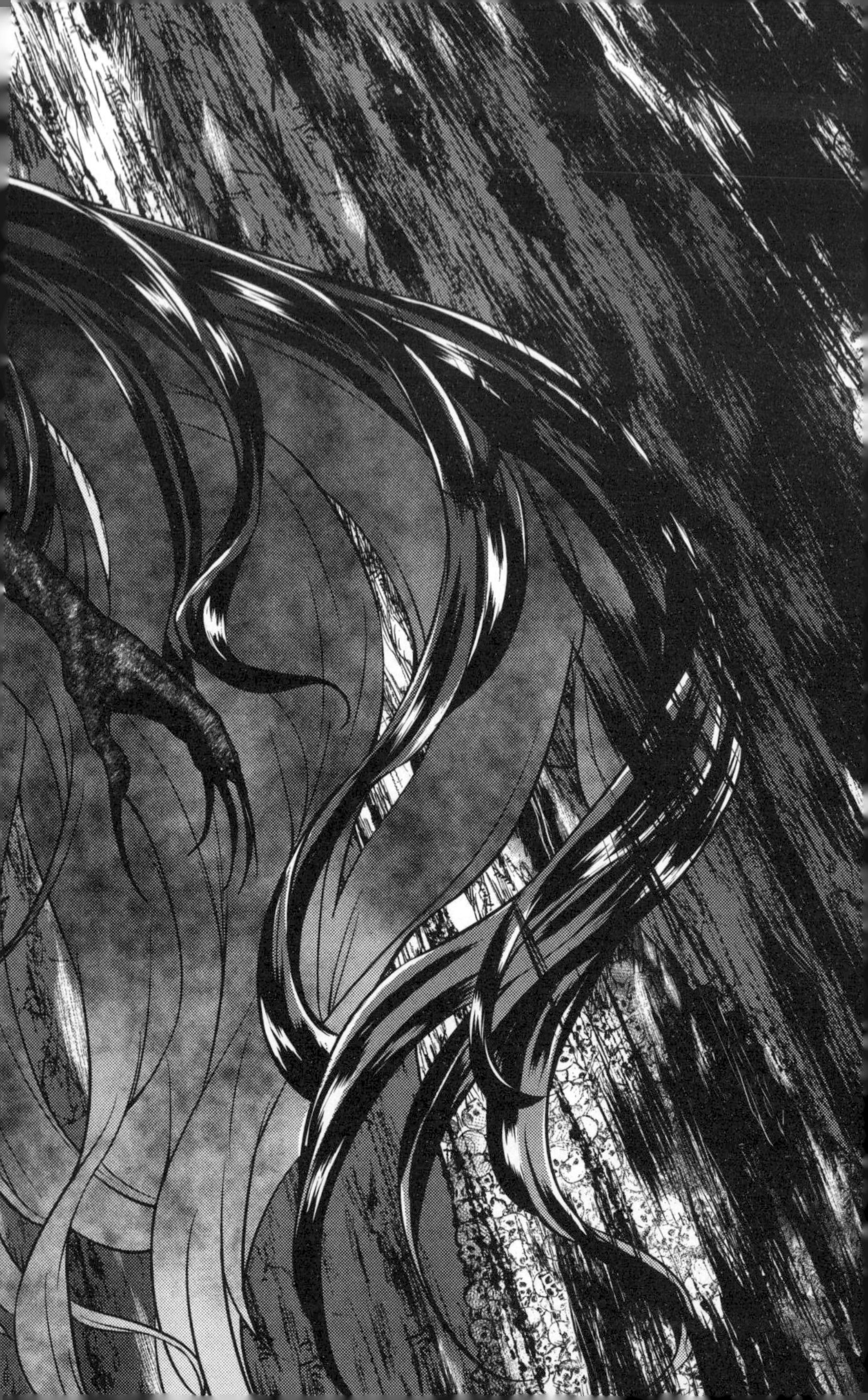

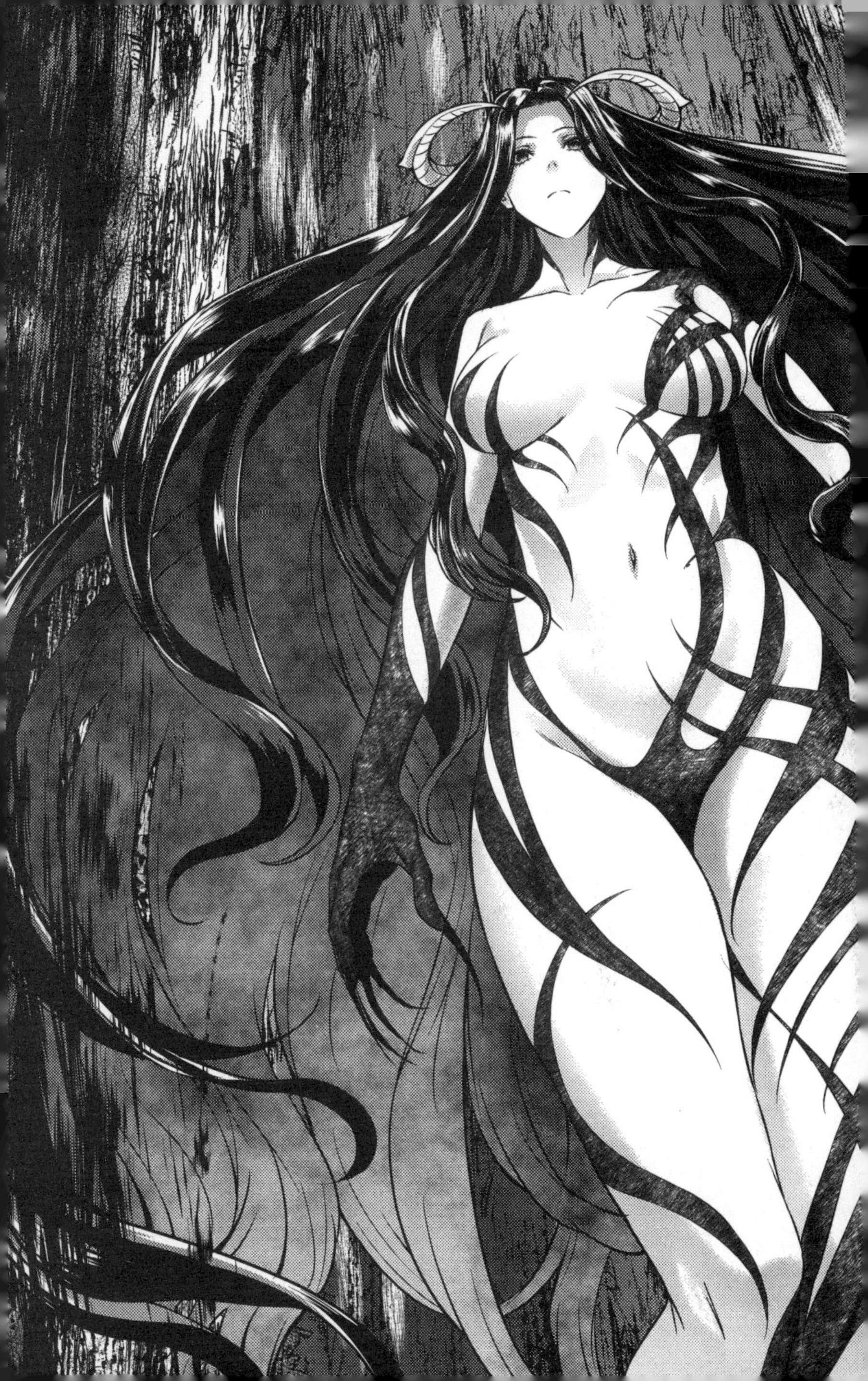

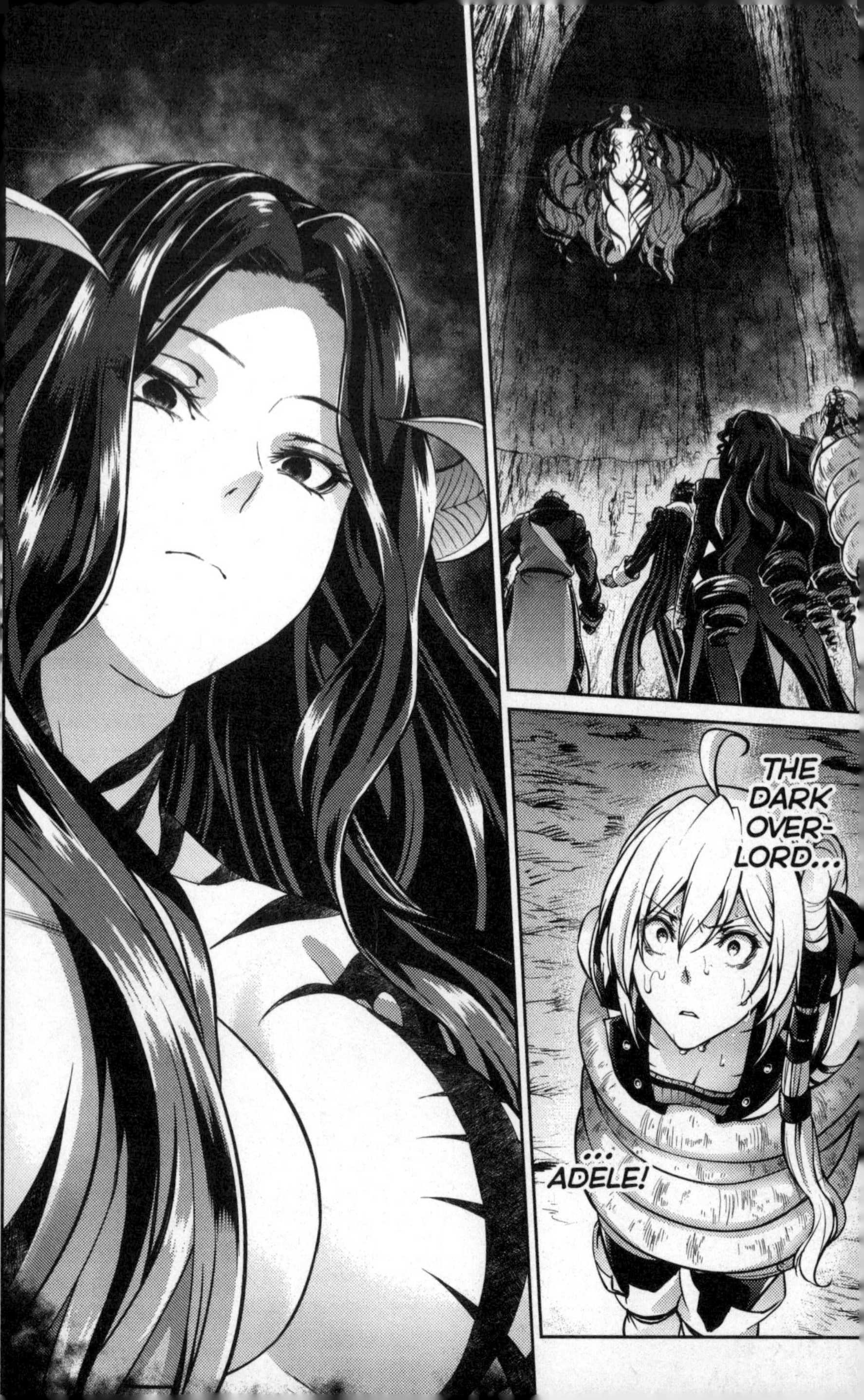
THE DARK OVER-LORD...
...ADELE!

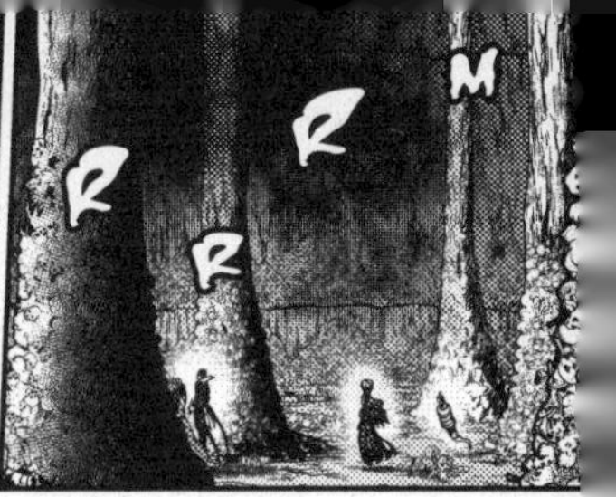
RRRRM

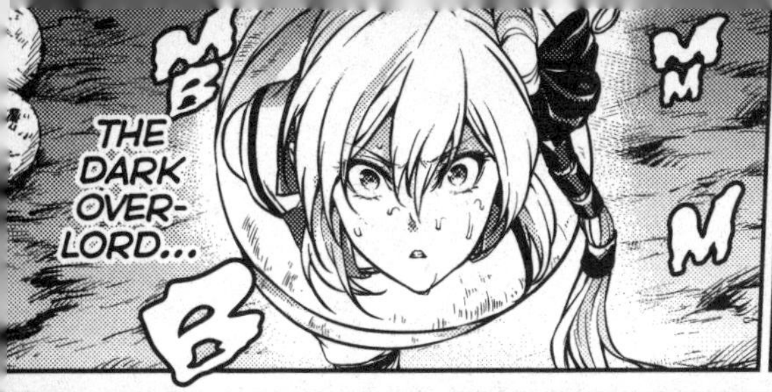
MMM
BB
THE DARK OVER-LORD...

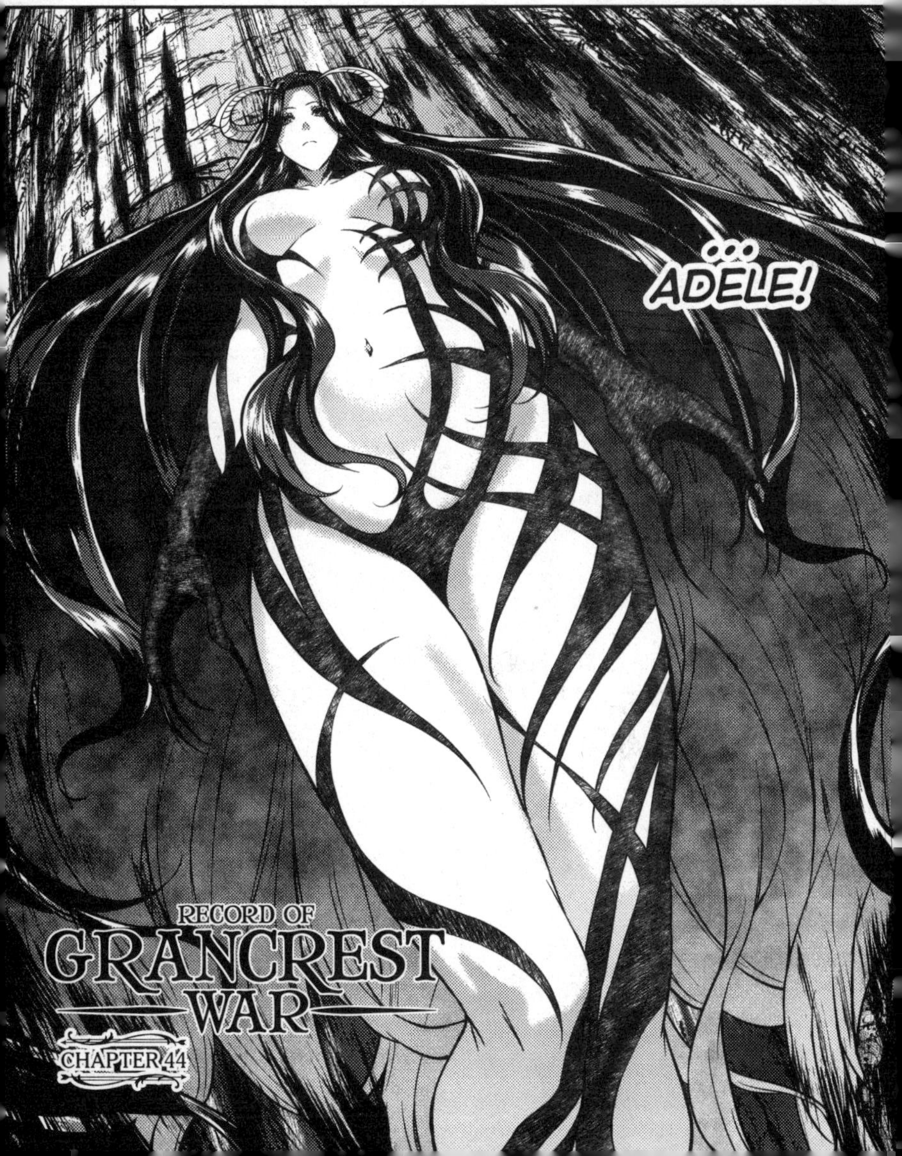
...ADÈLE!
RECORD OF GRANCREST WAR
CHAPTER 44

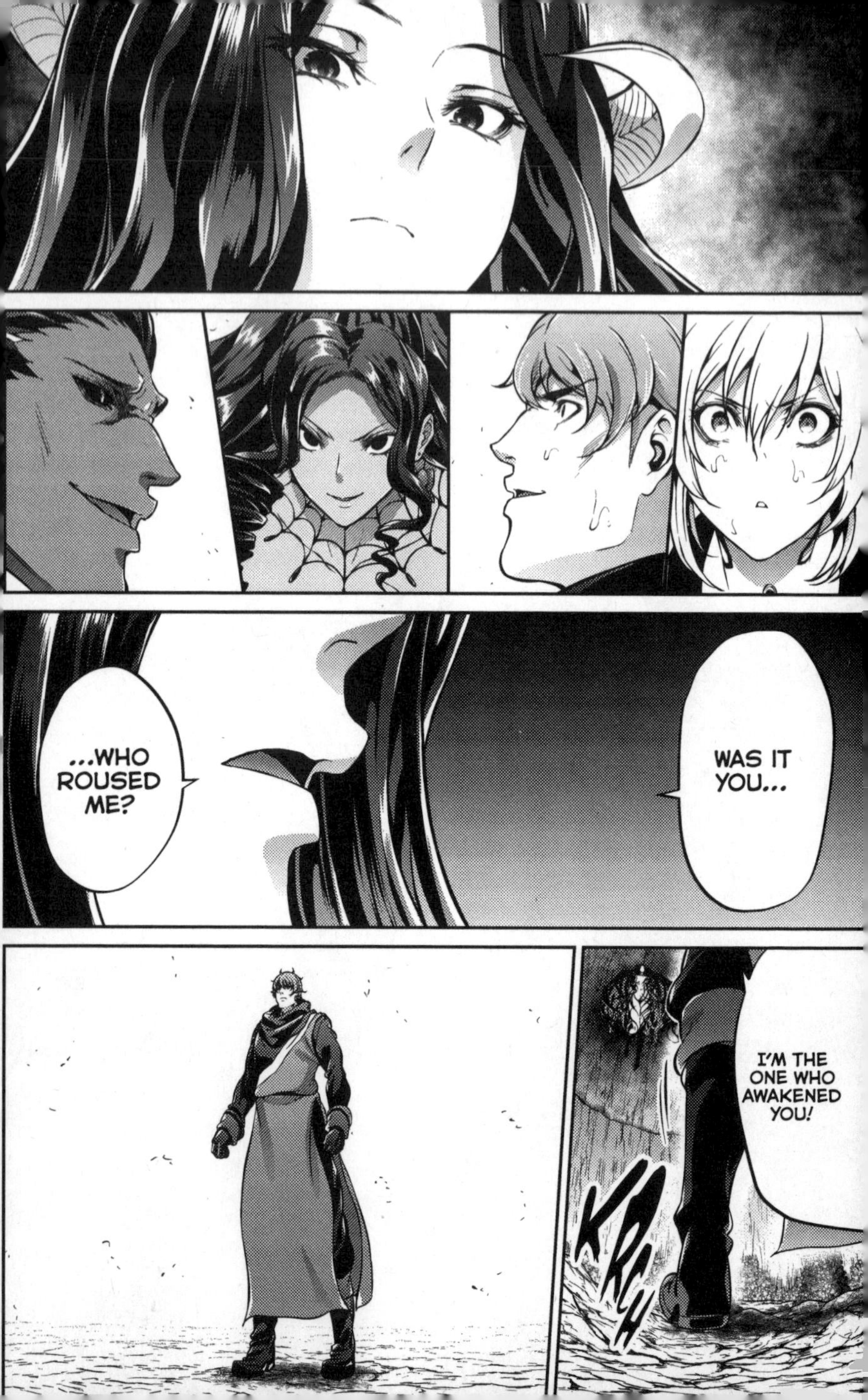
WAS IT YOU...
...WHO ROUSED ME?
I'M THE ONE WHO AWAKENED YOU!
KRCH

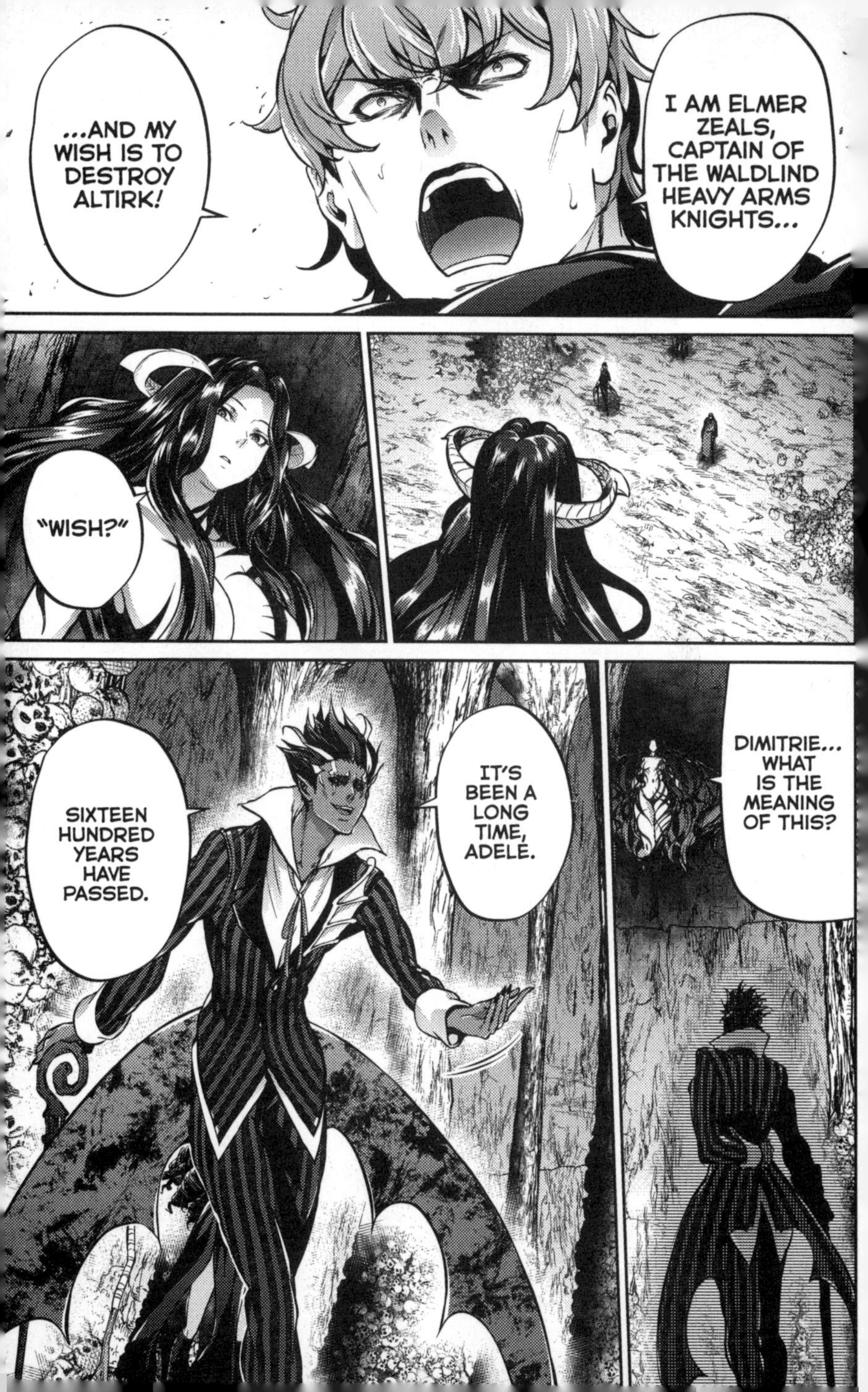
I AM ELMER ZEALS, CAPTAIN OF THE WALDLIND HEAVY ARMS KNIGHTS...
...AND MY WISH IS TO DESTROY ALTIRK!
"WISH?"
DIMITRIE... WHAT IS THE MEANING OF THIS?
IT'S BEEN A LONG TIME, ADELE.
SIXTEEN HUNDRED YEARS HAVE PASSED.

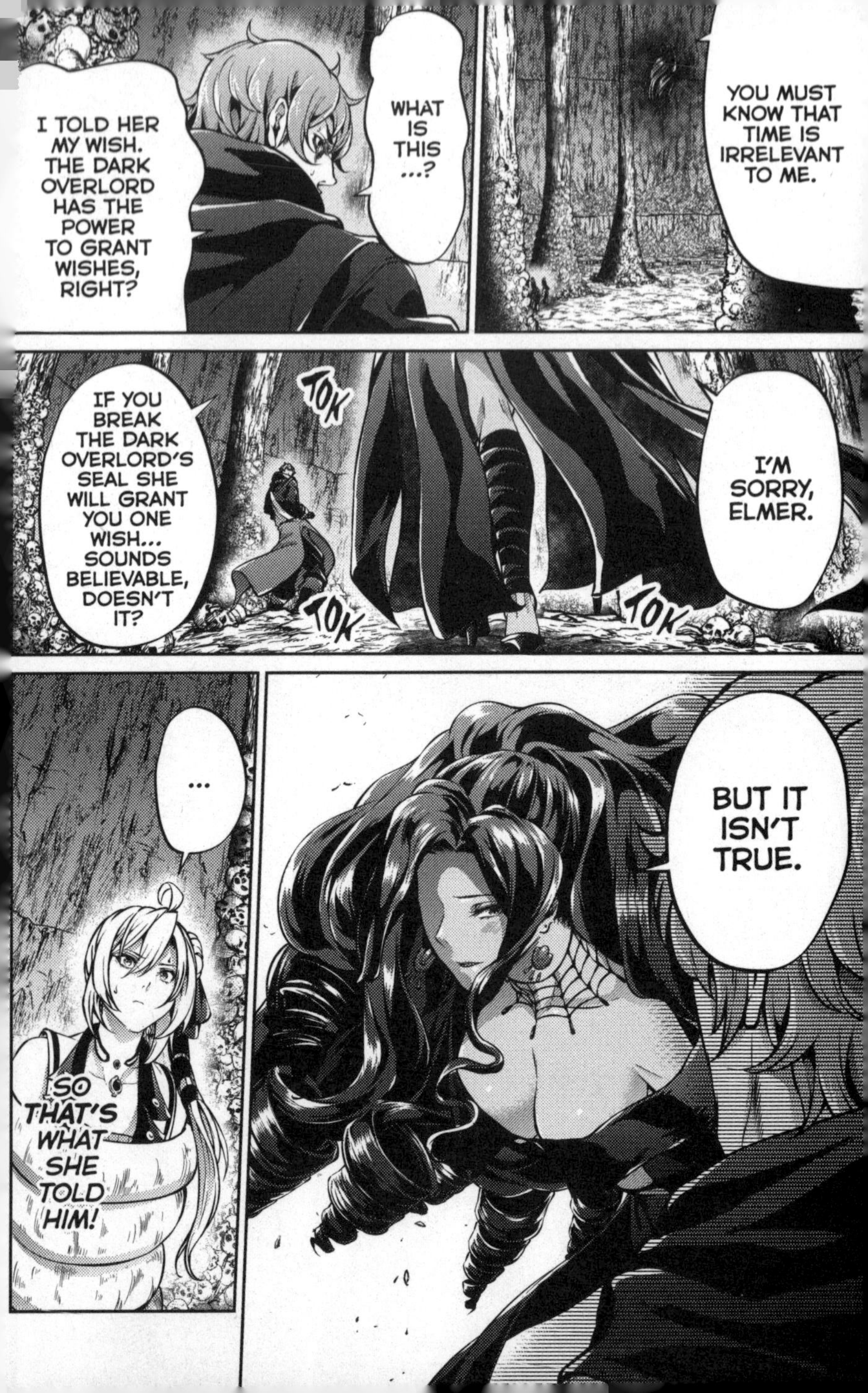
YOU MUST KNOW THAT TIME IS IRRELEVANT TO ME.
WHAT IS THIS ...?
I TOLD HER MY WISH. THE DARK OVERLORD HAS THE POWER TO GRANT WISHES, RIGHT?
I'M SORRY, ELMER.
TOK
TOK
TOK
IF YOU BREAK THE DARK OVERLORD'S SEAL SHE WILL GRANT YOU ONE WISH... SOUNDS BELIEVABLE, DOESN'T IT?
BUT IT ISN'T TRUE.
...
SO THAT'S WHAT SHE TOLD HIM!

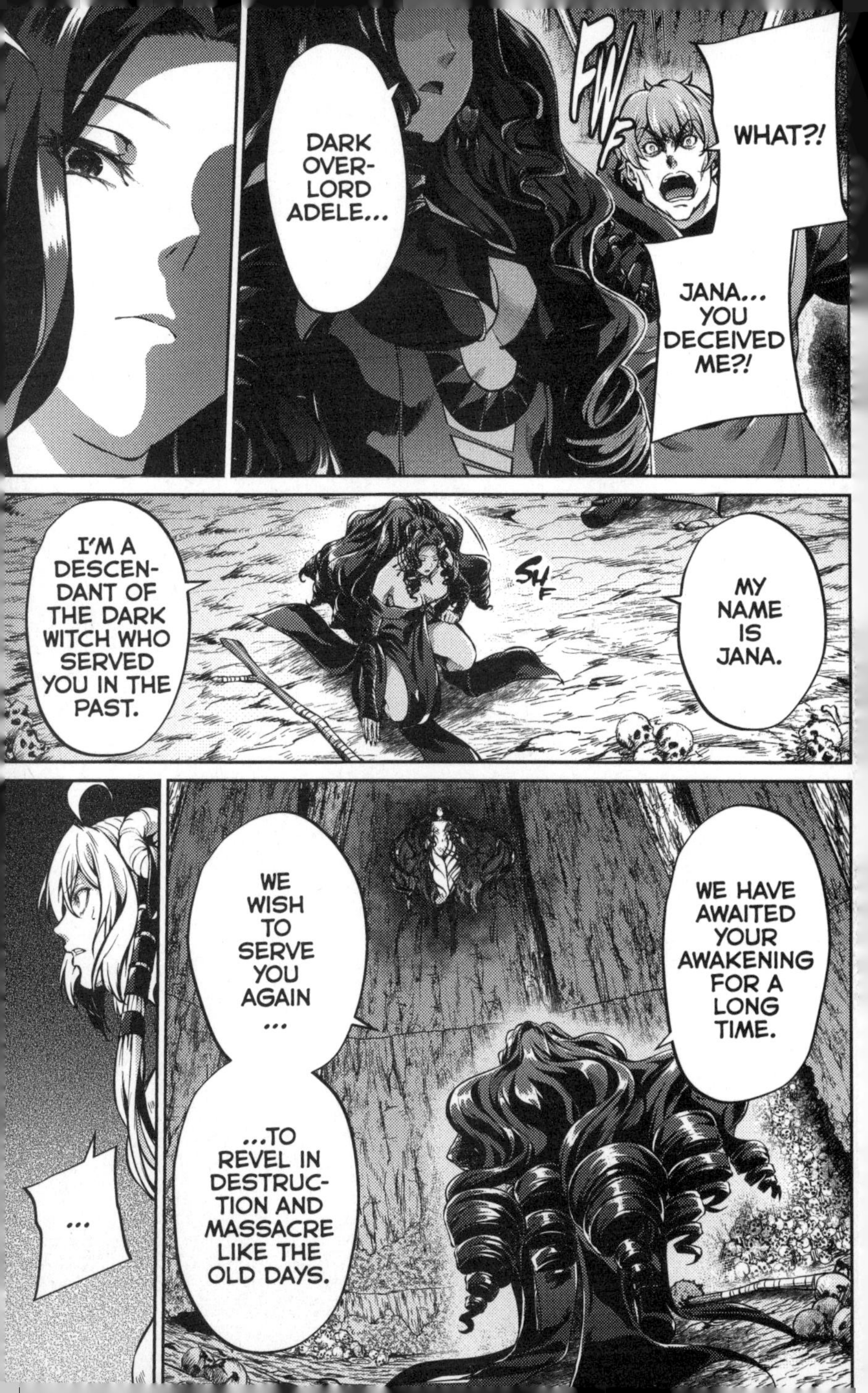
FWF
WHAT?!
JANA... YOU DECEIVED ME?!
DARK OVER-LORD ADELE...
MY NAME IS JANA.
SHF
I'M A DESCEN-DANT OF THE DARK WITCH WHO SERVED YOU IN THE PAST.
WE HAVE AWAITED YOUR AWAKENING FOR A LONG TIME.
WE WISH TO SERVE YOU AGAIN...
...TO REVEL IN DESTRUC-TION AND MASSACRE LIKE THE OLD DAYS.
...

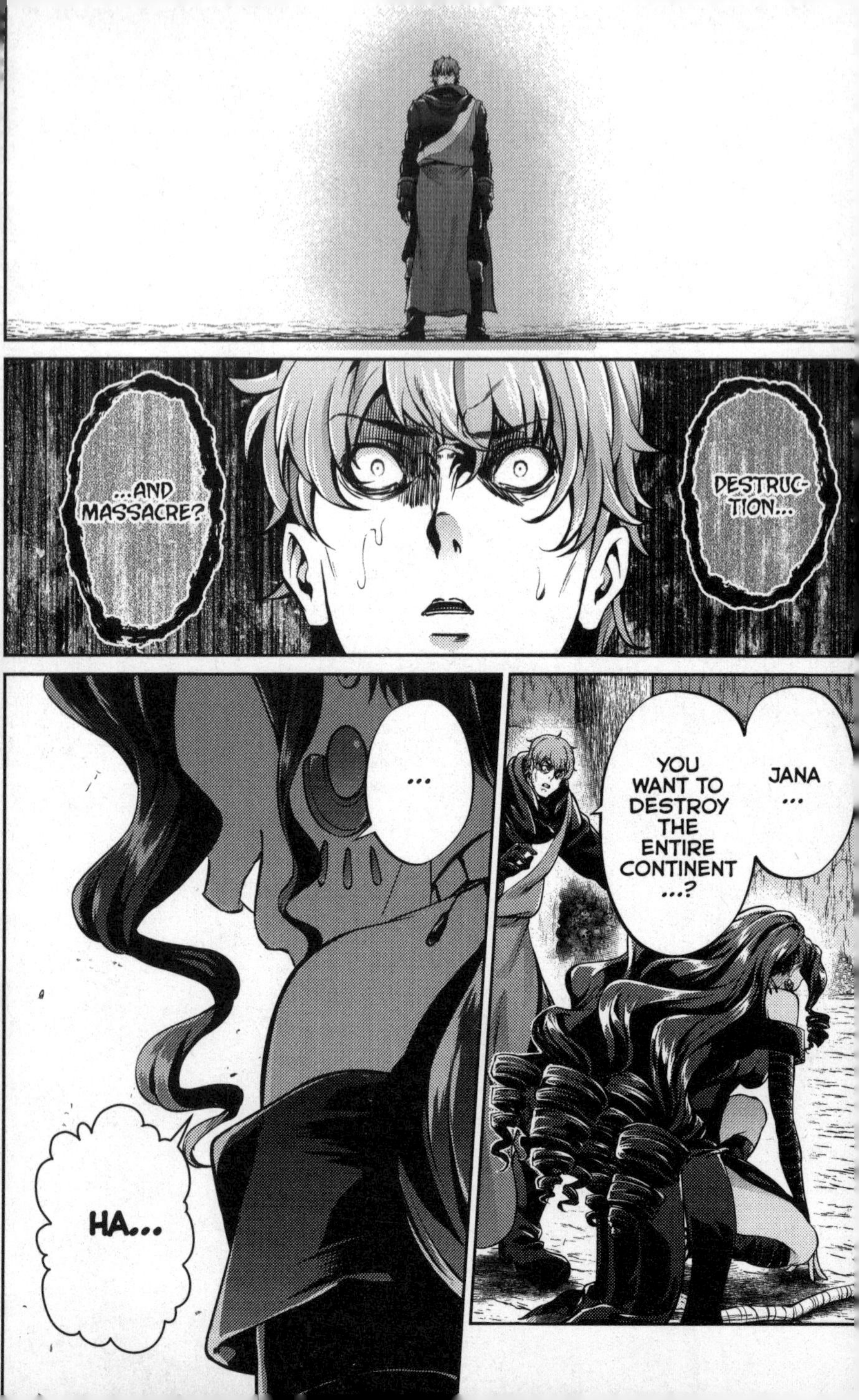
DESTRUC-TION...
...AND MASSACRE?
JANA ...
YOU WANT TO DESTROY THE ENTIRE CONTINENT ...?
...
HA...

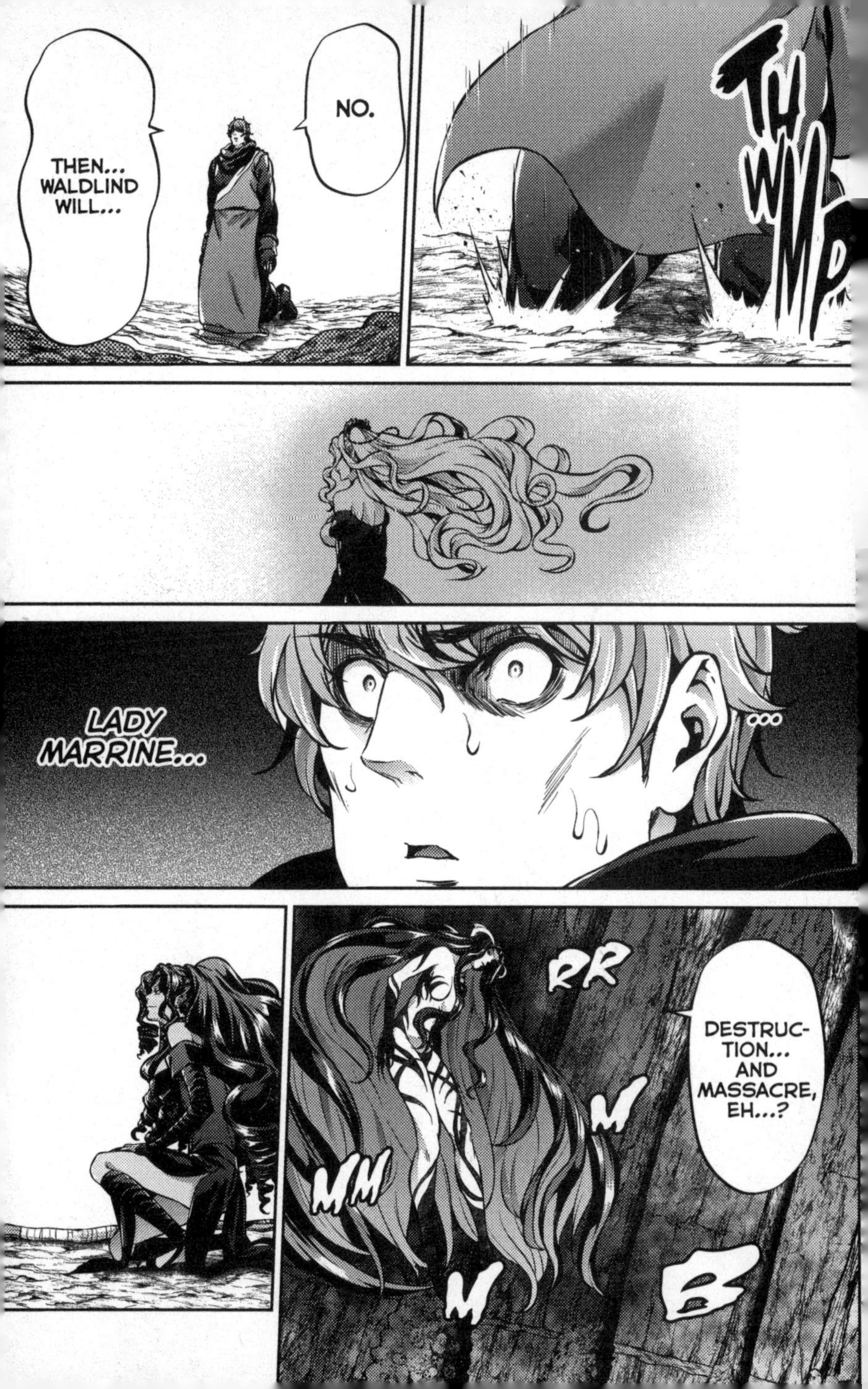
THWMP
NO.
THEN... WALDLIND WILL...
...
LADY MARRINE...
DESTRUCTION... AND MASSACRE, EH...?
RRMMMMMB

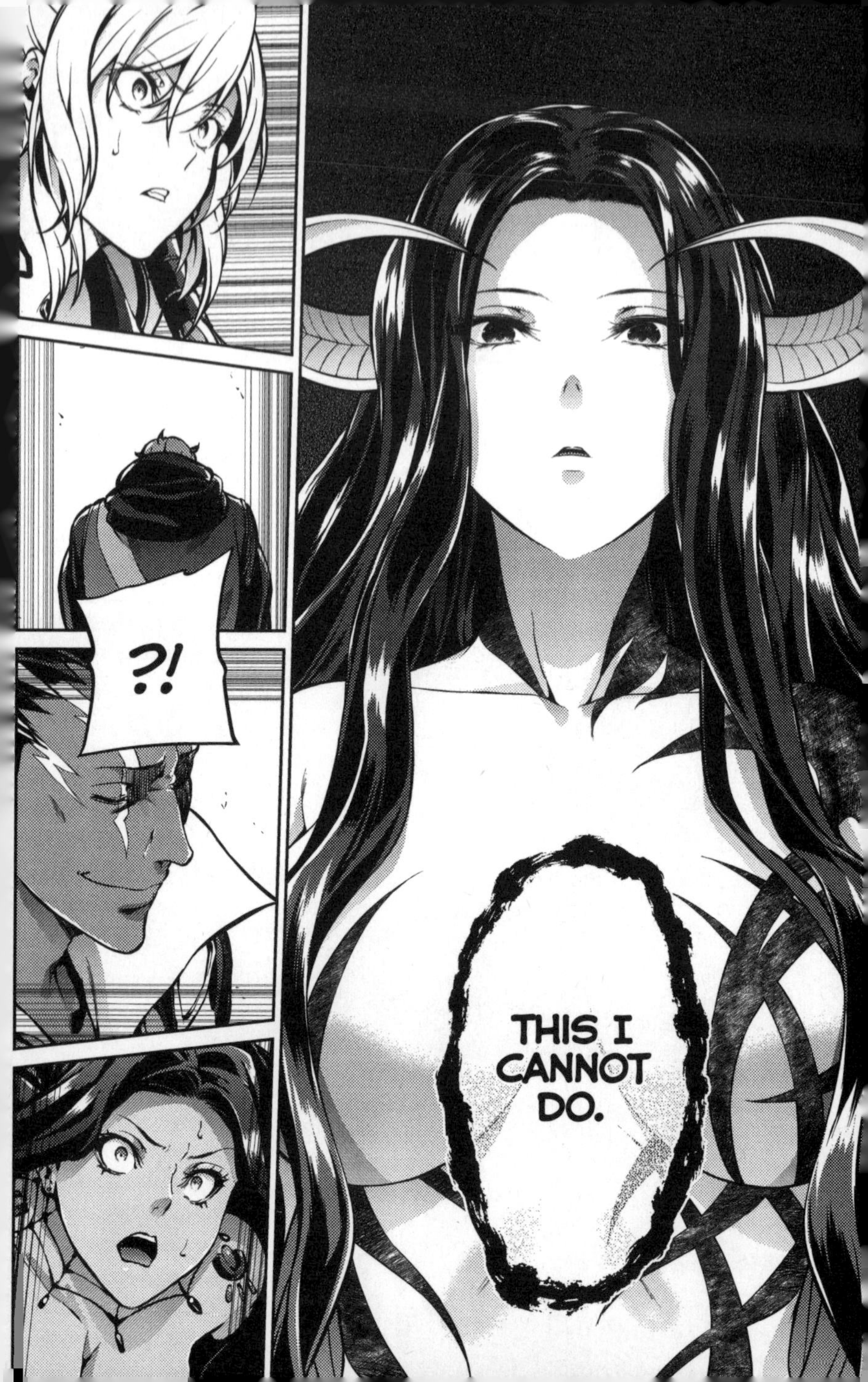
THIS I CANNOT DO.
?!

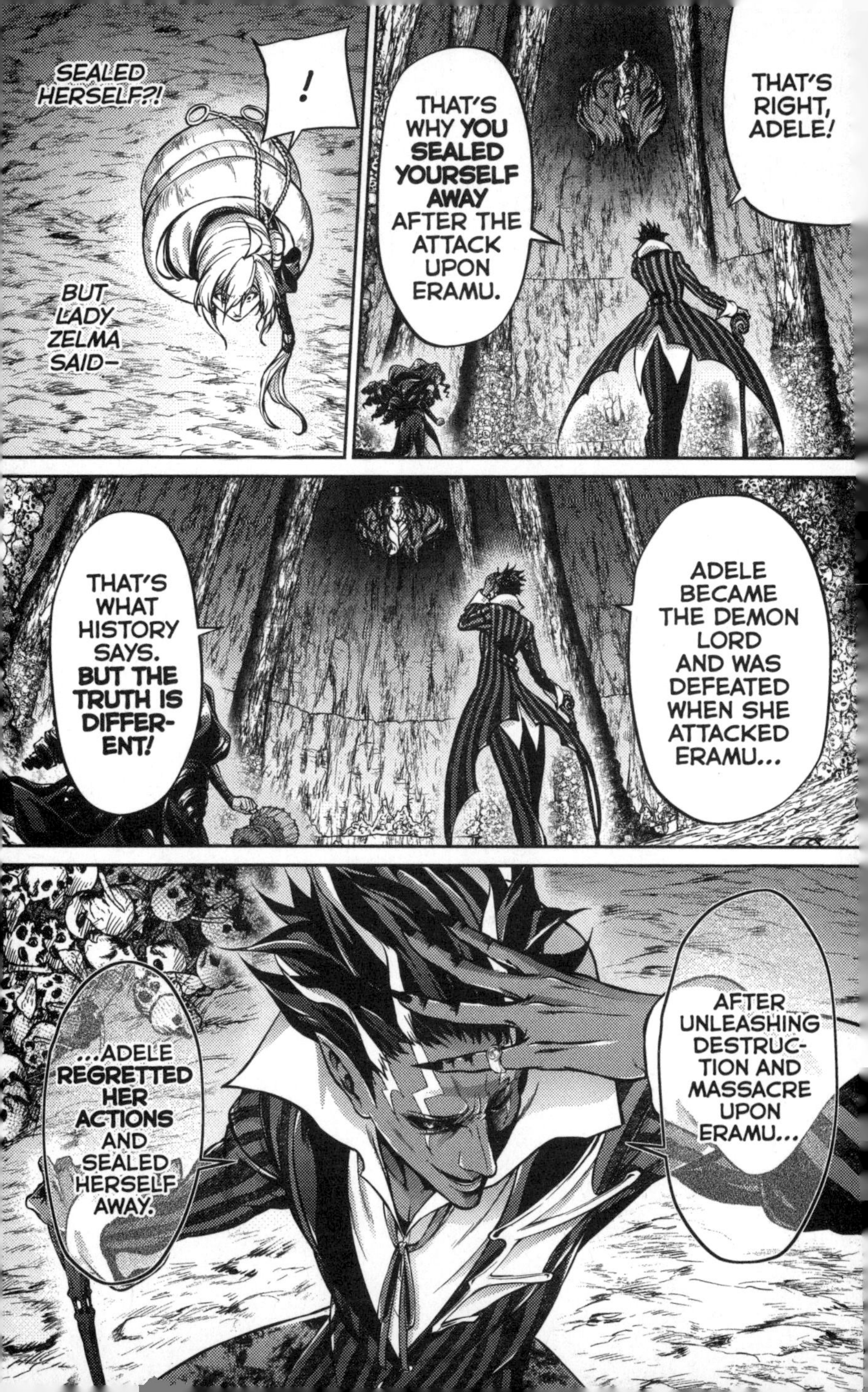
THAT'S RIGHT, ADELE!
THAT'S WHY YOU SEALED YOURSELF AWAY AFTER THE ATTACK UPON ERAMU.
!
SEALED HERSELF?!
BUT LADY ZELMA SAID—
ADELE BECAME THE DEMON LORD AND WAS DEFEATED WHEN SHE ATTACKED ERAMU...
THAT'S WHAT HISTORY SAYS. BUT THE TRUTH IS DIFFERENT!
AFTER UNLEASHING DESTRUCTION AND MASSACRE UPON ERAMU...
...ADELE REGRETTED HER ACTIONS AND SEALED HERSELF AWAY.

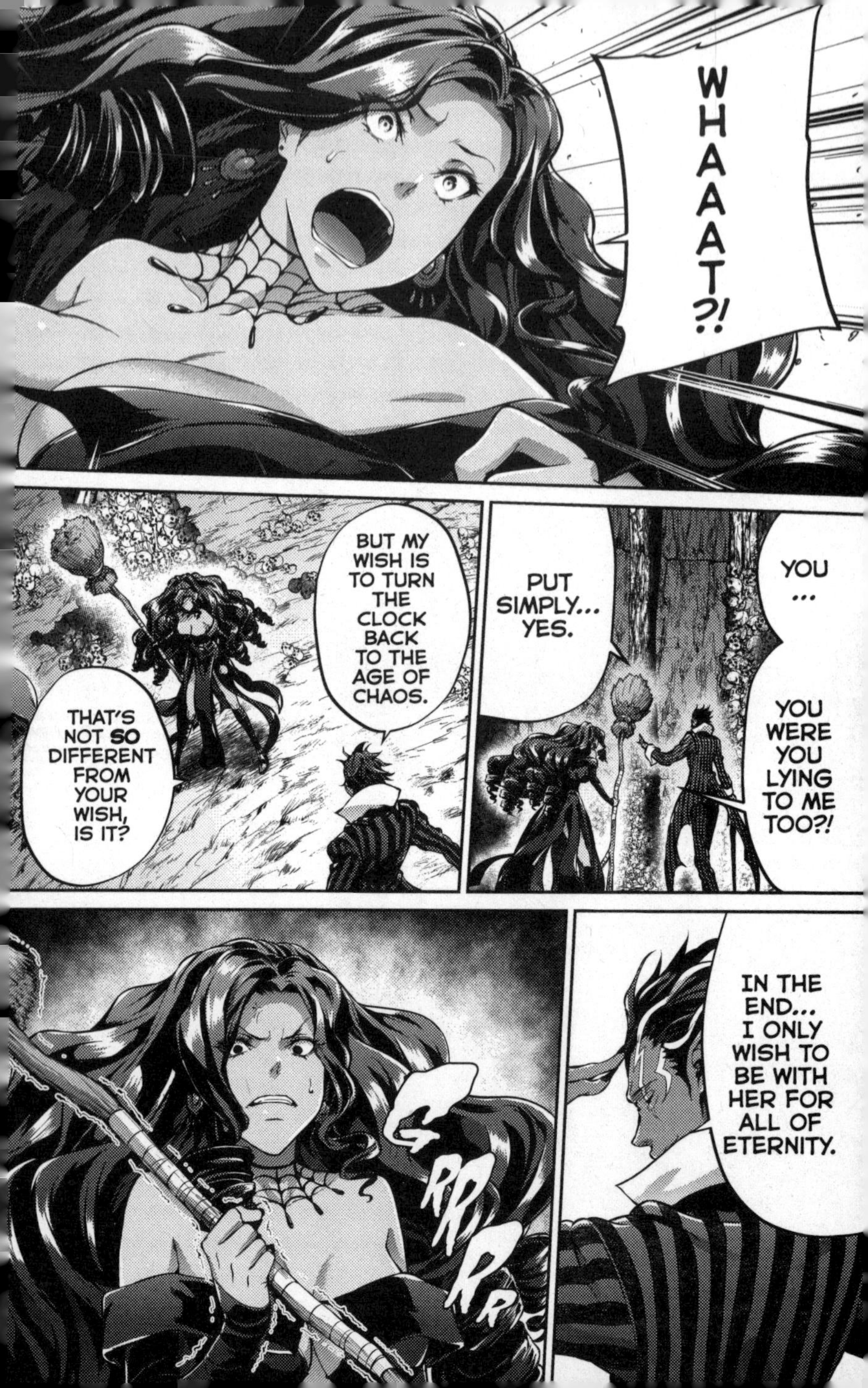
WHAAAT?!
YOU ...
YOU WERE YOU LYING TO ME TOO?!
PUT SIMPLY... YES.
BUT MY WISH IS TO TURN THE CLOCK BACK TO THE AGE OF CHAOS.
THAT'S NOT **SO** DIFFERENT FROM YOUR WISH, IS IT?
IN THE END... I ONLY WISH TO BE WITH HER FOR ALL OF ETERNITY.
GRRRR

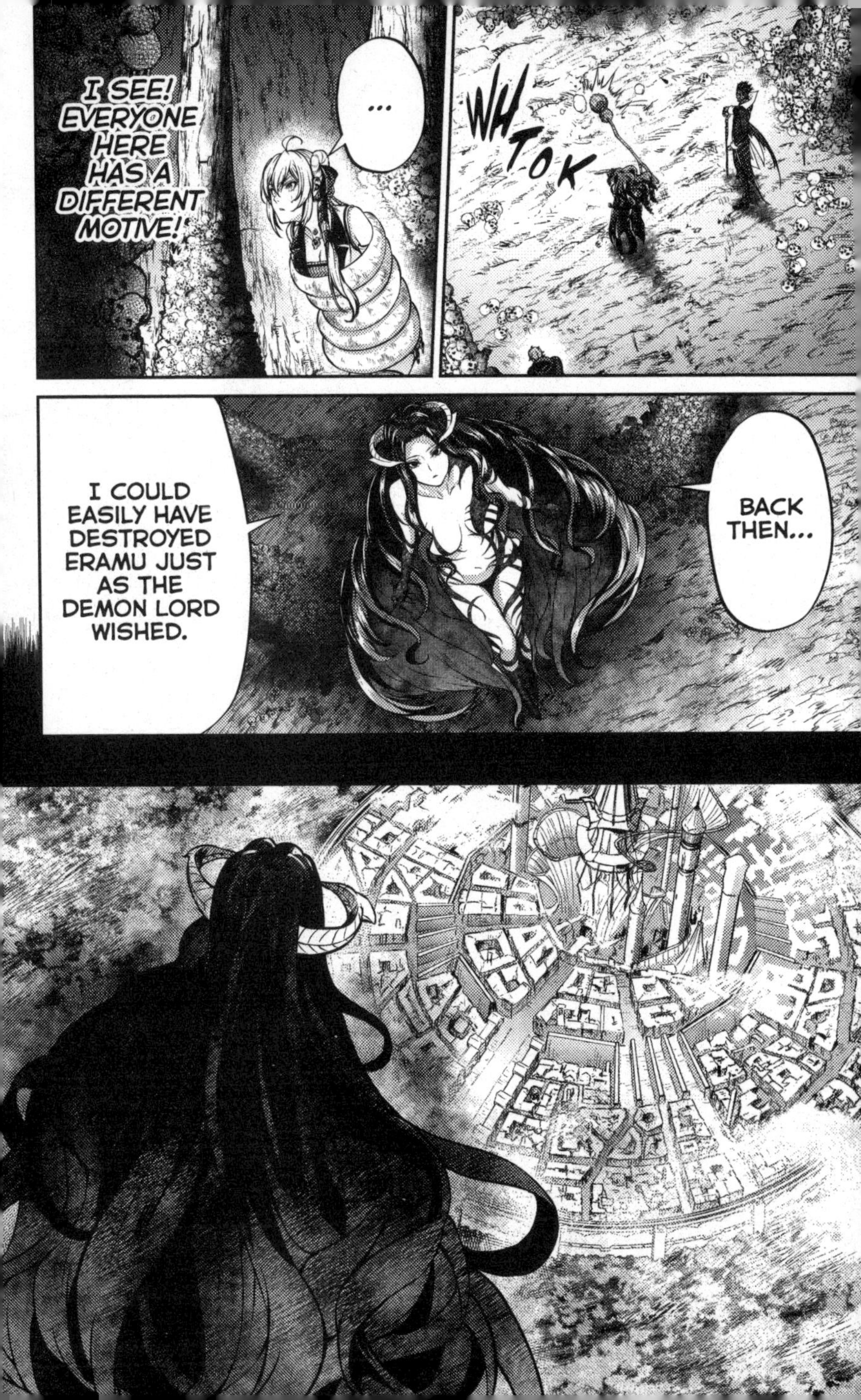
WHTOK
...
I SEE! EVERYONE HERE HAS A DIFFERENT MOTIVE!
BACK THEN...
I COULD EASILY HAVE DESTROYED ERAMU JUST AS THE DEMON LORD WISHED.

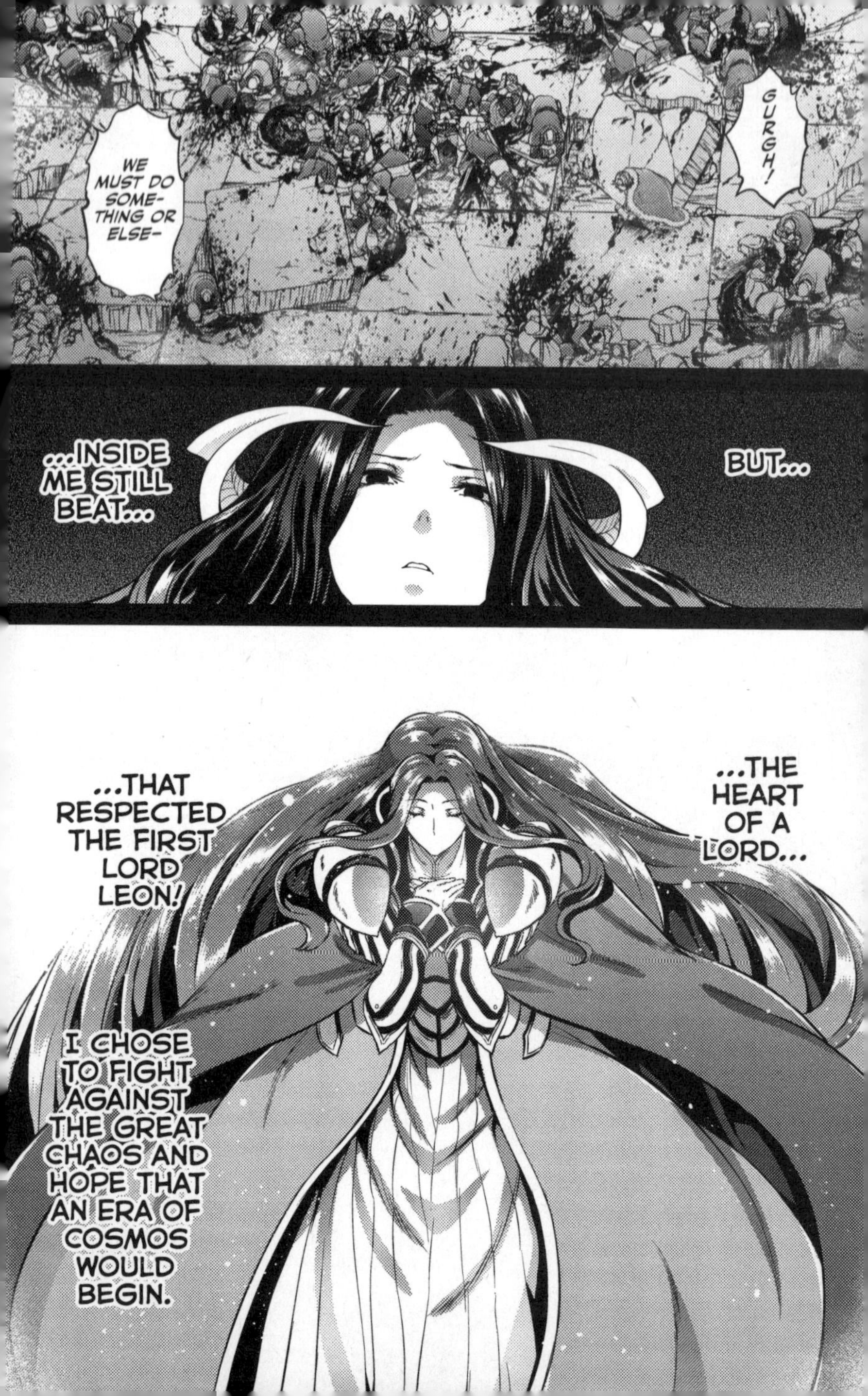
GURGH!
WE MUST DO SOME-THING OR ELSE–
BUT...
...INSIDE ME STILL BEAT...
...THE HEART OF A LORD...
...THAT RESPECTED THE FIRST LORD LEON!
I CHOSE TO FIGHT AGAINST THE GREAT CHAOS AND HOPE THAT AN ERA OF COSMOS WOULD BEGIN.

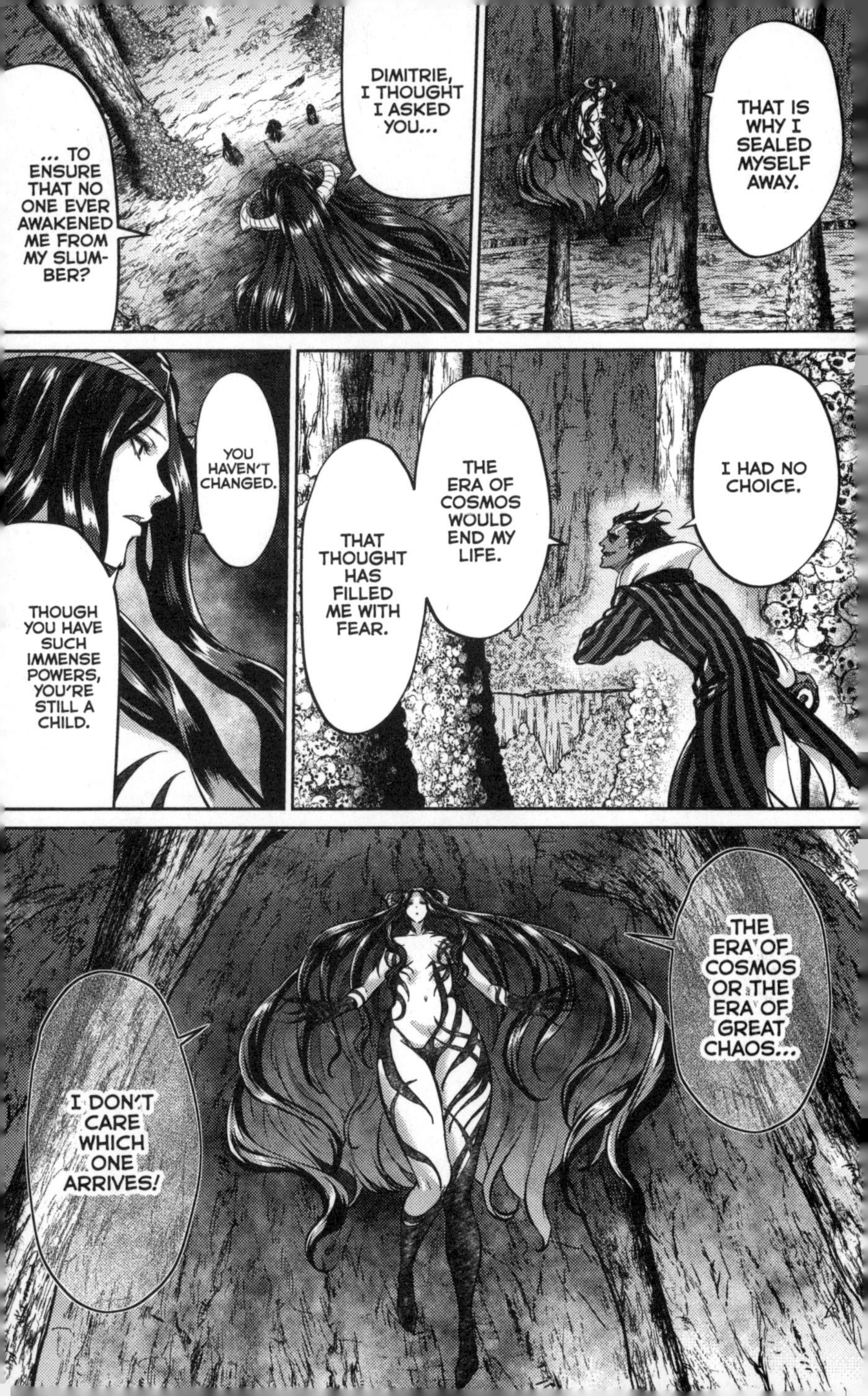
THAT IS WHY I SEALED MYSELF AWAY.
DIMITRIE, I THOUGHT I ASKED YOU...
... TO ENSURE THAT NO ONE EVER AWAKENED ME FROM MY SLUMBER?
I HAD NO CHOICE.
THE ERA OF COSMOS WOULD END MY LIFE.
THAT THOUGHT HAS FILLED ME WITH FEAR.
YOU HAVEN'T CHANGED.
THOUGH YOU HAVE SUCH IMMENSE POWERS, YOU'RE STILL A CHILD.
THE ERA OF COSMOS OR THE ERA OF GREAT CHAOS...
I DON'T CARE WHICH ONE ARRIVES!

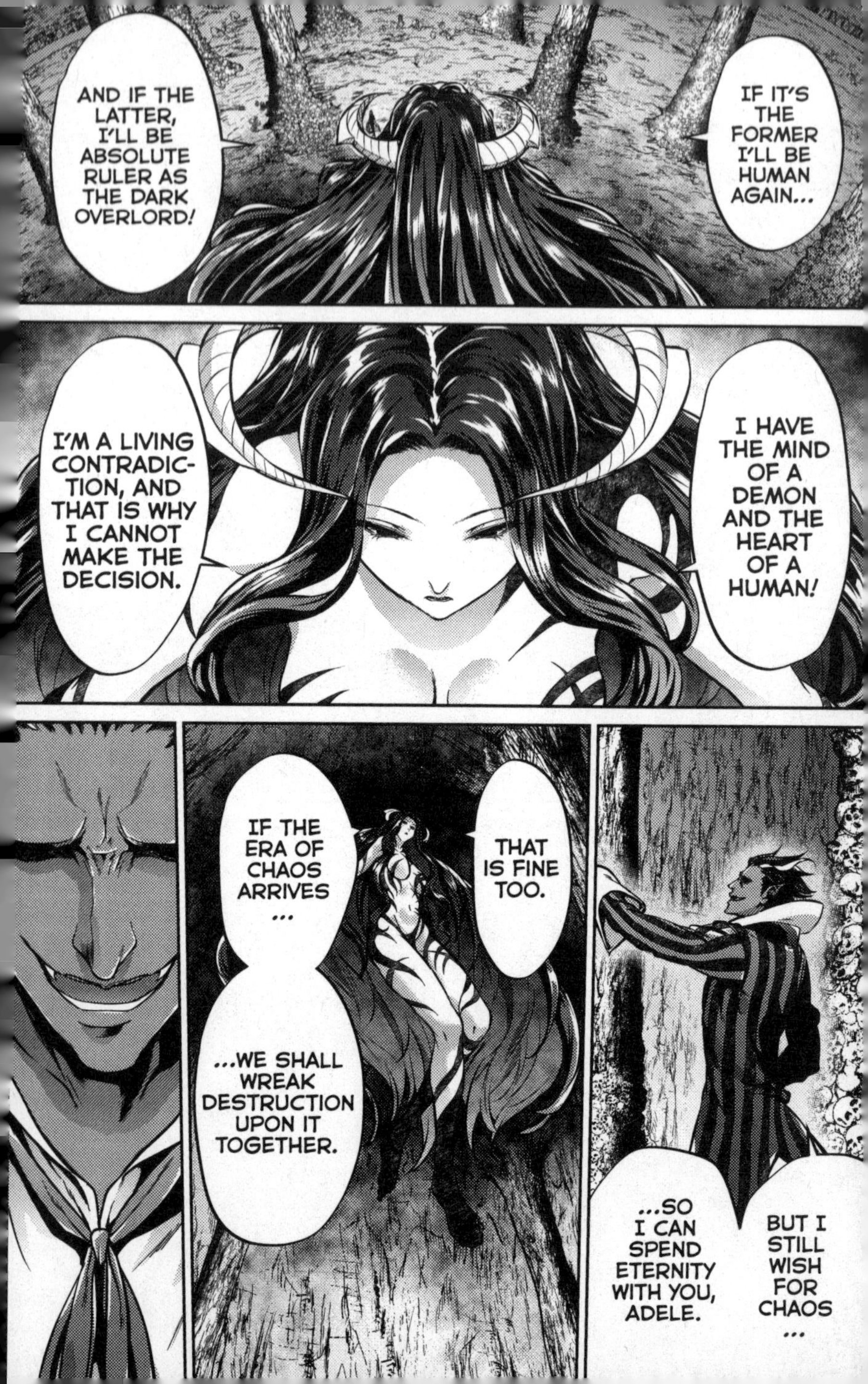
IF IT'S THE FORMER I'LL BE HUMAN AGAIN...
AND IF THE LATTER, I'LL BE ABSOLUTE RULER AS THE DARK OVERLORD!
I HAVE THE MIND OF A DEMON AND THE HEART OF A HUMAN!
I'M A LIVING CONTRADICTION, AND THAT IS WHY I CANNOT MAKE THE DECISION.
BUT I STILL WISH FOR CHAOS...
...SO I CAN SPEND ETERNITY WITH YOU, ADELE.
THAT IS FINE TOO.
IF THE ERA OF CHAOS ARRIVES...
...WE SHALL WREAK DESTRUCTION UPON IT TOGETHER.

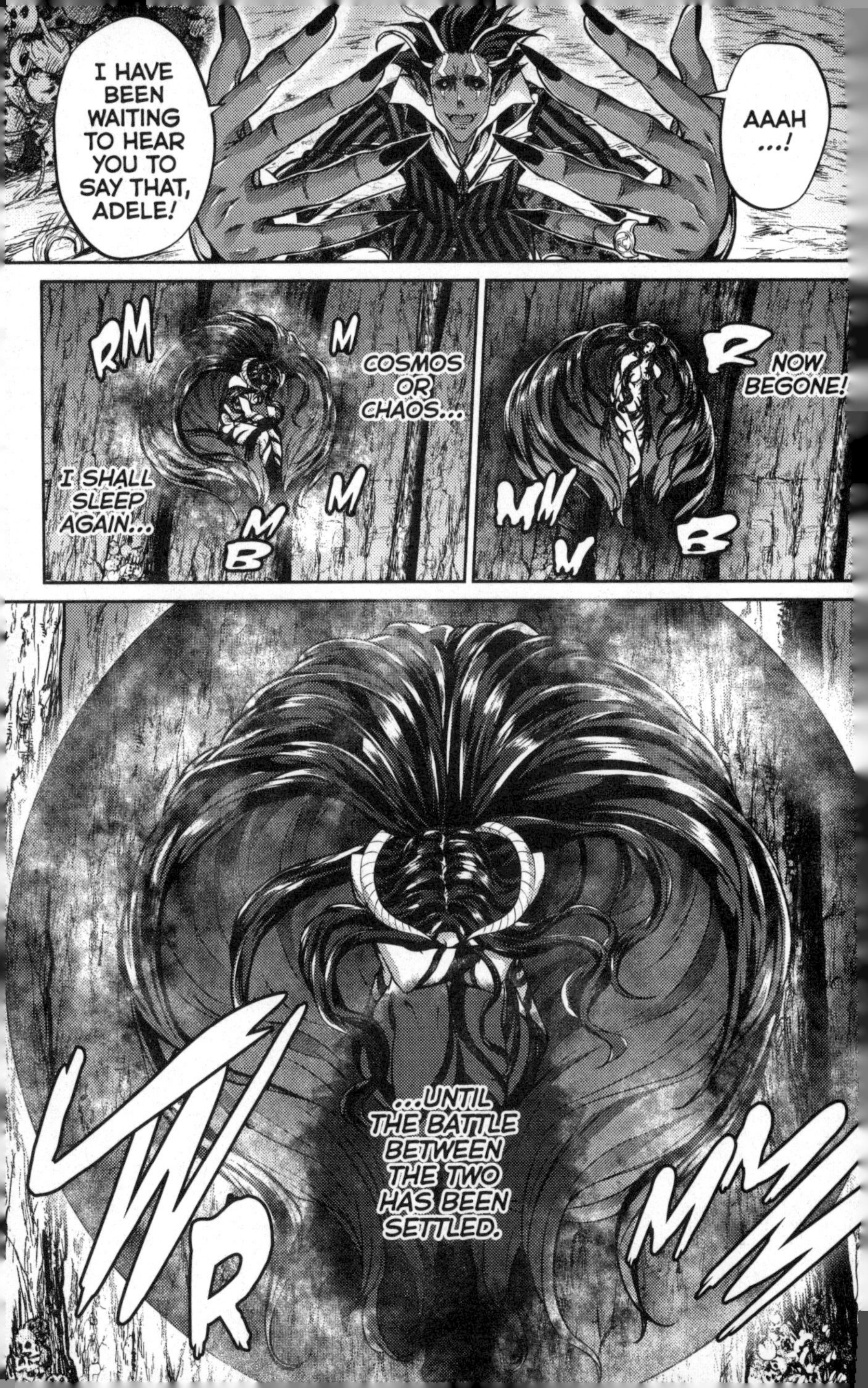
AAAH ...!
I HAVE BEEN WAITING TO HEAR YOU TO SAY THAT, ADELE!
R
NOW BEGONE!
MMMB
RM
M
COSMOS OR CHAOS...
I SHALL SLEEP AGAIN...
M
MB
...UNTIL THE BATTLE BETWEEN THE TWO HAS BEEN SETTLED.
MMM
WR

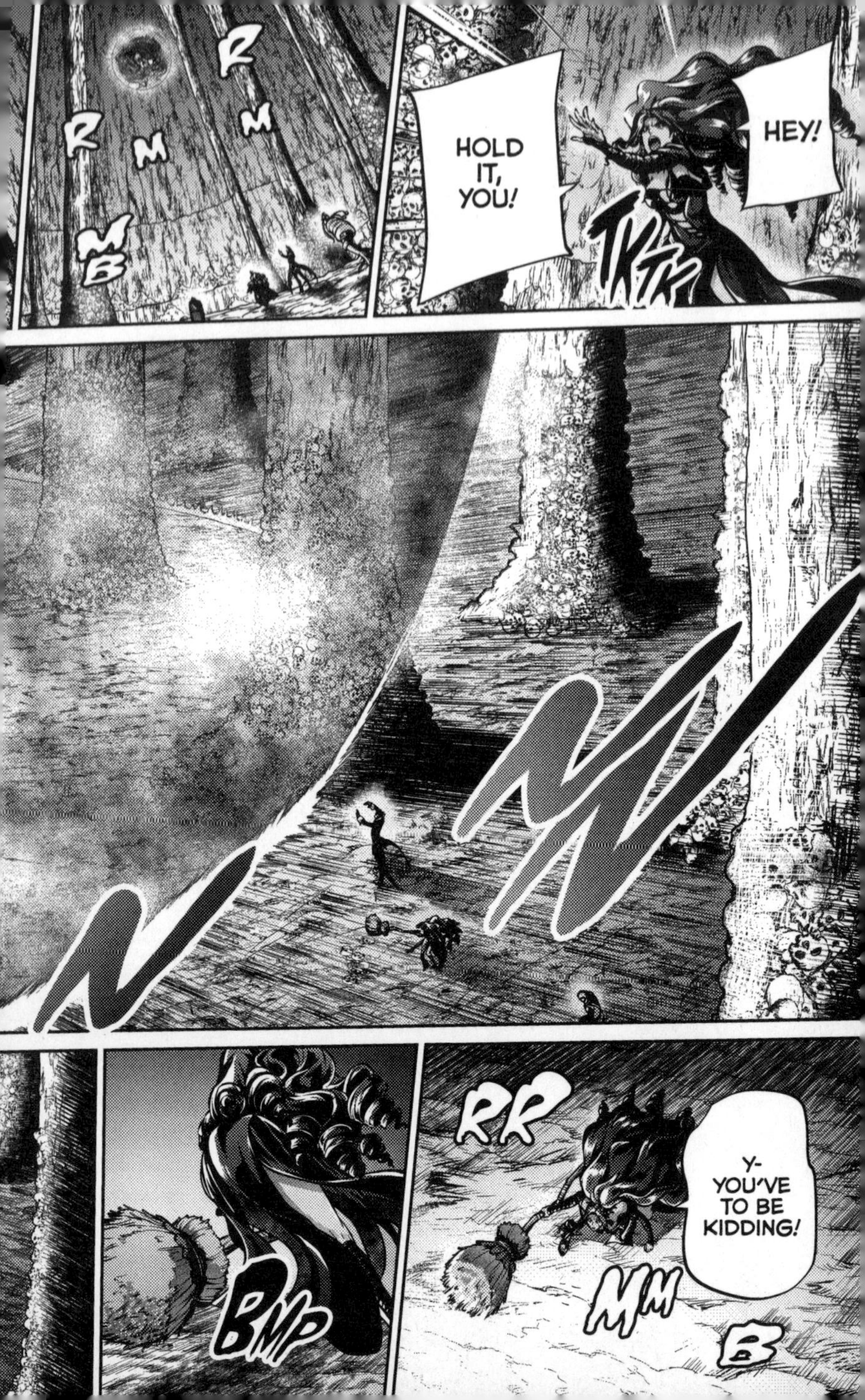
HEY!
HOLD IT, YOU!
TKTK
RRMMMB
RR
Y- YOU'VE TO BE KIDDING!
MMB
BMP

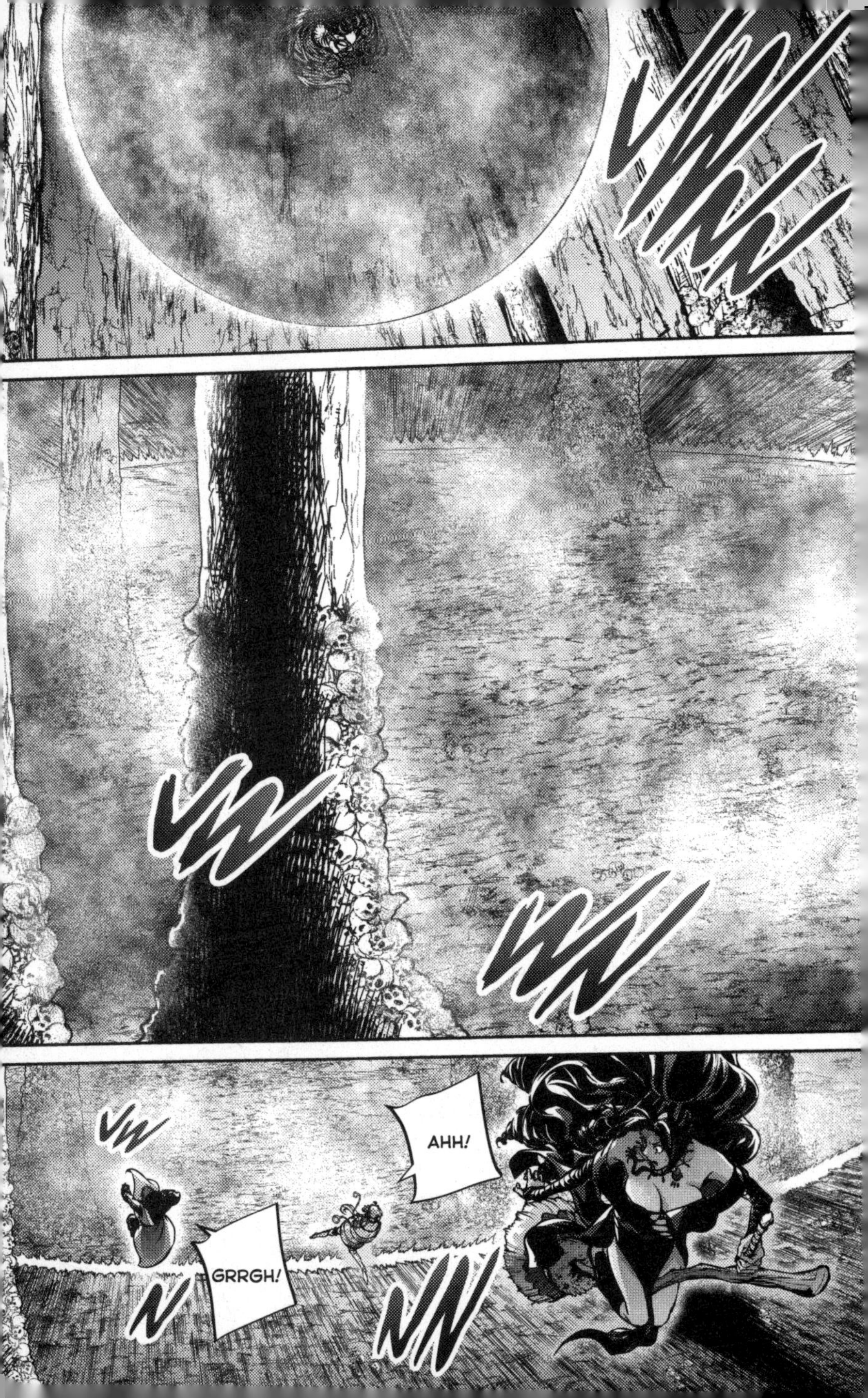
AHH!
GRRGH!

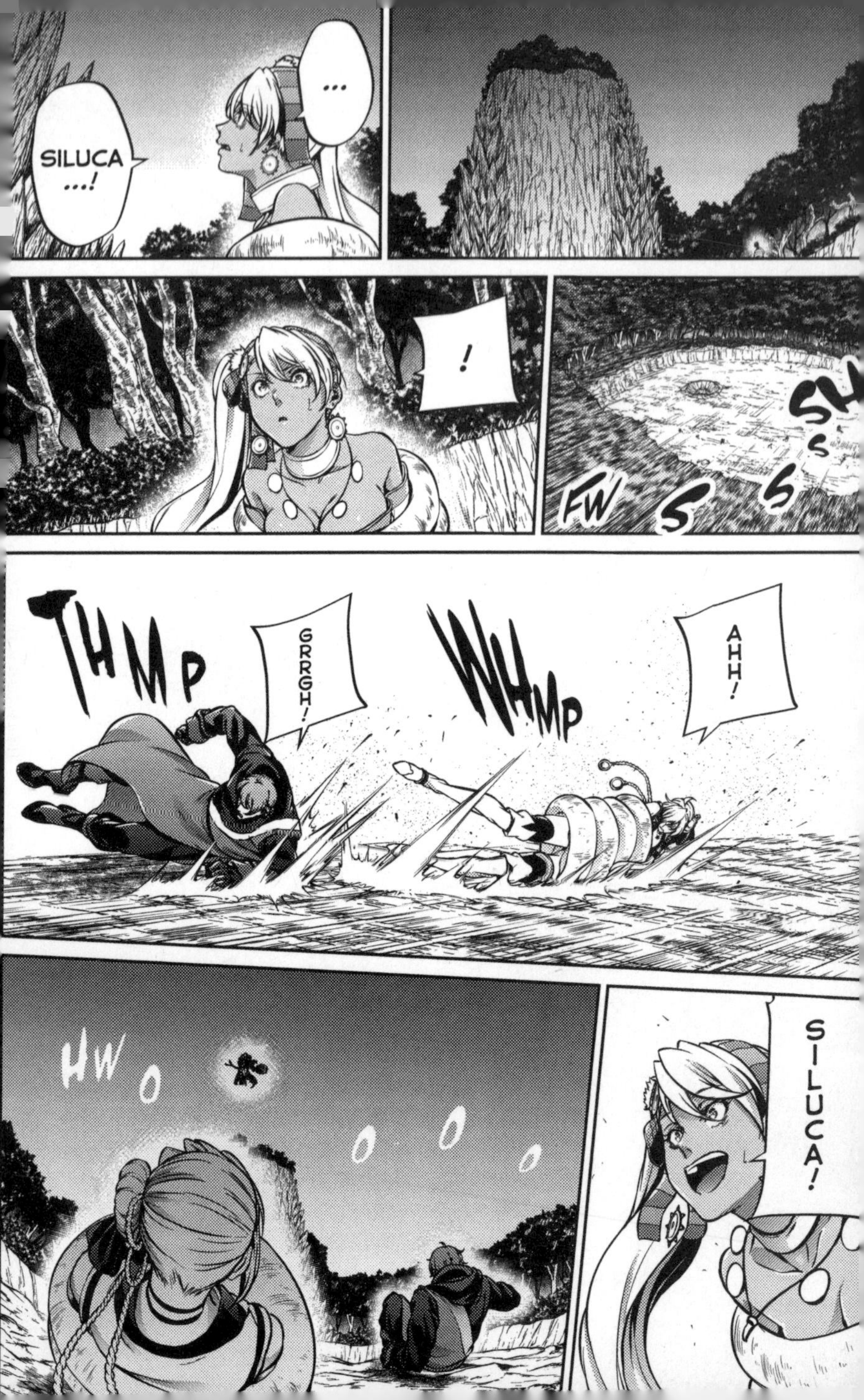
...
SILUCA ....!
SHSS
FW S S S
!
AHH!
WHMP
GRRGH!
THMP
SILUCA!
HWOOOO

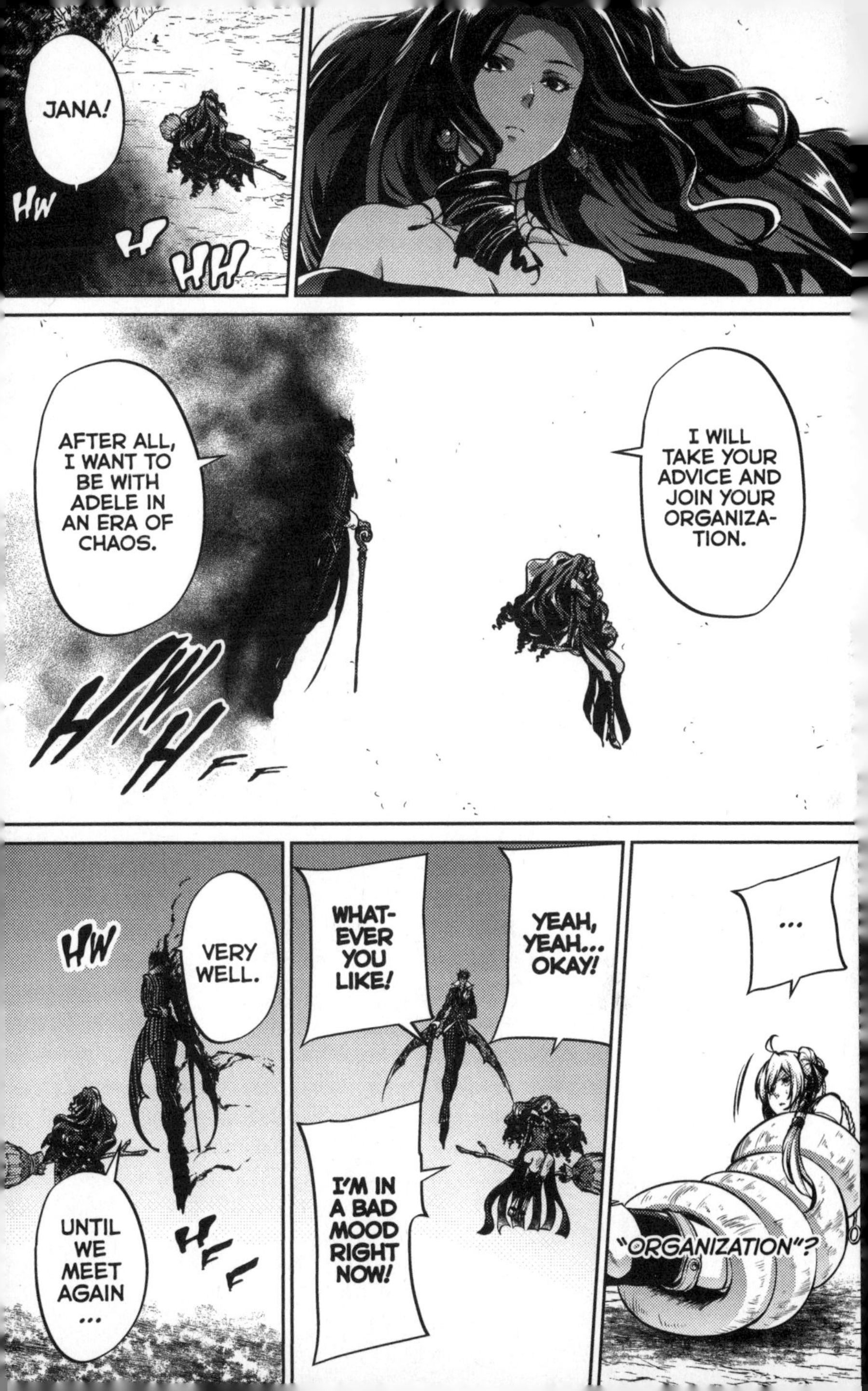
JANA!
HW
H
HH
I WILL TAKE YOUR ADVICE AND JOIN YOUR ORGANIZATION.
AFTER ALL, I WANT TO BE WITH ADELE IN AN ERA OF CHAOS.
...
"ORGANIZATION"?
YEAH, YEAH... OKAY!
WHATEVER YOU LIKE!
I'M IN A BAD MOOD RIGHT NOW!
HW
VERY WELL.
UNTIL WE MEET AGAIN...
HFF

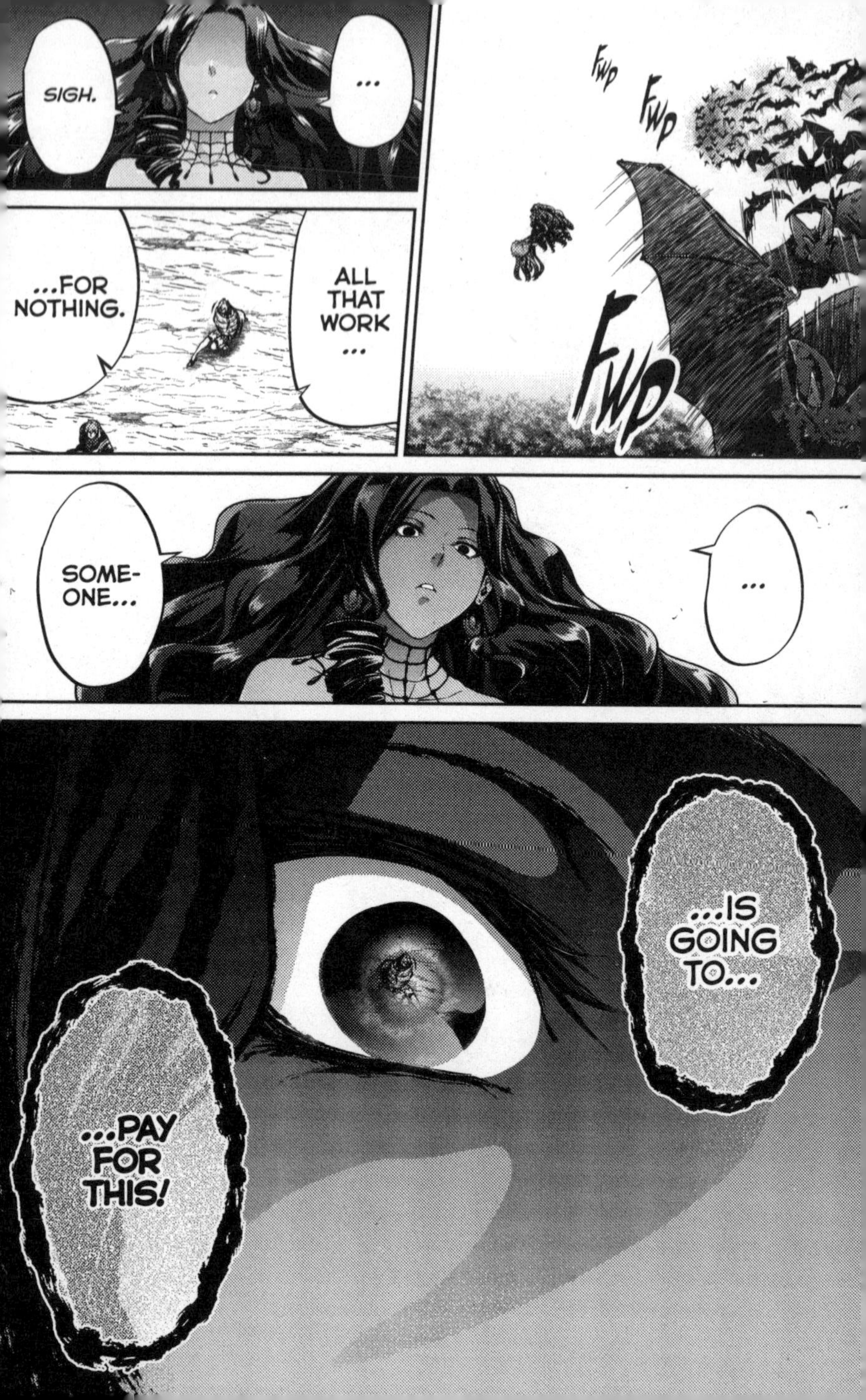
FWP
FWP
FWP
...
SIGH.
ALL THAT WORK...
...FOR NOTHING.
...
SOME-ONE...
...IS GOING TO...
...PAY FOR THIS!

※IMAGE OF ELMER BEING TOO SHOCKED TO EVEN FLINCH WHEN JANA USED HER COMET SPELL.

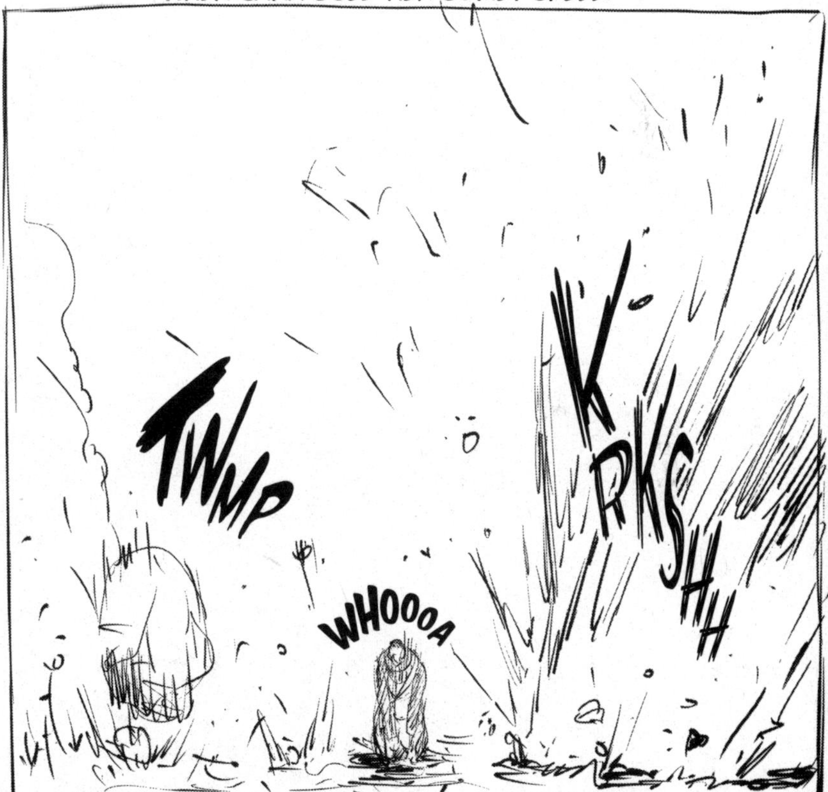
KRKSHH
TWMP
WHOOOA

RECORD OF
GRANCREST
WAR

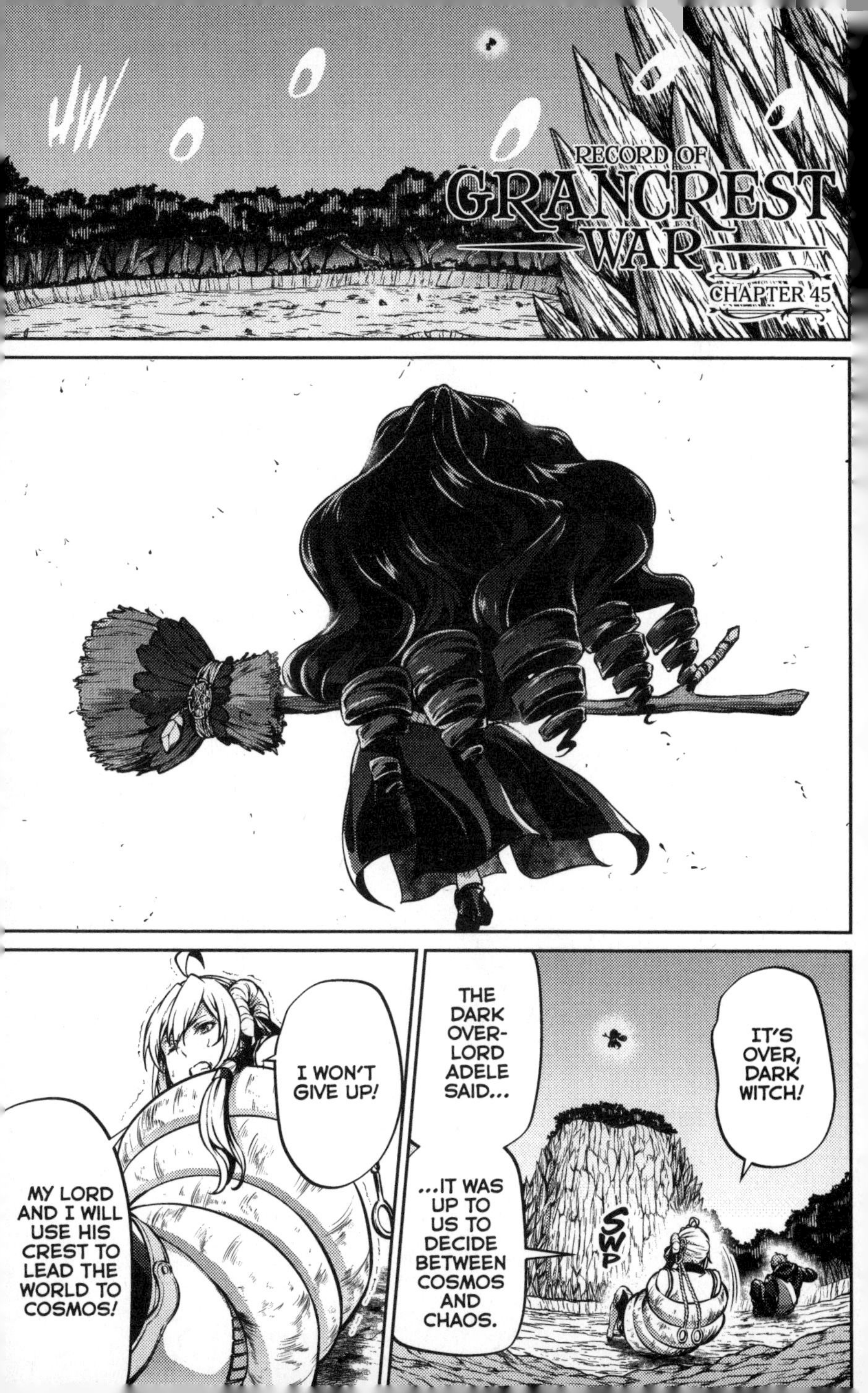
RECORD OF GRANCREST WAR
CHAPTER 45
IT'S OVER, DARK WITCH!
SWP
THE DARK OVER-LORD ADELE SAID...
...IT WAS UP TO US TO DECIDE BETWEEN COSMOS AND CHAOS.
I WON'T GIVE UP!
MY LORD AND I WILL USE HIS CREST TO LEAD THE WORLD TO COSMOS!

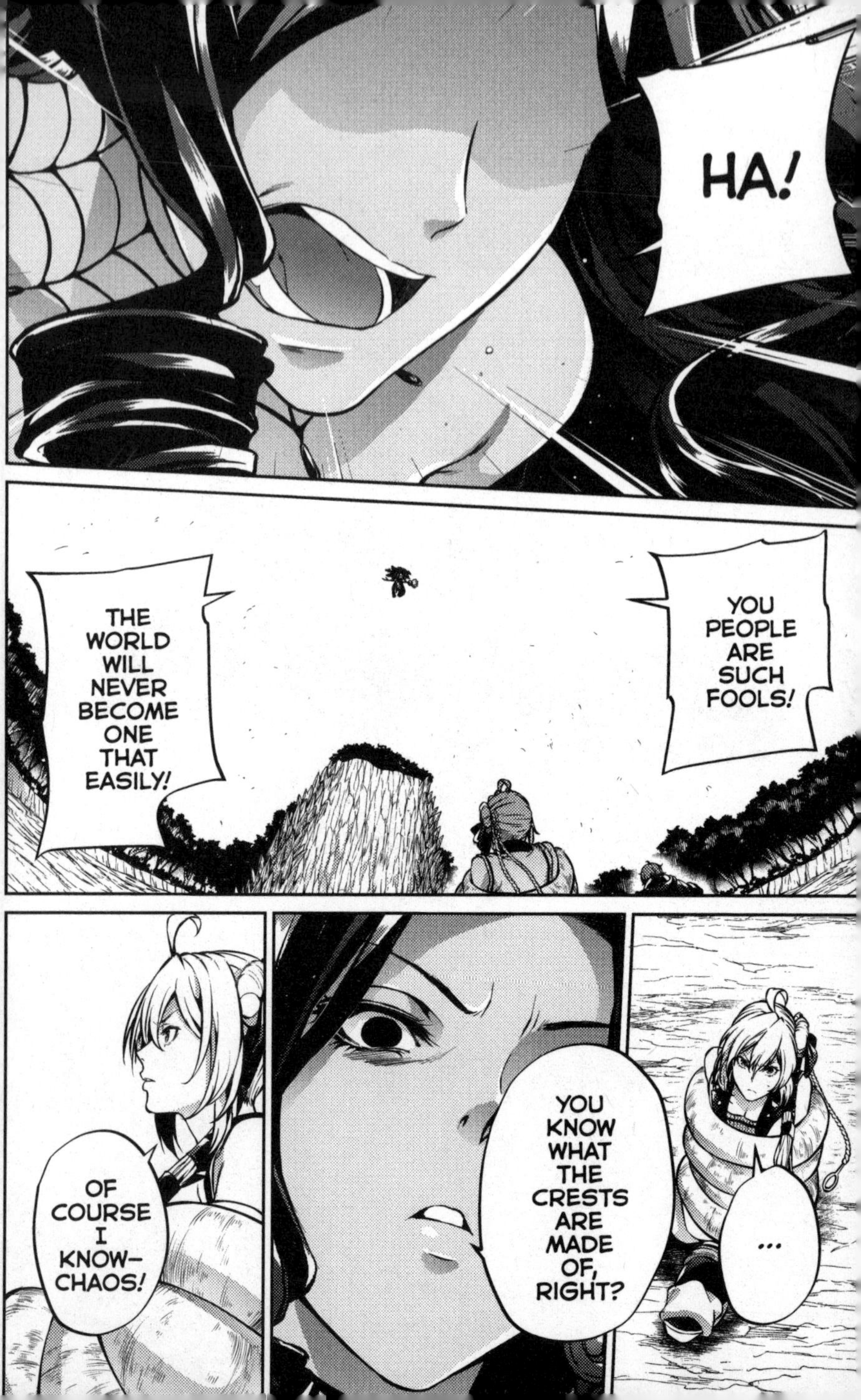
HA!
YOU PEOPLE ARE SUCH FOOLS!
THE WORLD WILL NEVER BECOME ONE THAT EASILY!
...
YOU KNOW WHAT THE CRESTS ARE MADE OF, RIGHT?
OF COURSE I KNOW—CHAOS!

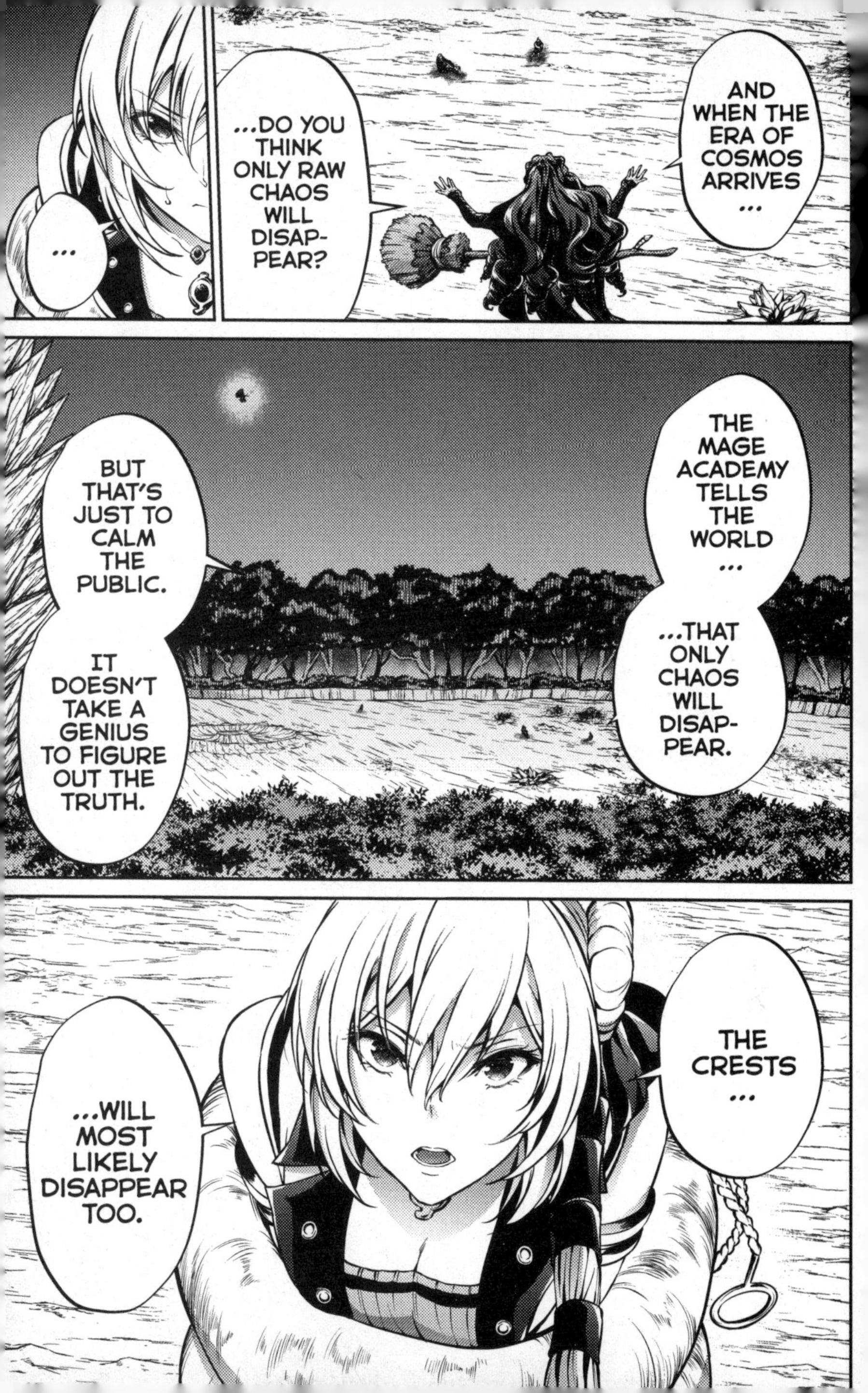
AND WHEN THE ERA OF COSMOS ARRIVES ...
...DO YOU THINK ONLY RAW CHAOS WILL DISAPPEAR?
...
THE MAGE ACADEMY TELLS THE WORLD ...
...THAT ONLY CHAOS WILL DISAPPEAR.
BUT THAT'S JUST TO CALM THE PUBLIC.
IT DOESN'T TAKE A GENIUS TO FIGURE OUT THE TRUTH.
THE CRESTS ...
...WILL MOST LIKELY DISAPPEAR TOO.

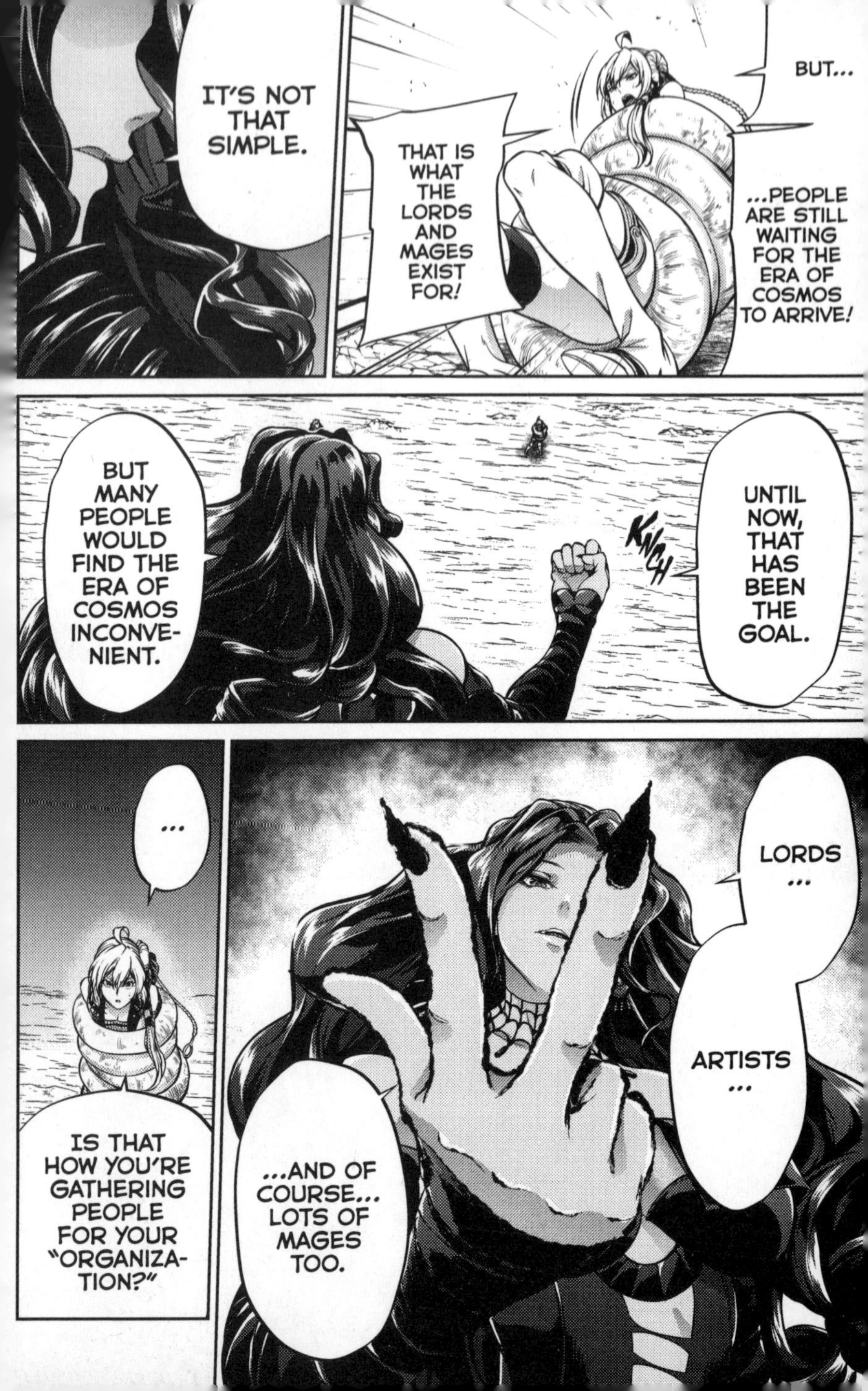
BUT...
...PEOPLE ARE STILL WAITING FOR THE ERA OF COSMOS TO ARRIVE!
THAT IS WHAT THE LORDS AND MAGES EXIST FOR!
IT'S NOT THAT SIMPLE.
UNTIL NOW, THAT HAS BEEN THE GOAL.
KNCH
BUT MANY PEOPLE WOULD FIND THE ERA OF COSMOS INCONVENIENT.
LORDS...
ARTISTS...
...AND OF COURSE... LOTS OF MAGES TOO.
...
IS THAT HOW YOU'RE GATHERING PEOPLE FOR YOUR "ORGANIZATION?"

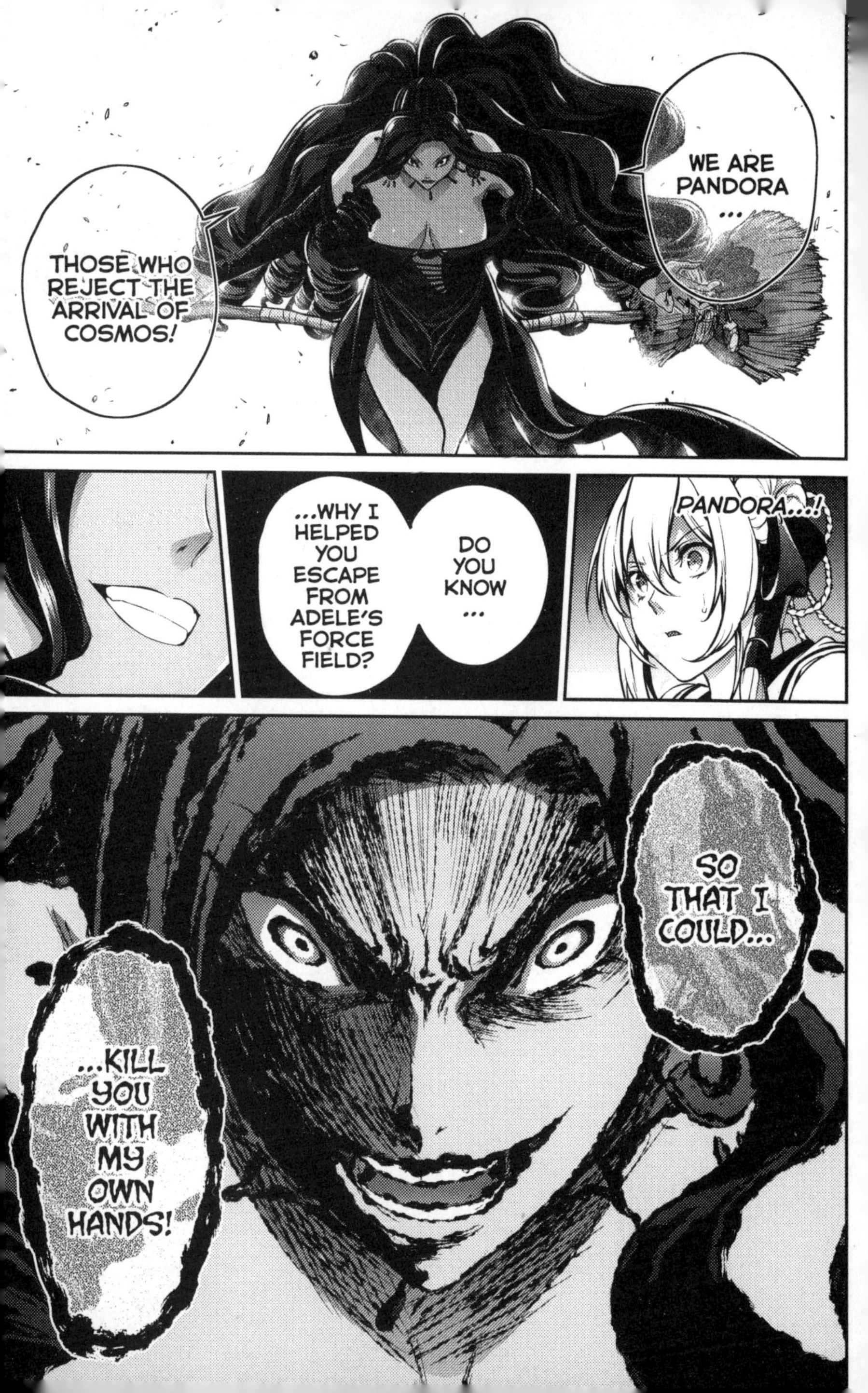
WE ARE PANDORA ...
THOSE WHO REJECT THE ARRIVAL OF COSMOS!
PANDORA...!
DO YOU KNOW ...
...WHY I HELPED YOU ESCAPE FROM ADELE'S FORCE FIELD?
SO THAT I COULD...
...KILL YOU WITH MY OWN HANDS!

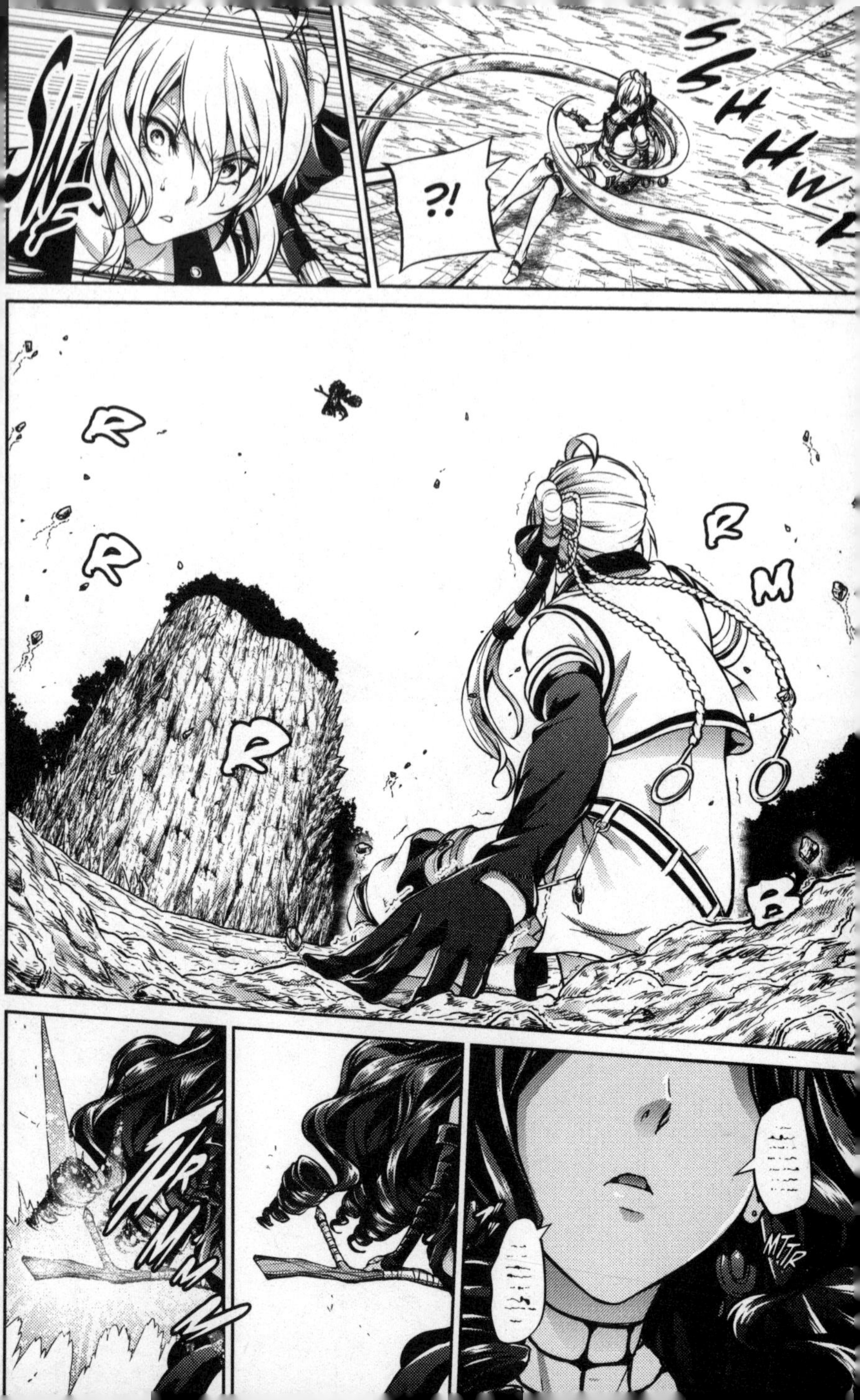
SHHWP
?!
RRR
RMB
MTTR

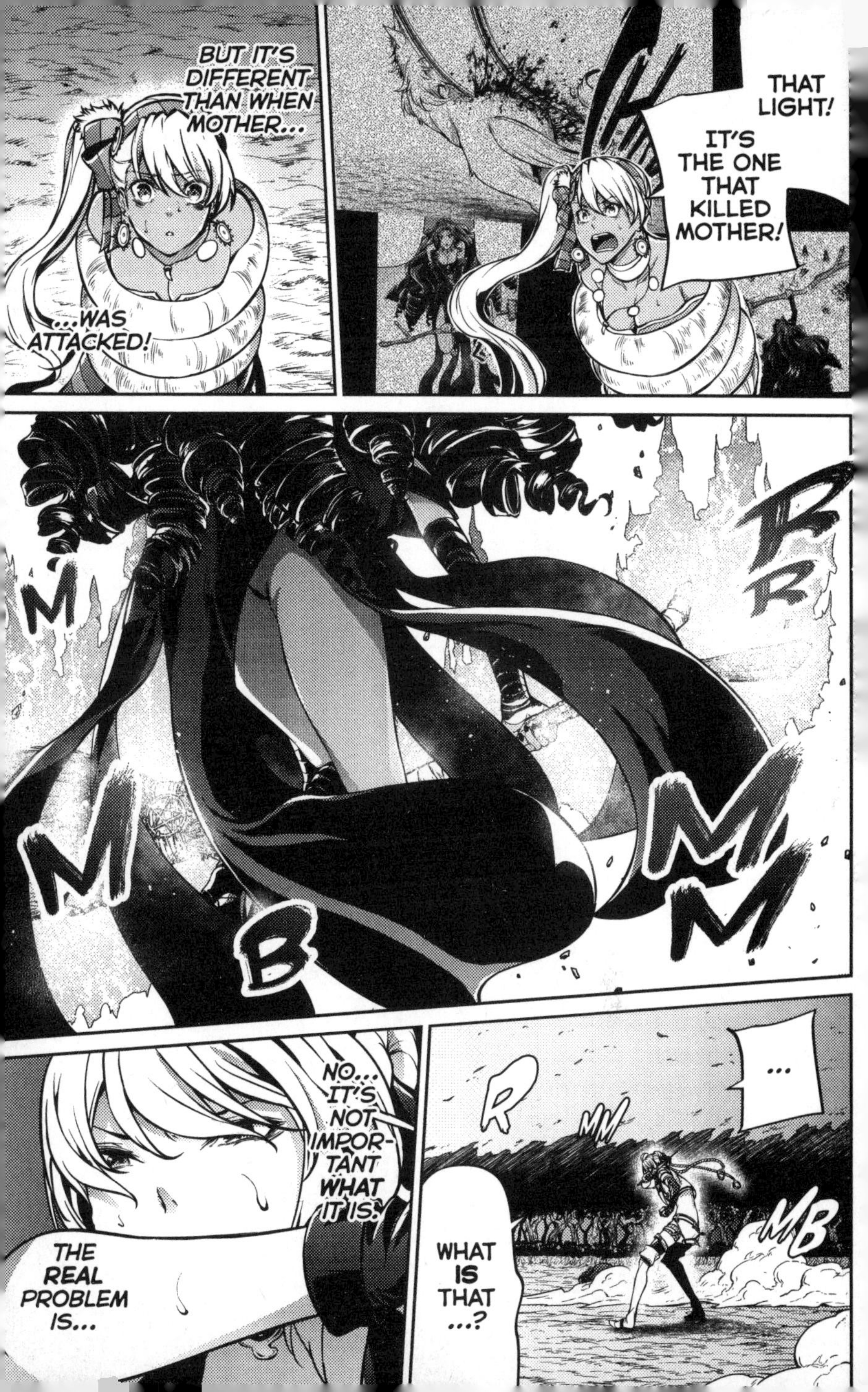
THAT LIGHT!
IT'S THE ONE THAT KILLED MOTHER!
BUT IT'S DIFFERENT THAN WHEN MOTHER...
...WAS ATTACKED!
RR
MMM
MM
B
...
R
MM
MB
WHAT IS THAT ...?
NO... IT'S NOT IMPOR-TANT WHAT IT IS.
THE REAL PROBLEM IS...

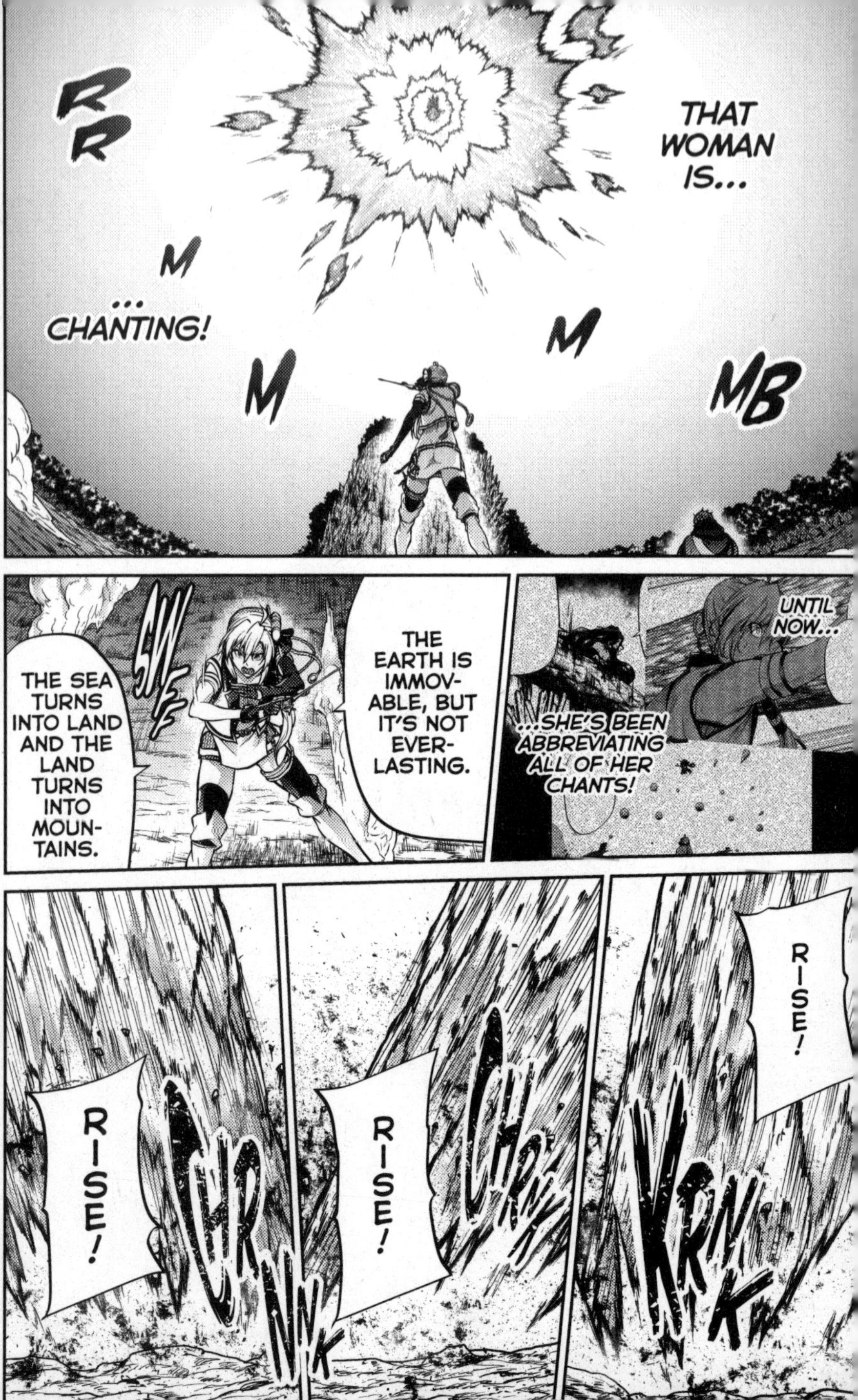
THAT WOMAN IS...
RR
M
M
M
MB
...CHANTING!
UNTIL NOW...
...SHE'S BEEN ABBREVIATING ALL OF HER CHANTS!
THE EARTH IS IMMOVABLE, BUT IT'S NOT EVERLASTING.
SWF
THE SEA TURNS INTO LAND AND THE LAND TURNS INTO MOUNTAINS.
RISE!
RISE!
RISE!

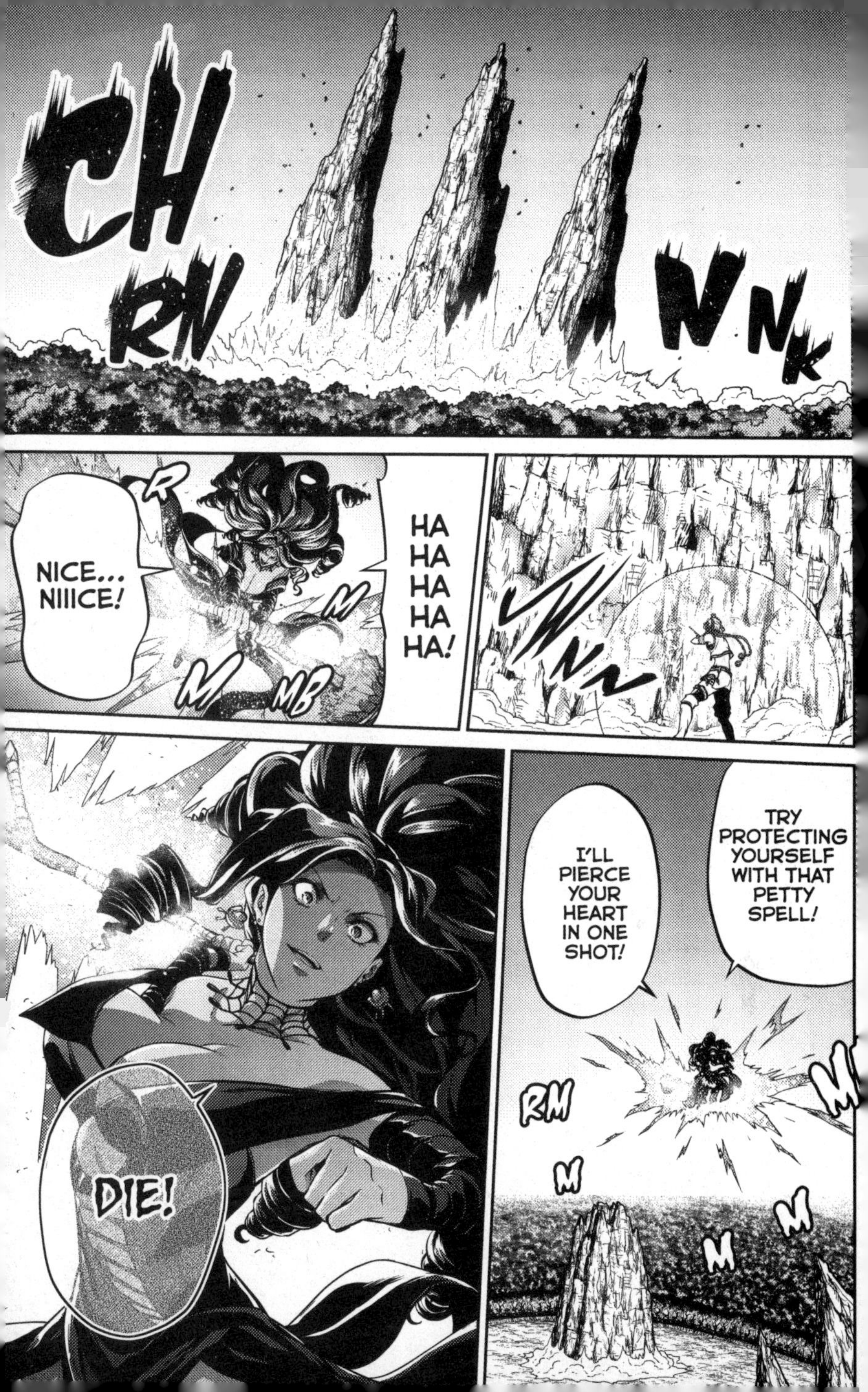

CHRNNNK
WNN
HA HA HA HA HA!
NICE... NIIICE!
RMMMB
TRY PROTECTING YOURSELF WITH THAT PETTY SPELL!
I'LL PIERCE YOUR HEART IN ONE SHOT!
RMMMMMM
DIE!

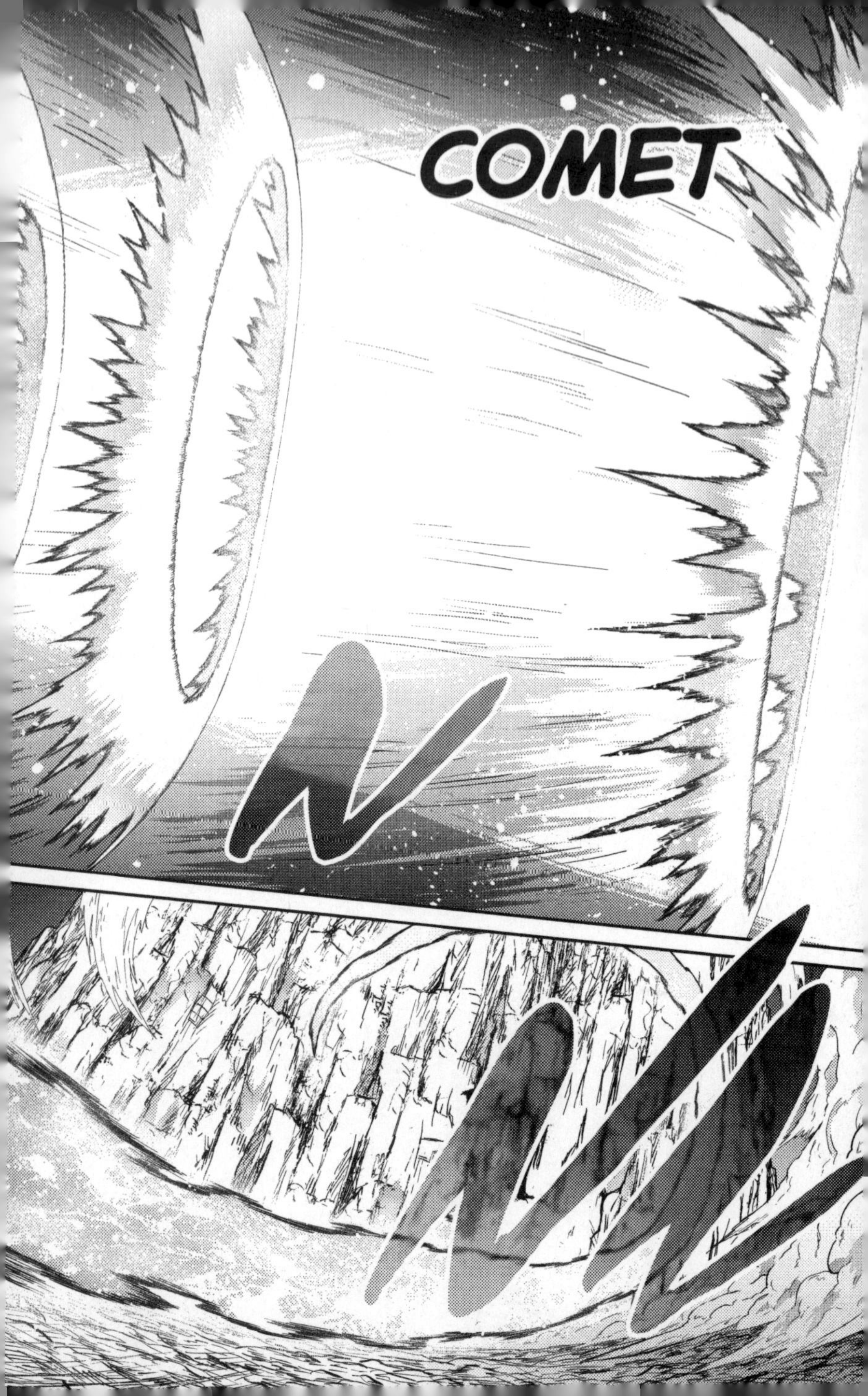
COMET

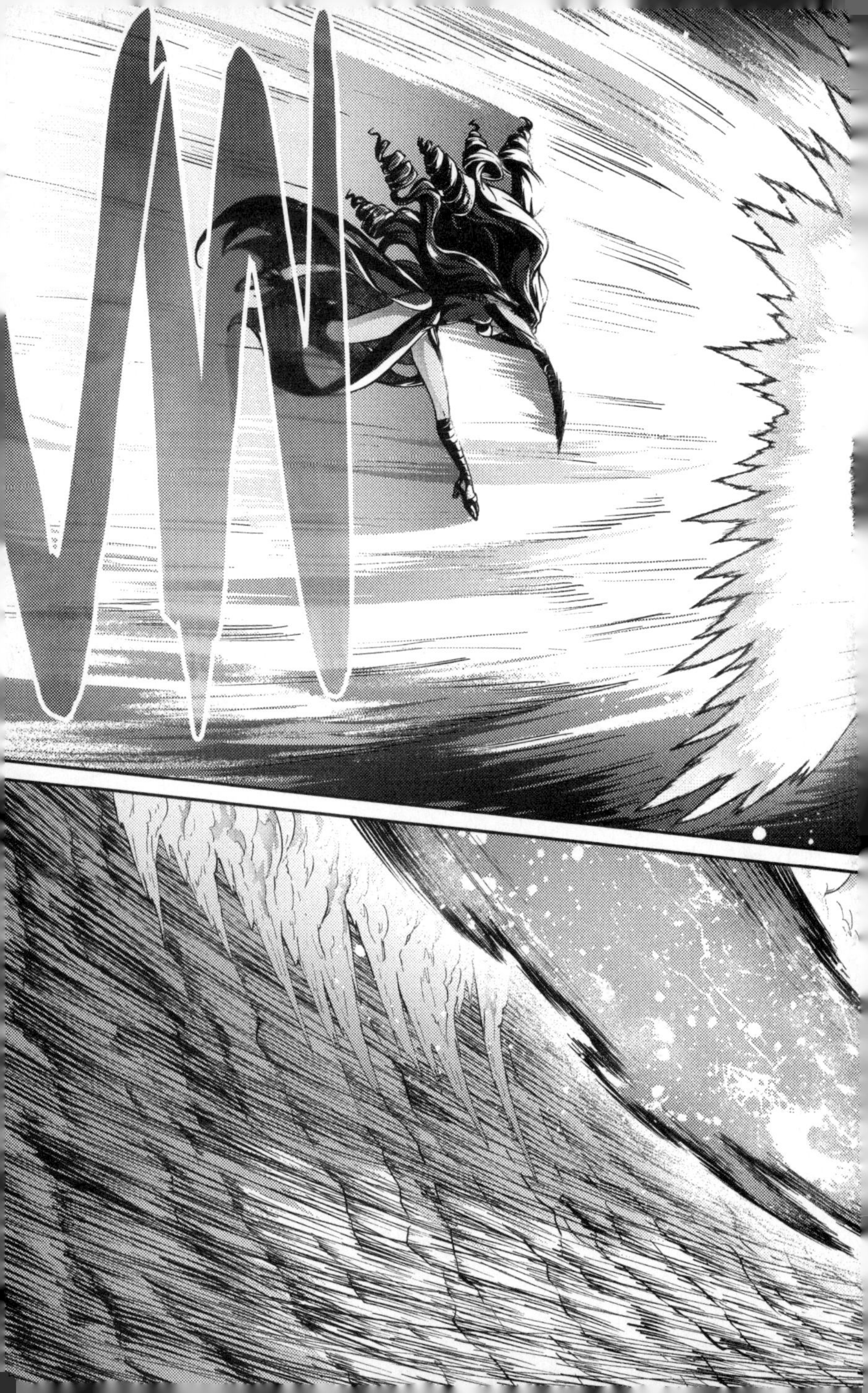

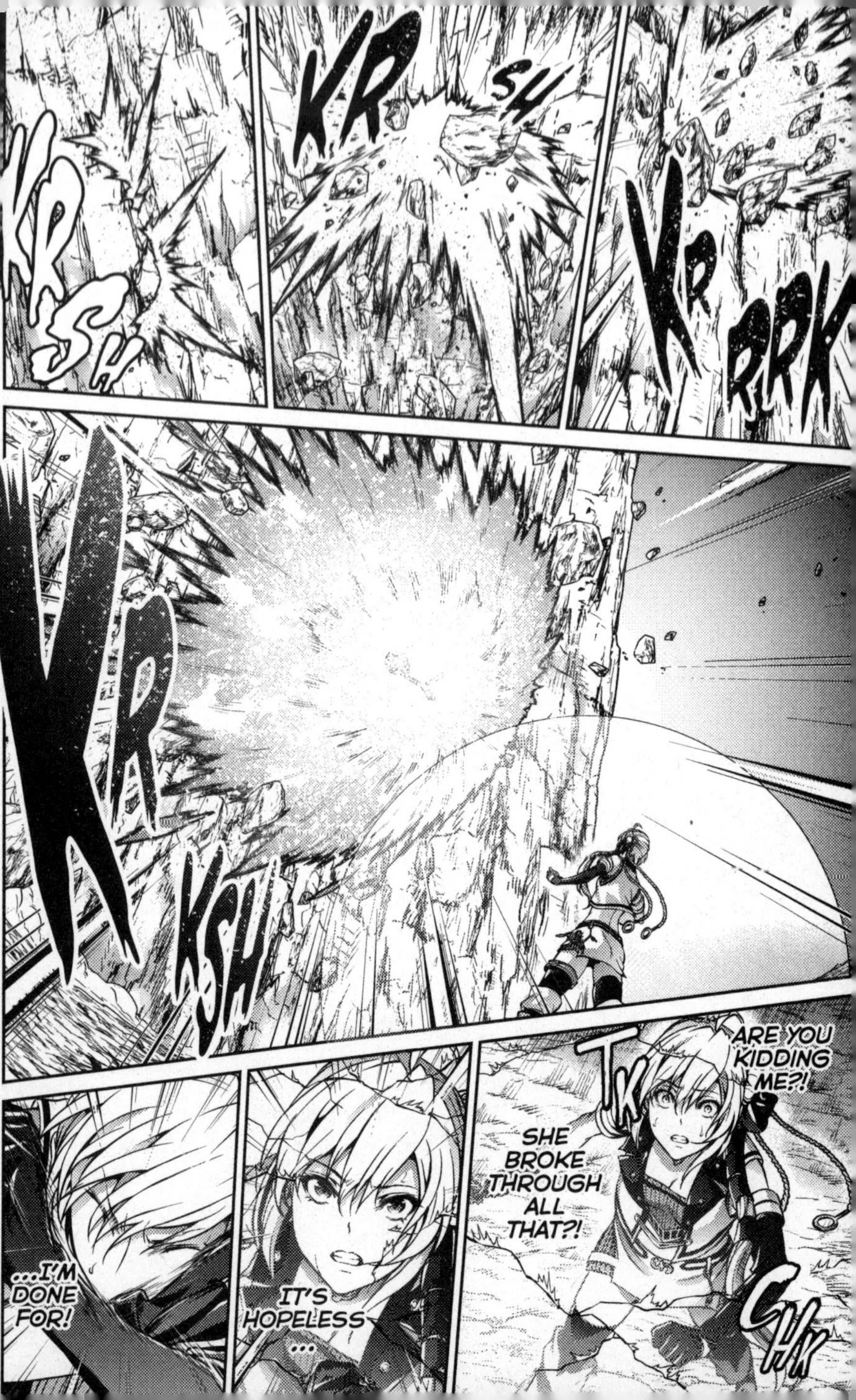
KRRRK
KRSH
KRSH
KRKSH
TK
ARE YOU KIDDING ME?!
SHE BROKE THROUGH ALL THAT?!
CHK
IT'S HOPELESS...
...I'M DONE FOR!

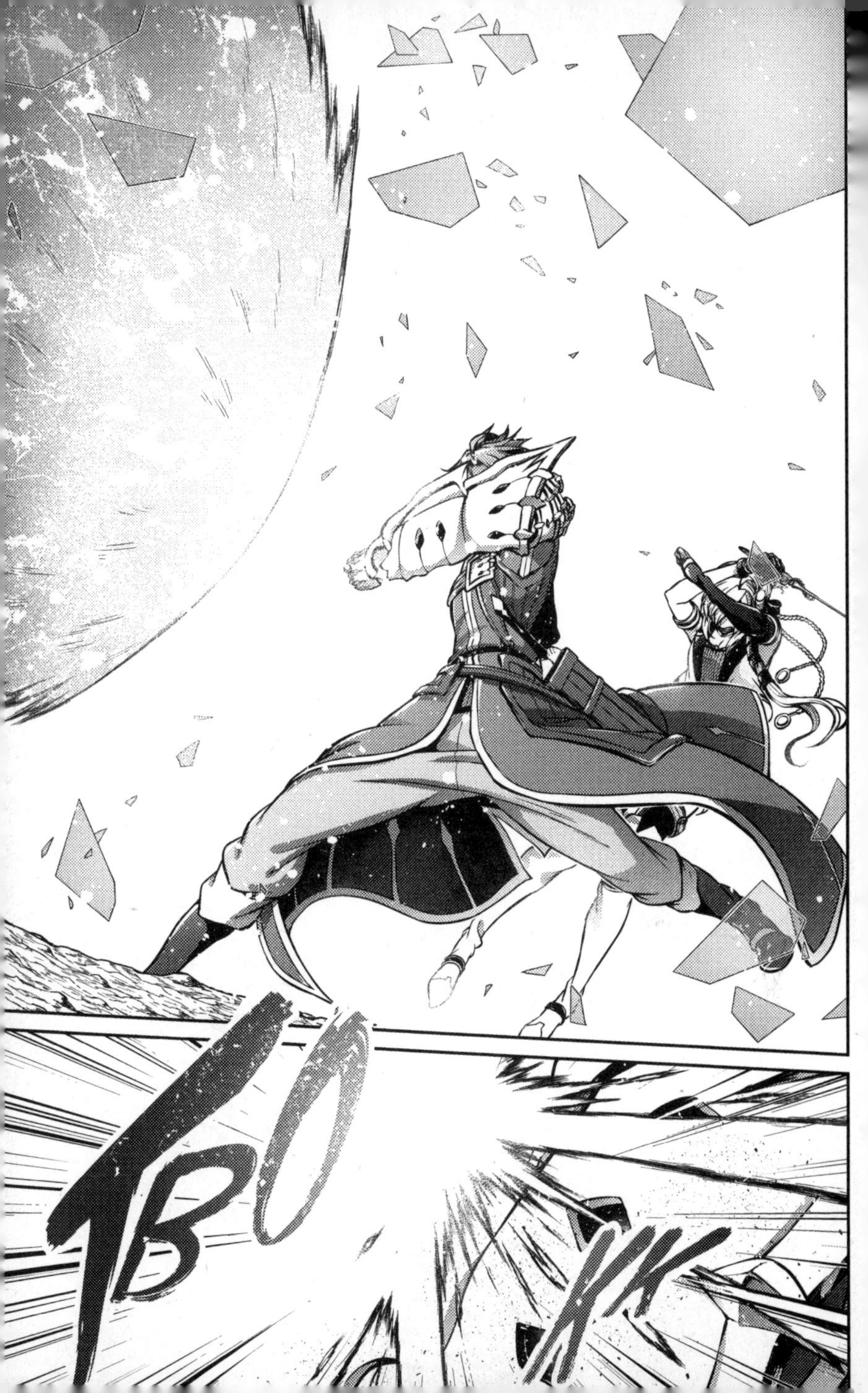

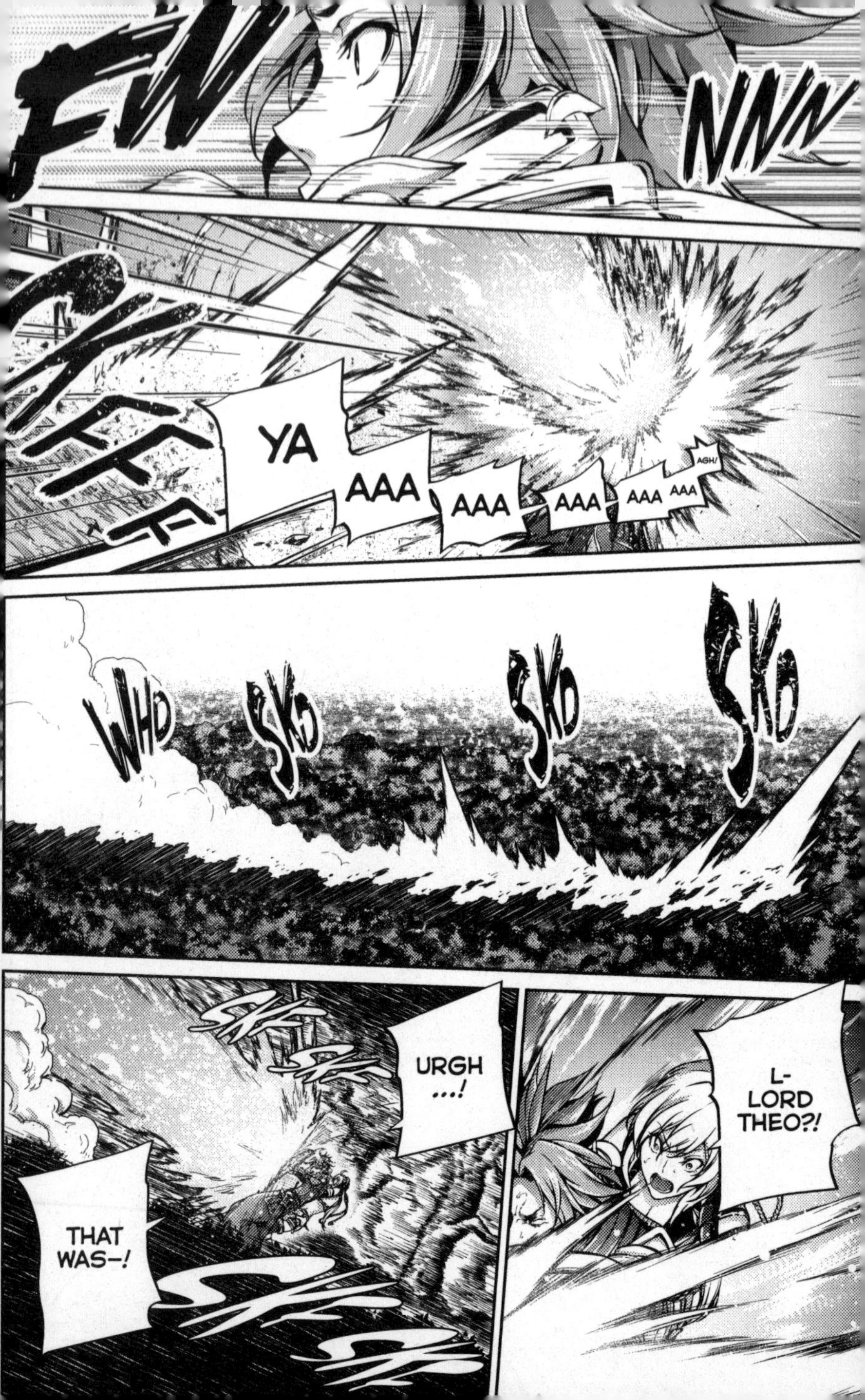

NINN
FW
FFF
YA AAA AAA AAA AAA AAA
AGH!
SKD SKD SKD WHD
L- LORD THEO?!
SK SK SK
URGH ...!
THAT WAS--!
SH SH SK

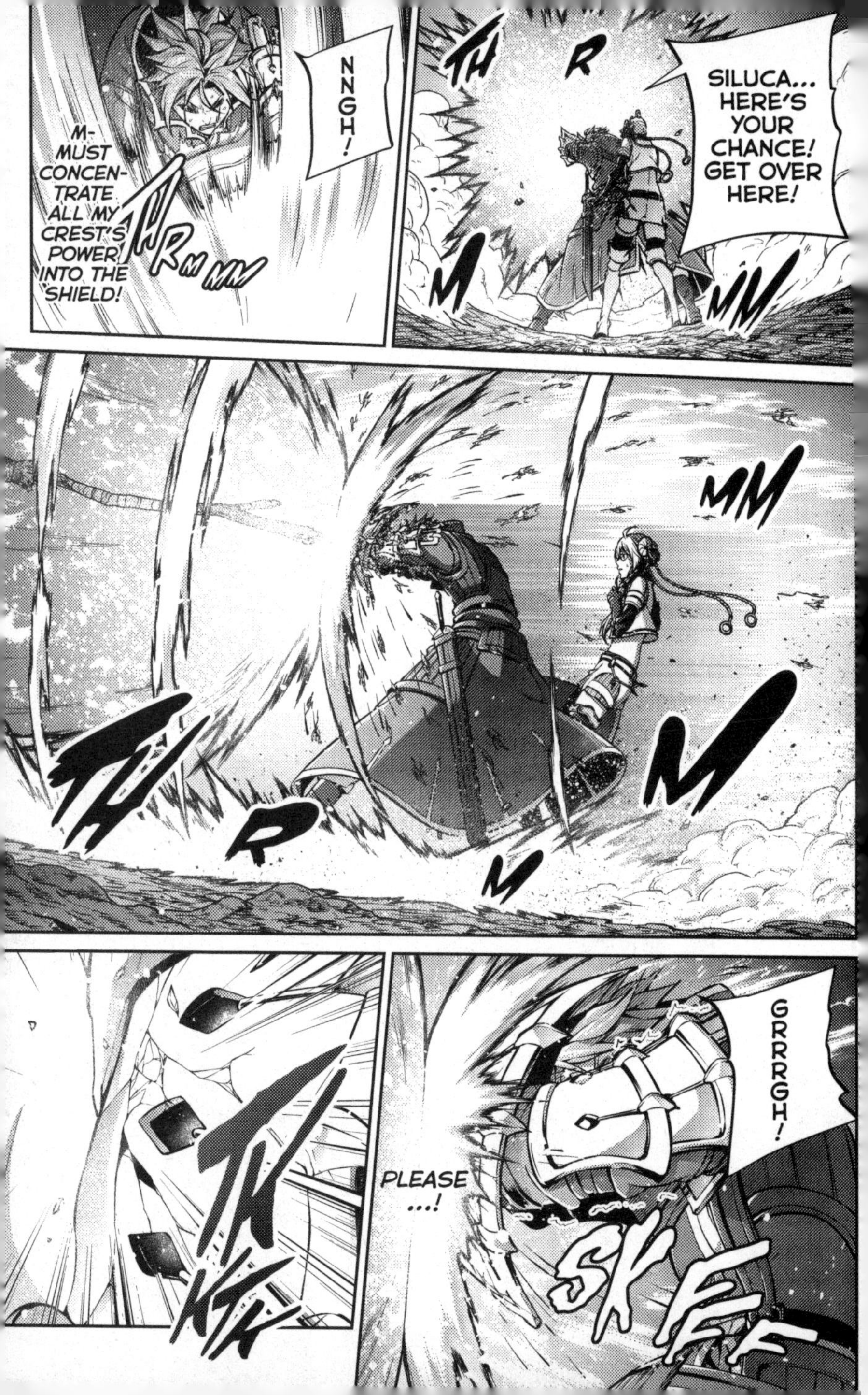

TH R
SILUCA... HERE'S YOUR CHANCE! GET OVER HERE!
M MM
NNGH!
M-MUST CONCENTRATE ALL MY CREST'S POWER INTO THE SHIELD!
THRMMM
MM
M
TH R M
GRRRGH!
SKEFF
PLEASE ...!
TK KTK

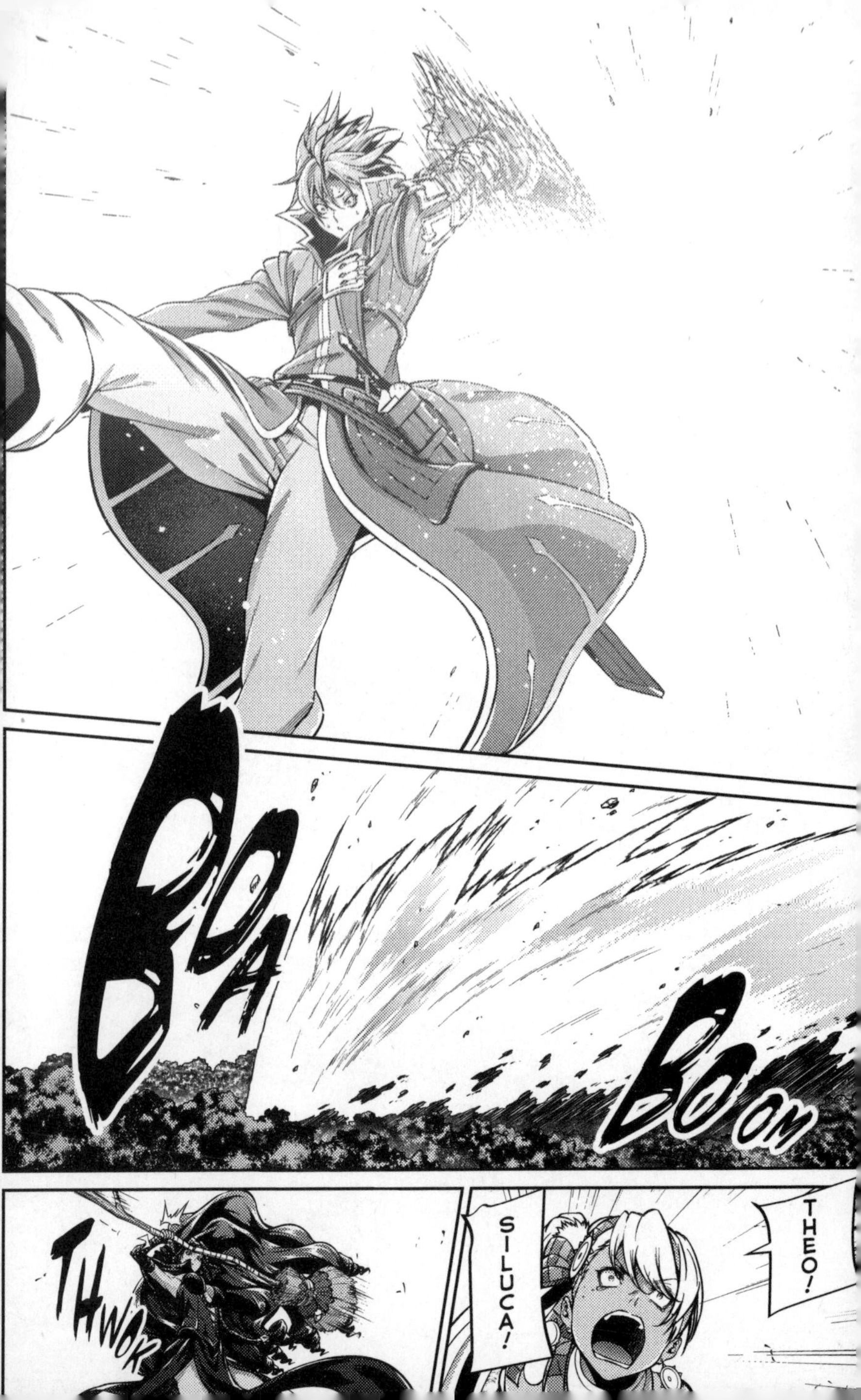
BOOM
THEO!
SILUCA!
THWOK

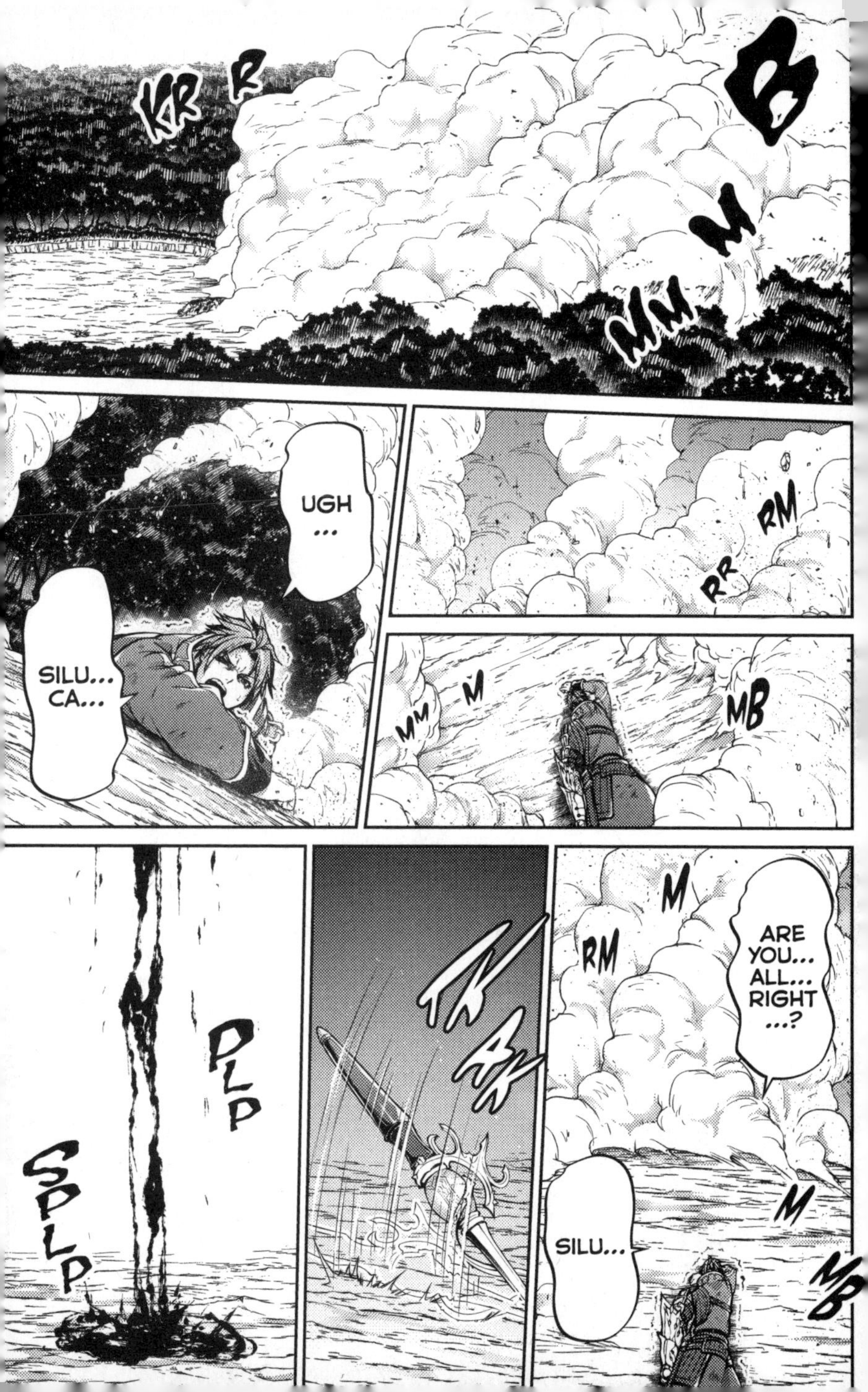
B
M
MM
KR R
RM
RR
MB
M
MM
UGH...
SILU... CA...
ARE YOU... ALL... RIGHT...?
M
RM
SILU...
M
MB
THAK
PLP
SPLP

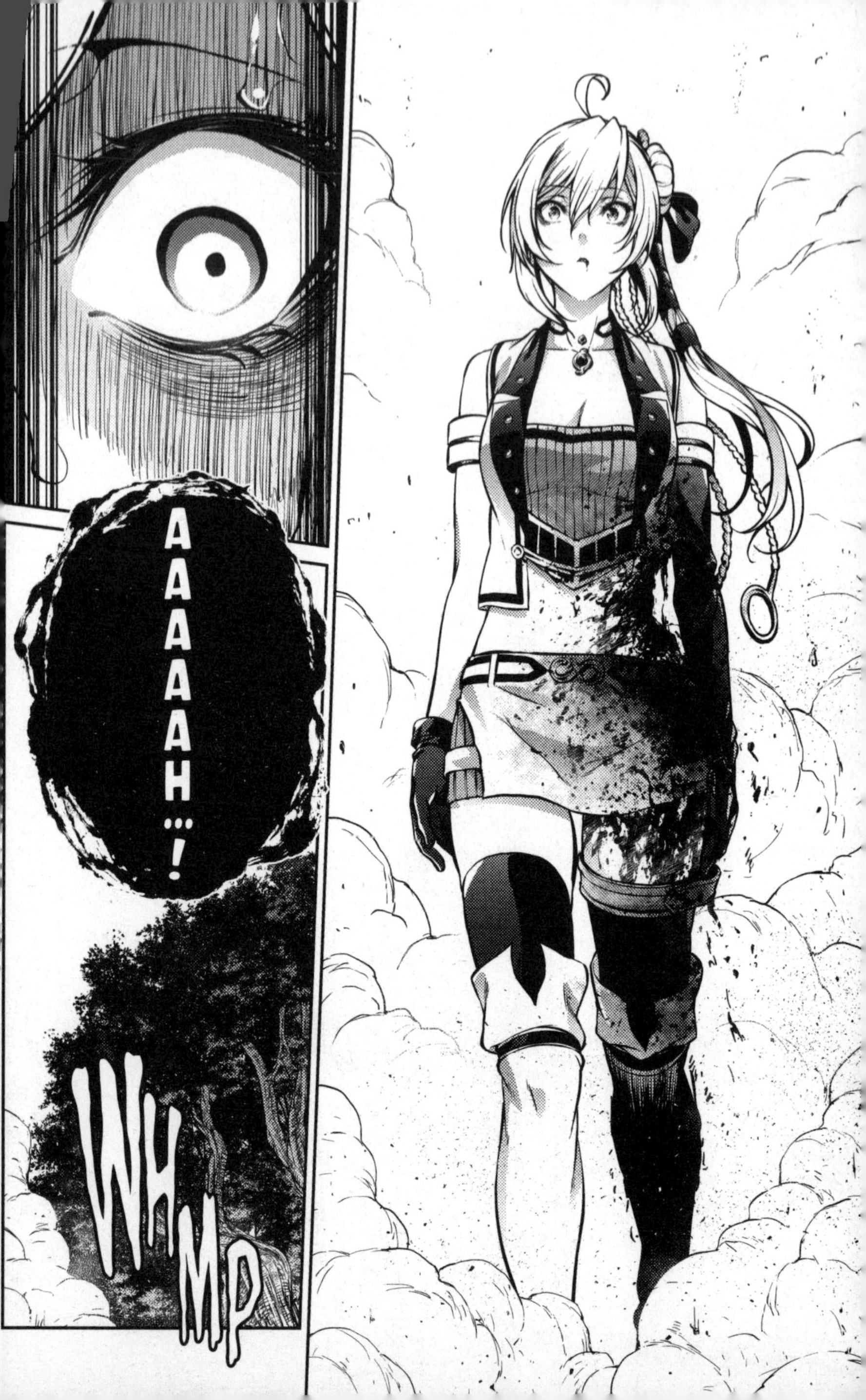
AAAAAH...!
WHMP

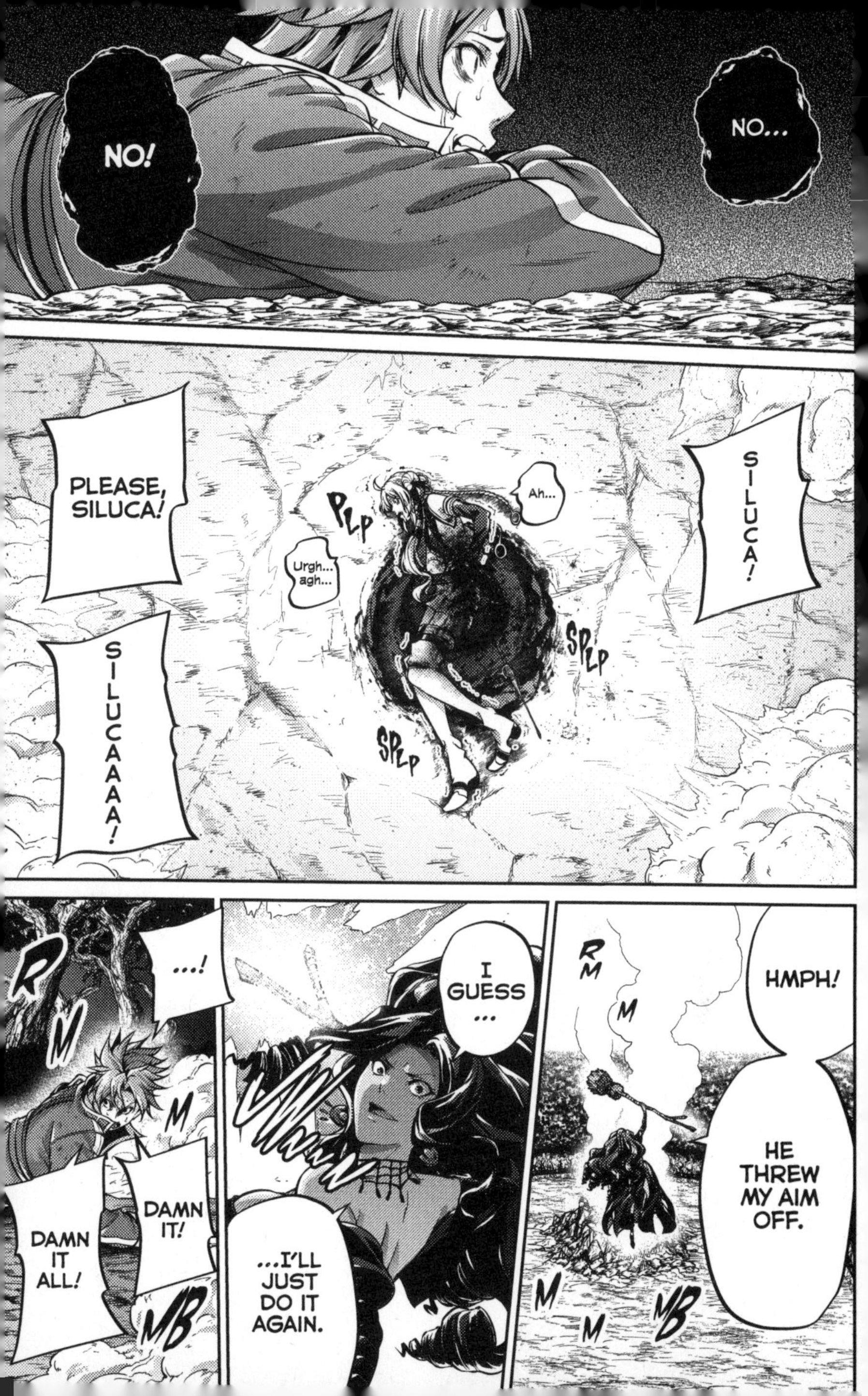
NO...
NO!
SILUCA!
Ah...
PLP
Urgh... agh...
SPLP
SPLP
PLEASE, SILUCA!
SILUCAAAA!
RM
M
HMPH!
HE THREW MY AIM OFF.
M
M
MB
I GUESS...
...I'LL JUST DO IT AGAIN.
...!
R
M
M
DAMN IT!
DAMN IT ALL!
MB

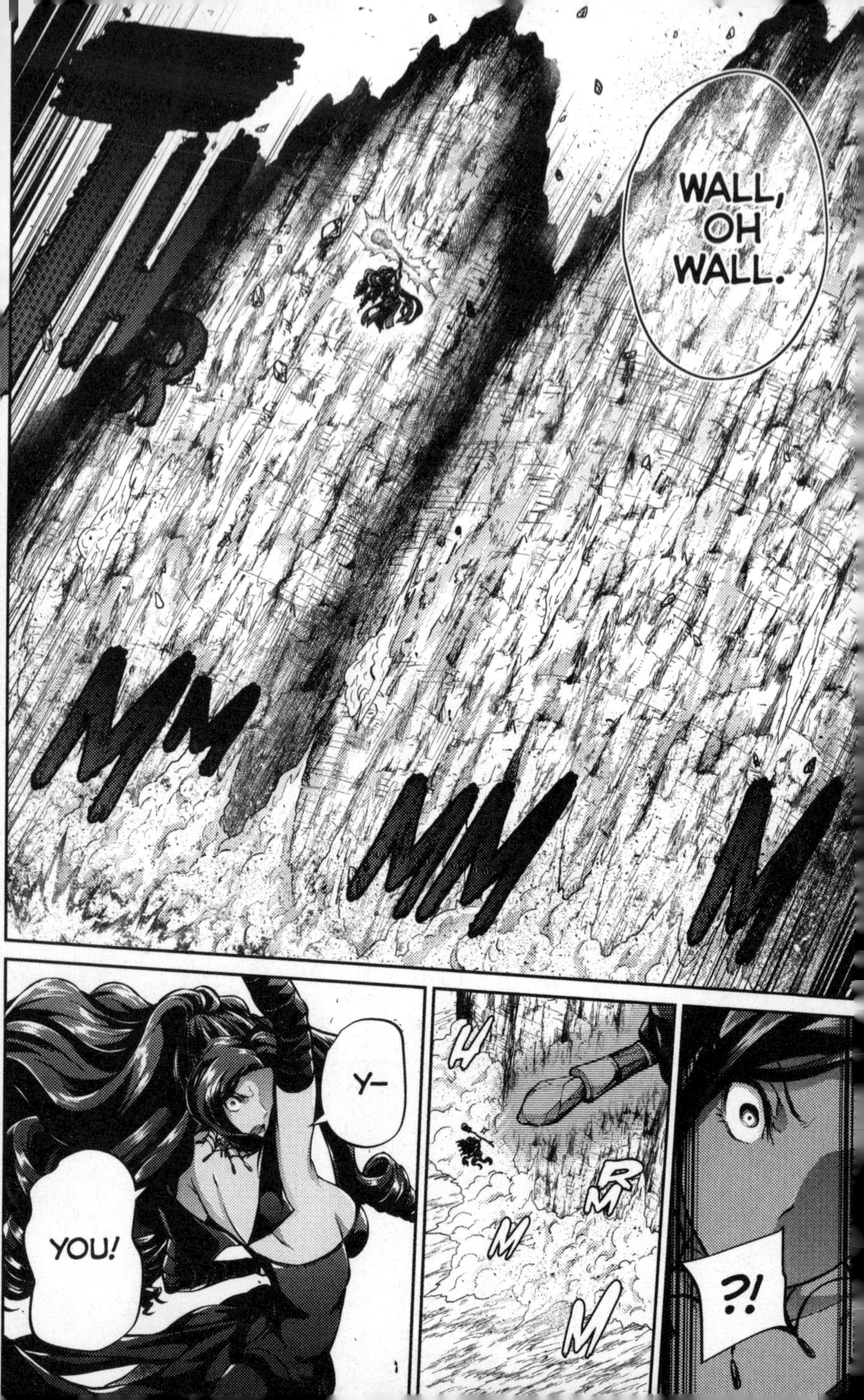
WALL, OH WALL.
?!
Y-
YOU!

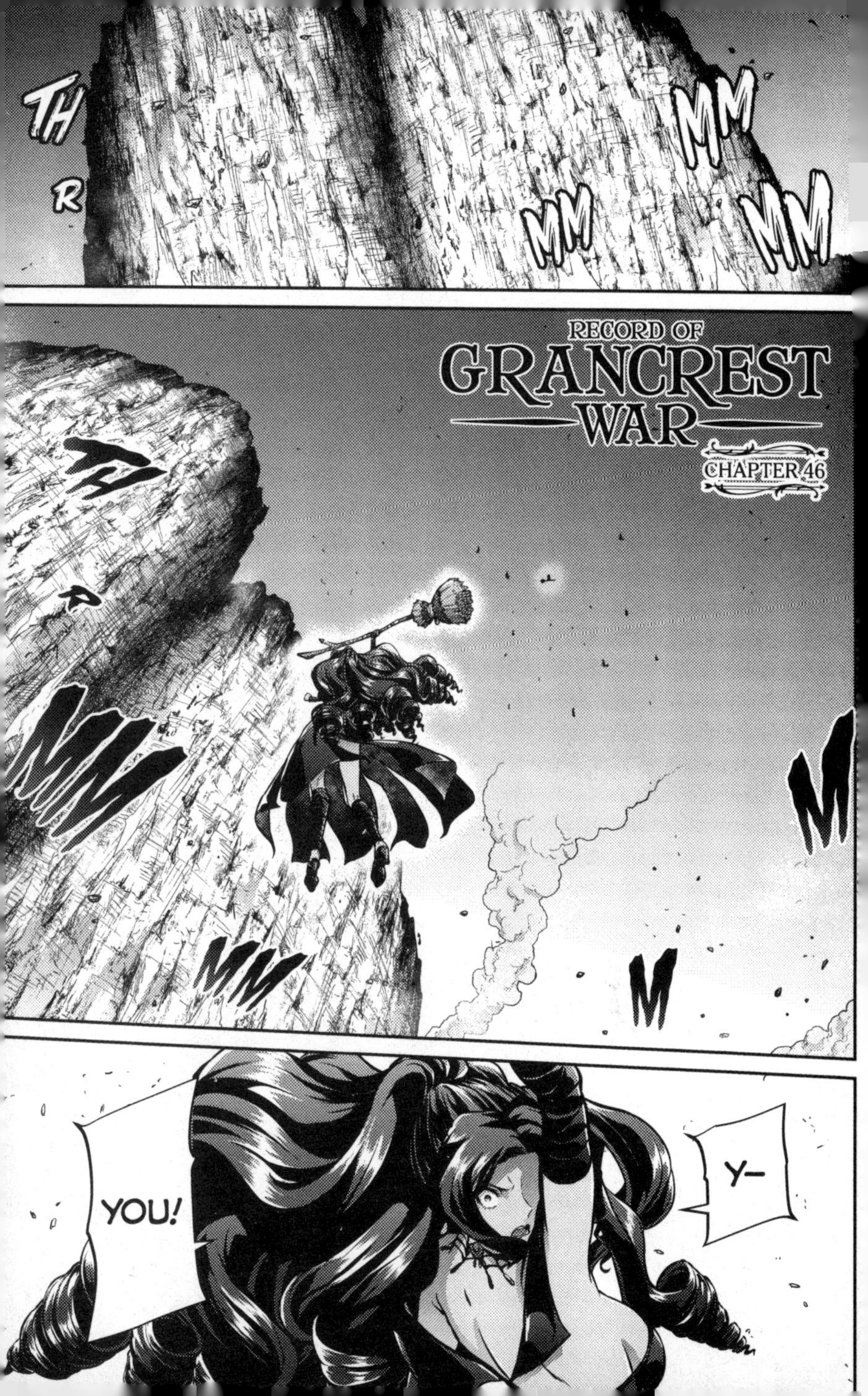
TH
R
MM
MM
MM
RECORD OF
GRANCREST
WAR
CHAPTER 46
TH
R
MM
MM
M
M
Y—
YOU!

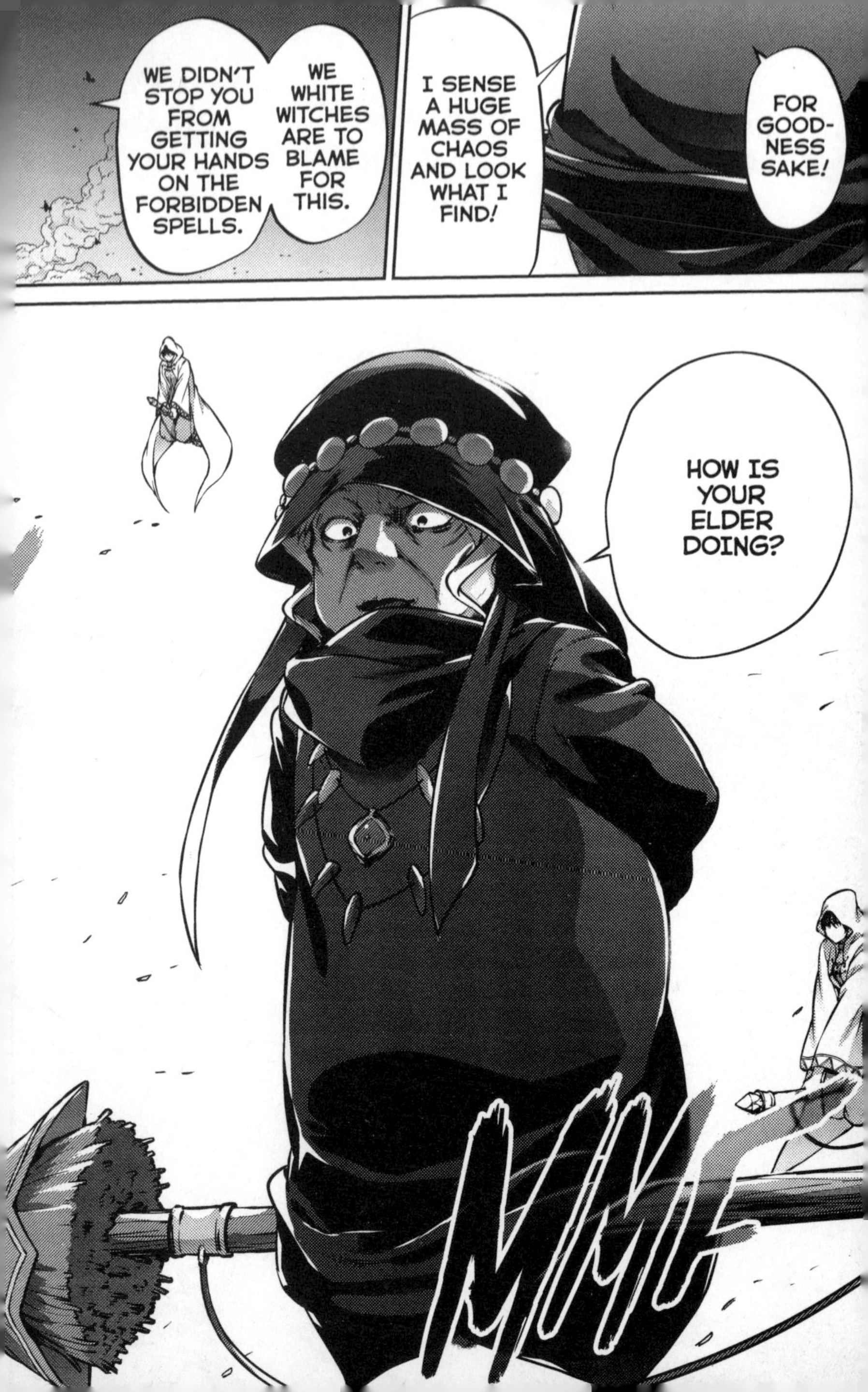
FOR GOODNESS SAKE!
I SENSE A HUGE MASS OF CHAOS AND LOOK WHAT I FIND!
WE WHITE WITCHES ARE TO BLAME FOR THIS.
WE DIDN'T STOP YOU FROM GETTING YOUR HANDS ON THE FORBIDDEN SPELLS.
HOW IS YOUR ELDER DOING?

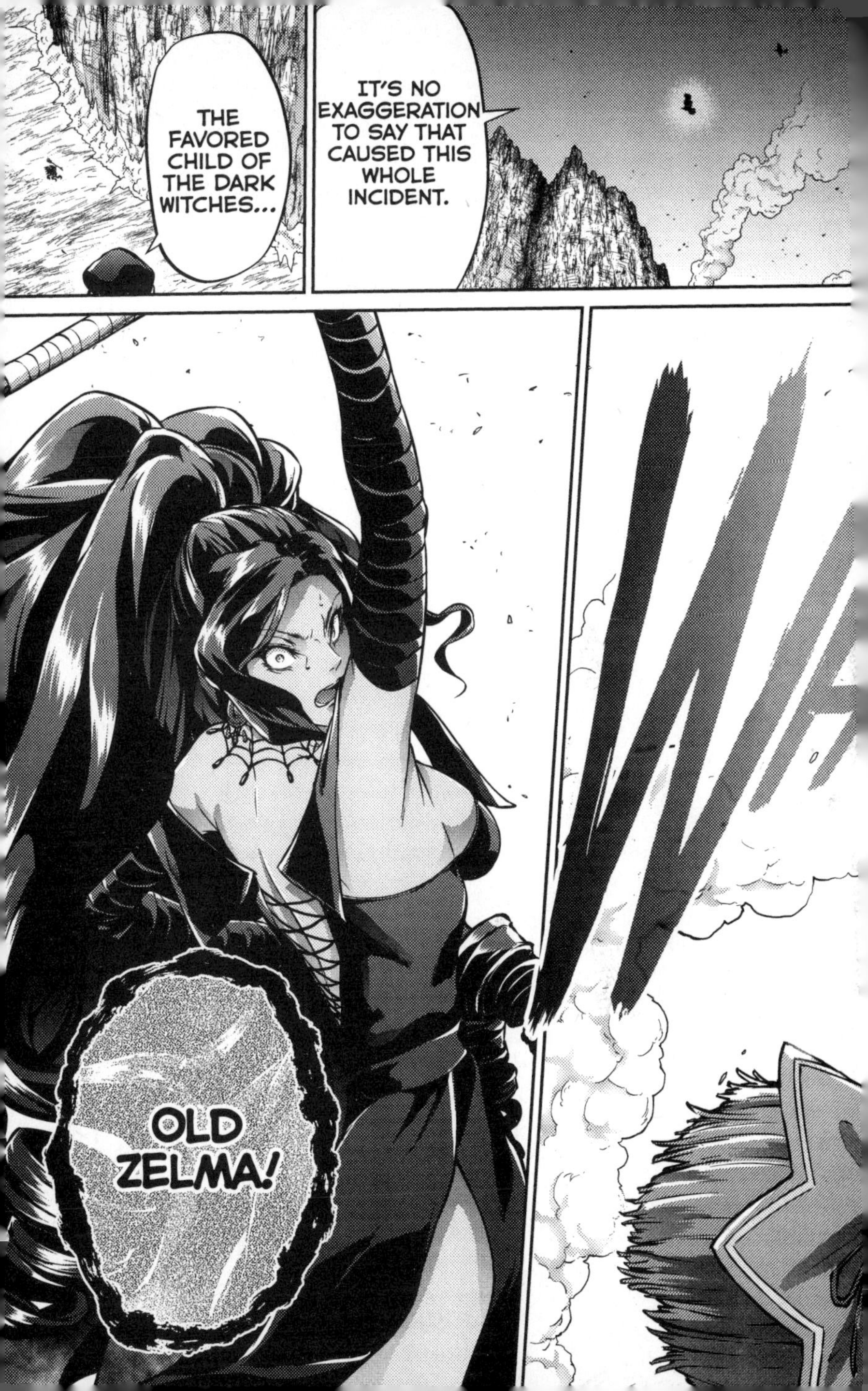
IT'S NO EXAGGERATION TO SAY THAT CAUSED THIS WHOLE INCIDENT.
THE FAVORED CHILD OF THE DARK WITCHES...
OLD ZELMA!

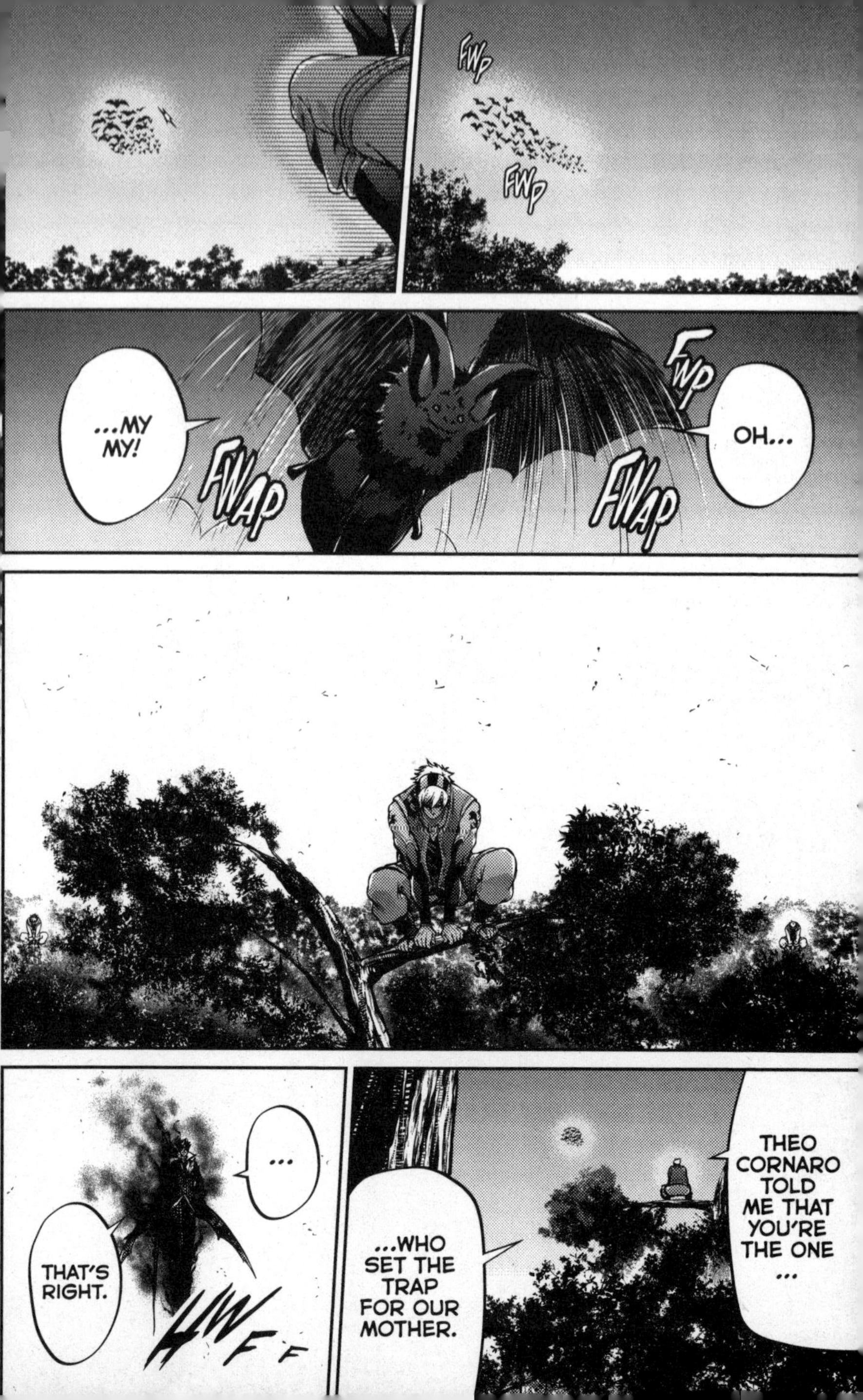
FWP
FWP
FWP
OH...
FWAP
FWAP
...MY MY!
THEO CORNARO TOLD ME THAT YOU'RE THE ONE ...
...WHO SET THE TRAP FOR OUR MOTHER.
...
THAT'S RIGHT.
HWFF

AFTER WHAT YOU'VE DONE...

GRRRR...

...I HOPE YOU DON'T THINK YOU'RE GONNA SOMEHOW ESCAPE.

RR

M

M

M

B

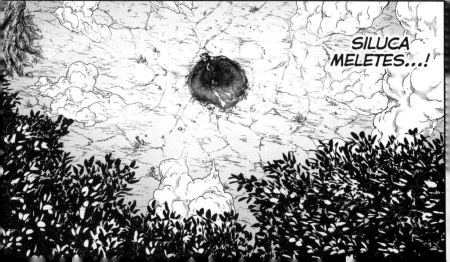

SILUCA MELETES...!

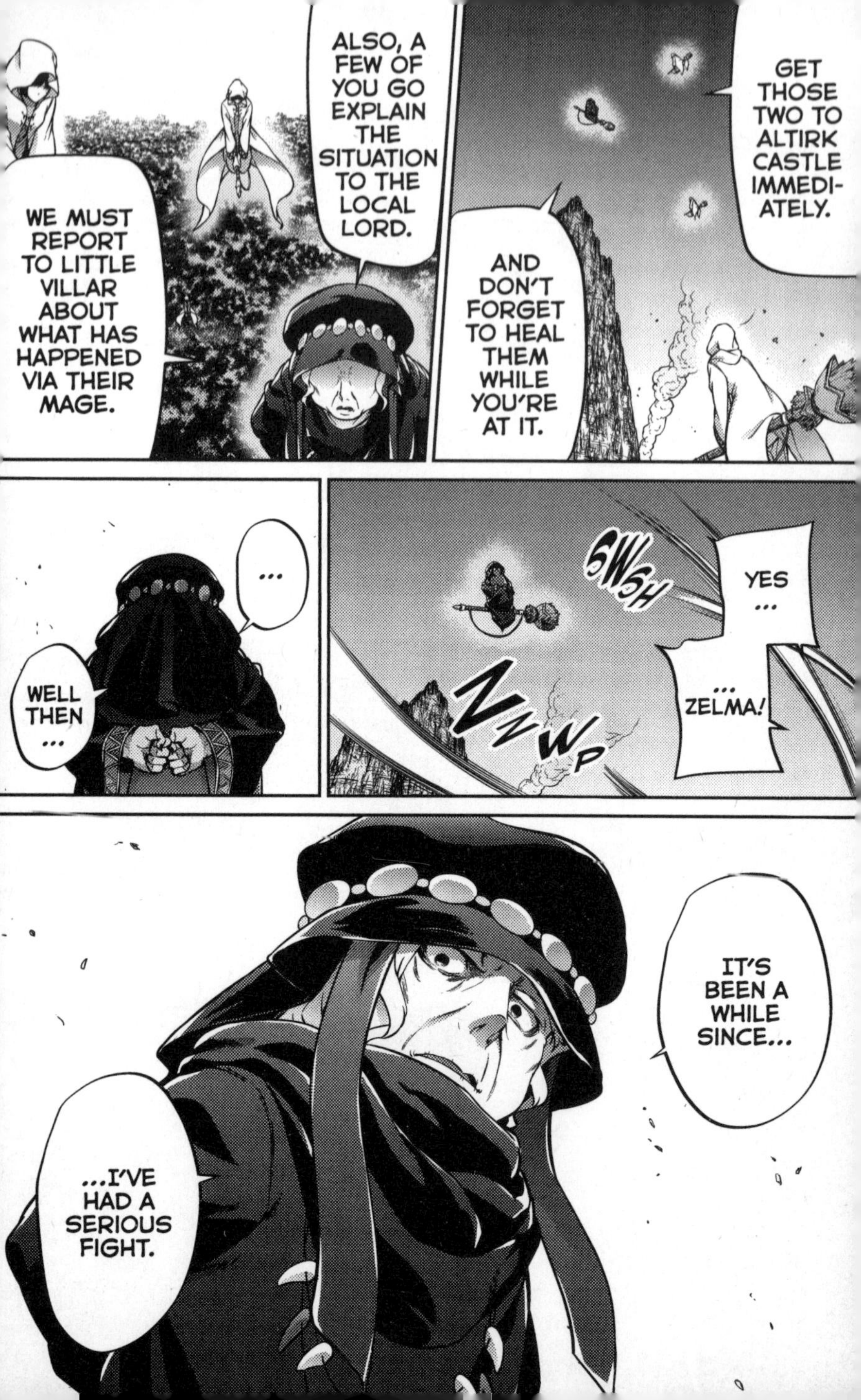
GET THOSE TWO TO ALTIRK CASTLE IMMEDI-ATELY.
AND DON'T FORGET TO HEAL THEM WHILE YOU'RE AT IT.
ALSO, A FEW OF YOU GO EXPLAIN THE SITUATION TO THE LOCAL LORD.
WE MUST REPORT TO LITTLE VILLAR ABOUT WHAT HAS HAPPENED VIA THEIR MAGE.
SWSH
YES ...
... ZELMA!
NNWP
...
WELL THEN ...
IT'S BEEN A WHILE SINCE...
...I'VE HAD A SERIOUS FIGHT.

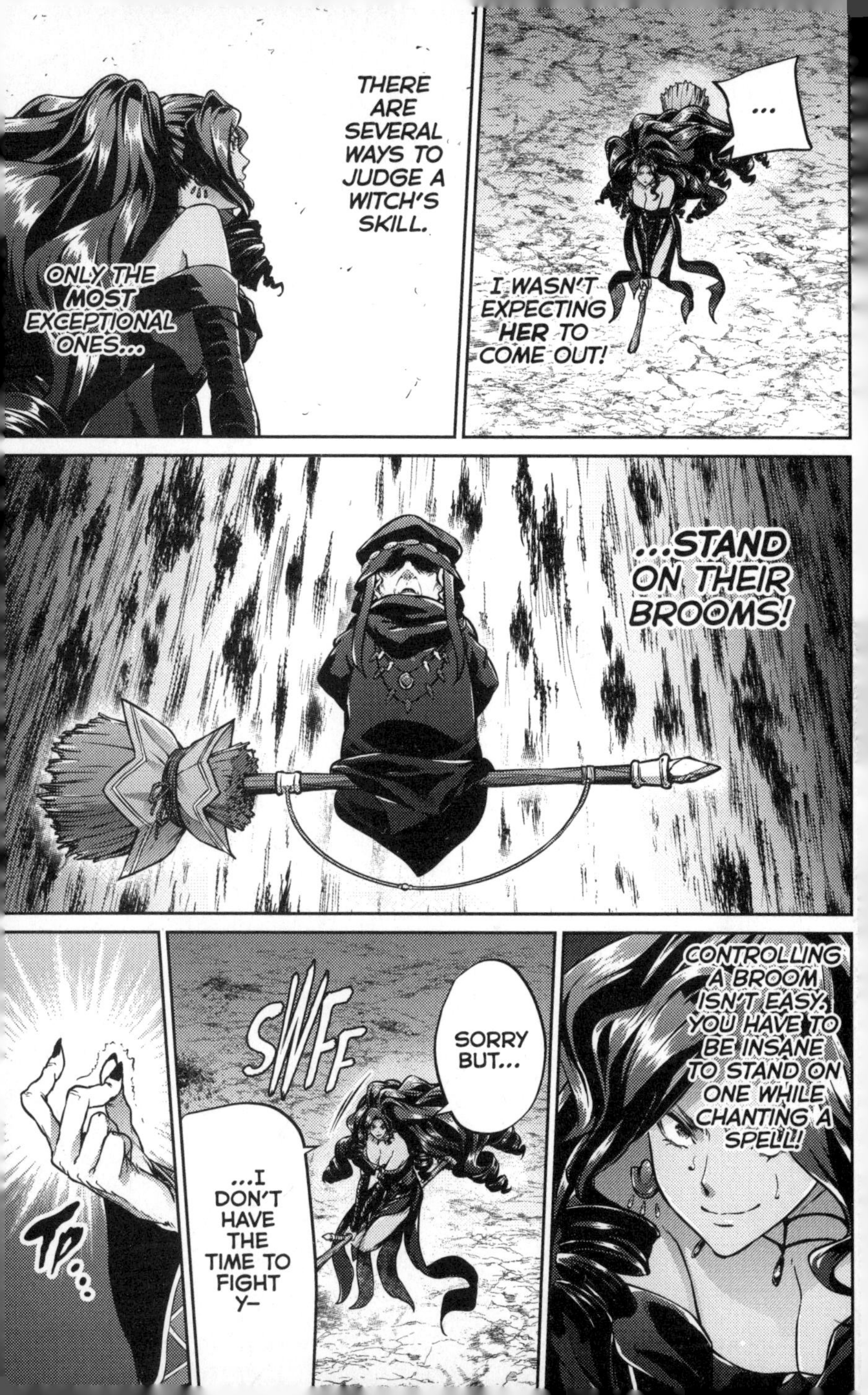
...
I WASN'T EXPECTING HER TO COME OUT!
THERE ARE SEVERAL WAYS TO JUDGE A WITCH'S SKILL.
ONLY THE MOST EXCEPTIONAL ONES...
...STAND ON THEIR BROOMS!
CONTROLLING A BROOM ISN'T EASY. YOU HAVE TO BE INSANE TO STAND ON ONE WHILE CHANTING A SPELL!
SWFF
SORRY BUT...
...I DON'T HAVE THE TIME TO FIGHT Y–
TP...

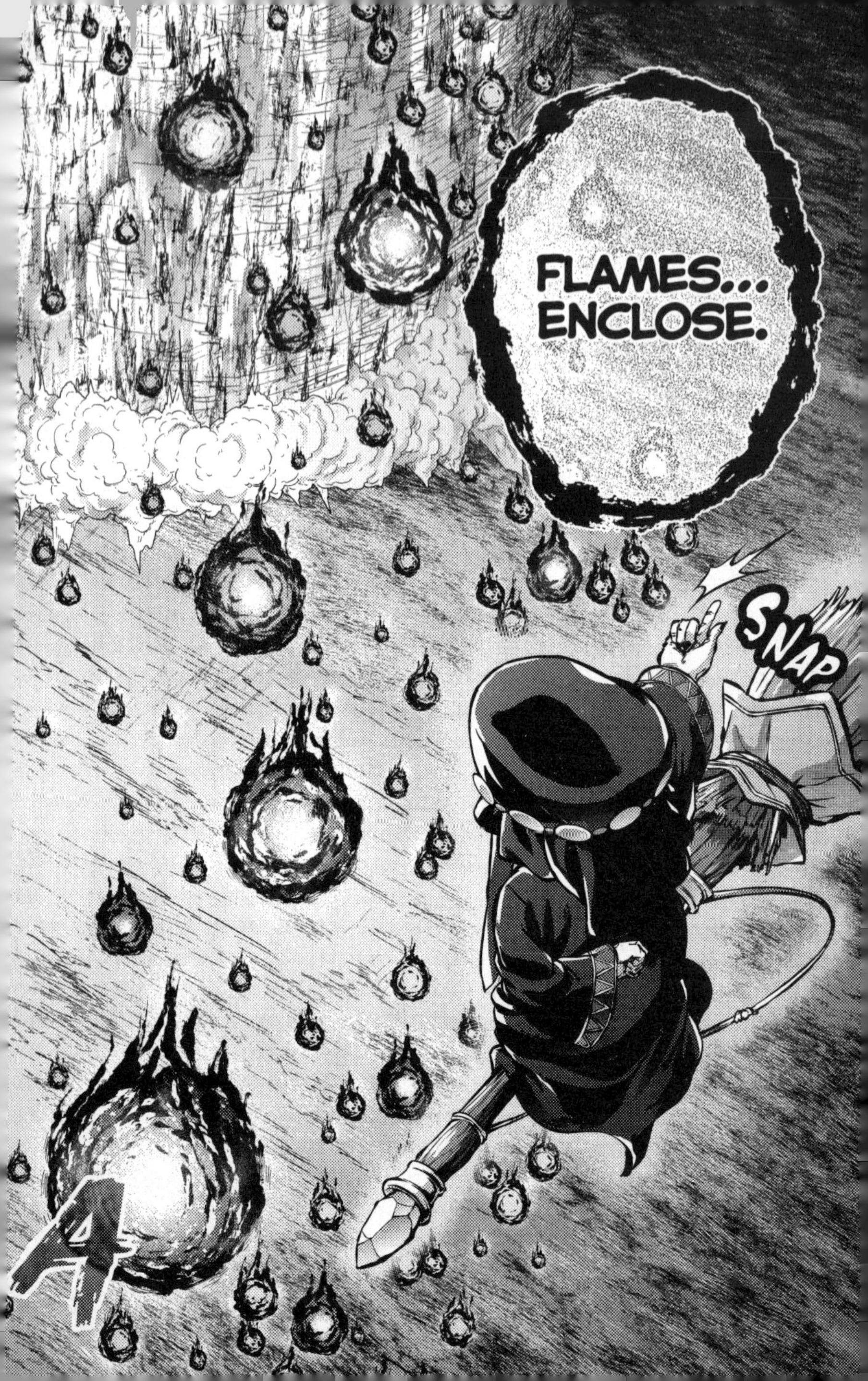
FLAMES... ENCLOSE.
SNAP

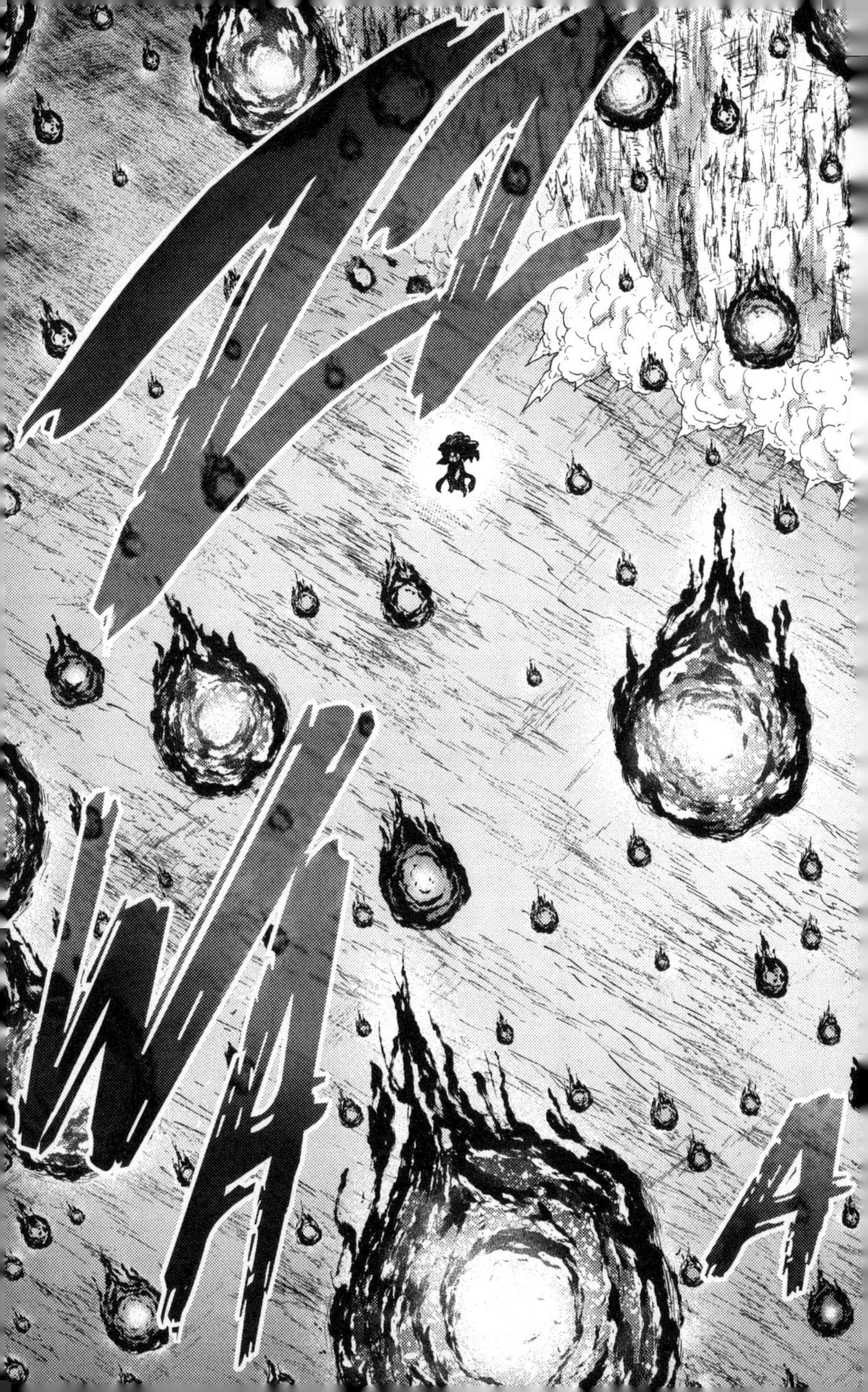

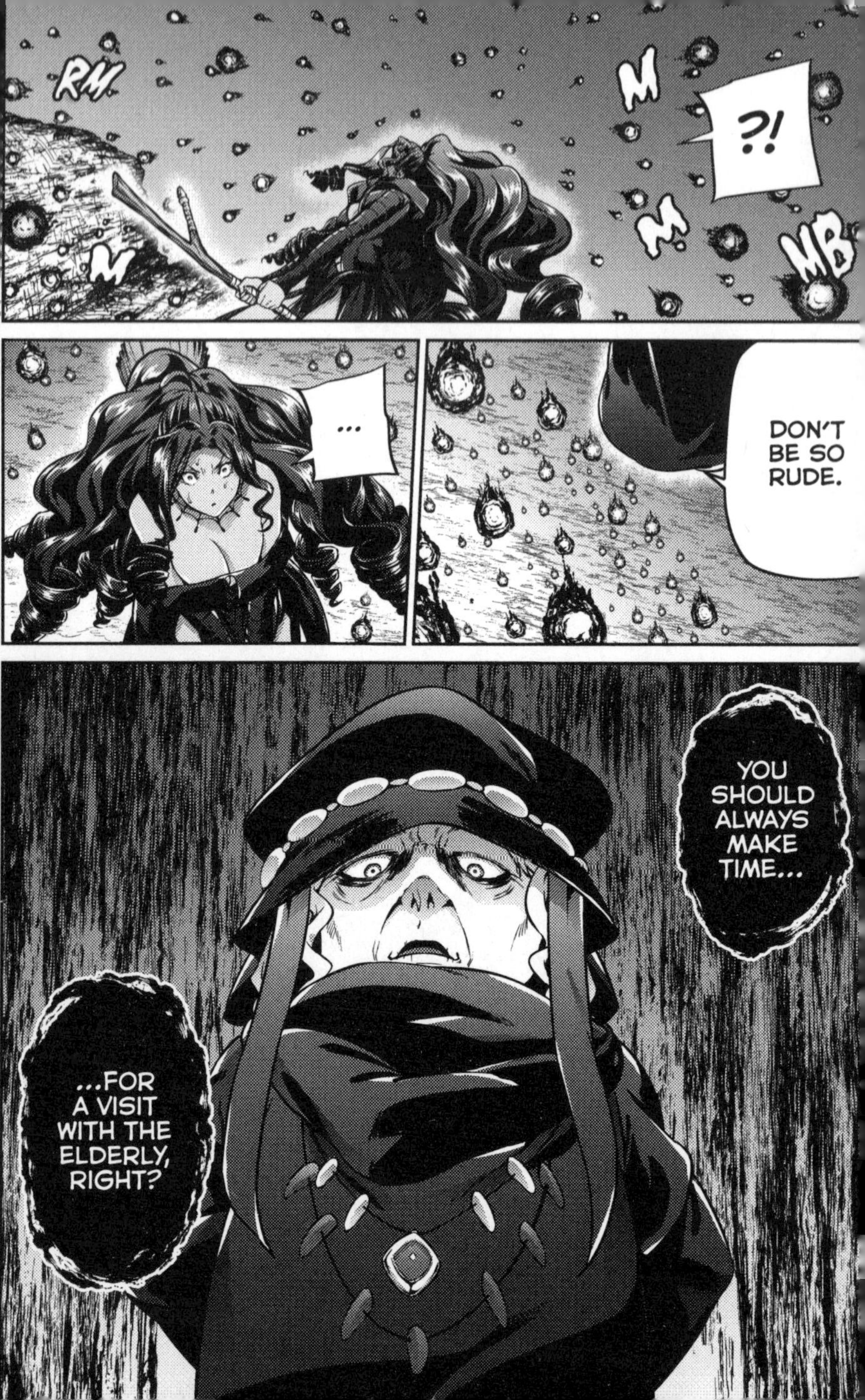

MMMB
?!
RM
M
DON'T BE SO RUDE.
...
YOU SHOULD ALWAYS MAKE TIME...
...FOR A VISIT WITH THE ELDERLY, RIGHT?

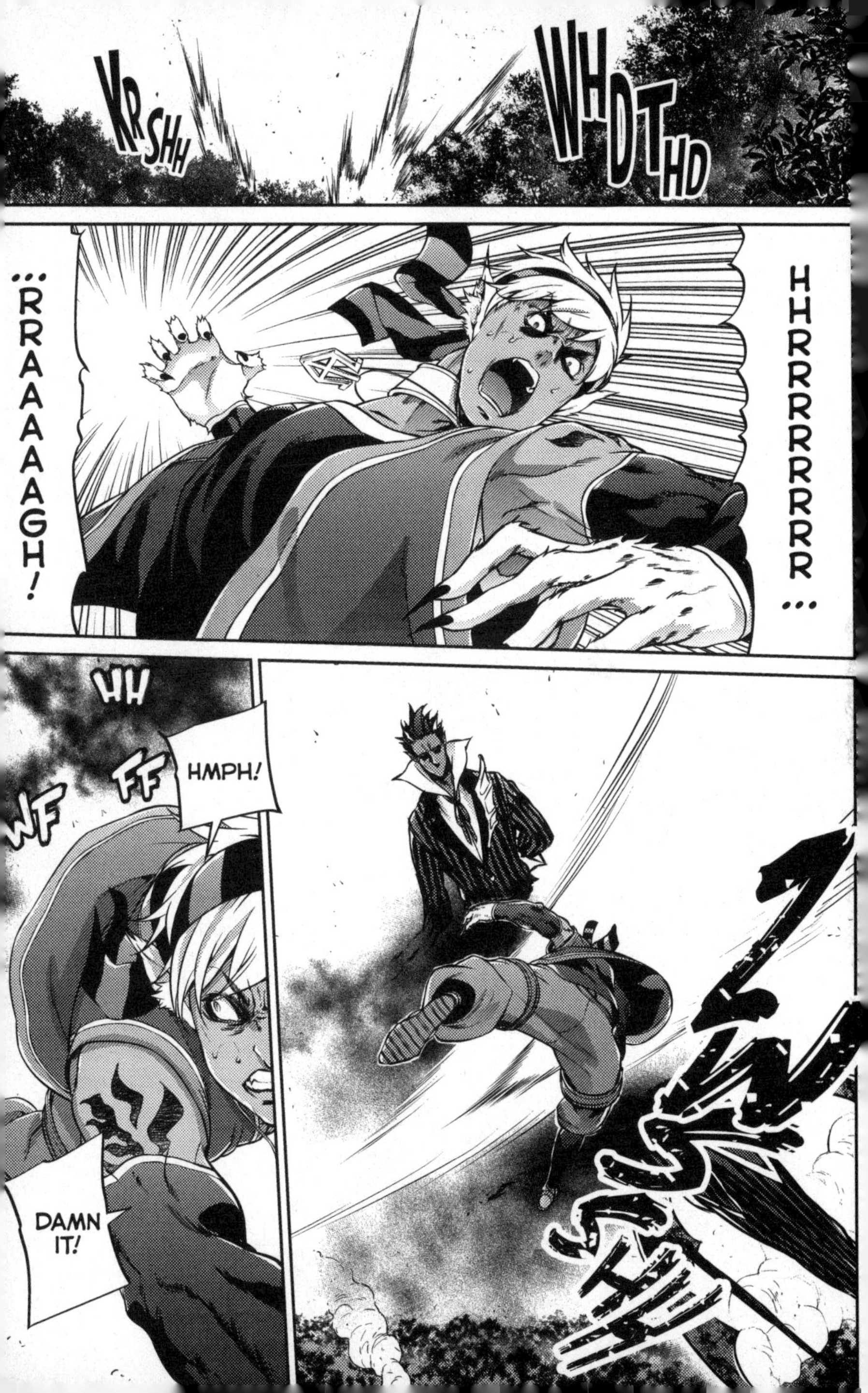
WHDTHD
KRSHH
HHRRRRRRRR...
...RRAAAAAGH!
HH
FF
WF
HMPH!
DAMN IT!

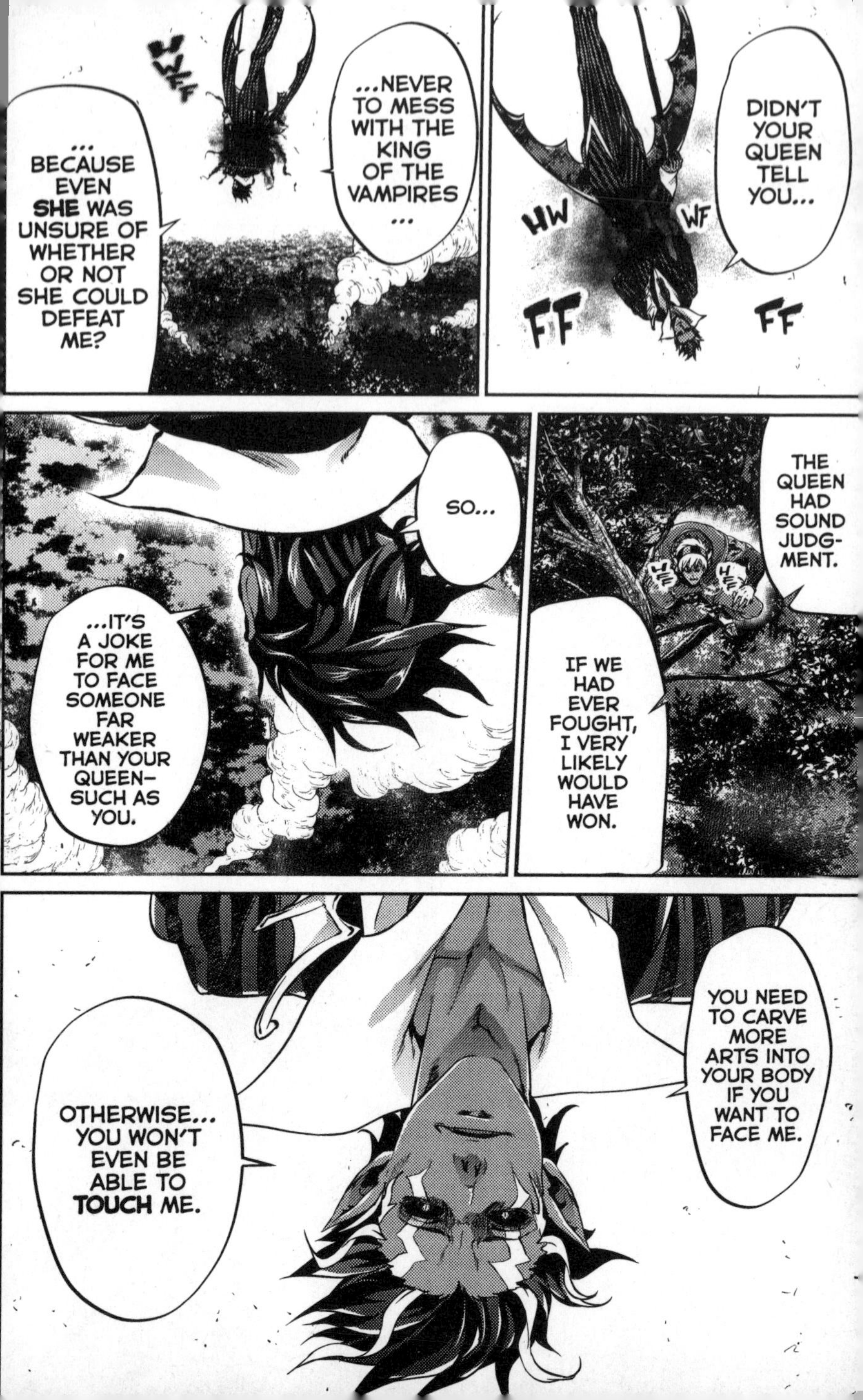
DIDN'T YOUR QUEEN TELL YOU...
HW
WF
FF
FF
...NEVER TO MESS WITH THE KING OF THE VAMPIRES...
...BECAUSE EVEN **SHE** WAS UNSURE OF WHETHER OR NOT SHE COULD DEFEAT ME?
HWFF
THE QUEEN HAD SOUND JUDG-MENT.
HFF
HFF
IF WE HAD EVER FOUGHT, I VERY LIKELY WOULD HAVE WON.
SO...
...IT'S A JOKE FOR ME TO FACE SOMEONE FAR WEAKER THAN YOUR QUEEN—SUCH AS YOU.
YOU NEED TO CARVE MORE ARTS INTO YOUR BODY IF YOU WANT TO FACE ME.
OTHERWISE... YOU WON'T EVEN BE ABLE TO **TOUCH** ME.

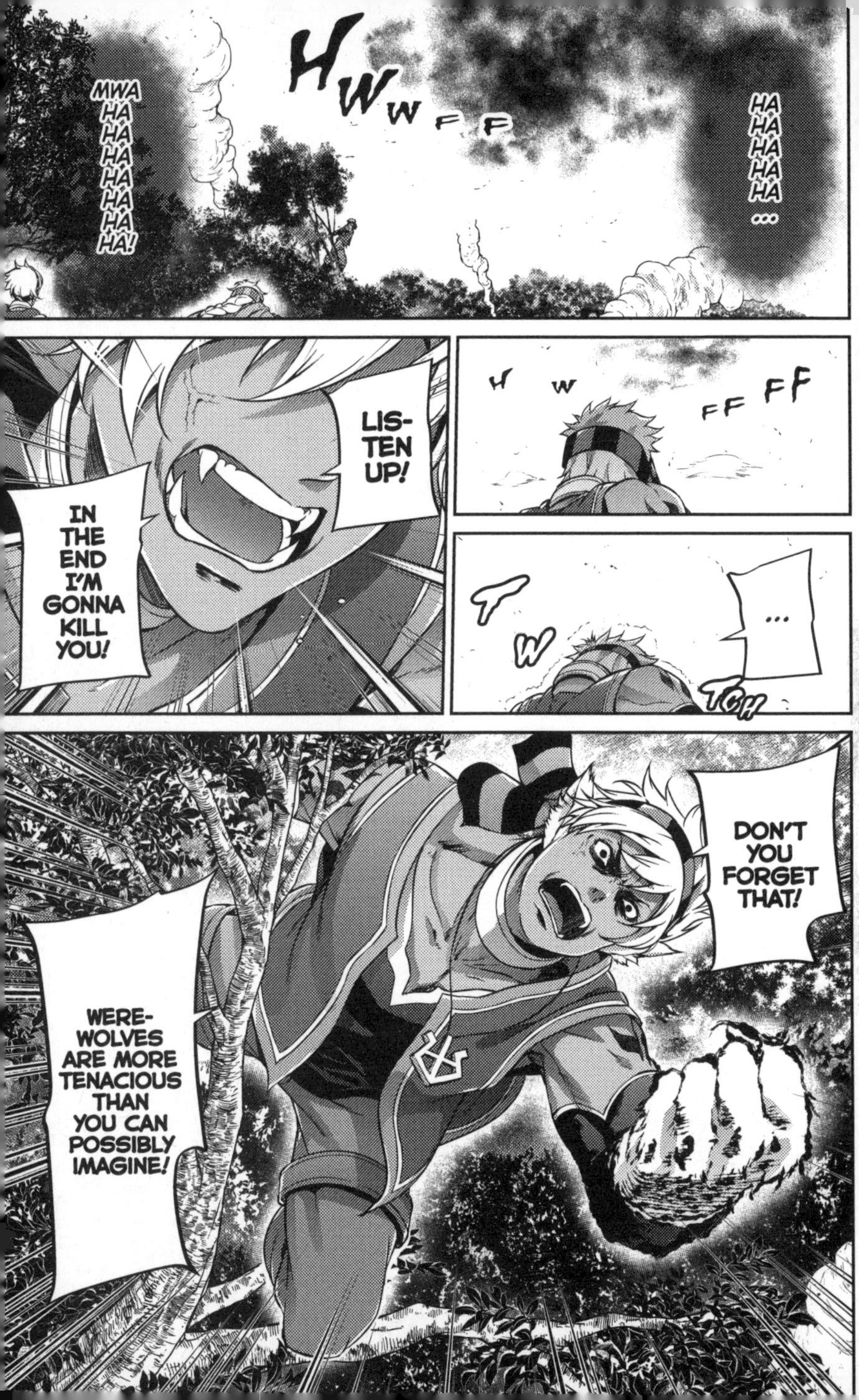
HA HA HA HA HA ...
HWWFF
MWA HA HA HA HA HA HA HA!
HWFFFF
TW
...
TCH
LIS-TEN UP!
IN THE END I'M GONNA KILL YOU!
DON'T YOU FORGET THAT!
WERE-WOLVES ARE MORE TENACIOUS THAN YOU CAN POSSIBLY IMAGINE!

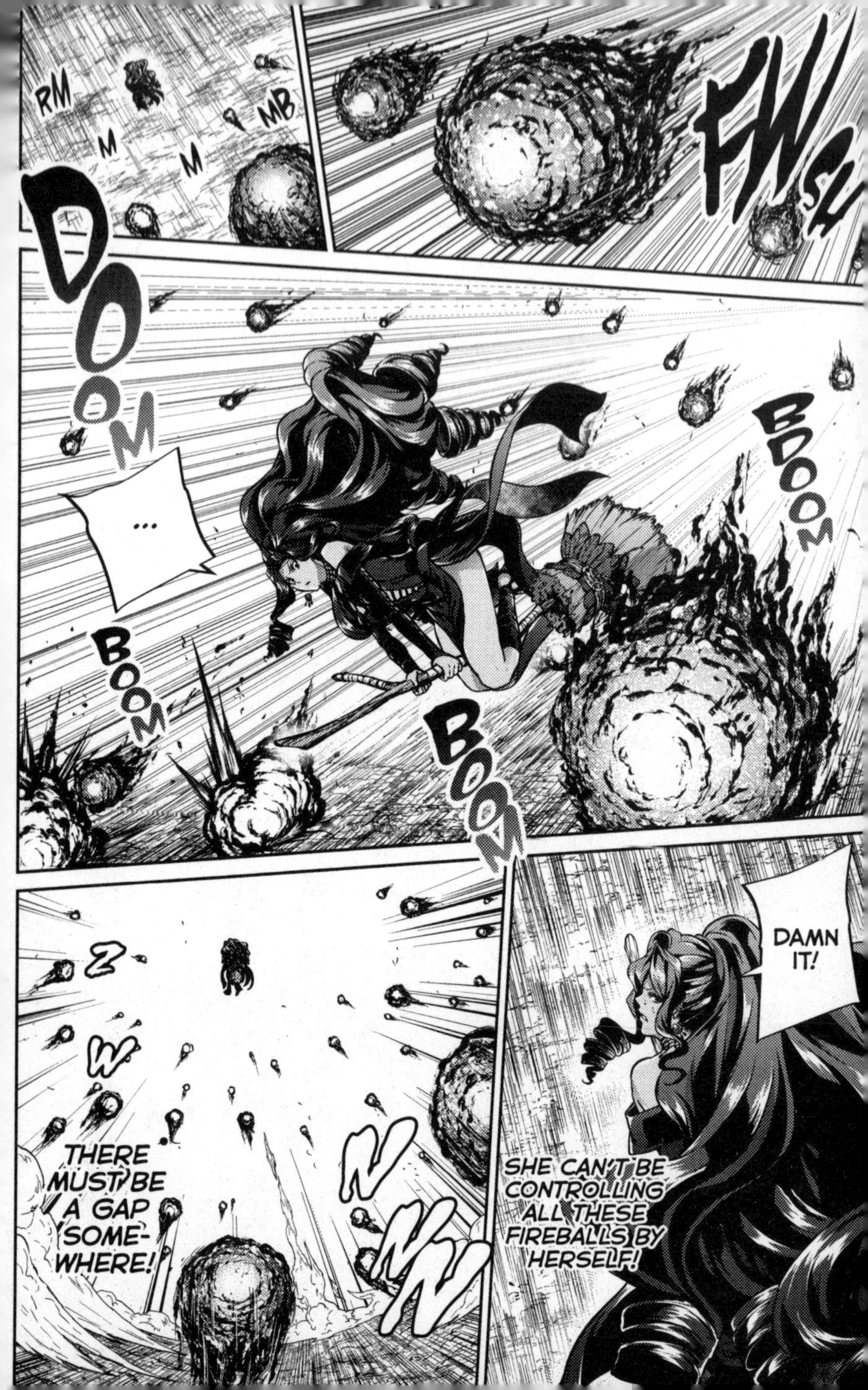
FWSH
RMMMB
DOOOM
...
BDOOOM
BOOOM
BOOOM
DAMN IT!
SHE CAN'T BE CONTROLLING ALL THESE FIREBALLS BY HERSELF!
ZWNNN
THERE MUST BE A GAP SOME-WHERE!

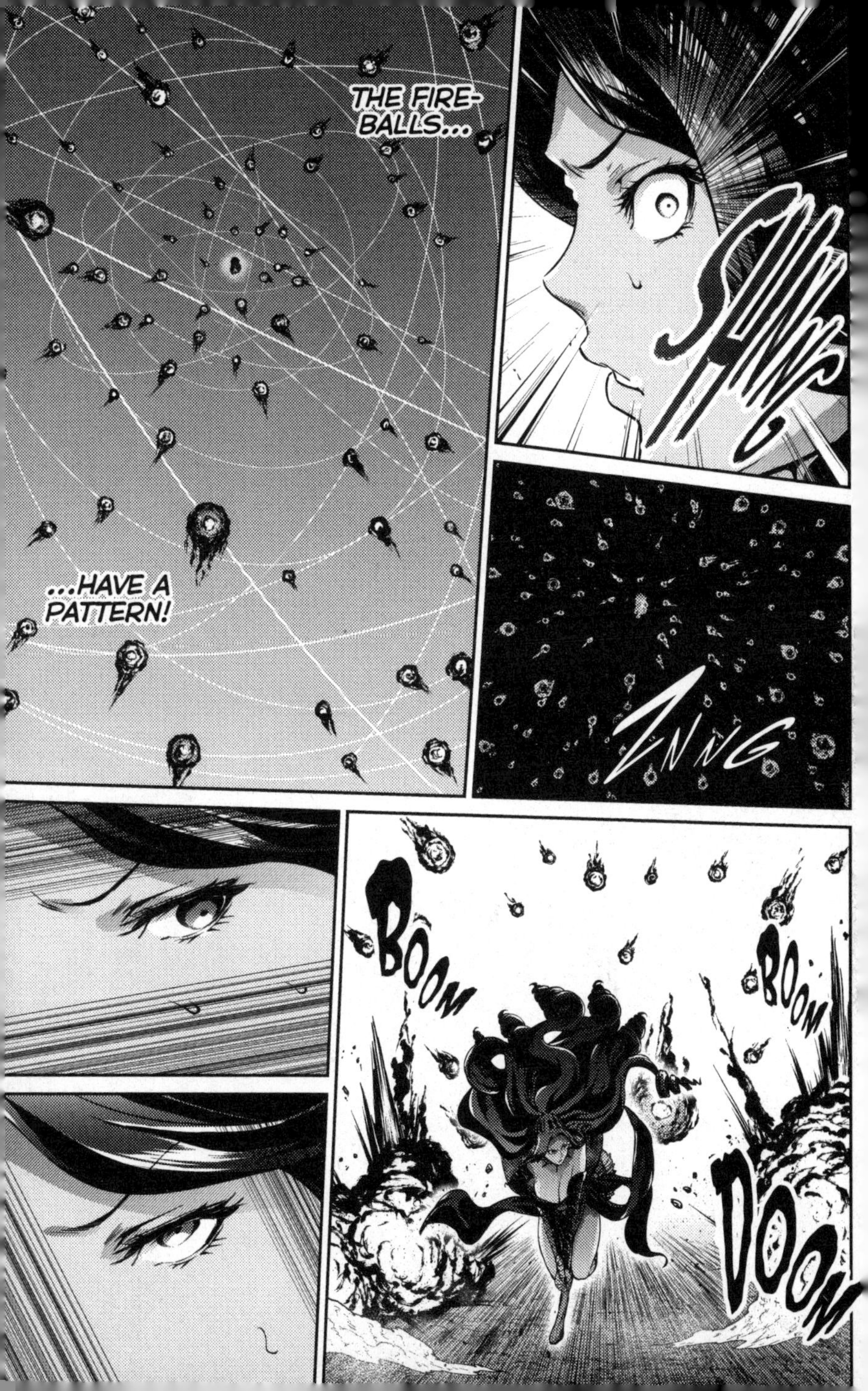
SHING
ZNNG
THE FIRE-BALLS...
...HAVE A PATTERN!
BOOM
BOOM
DOOM

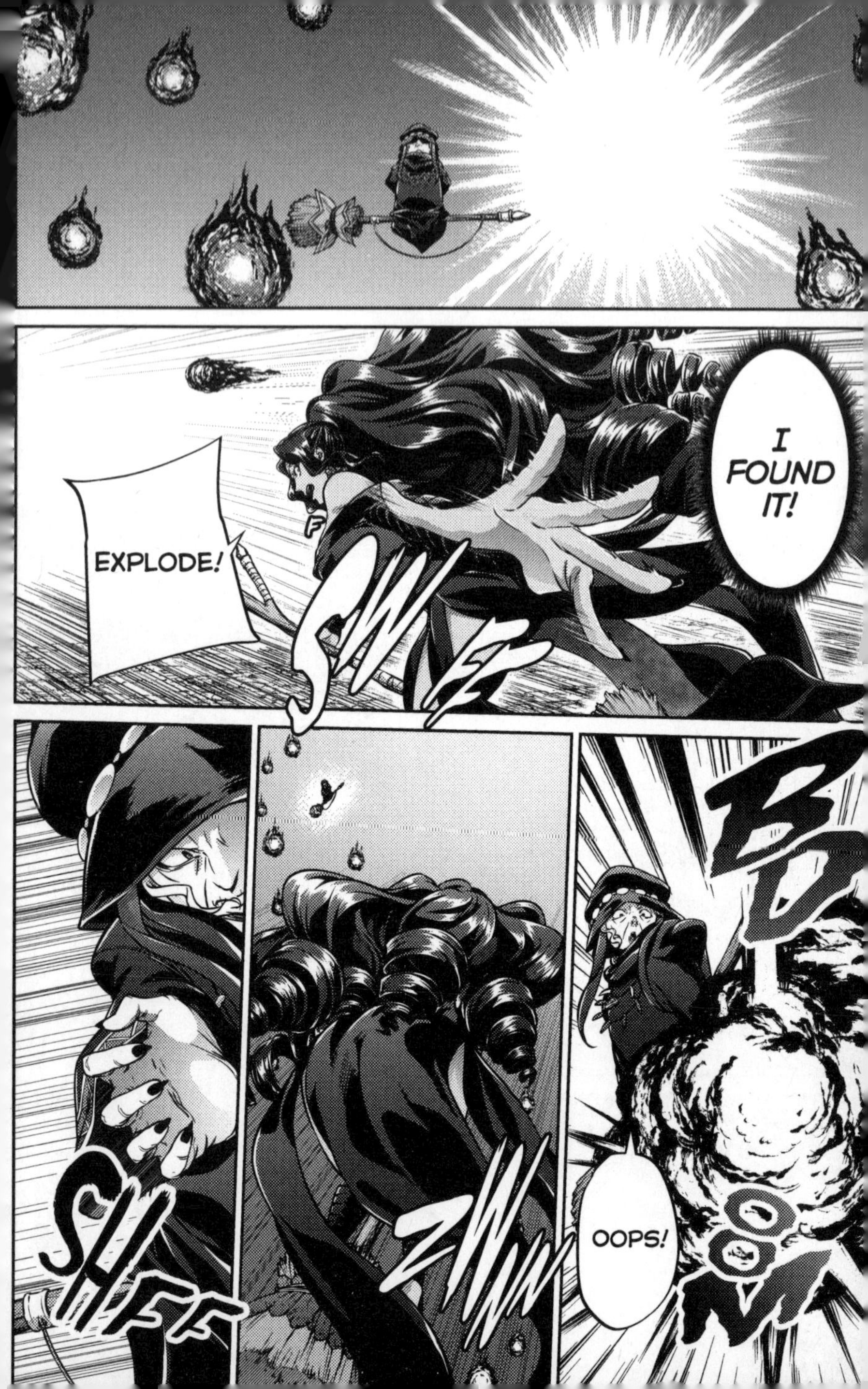
I FOUND IT!
EXPLODE!
OOPS!

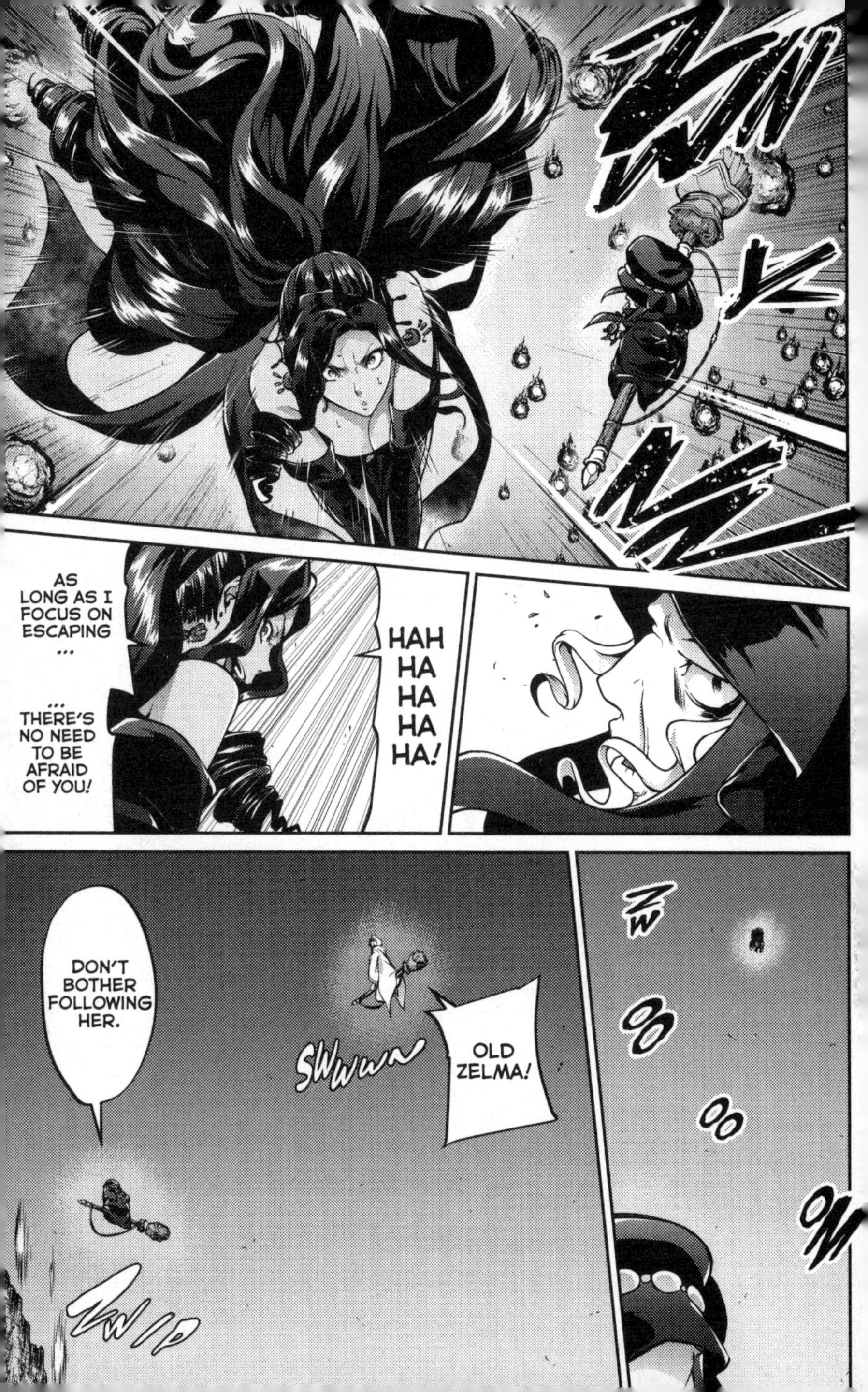
HAH HA HA HA HA!
AS LONG AS I FOCUS ON ESCAPING ...
... THERE'S NO NEED TO BE AFRAID OF YOU!
ZWOOOOOM
OLD ZELMA!
SWWWN
DON'T BOTHER FOLLOWING HER.
ZWIP

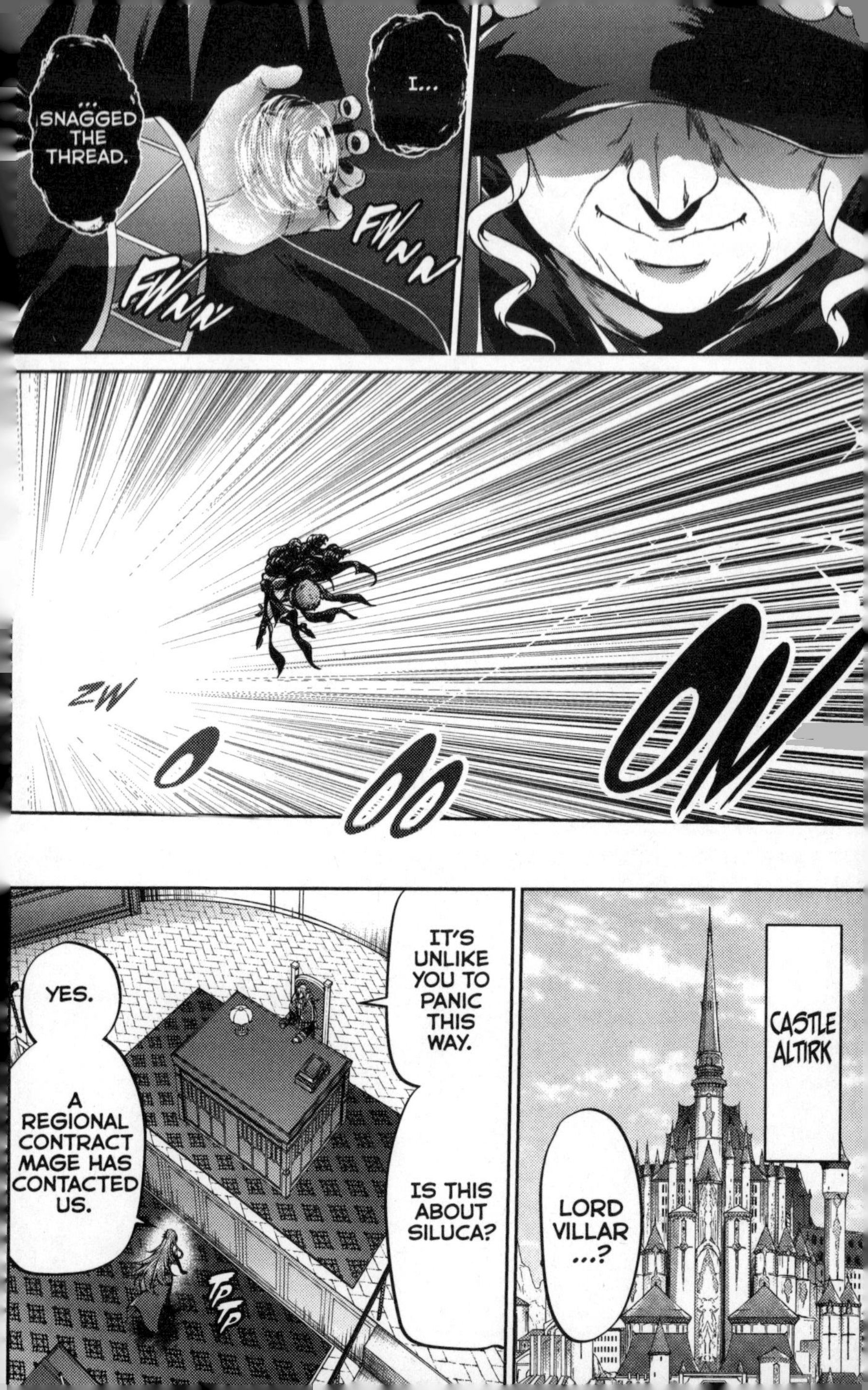
I...
...SNAGGED THE THREAD.
FWNN
FWNNN
ZWOOOM
CASTLE ALTIRK
LORD VILLAR ...?
IT'S UNLIKE YOU TO PANIC THIS WAY.
IS THIS ABOUT SILUCA?
YES.
A REGIONAL CONTRACT MAGE HAS CONTACTED US.
TPTP

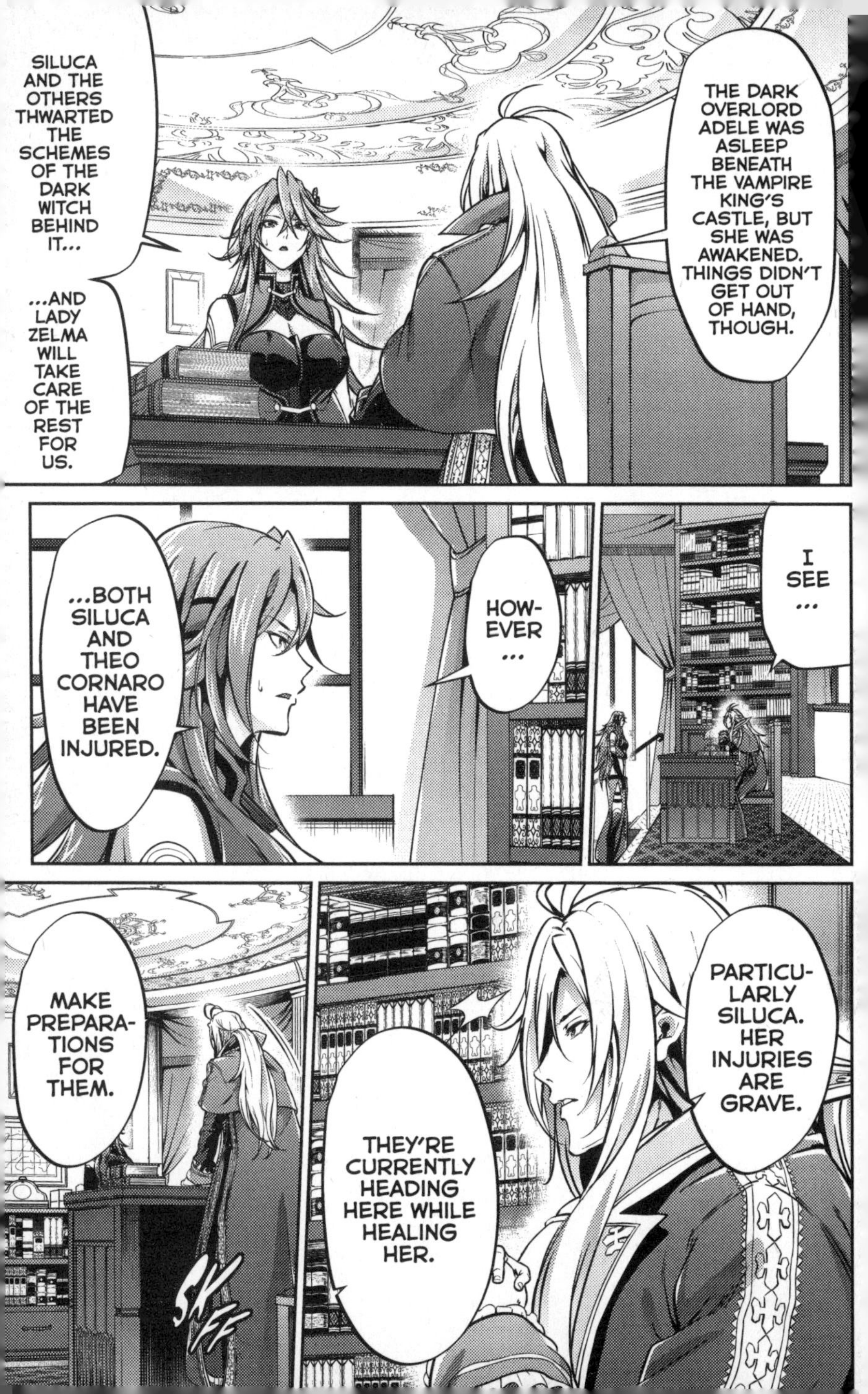
THE DARK OVERLORD ADELE WAS ASLEEP BENEATH THE VAMPIRE KING'S CASTLE, BUT SHE WAS AWAKENED. THINGS DIDN'T GET OUT OF HAND, THOUGH.
SILUCA AND THE OTHERS THWARTED THE SCHEMES OF THE DARK WITCH BEHIND IT...
...AND LADY ZELMA WILL TAKE CARE OF THE REST FOR US.
I SEE...
HOW-EVER...
...BOTH SILUCA AND THEO CORNARO HAVE BEEN INJURED.
PARTICU-LARLY SILUCA. HER INJURIES ARE GRAVE.
THEY'RE CURRENTLY HEADING HERE WHILE HEALING HER.
MAKE PREPARA-TIONS FOR THEM.

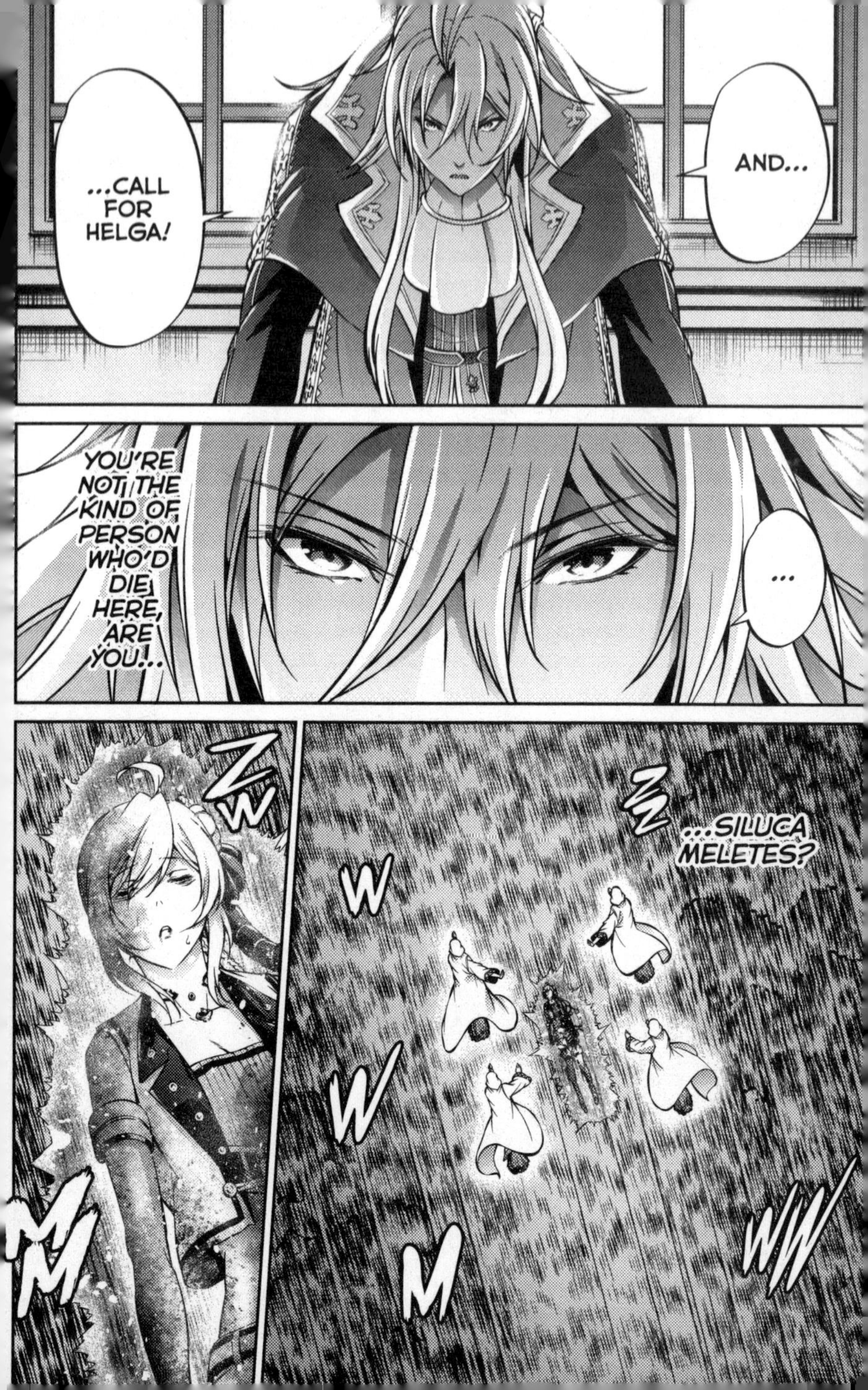
AND...
...CALL FOR HELGA!
...
YOU'RE NOT THE KIND OF PERSON WHO'D DIE HERE, ARE YOU...
ZZ
...SILUCA MELETES?
W
W
WW
M
ZW
MM

INSULT TO INJURY

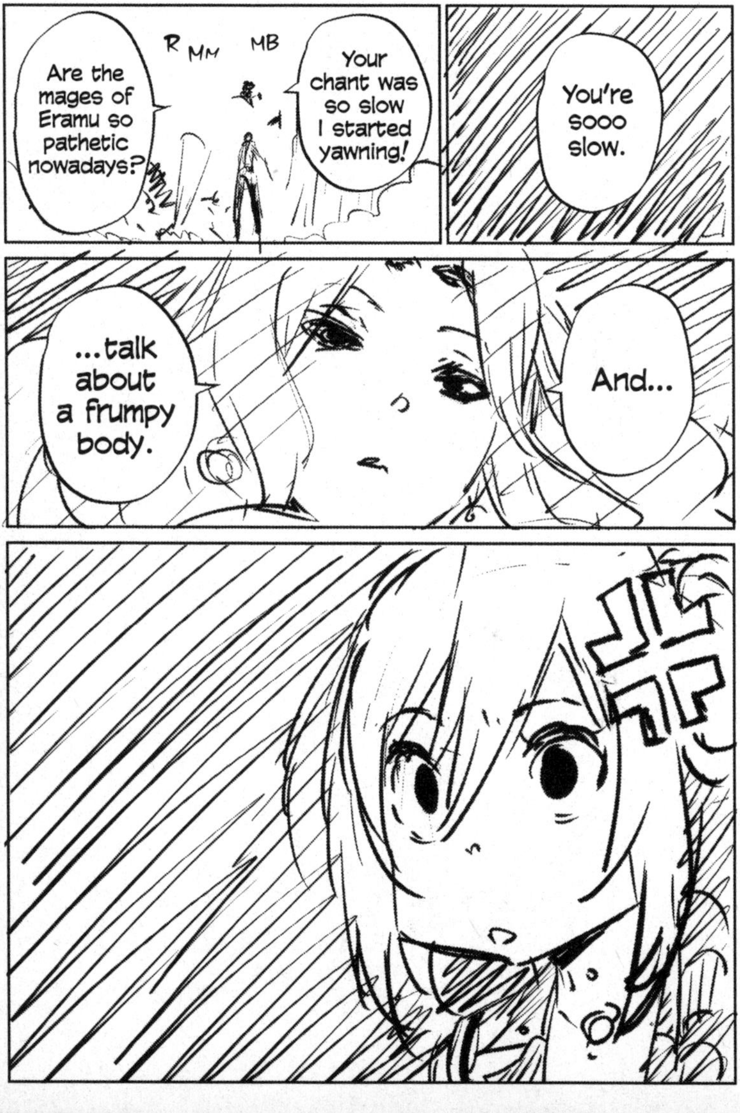

You're sooo slow.
Your chant was so slow I started yawning!
RMM MB
Are the mages of Eramu so pathetic nowadays?
And...
...talk about a frumpy body.

RECORD OF
GRANCREST
WAR

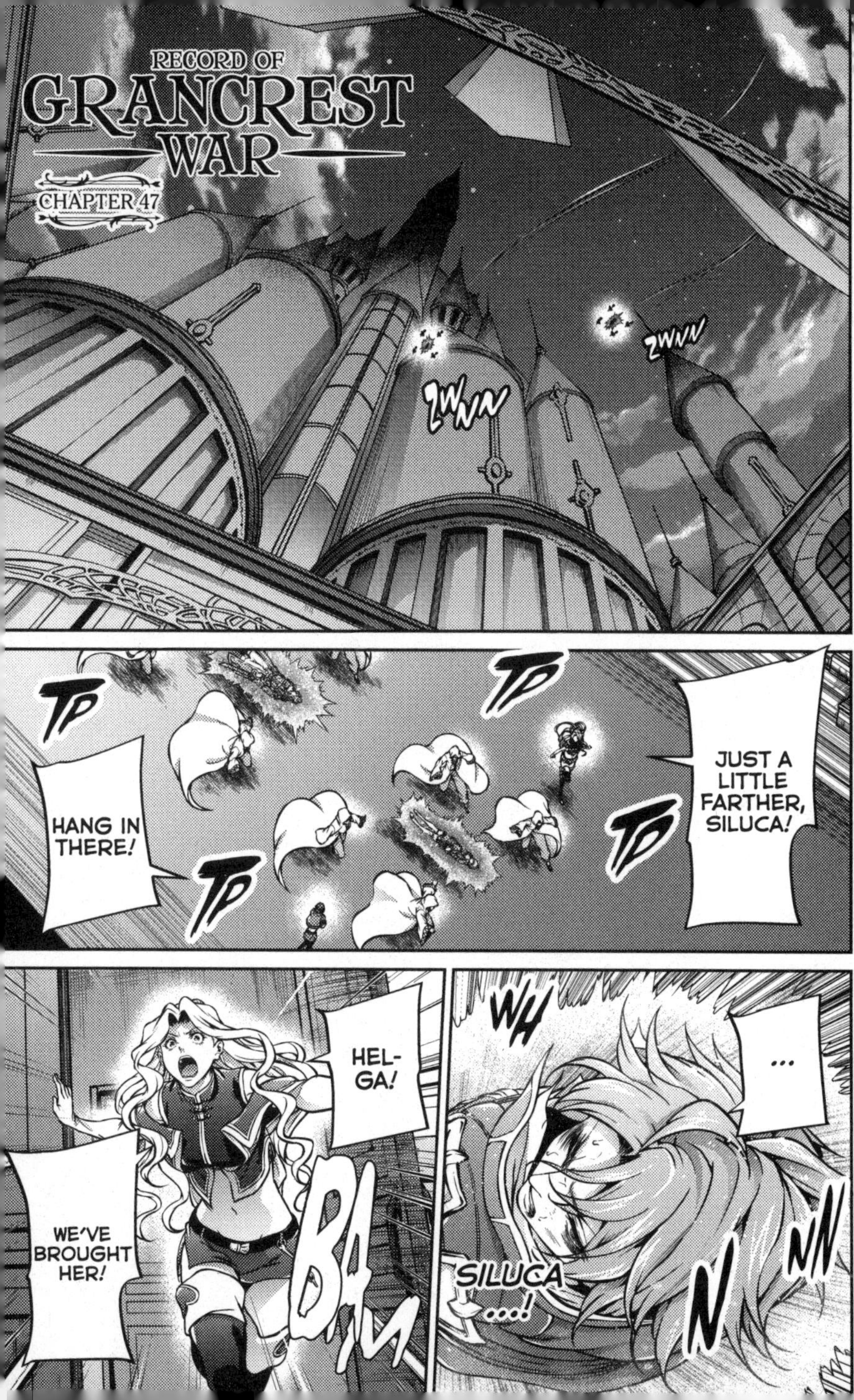
RECORD OF GRANCREST WAR
CHAPTER 47
ZWNN
ZWNN
TP
JUST A LITTLE FARTHER, SILUCA!
TP
TP
TP
HANG IN THERE!
WH
...
NN
N
SILUCA ...!
HEL-GA!
WE'VE BROUGHT HER!
BAM

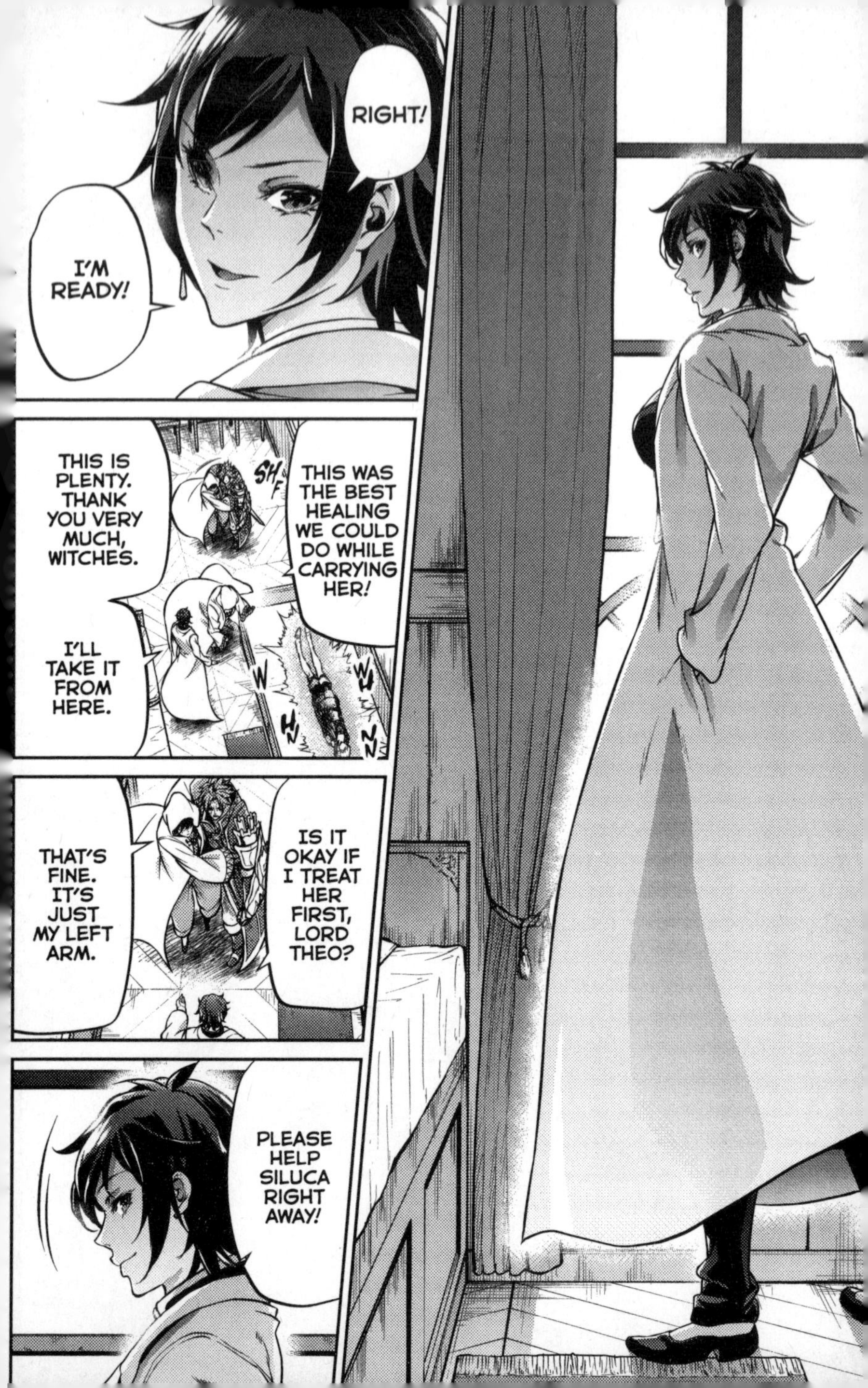
RIGHT!
I'M READY!
THIS WAS THE BEST HEALING WE COULD DO WHILE CARRYING HER!
THIS IS PLENTY. THANK YOU VERY MUCH, WITCHES.
I'LL TAKE IT FROM HERE.
IS IT OKAY IF I TREAT HER FIRST, LORD THEO?
THAT'S FINE. IT'S JUST MY LEFT ARM.
PLEASE HELP SILUCA RIGHT AWAY!

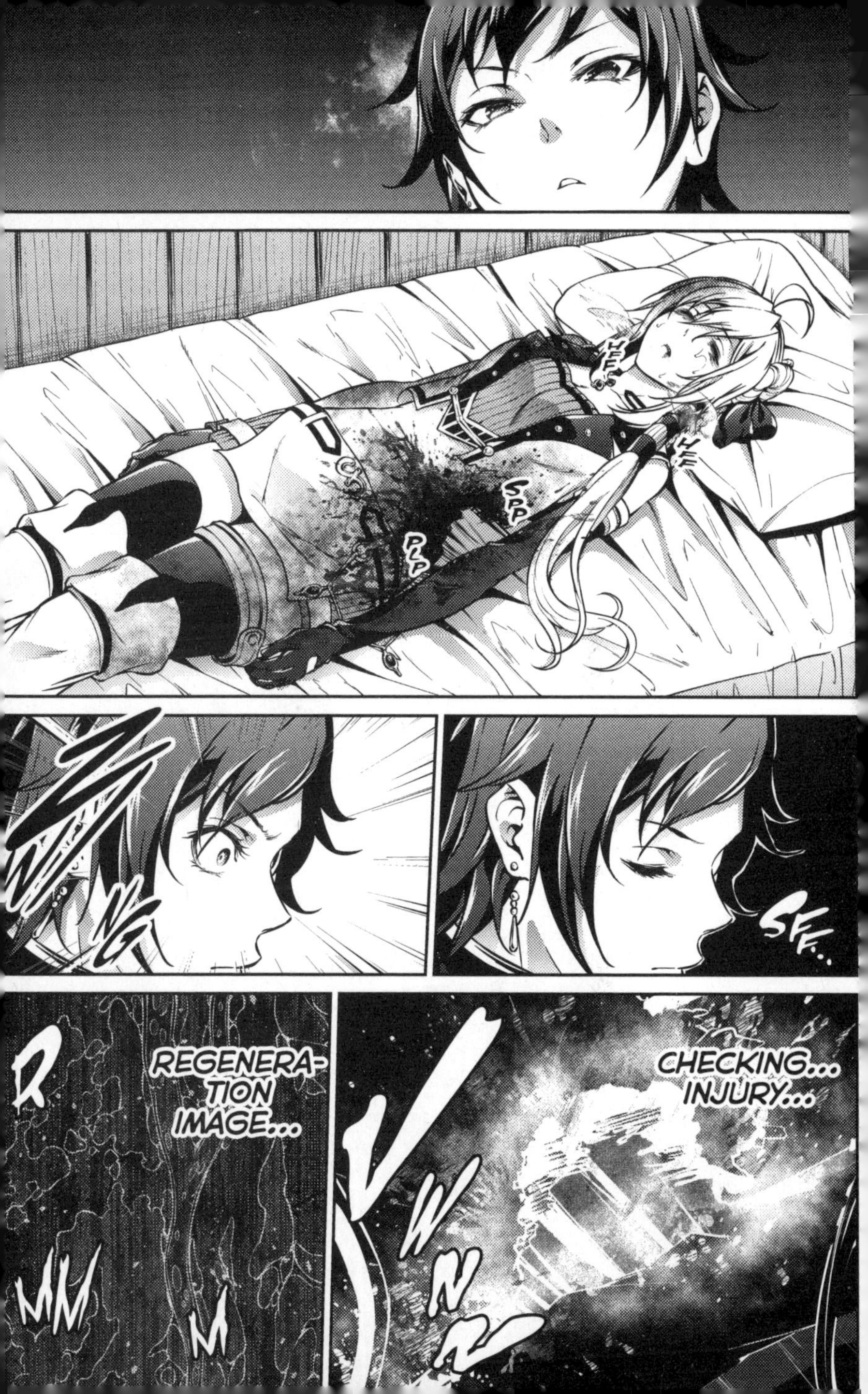
HFF
HFF
SPP
PLP
SFF...
CHECKING... INJURY...
REGENERA-TION IMAGE...

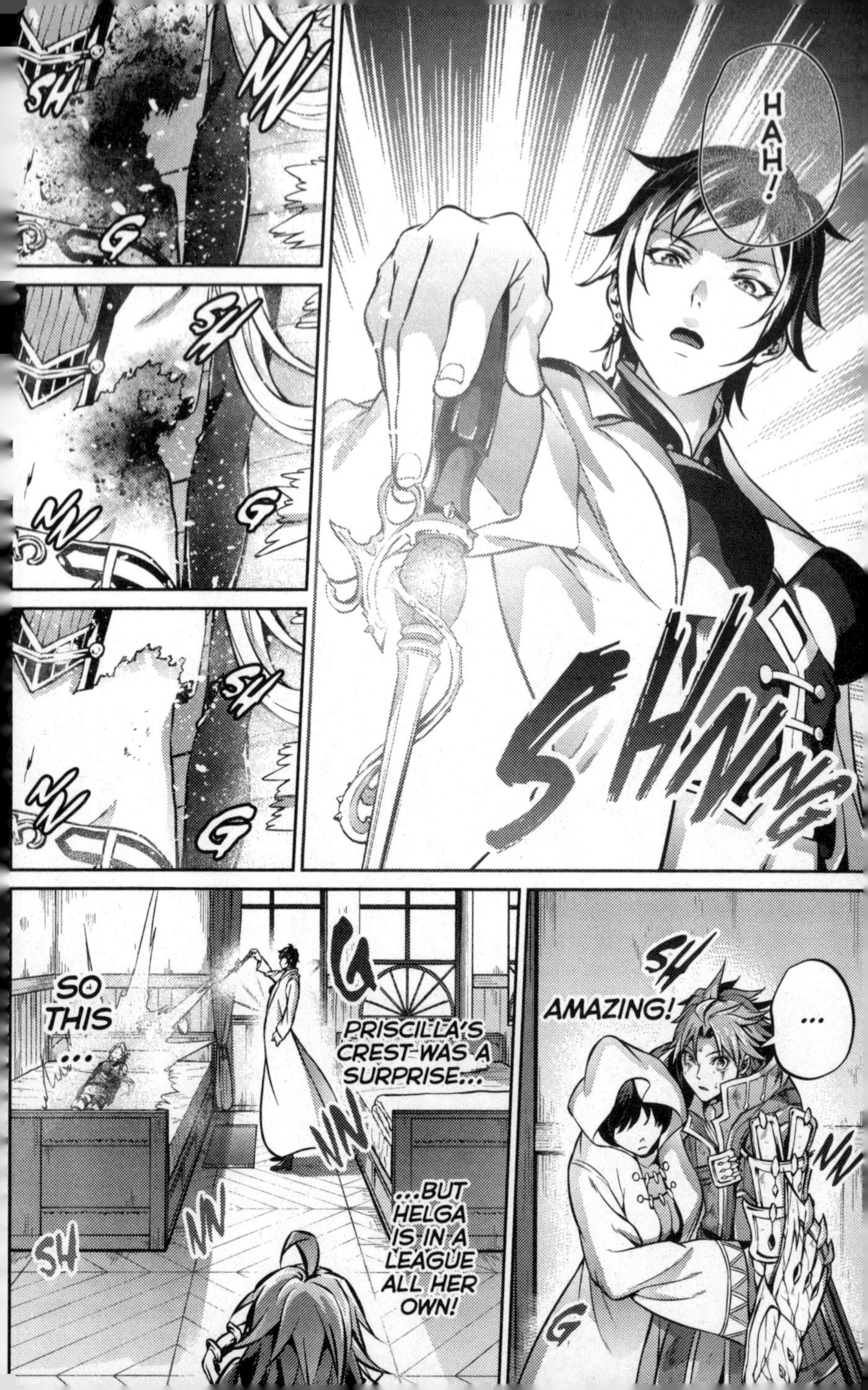
HAH!
SHING
SH
NN
G
SH
NN
G
SH
NN
G
...
SH
AMAZING!
NN
G
G
PRISCILLA'S CREST WAS A SURPRISE...
SO THIS...
NN
...BUT HELGA IS IN A LEAGUE ALL HER OWN!
NN
SH

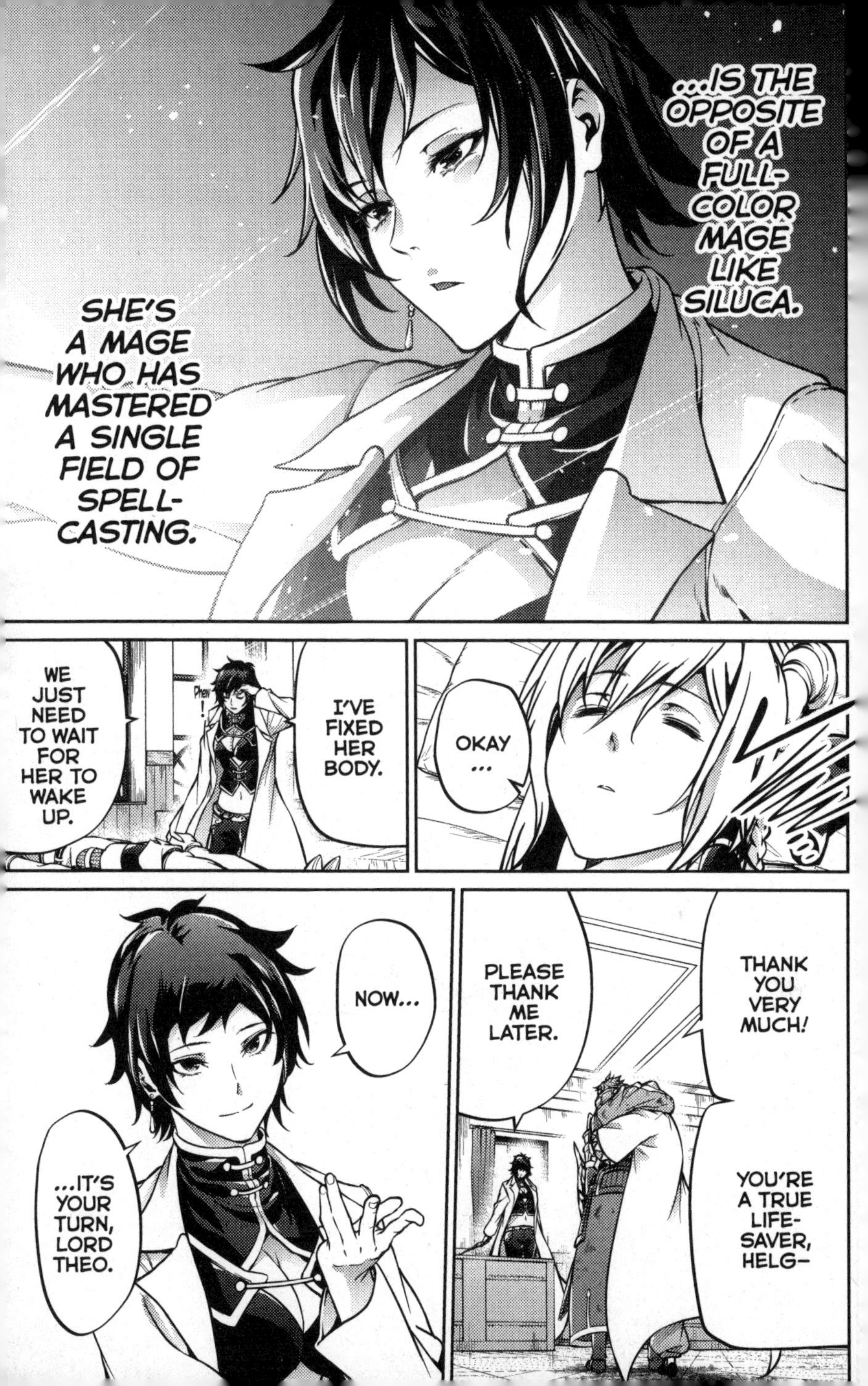
...IS THE OPPOSITE OF A FULL-COLOR MAGE LIKE SILUCA.
SHE'S A MAGE WHO HAS MASTERED A SINGLE FIELD OF SPELL-CASTING.
OKAY...
I'VE FIXED HER BODY.
Phew!
WE JUST NEED TO WAIT FOR HER TO WAKE UP.
THANK YOU VERY MUCH!
PLEASE THANK ME LATER.
YOU'RE A TRUE LIFE-SAVER, HELG—
NOW...
...IT'S YOUR TURN, LORD THEO.

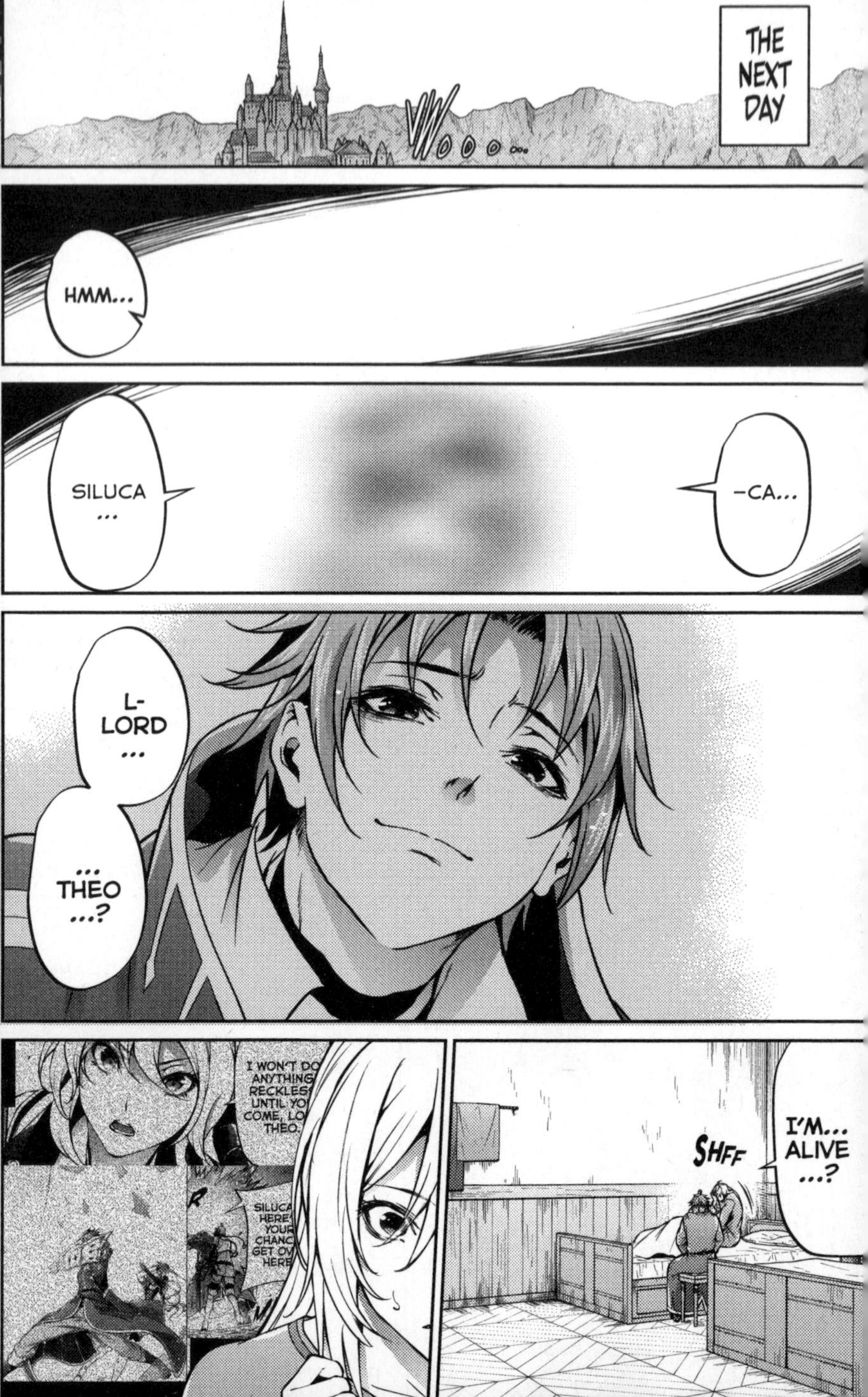
THE NEXT DAY
HMM...
-CA...
SILUCA ...
L- LORD ...
... THEO ...?
I'M... ALIVE ...?
SHFF
I WON'T DO ANYTHING RECKLES UNTIL YO COME, LO THEO.
SILUCA HERE YOUR CHANC GET OV HERE

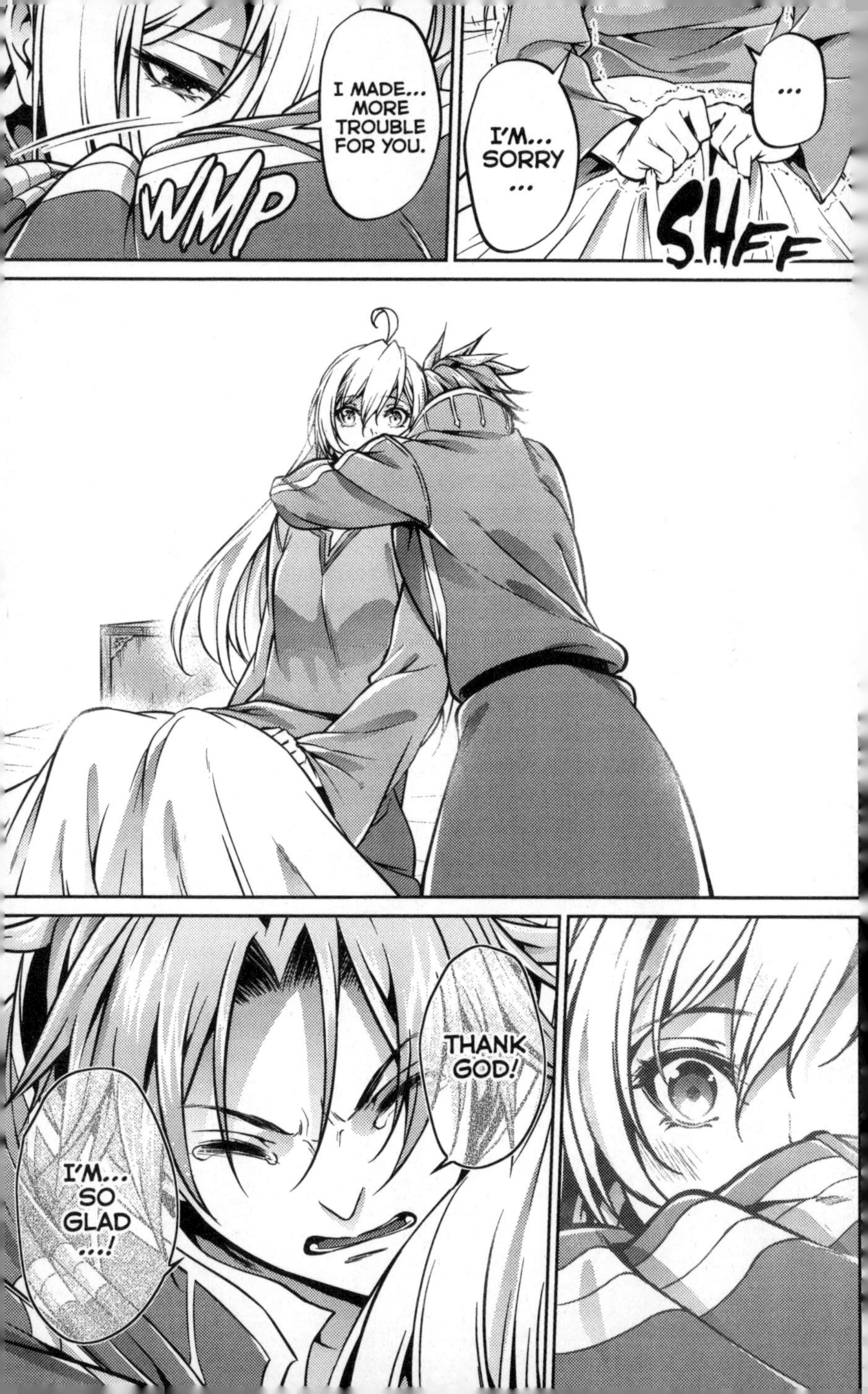
...
I'M... SORRY ...
SHFF
I MADE... MORE TROUBLE FOR YOU.
WMP
THANK GOD!
I'M... SO GLAD ...!

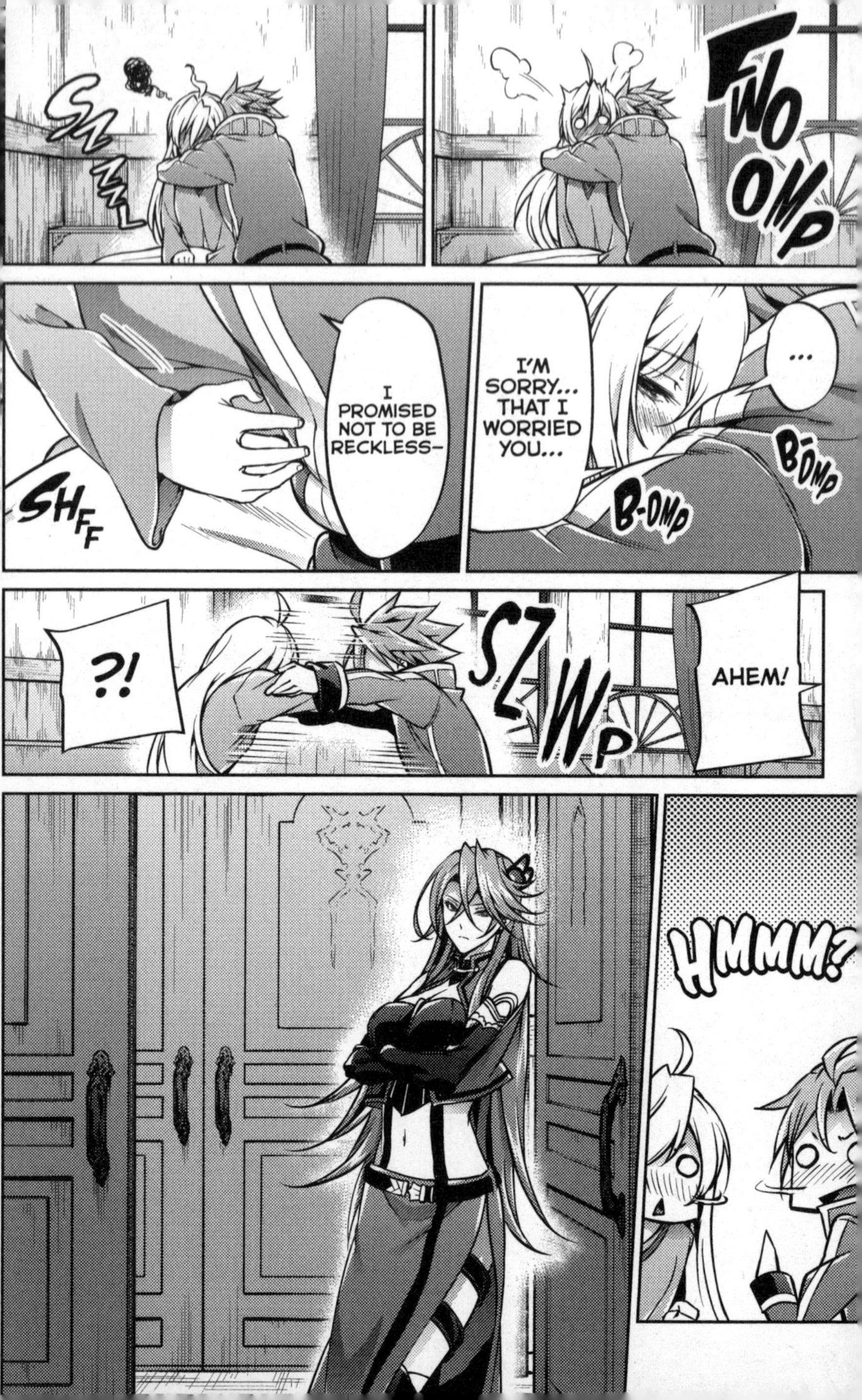
FWOOMP
SNNNL
...
B-OMP
B-OMP
I'M SORRY... THAT I WORRIED YOU...
I PROMISED NOT TO BE RECKLESS–
SHFF
AHEM!
SZWP
?!
HMMM?!

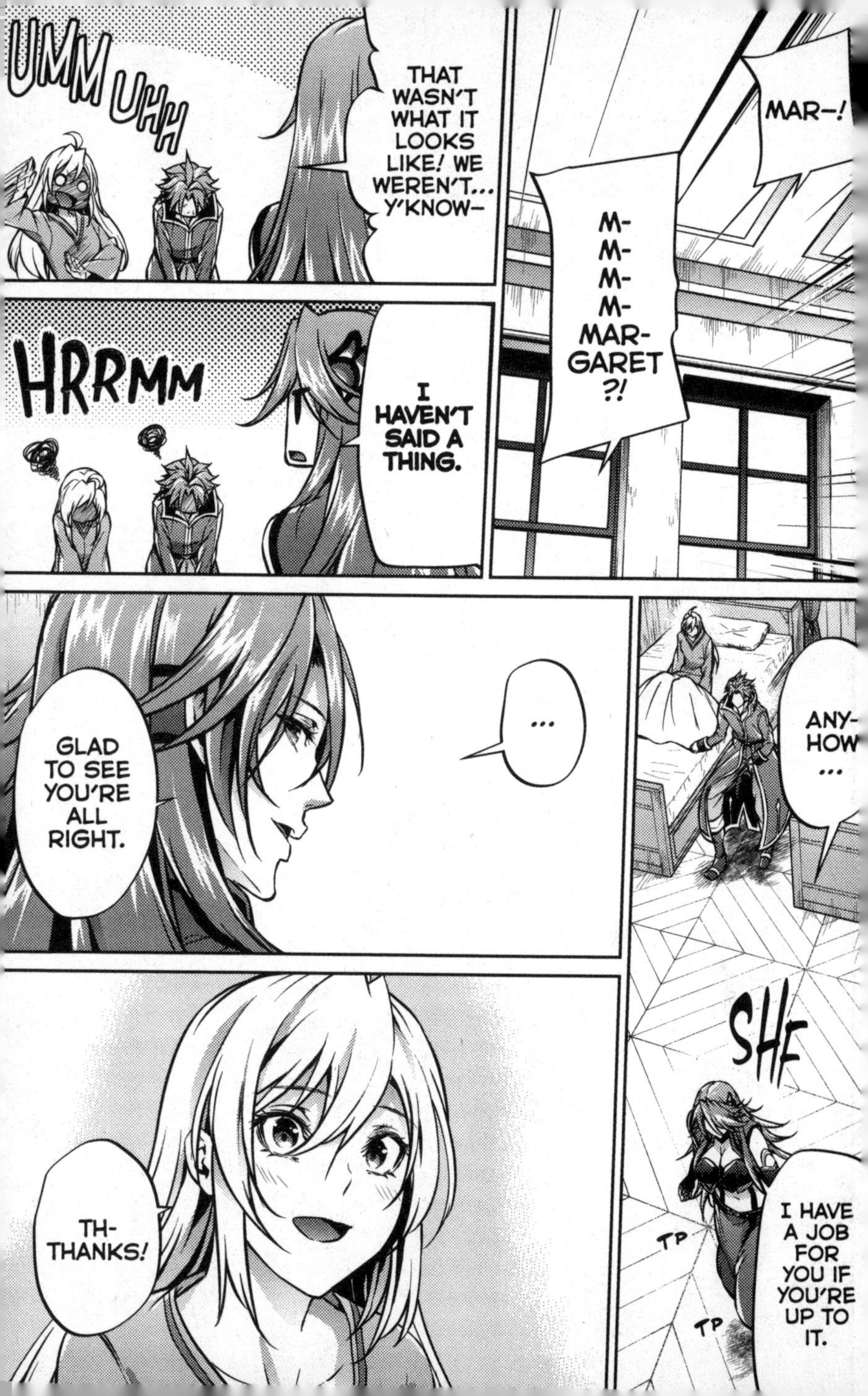
MAR-!
M-M-M-M-MAR-GARET?!
THAT WASN'T WHAT IT LOOKS LIKE! WE WEREN'T... Y'KNOW-
UMM UHH
I HAVEN'T SAID A THING.
HRRMM
ANY-HOW...
SHF
I HAVE A JOB FOR YOU IF YOU'RE UP TO IT.
TP
TP
...
GLAD TO SEE YOU'RE ALL RIGHT.
TH-THANKS!

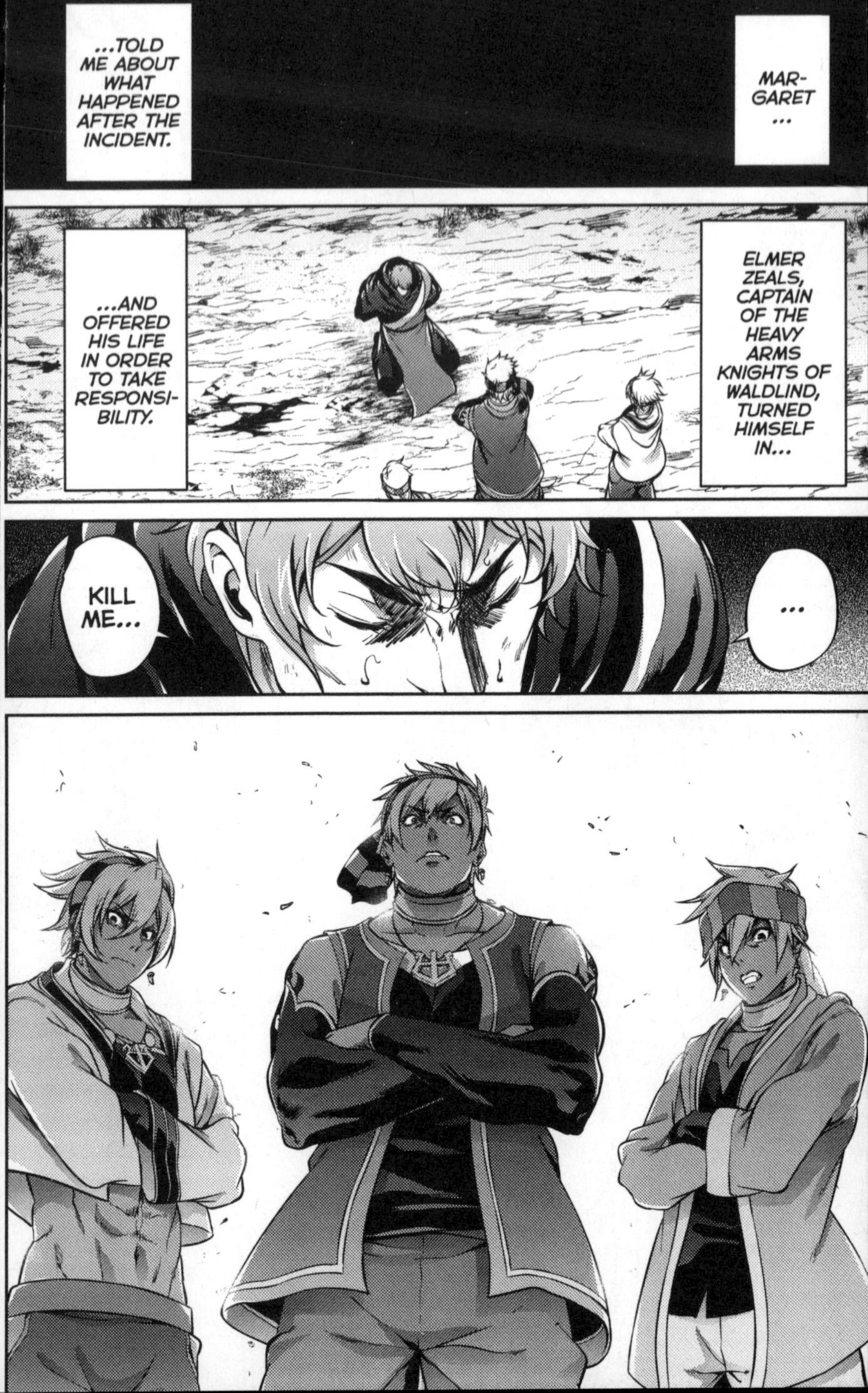
MAR-
GARET
...
...TOLD ME ABOUT WHAT HAPPENED AFTER THE INCIDENT.
ELMER ZEALS, CAPTAIN OF THE HEAVY ARMS KNIGHTS OF WALDLIND, TURNED HIMSELF IN...
...AND OFFERED HIS LIFE IN ORDER TO TAKE RESPONSI-BILITY.
...
KILL ME...

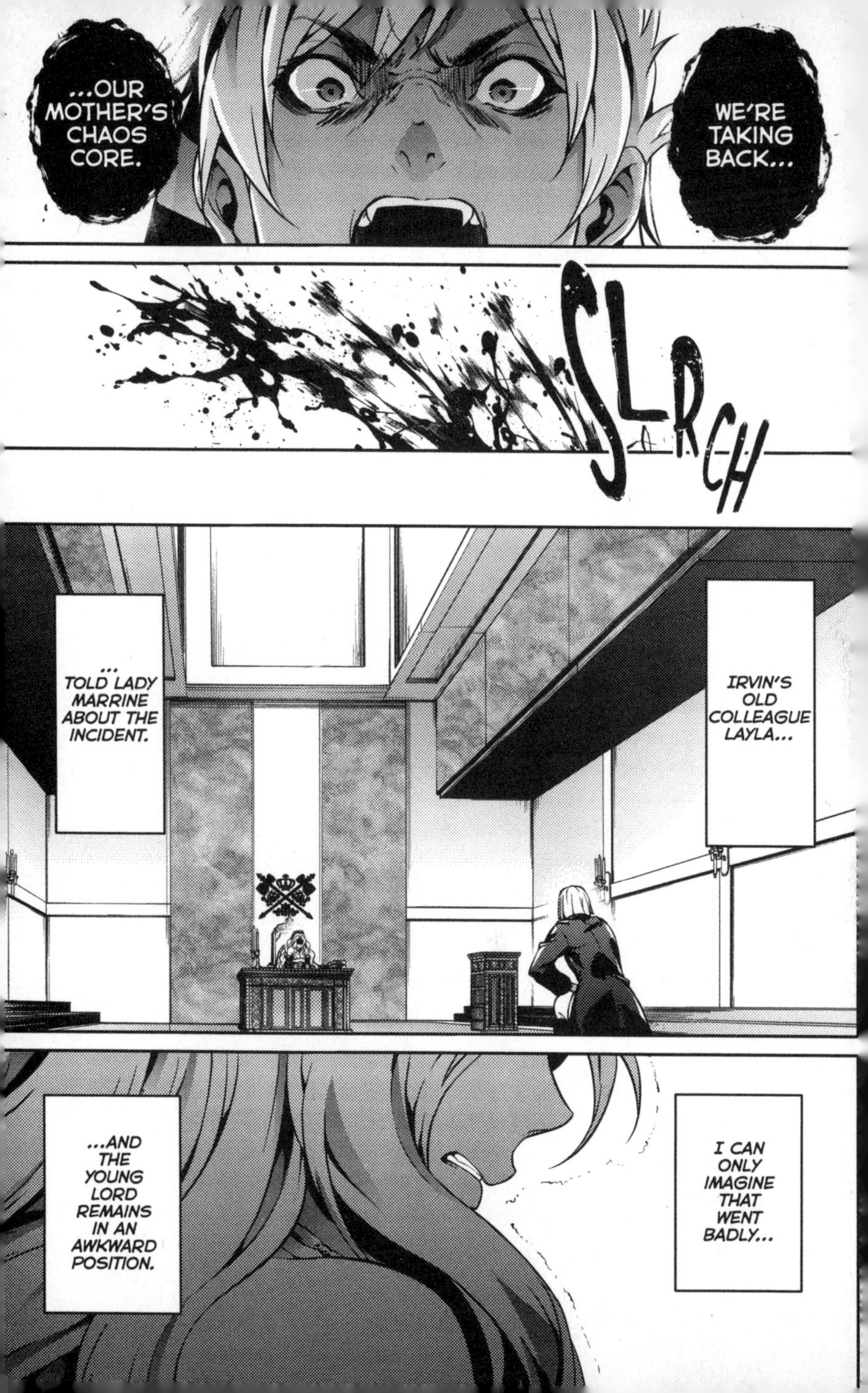
WE'RE TAKING BACK...
...OUR MOTHER'S CHAOS CORE.
SLRCH
IRVIN'S OLD COLLEAGUE LAYLA...
... TOLD LADY MARRINE ABOUT THE INCIDENT.
I CAN ONLY IMAGINE THAT WENT BADLY...
...AND THE YOUNG LORD REMAINS IN AN AWKWARD POSITION.

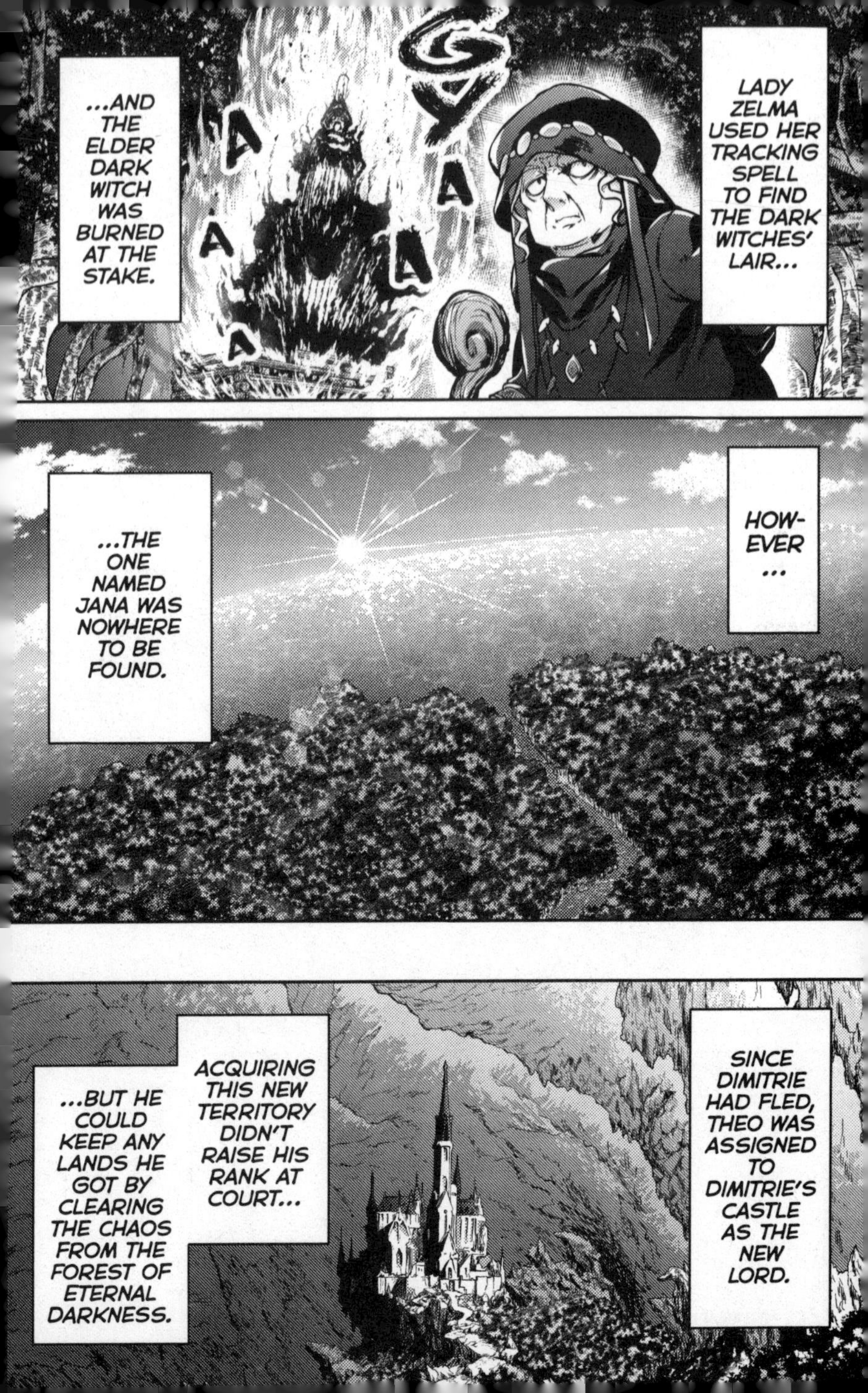
LADY ZELMA USED HER TRACKING SPELL TO FIND THE DARK WITCHES' LAIR...
GYAAAAA
...AND THE ELDER DARK WITCH WAS BURNED AT THE STAKE.
HOW-EVER...
...THE ONE NAMED JANA WAS NOWHERE TO BE FOUND.
SINCE DIMITRIE HAD FLED, THEO WAS ASSIGNED TO DIMITRIE'S CASTLE AS THE NEW LORD.
ACQUIRING THIS NEW TERRITORY DIDN'T RAISE HIS RANK AT COURT...
...BUT HE COULD KEEP ANY LANDS HE GOT BY CLEARING THE CHAOS FROM THE FOREST OF ETERNAL DARKNESS.

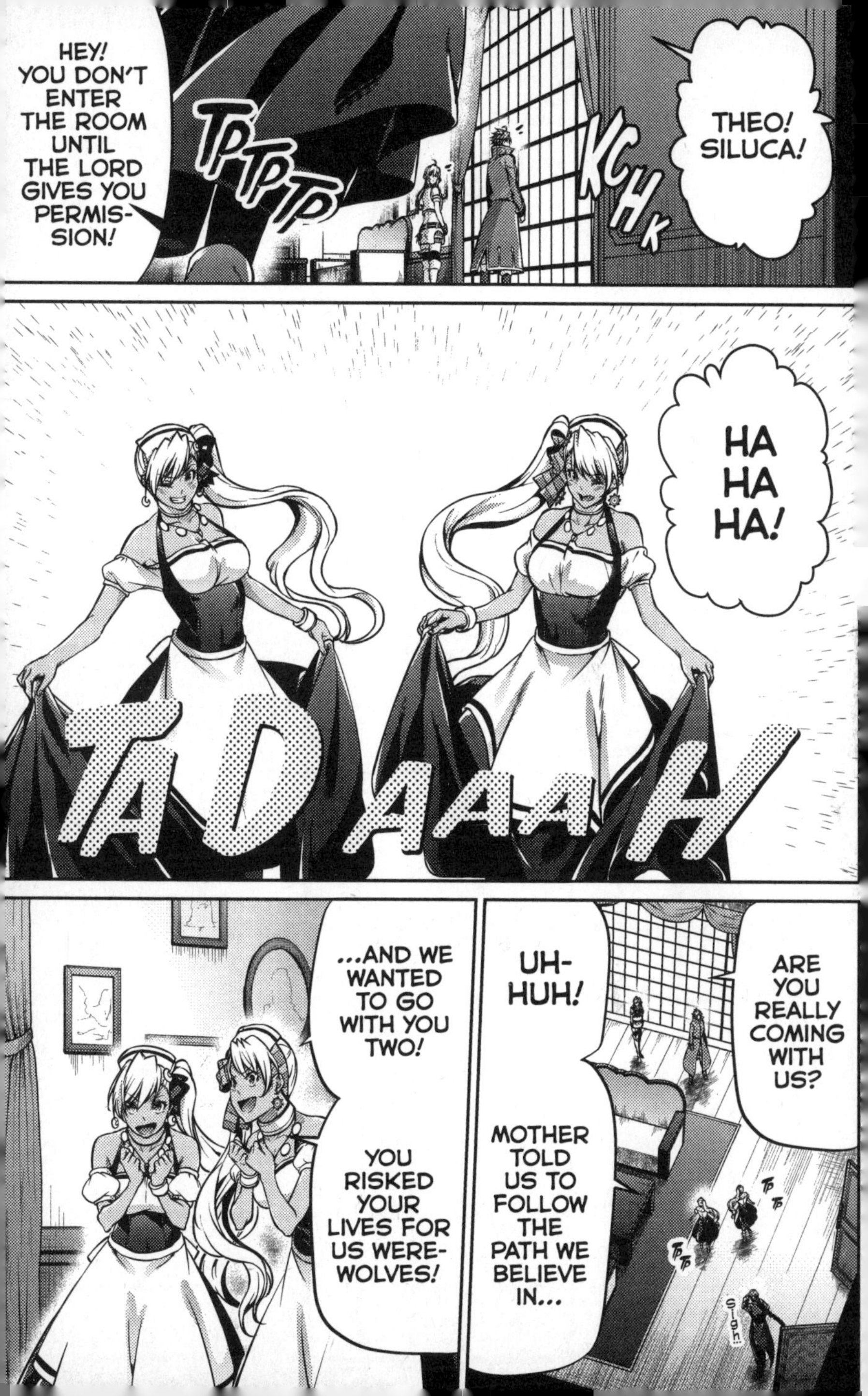
THEO! SILUCA!
KCHK
TPTPTP
HEY! YOU DON'T ENTER THE ROOM UNTIL THE LORD GIVES YOU PERMIS-SION!
HA HA HA!
TADAAAH
ARE YOU REALLY COMING WITH US?
UH-HUH!
MOTHER TOLD US TO FOLLOW THE PATH WE BELIEVE IN...
Tp Tp
Tp Tp
Sigh...
...AND WE WANTED TO GO WITH YOU TWO!
YOU RISKED YOUR LIVES FOR US WERE-WOLVES!

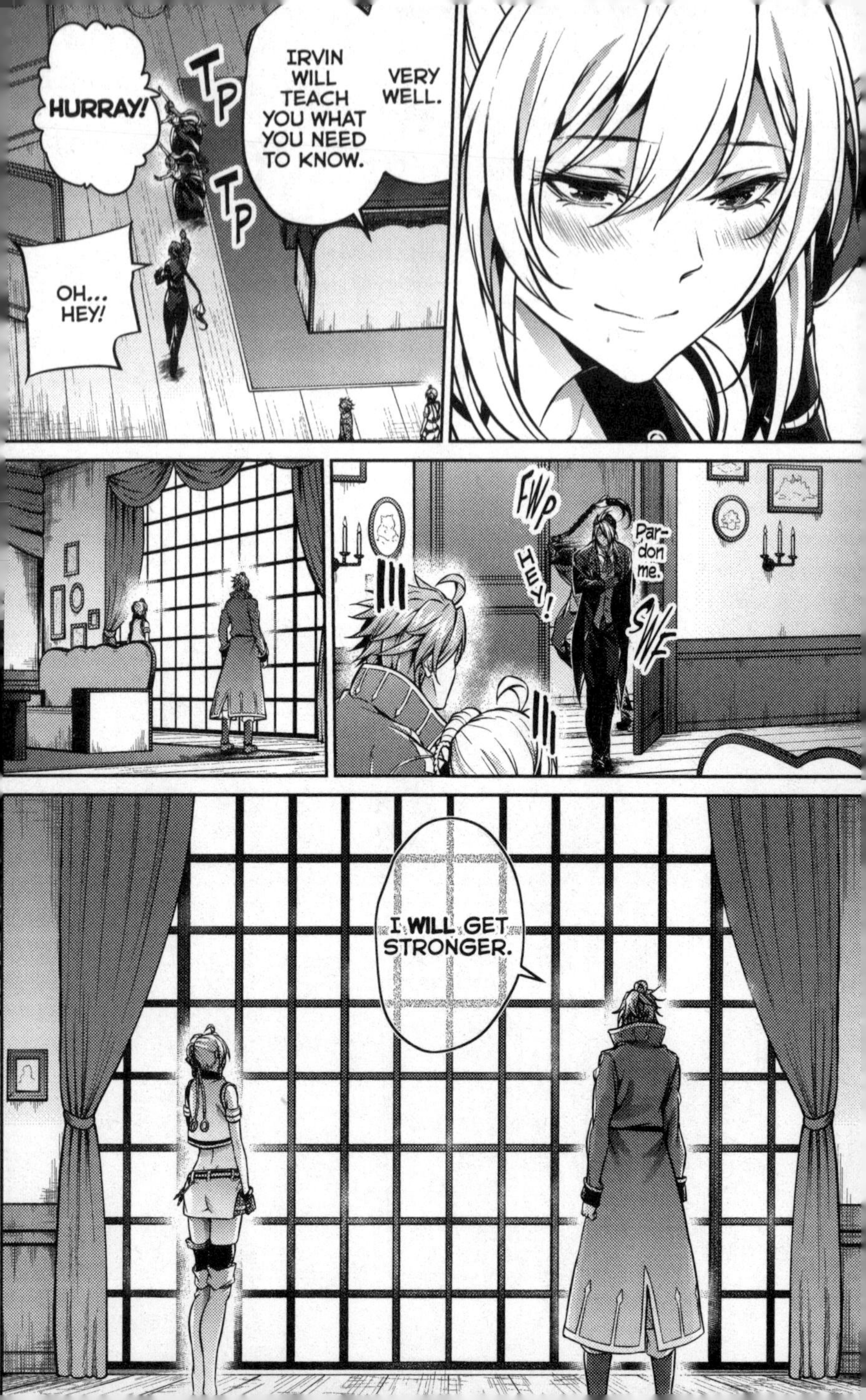
VERY WELL.
IRVIN WILL TEACH YOU WHAT YOU NEED TO KNOW.
TP
HURRAY!
TP
OH... HEY!
Par-don me.
FWP
HEY!
SWE
I WILL GET STRONGER.

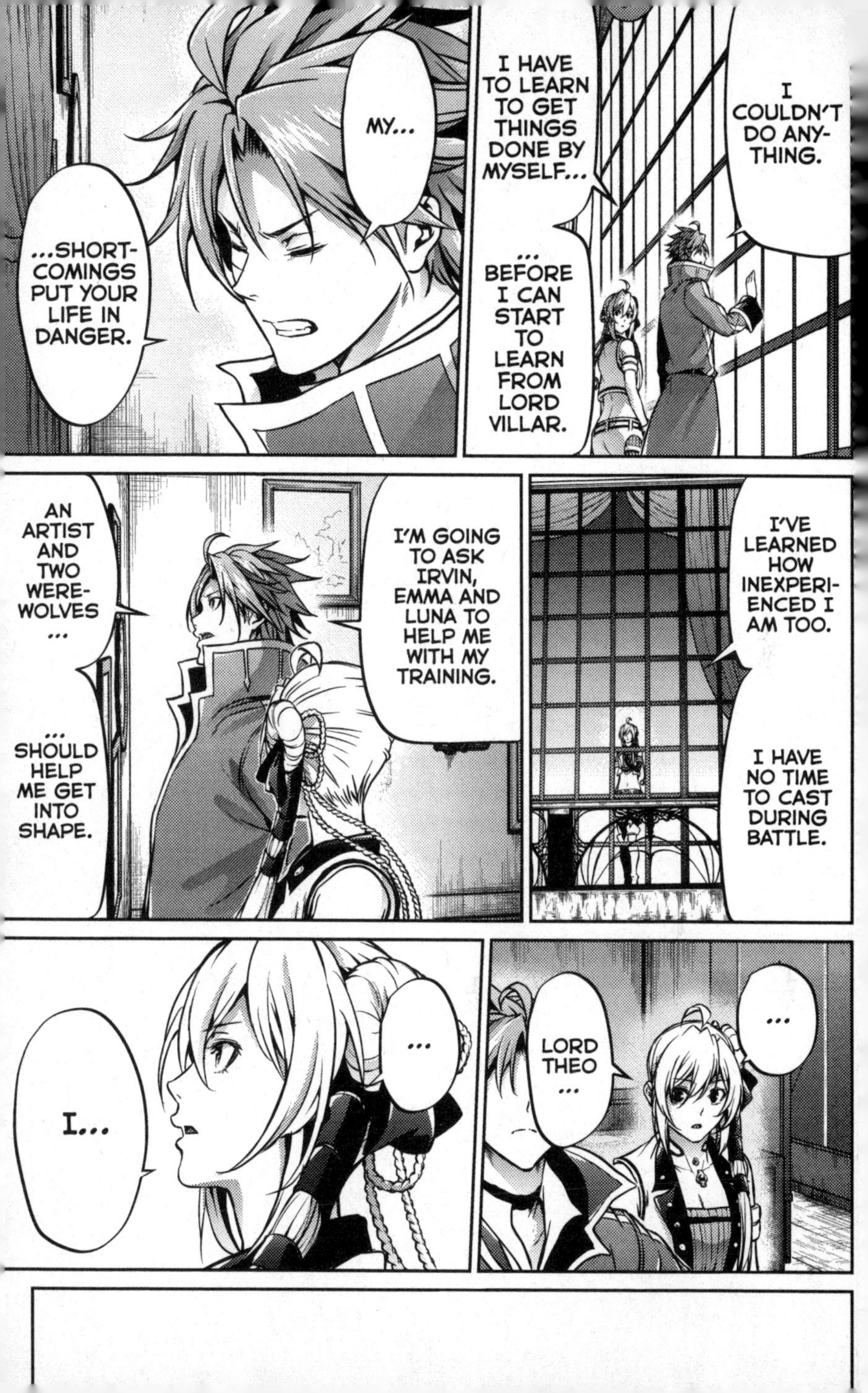
I COULDN'T DO ANY-THING.
I HAVE TO LEARN TO GET THINGS DONE BY MYSELF...
... BEFORE I CAN START TO LEARN FROM LORD VILLAR.
MY...
...SHORT-COMINGS PUT YOUR LIFE IN DANGER.
I'VE LEARNED HOW INEXPERI-ENCED I AM TOO.
I HAVE NO TIME TO CAST DURING BATTLE.
I'M GOING TO ASK IRVIN, EMMA AND LUNA TO HELP ME WITH MY TRAINING.
AN ARTIST AND TWO WERE-WOLVES ...
... SHOULD HELP ME GET INTO SHAPE.
...
LORD THEO ...
...
I...

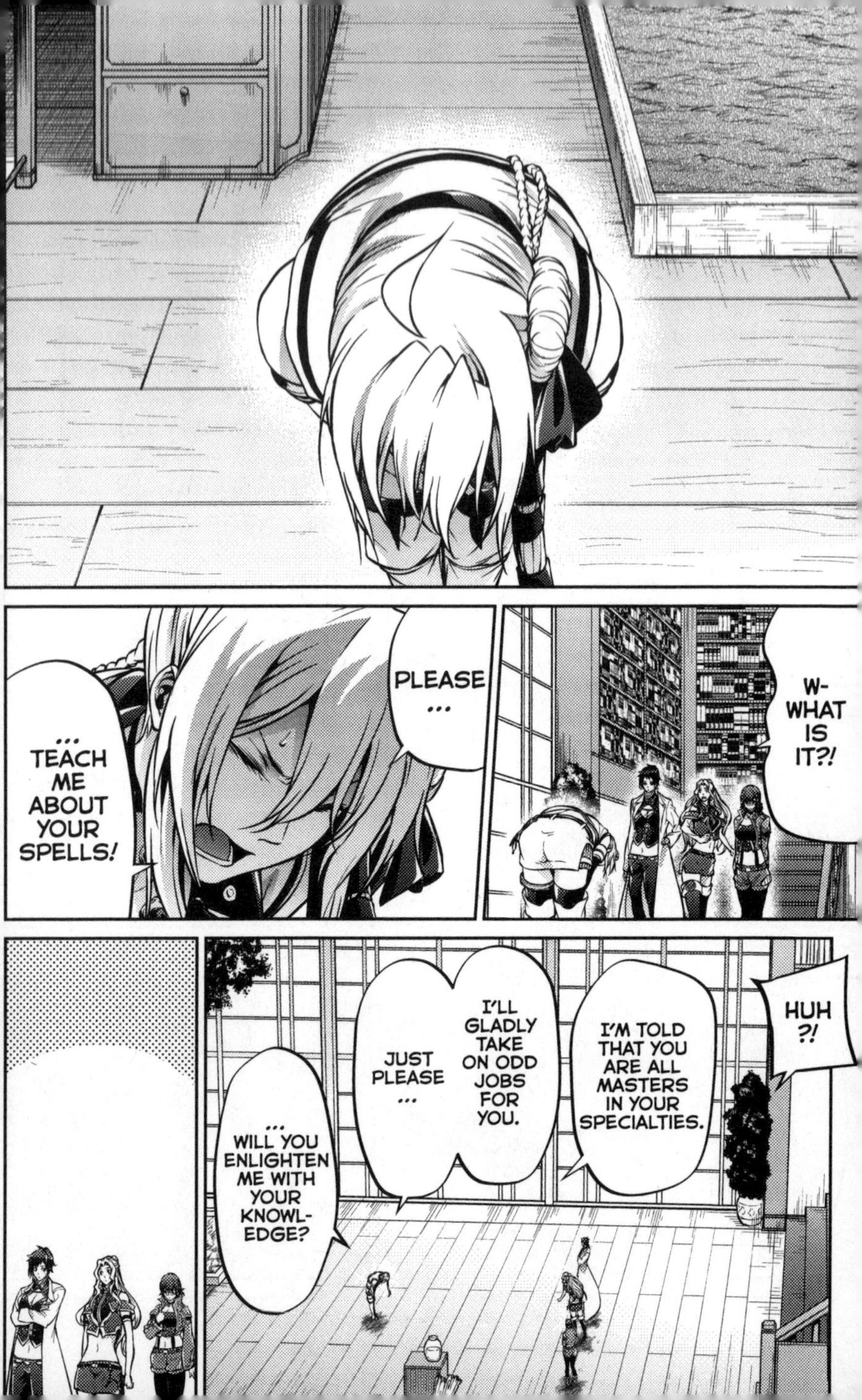
W-WHAT IS IT?!
PLEASE...
...TEACH ME ABOUT YOUR SPELLS!
HUH?!
I'M TOLD THAT YOU ARE ALL MASTERS IN YOUR SPECIALTIES.
I'LL GLADLY TAKE ON ODD JOBS FOR YOU.
JUST PLEASE...
...WILL YOU ENLIGHTEN ME WITH YOUR KNOWL-EDGE?

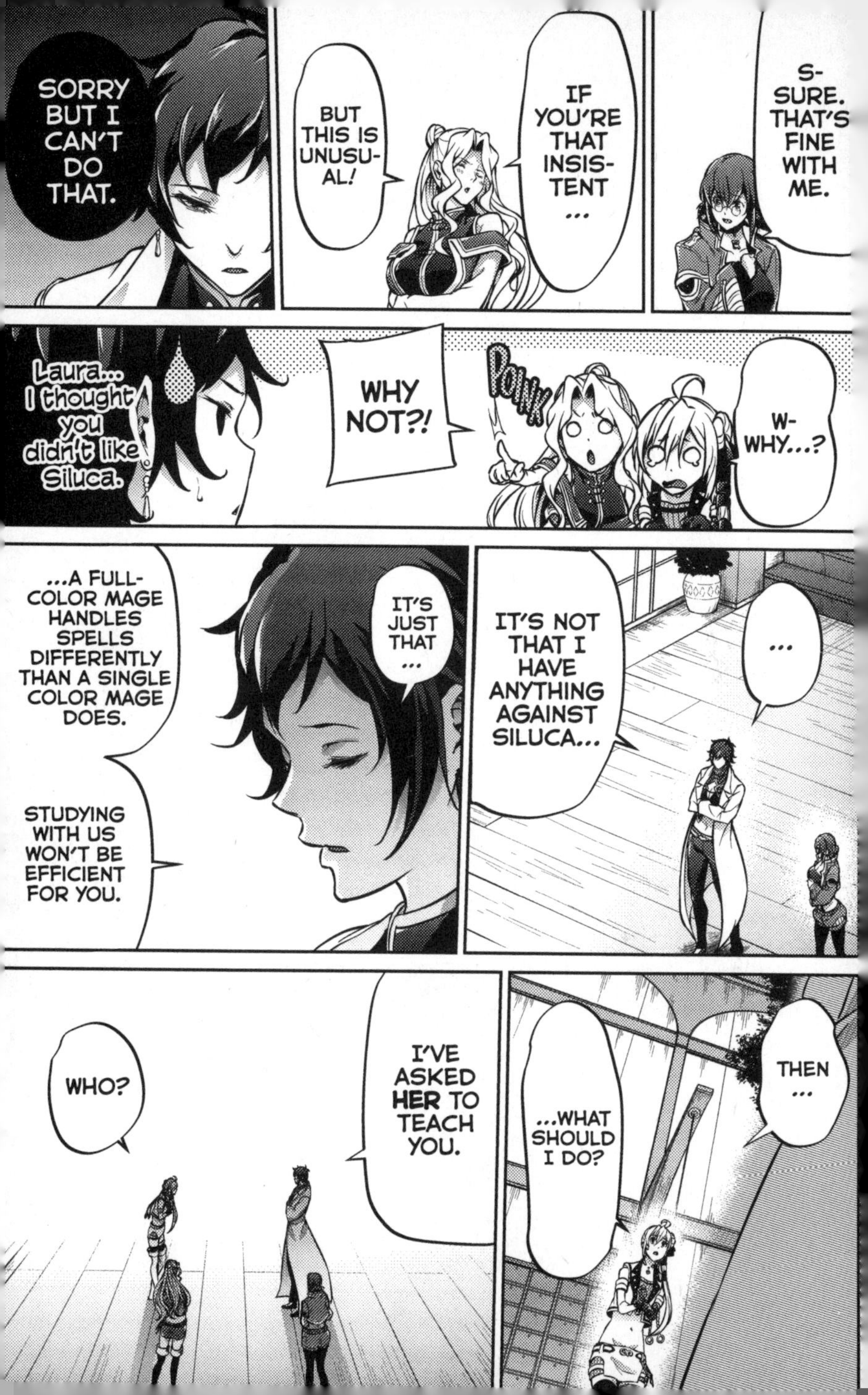
S-SURE. THAT'S FINE WITH ME.
IF YOU'RE THAT INSISTENT...
BUT THIS IS UNUSUAL!
SORRY BUT I CAN'T DO THAT.
W-WHY...?
POINK
WHY NOT?!
Laura... I thought you didn't like Siluca.
...
IT'S NOT THAT I HAVE ANYTHING AGAINST SILUCA...
IT'S JUST THAT...
...A FULL-COLOR MAGE HANDLES SPELLS DIFFERENTLY THAN A SINGLE COLOR MAGE DOES.
STUDYING WITH US WON'T BE EFFICIENT FOR YOU.
THEN...
...WHAT SHOULD I DO?
I'VE ASKED **HER** TO TEACH YOU.
WHO?

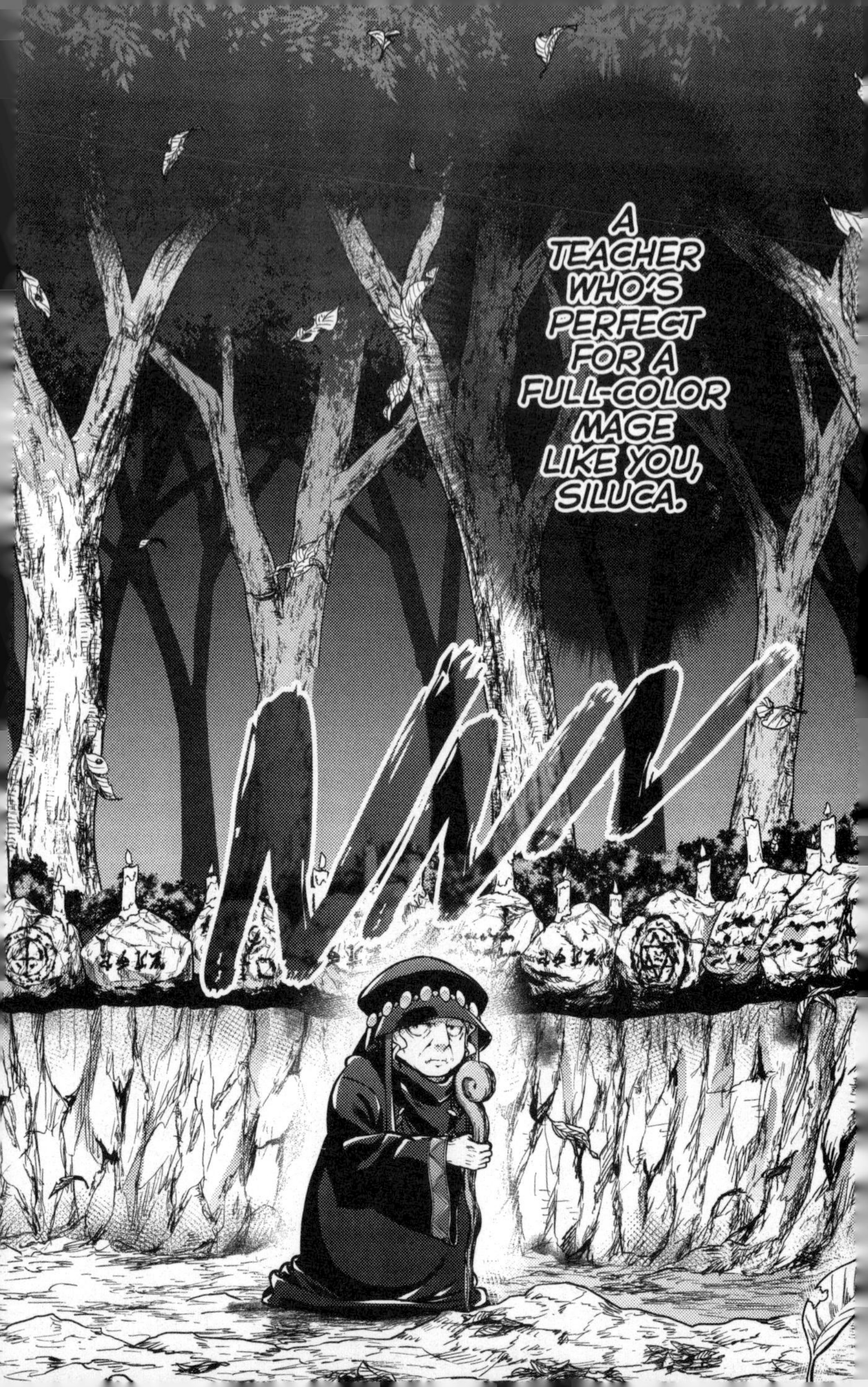
A TEACHER WHO'S PERFECT FOR A FULL-COLOR MAGE LIKE YOU, SILUCA.

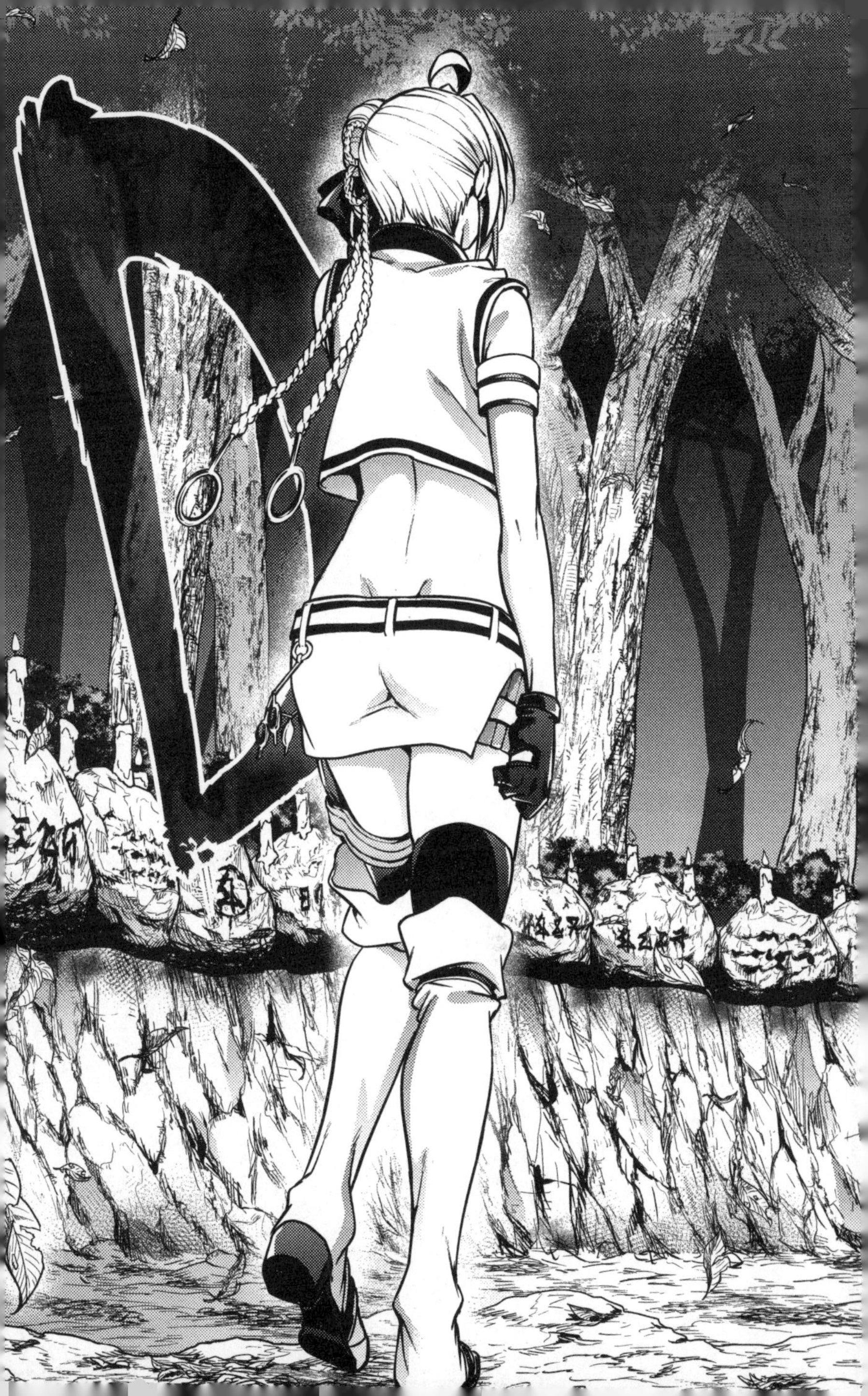

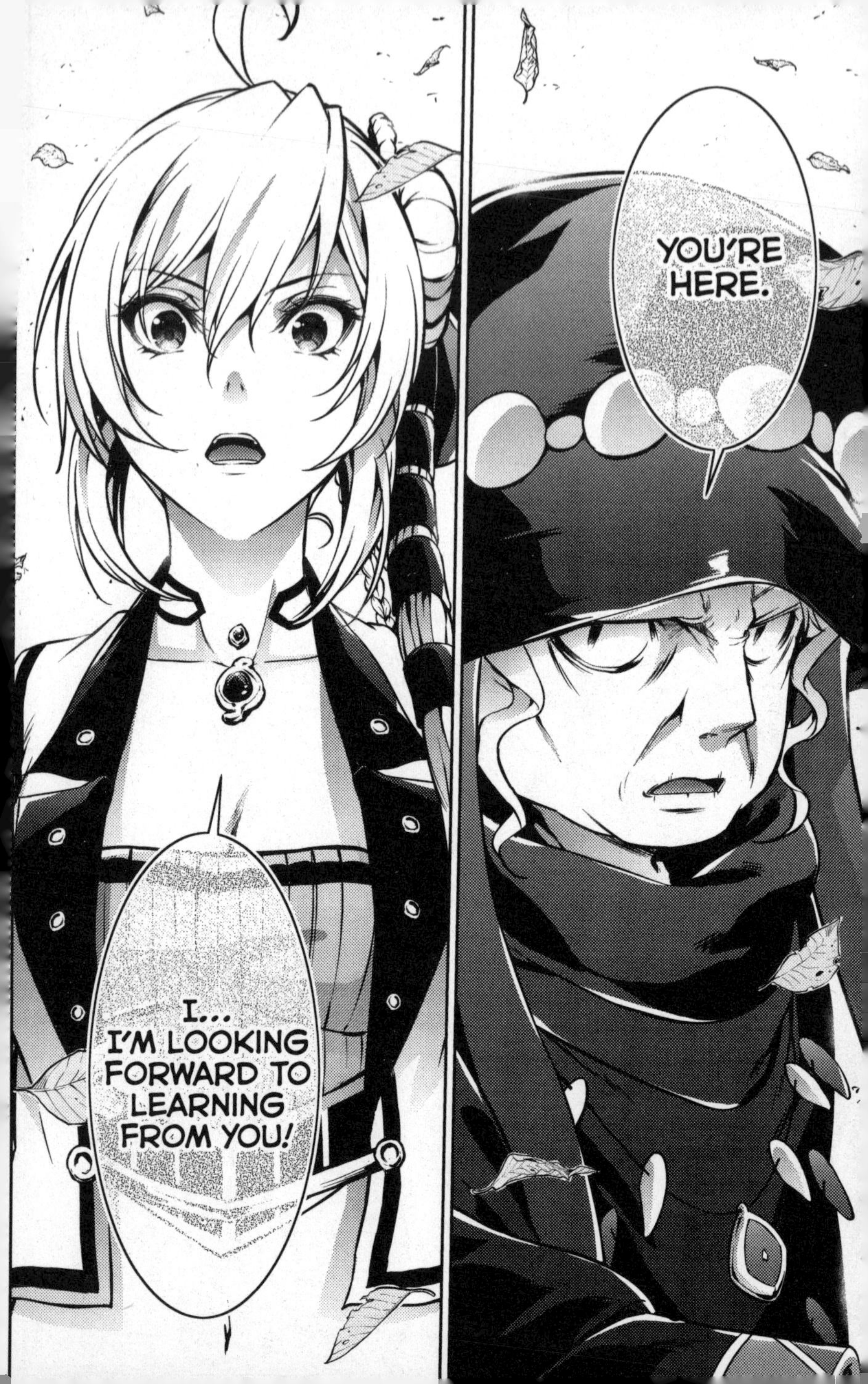
YOU'RE HERE.
I... I'M LOOKING FORWARD TO LEARNING FROM YOU!

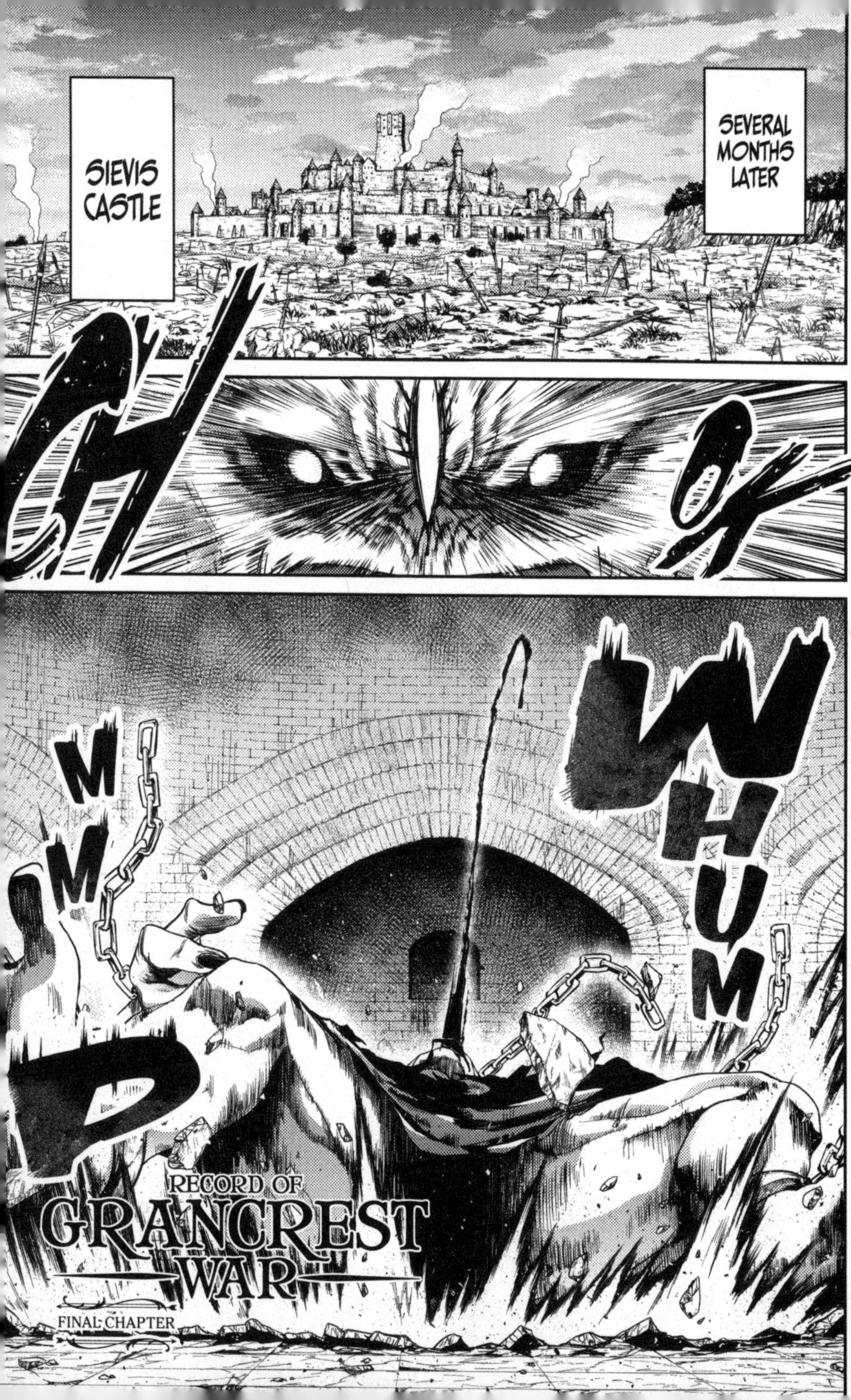
SEVERAL MONTHS LATER
SIEVIS CASTLE
CHOK
WHUMP
MM
RECORD OF GRANCREST WAR
FINAL CHAPTER

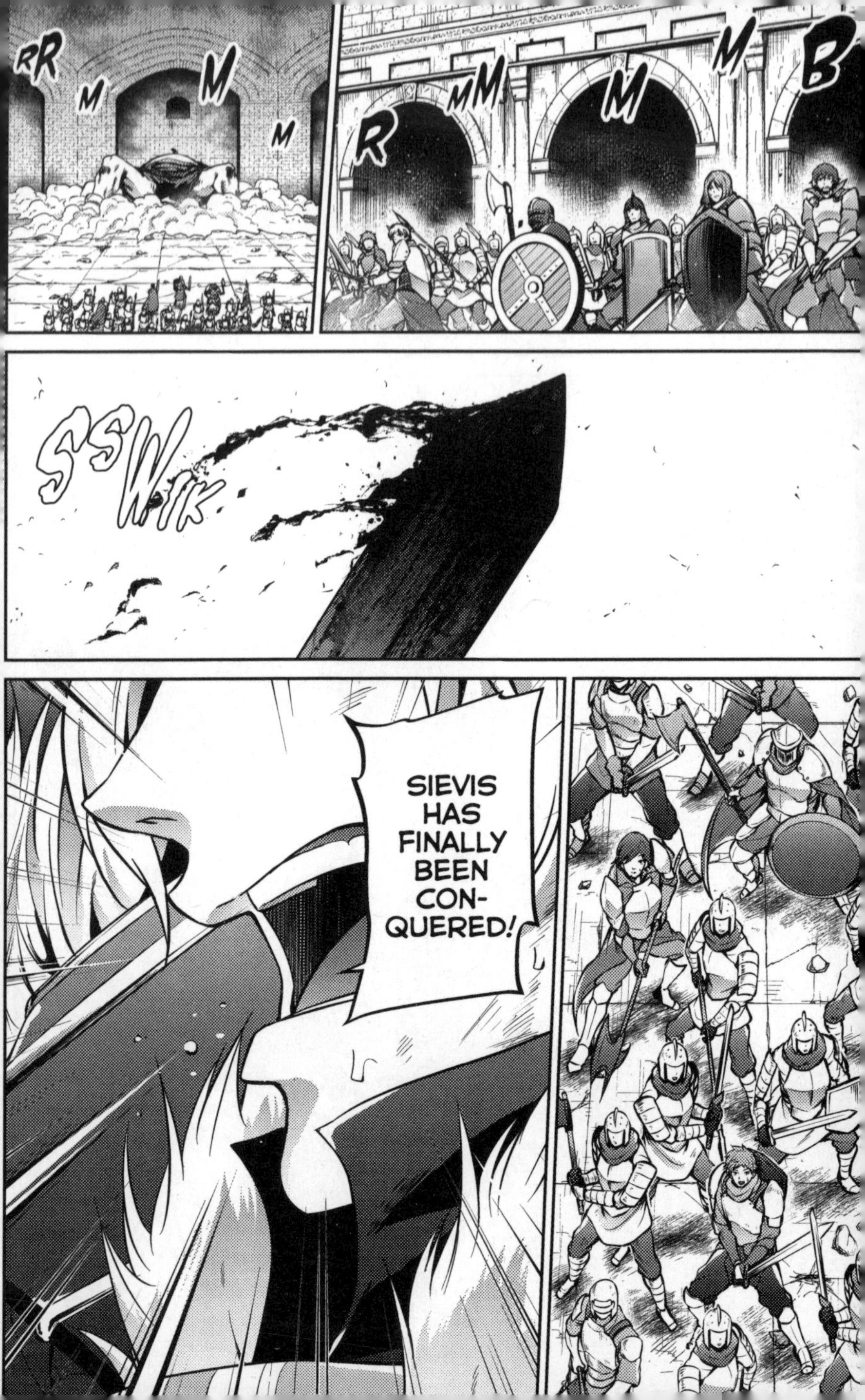
RRMMMM
RMMMMB
SSWIK
SIEVIS HAS FINALLY BEEN CON-QUERED!

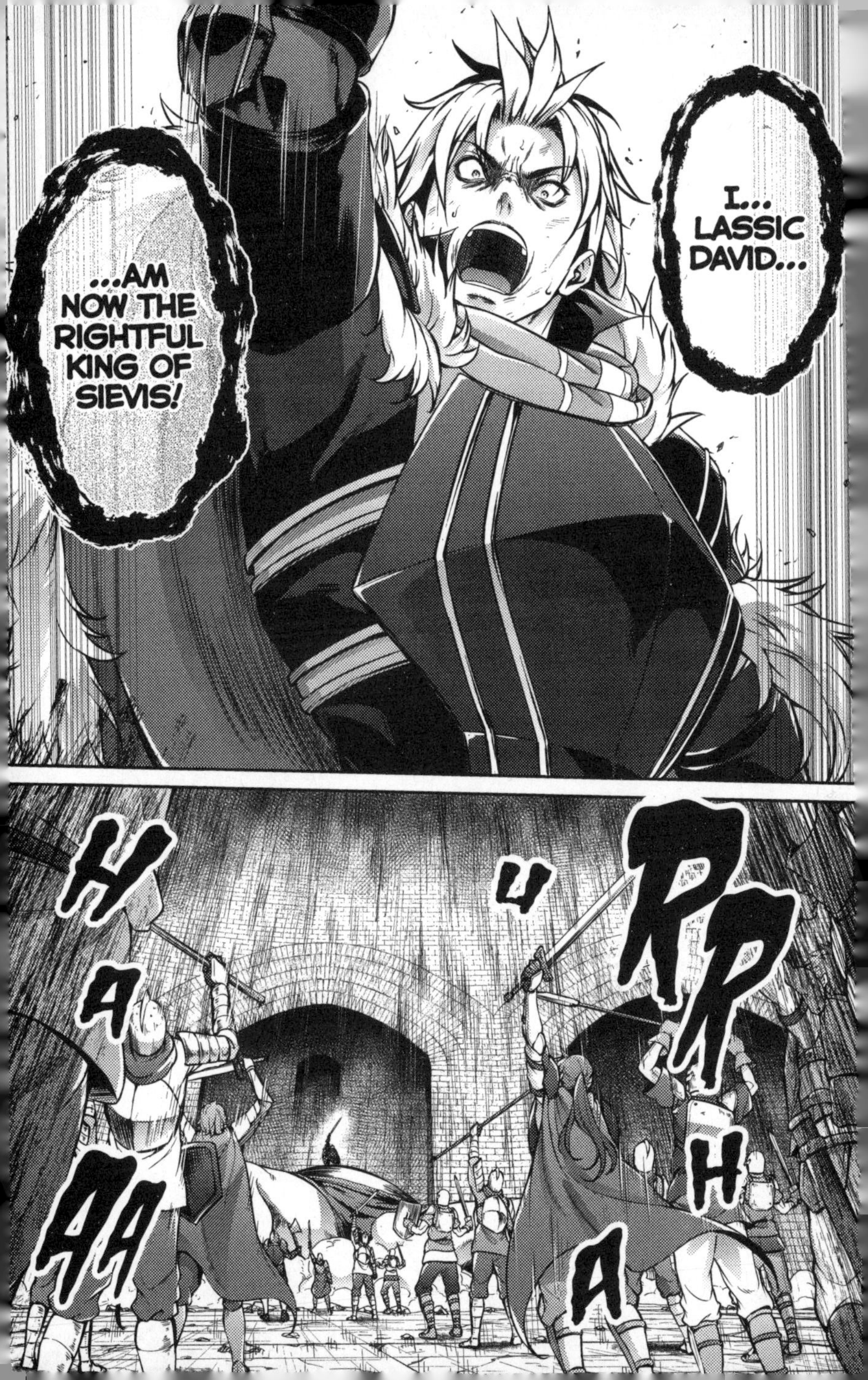
I... LASSIC DAVID...
...AM NOW THE RIGHTFUL KING OF SIEVIS!
URRHA
HAAA

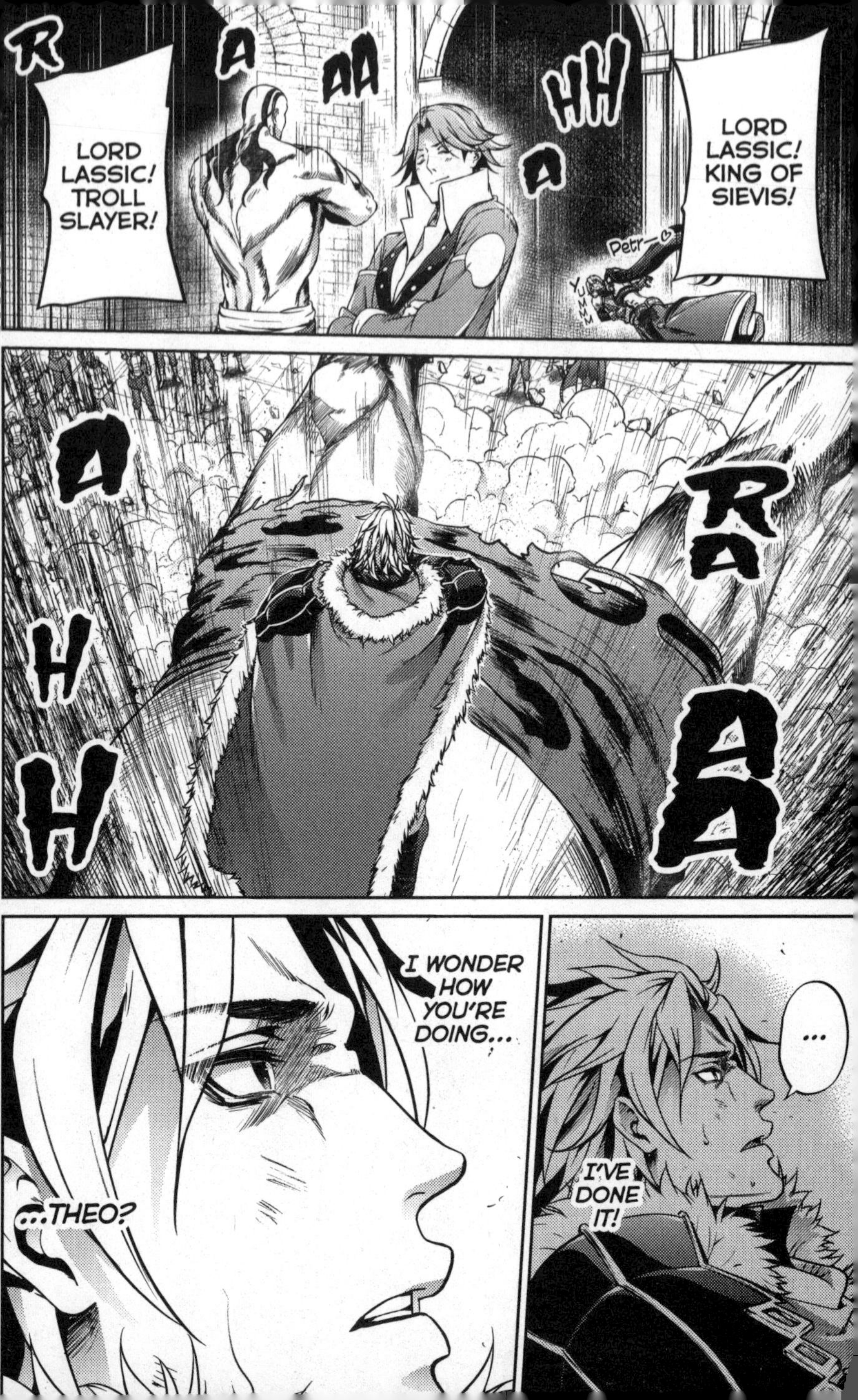
RAAAHHA
LORD LASSIC! KING OF SIEVIS!
Petr—♡
YUMMM
LORD LASSIC! TROLL SLAYER!
RAAA
AHH
...
I'VE DONE IT!
I WONDER HOW YOU'RE DOING...
...THEO?

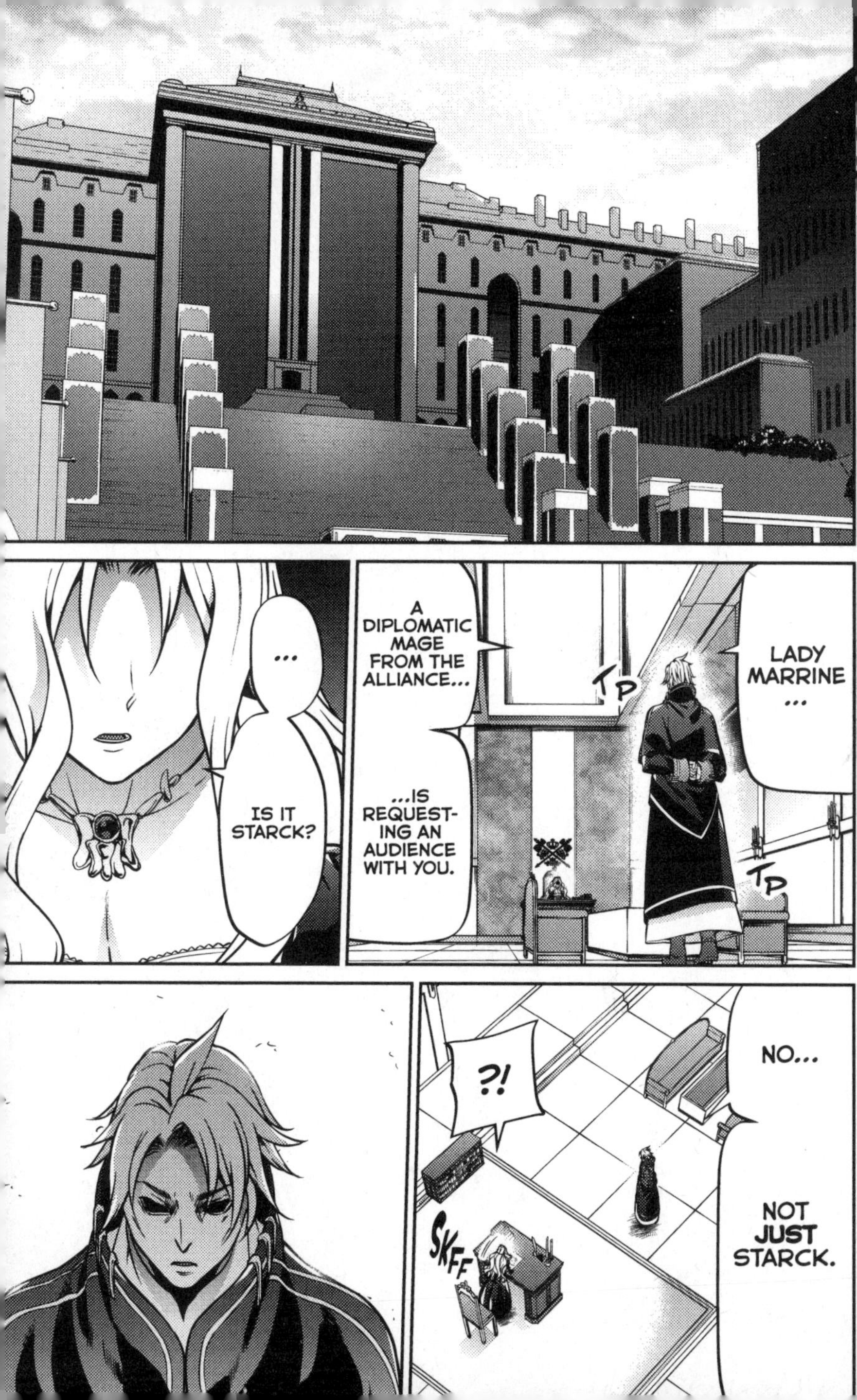
LADY MARRINE ...
A DIPLOMATIC MAGE FROM THE ALLIANCE...
TP
...IS REQUEST-ING AN AUDIENCE WITH YOU.
TP
...
IS IT STARCK?
NO...
?!
NOT **JUST** STARCK.
SKFF

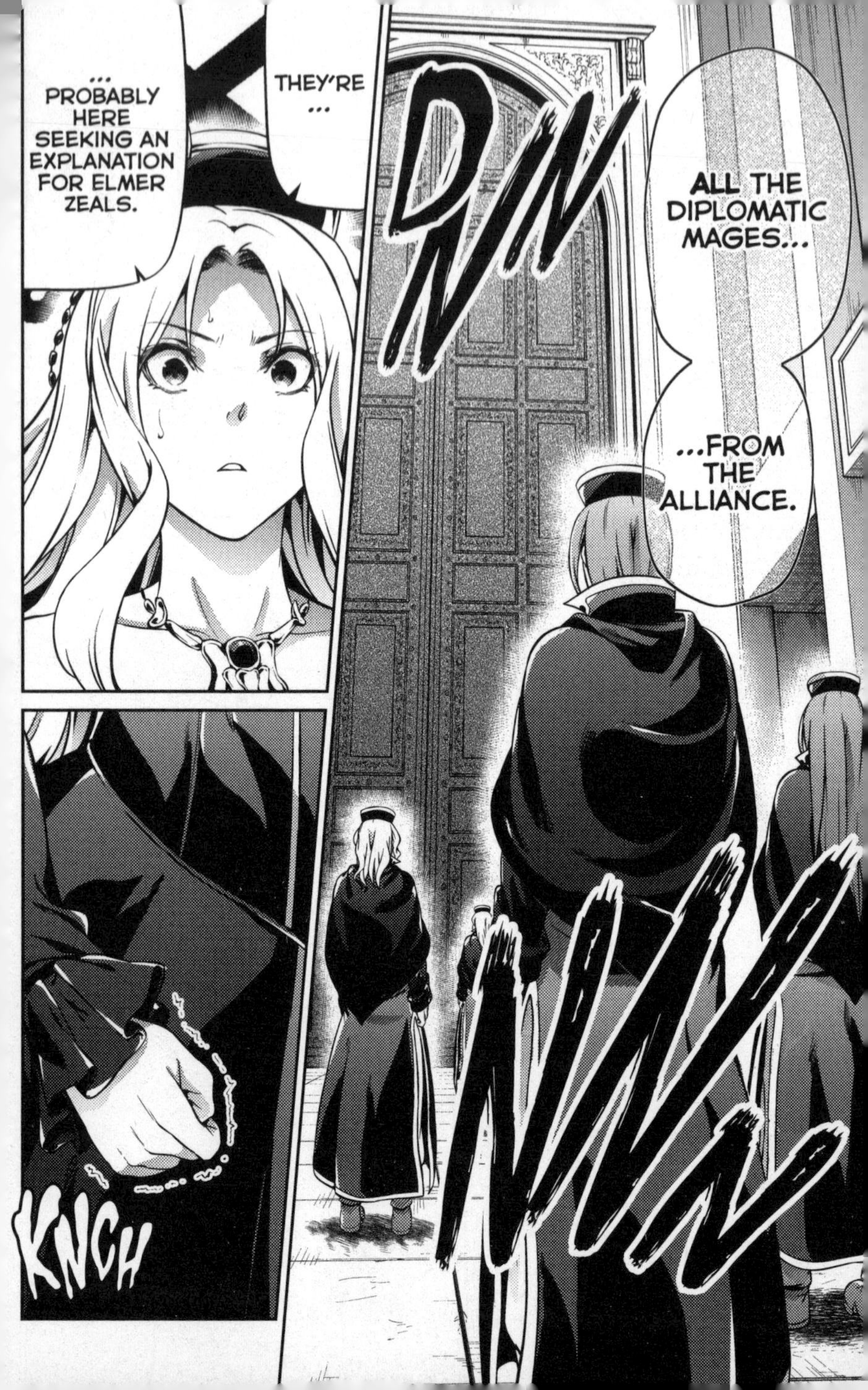
ALL THE DIPLOMATIC MAGES...
...FROM THE ALLIANCE.
THEY'RE ...
... PROBABLY HERE SEEKING AN EXPLANATION FOR ELMER ZEALS.
KNCH

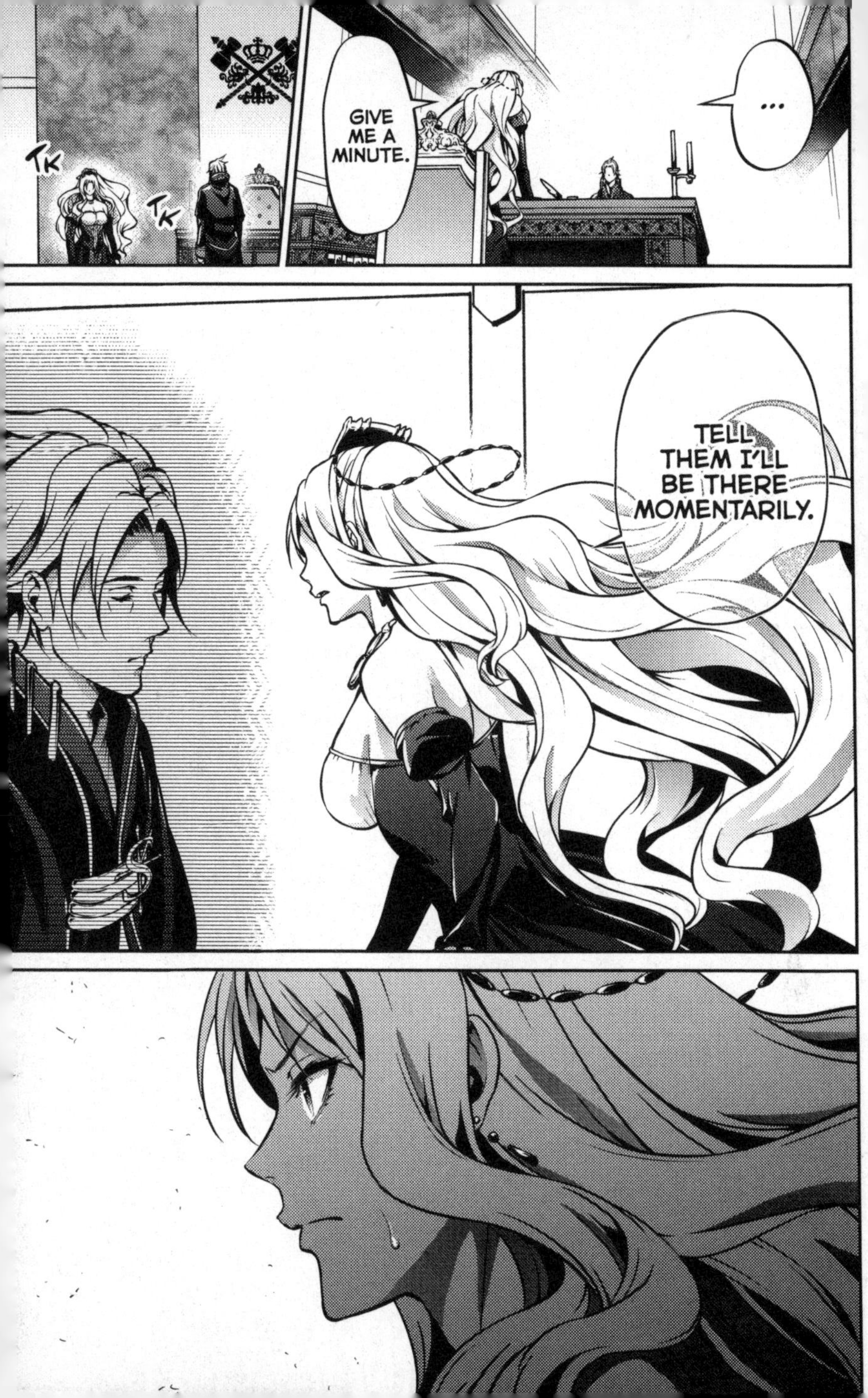
...
GIVE ME A MINUTE.
TK
TK
TELL THEM I'LL BE THERE MOMENTARILY.

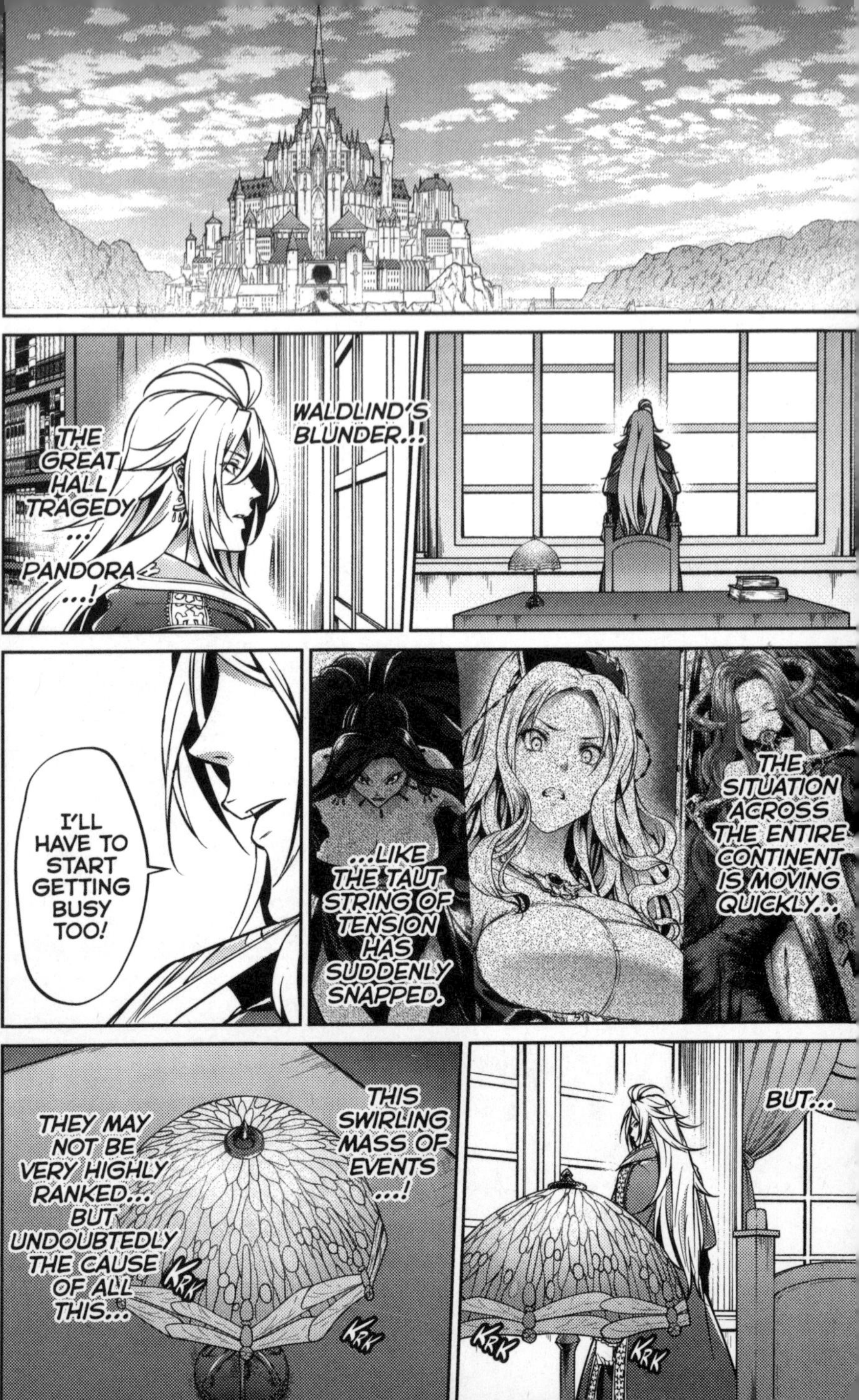
WALDLIND'S BLUNDER...
THE GREAT HALL TRAGEDY... PANDORA...!
THE SITUATION ACROSS THE ENTIRE CONTINENT IS MOVING QUICKLY...
...LIKE THE TAUT STRING OF TENSION HAS SUDDENLY SNAPPED.
I'LL HAVE TO START GETTING BUSY TOO!
BUT...
KRK
KRK
THIS SWIRLING MASS OF EVENTS...!
THEY MAY NOT BE VERY HIGHLY RANKED... BUT UNDOUBTEDLY THE CAUSE OF ALL THIS...
KRK
KRK

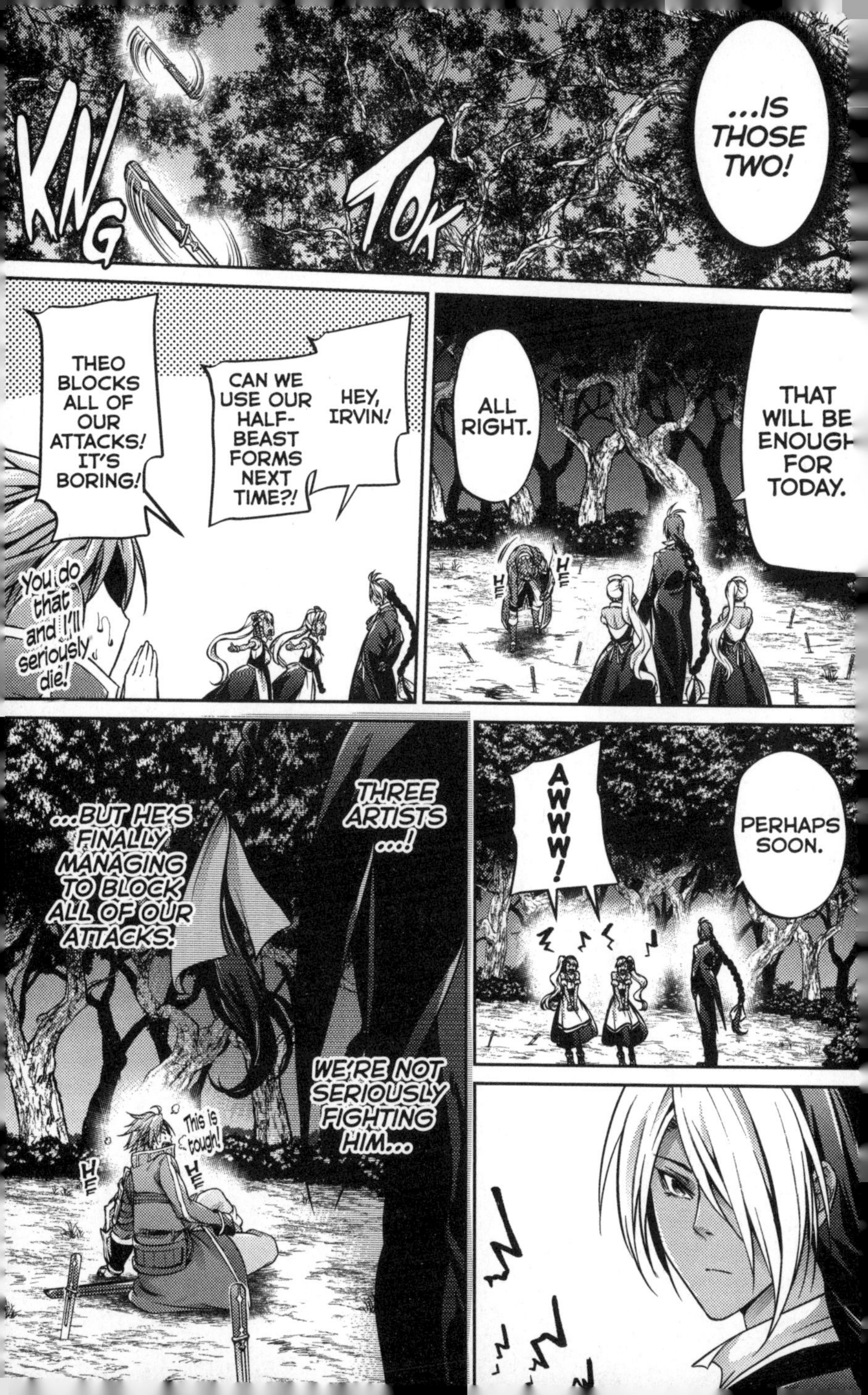
...IS THOSE TWO!
TOK
KNG
THAT WILL BE ENOUGH FOR TODAY.
ALL RIGHT.
HE HE
HEY, IRVIN!
CAN WE USE OUR HALF-BEAST FORMS NEXT TIME?!
THEO BLOCKS ALL OF OUR ATTACKS! IT'S BORING!
You do that and I'll seriously die!
PERHAPS SOON.
AWWW!
THREE ARTISTS ...!
...BUT HE'S FINALLY MANAGING TO BLOCK ALL OF OUR ATTACKS.
WE'RE NOT SERIOUSLY FIGHTING HIM...
This is tough!
HE HE

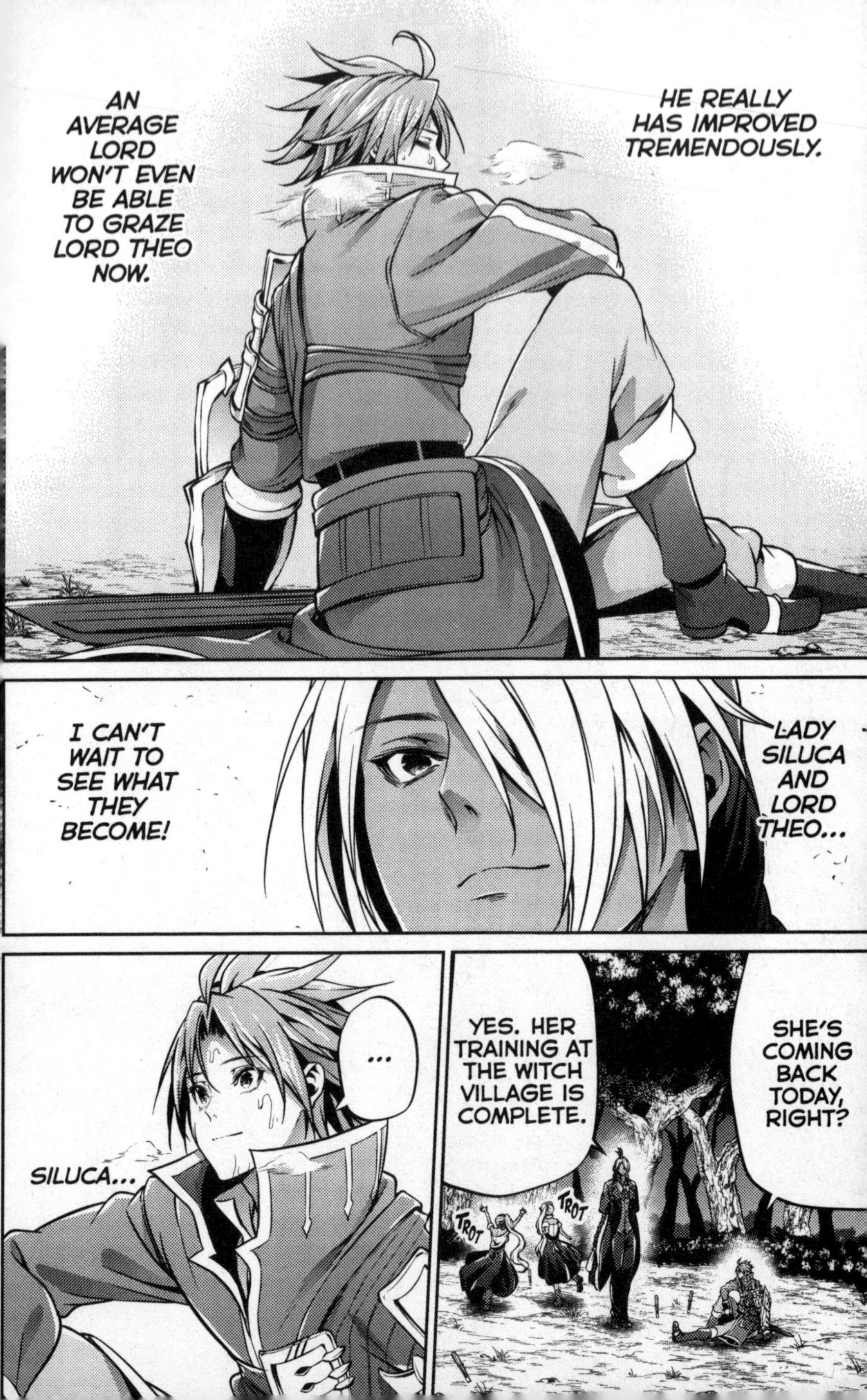
HE REALLY HAS IMPROVED TREMENDOUSLY.
AN AVERAGE LORD WON'T EVEN BE ABLE TO GRAZE LORD THEO NOW.
LADY SILUCA AND LORD THEO...
I CAN'T WAIT TO SEE WHAT THEY BECOME!
SHE'S COMING BACK TODAY, RIGHT?
YES. HER TRAINING AT THE WITCH VILLAGE IS COMPLETE.
TROT
TROT
...
SILUCA...

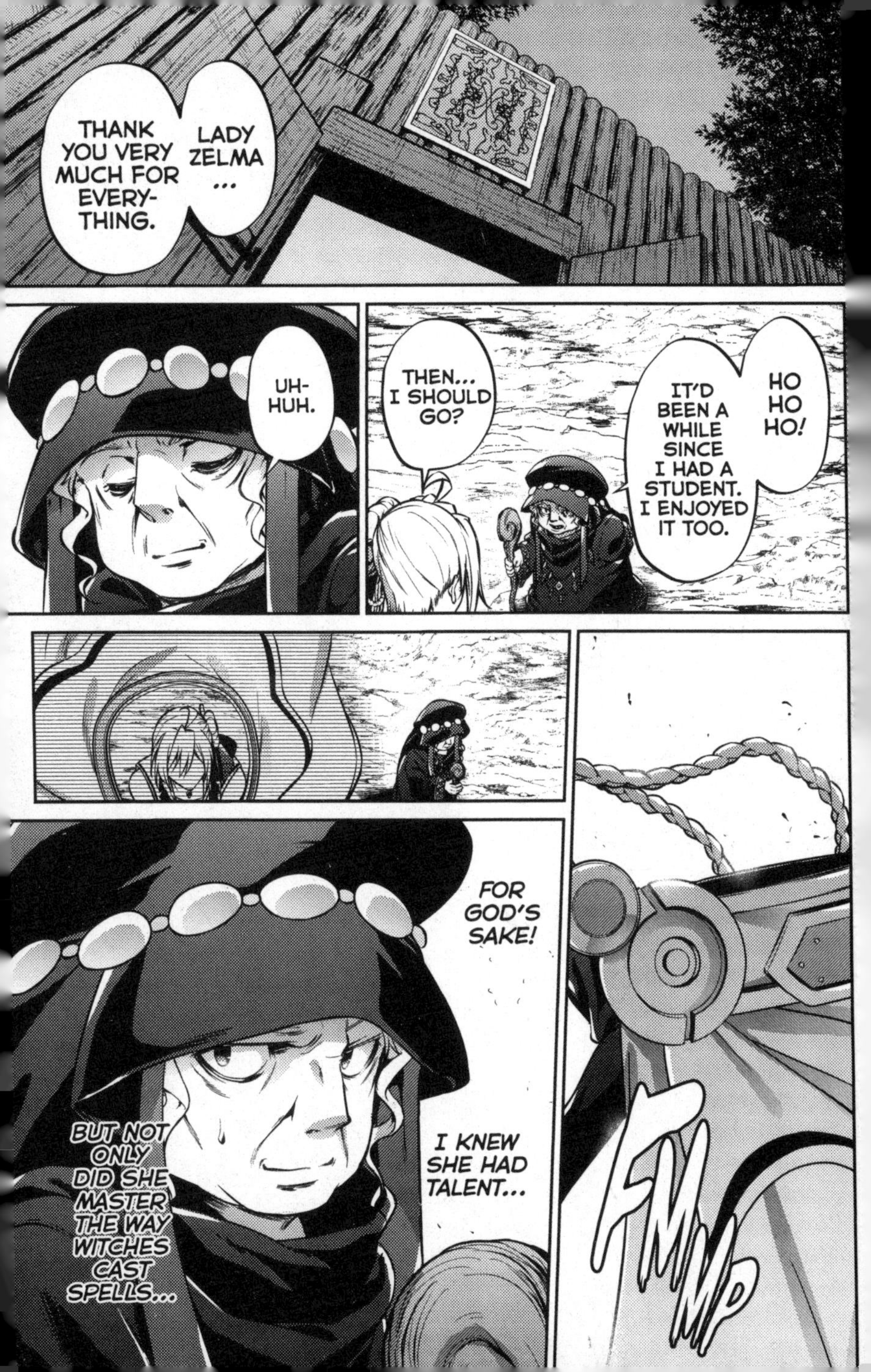
LADY ZELMA...
THANK YOU VERY MUCH FOR EVERY-THING.
HO HO HO!
IT'D BEEN A WHILE SINCE I HAD A STUDENT. I ENJOYED IT TOO.
THEN... I SHOULD GO?
UH-HUH.
FMMP
FOR GOD'S SAKE!
I KNEW SHE HAD TALENT...
BUT NOT ONLY DID SHE MASTER THE WAY WITCHES CAST SPELLS...

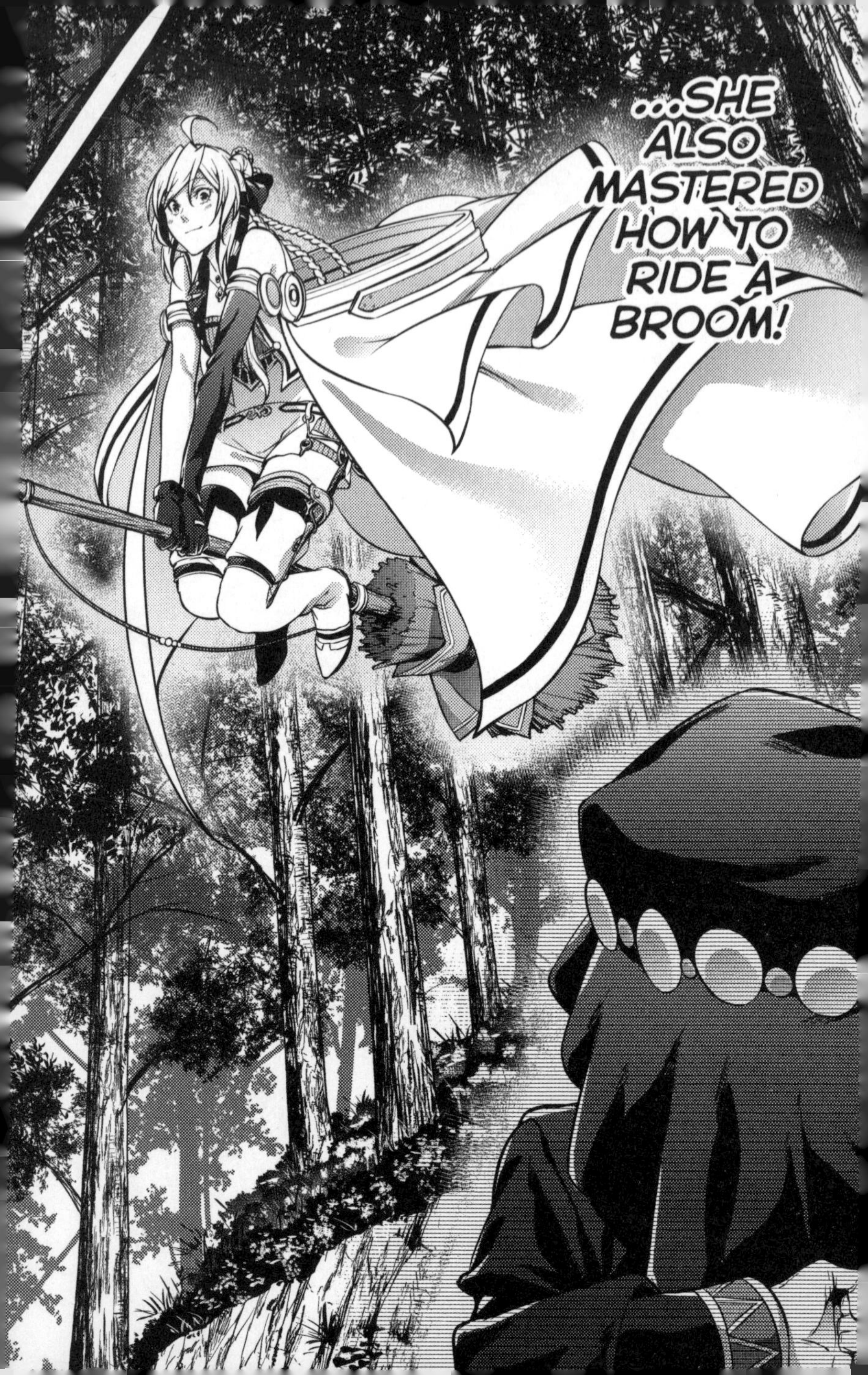
...SHE ALSO MASTERED HOW TO RIDE A BROOM!

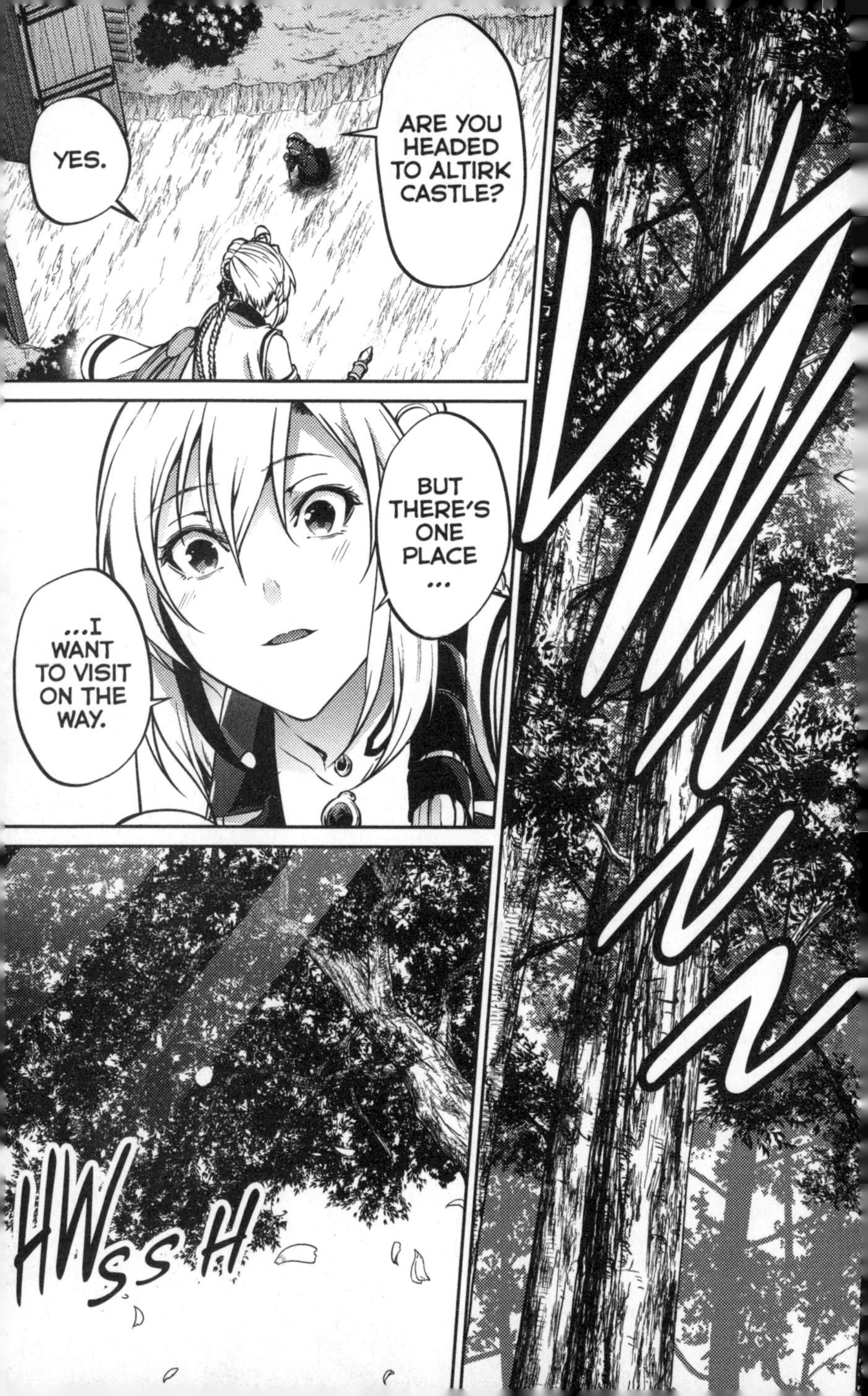
ARE YOU HEADED TO ALTIRK CASTLE?
YES.
BUT THERE'S ONE PLACE...
...I WANT TO VISIT ON THE WAY.
HWSSH

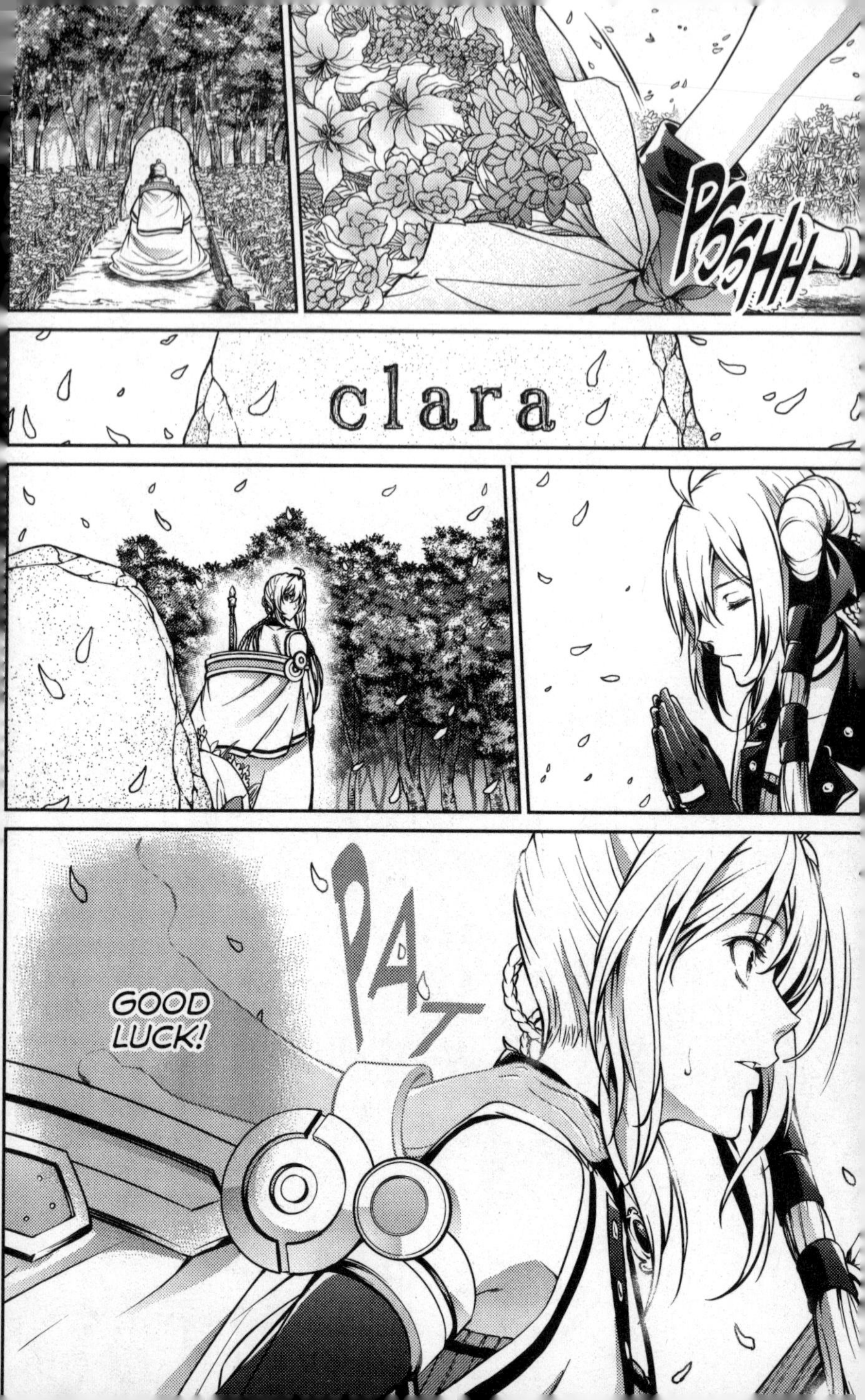
PSSHH
clara
PAT
GOOD LUCK!

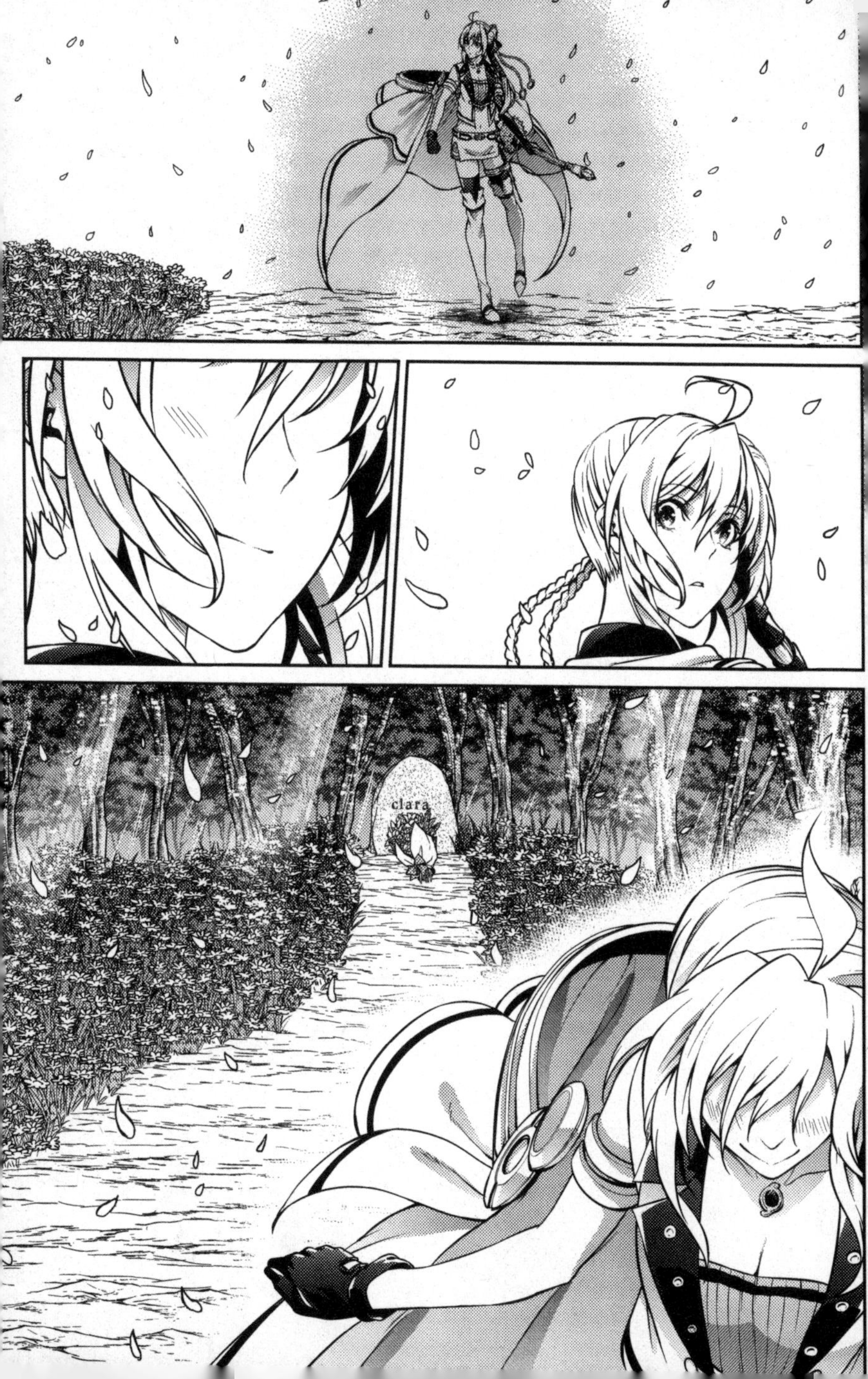
clara

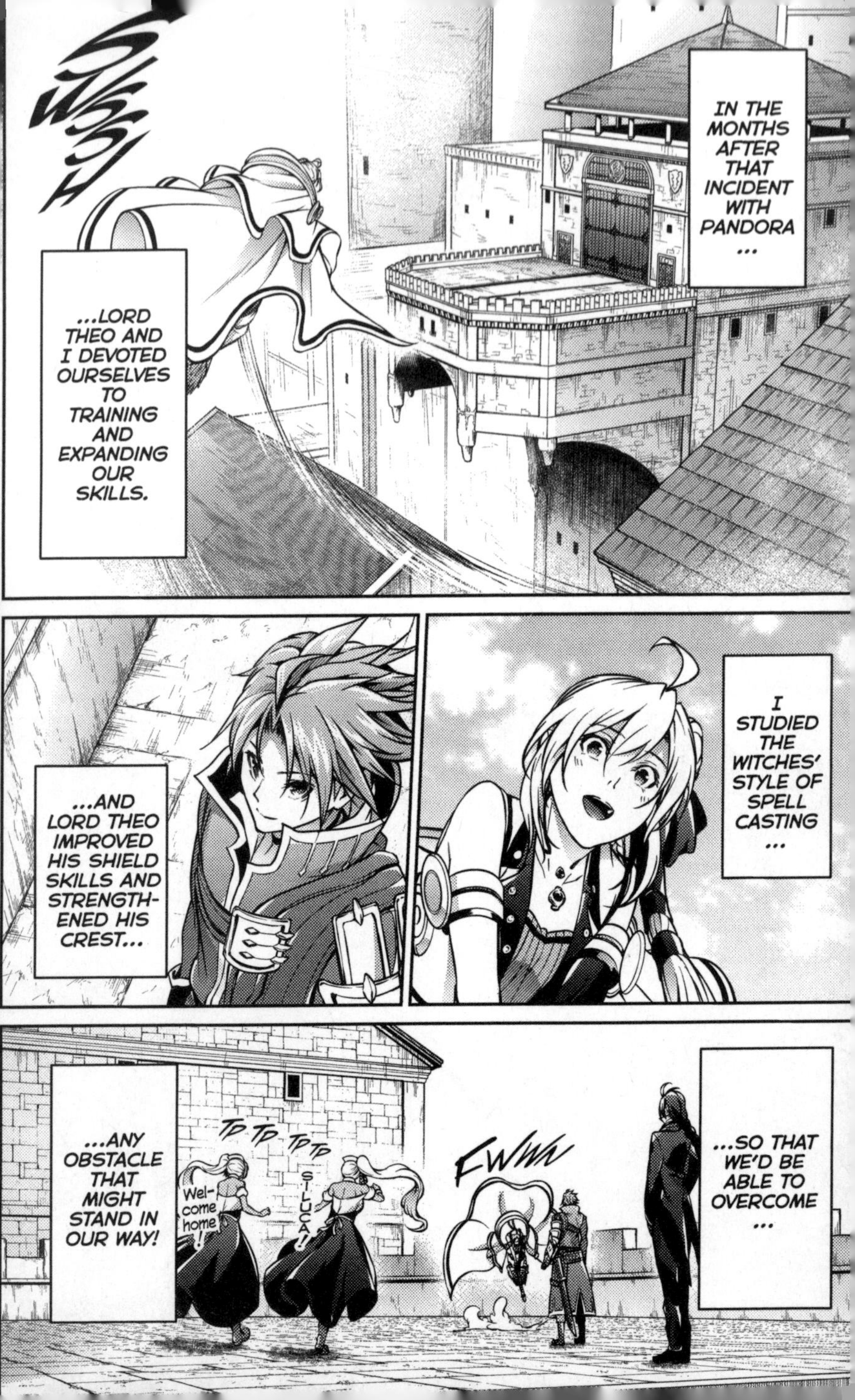
IN THE MONTHS AFTER THAT INCIDENT WITH PANDORA...
SWISSH
...LORD THEO AND I DEVOTED OURSELVES TO TRAINING AND EXPANDING OUR SKILLS.
I STUDIED THE WITCHES' STYLE OF SPELL CASTING...
...AND LORD THEO IMPROVED HIS SHIELD SKILLS AND STRENGTH-ENED HIS CREST...
...SO THAT WE'D BE ABLE TO OVERCOME...
FWIW
SILUCA!
TP TP TP TP
Wel-come home!
...ANY OBSTACLE THAT MIGHT STAND IN OUR WAY!

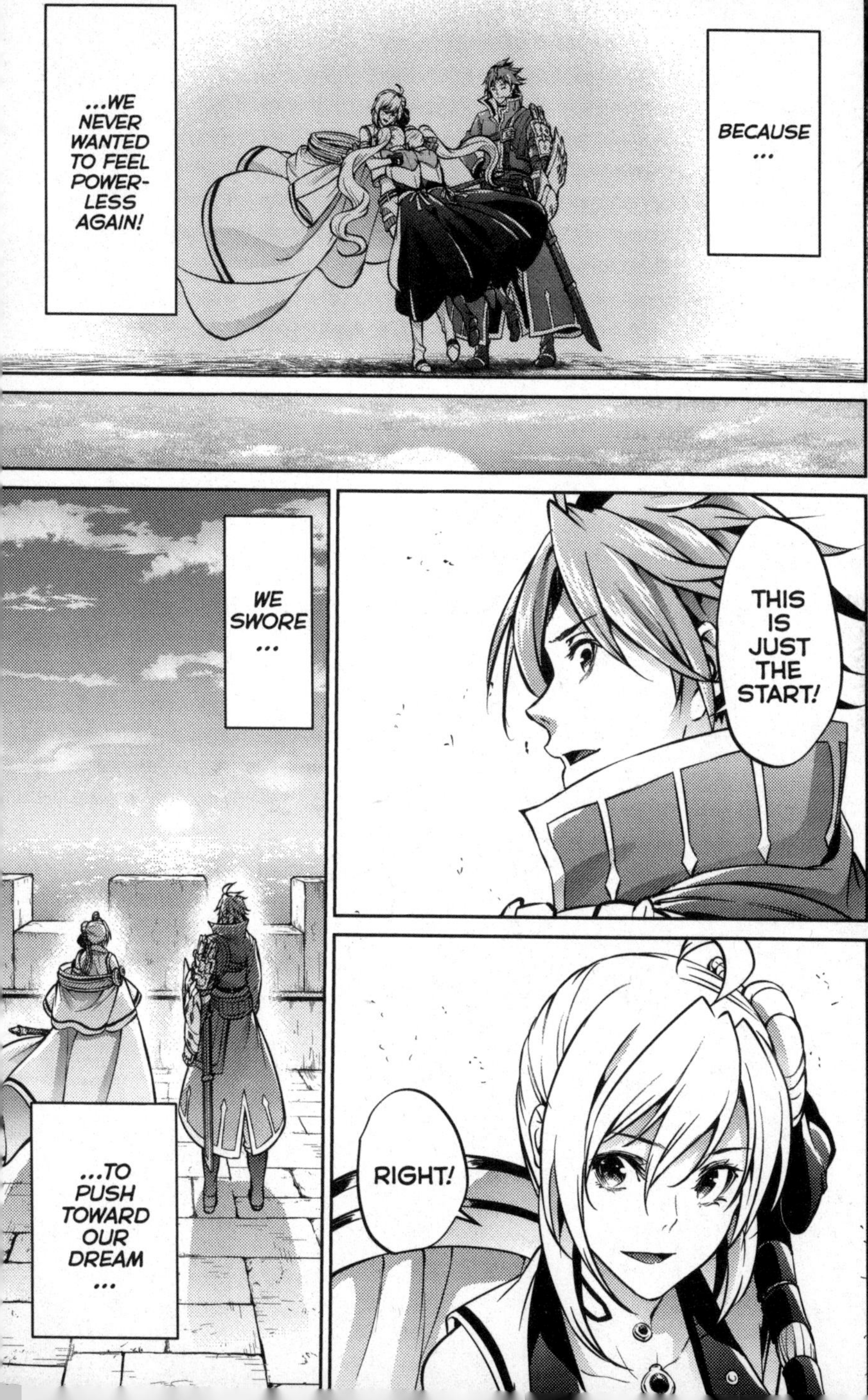
BECAUSE...
...WE NEVER WANTED TO FEEL POWER-LESS AGAIN!
THIS IS JUST THE START!
RIGHT!
WE SWORE...
...TO PUSH TOWARD OUR DREAM...

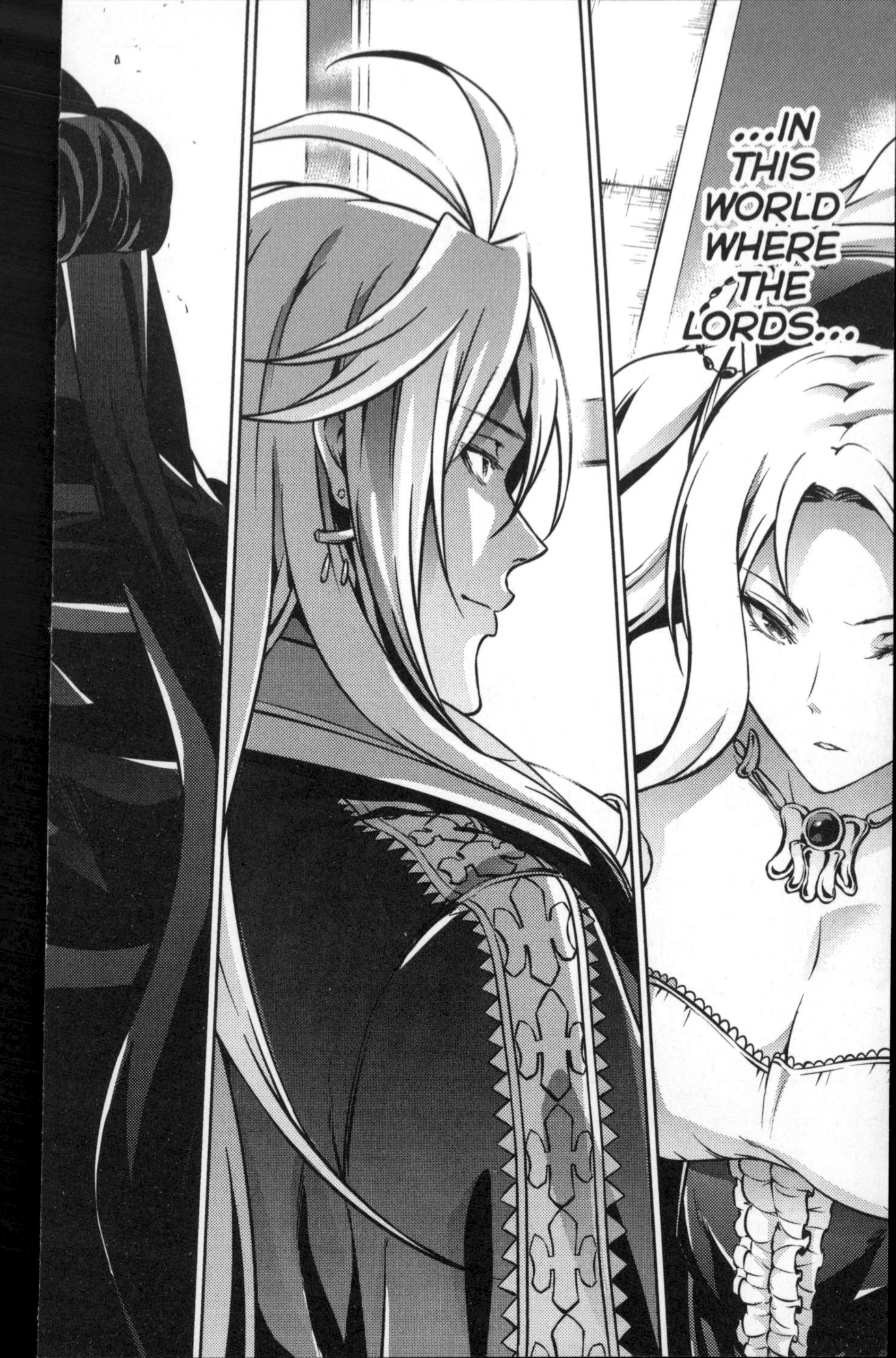
...IN THIS WORLD WHERE THE LORDS...

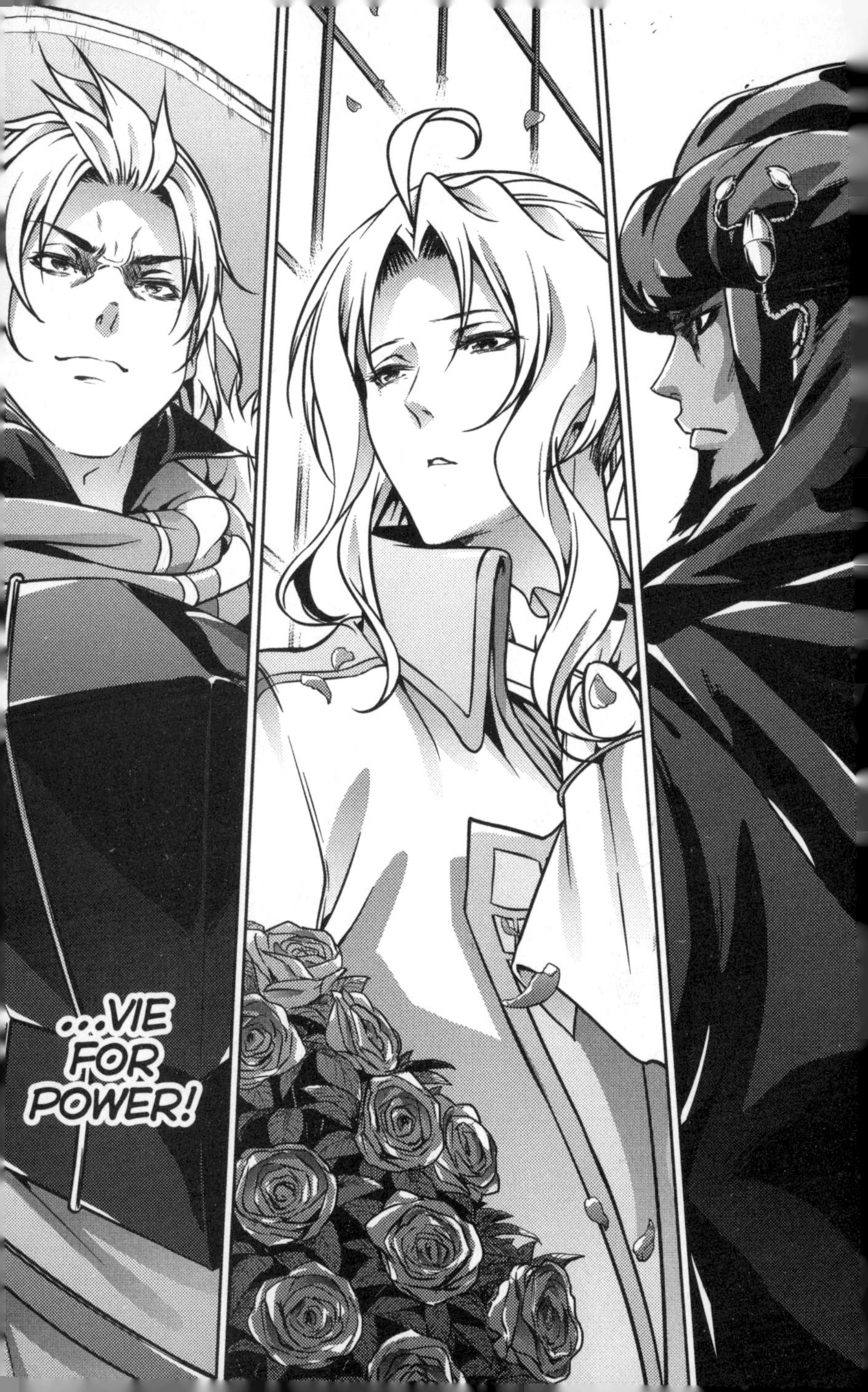
...VIE FOR POWER!

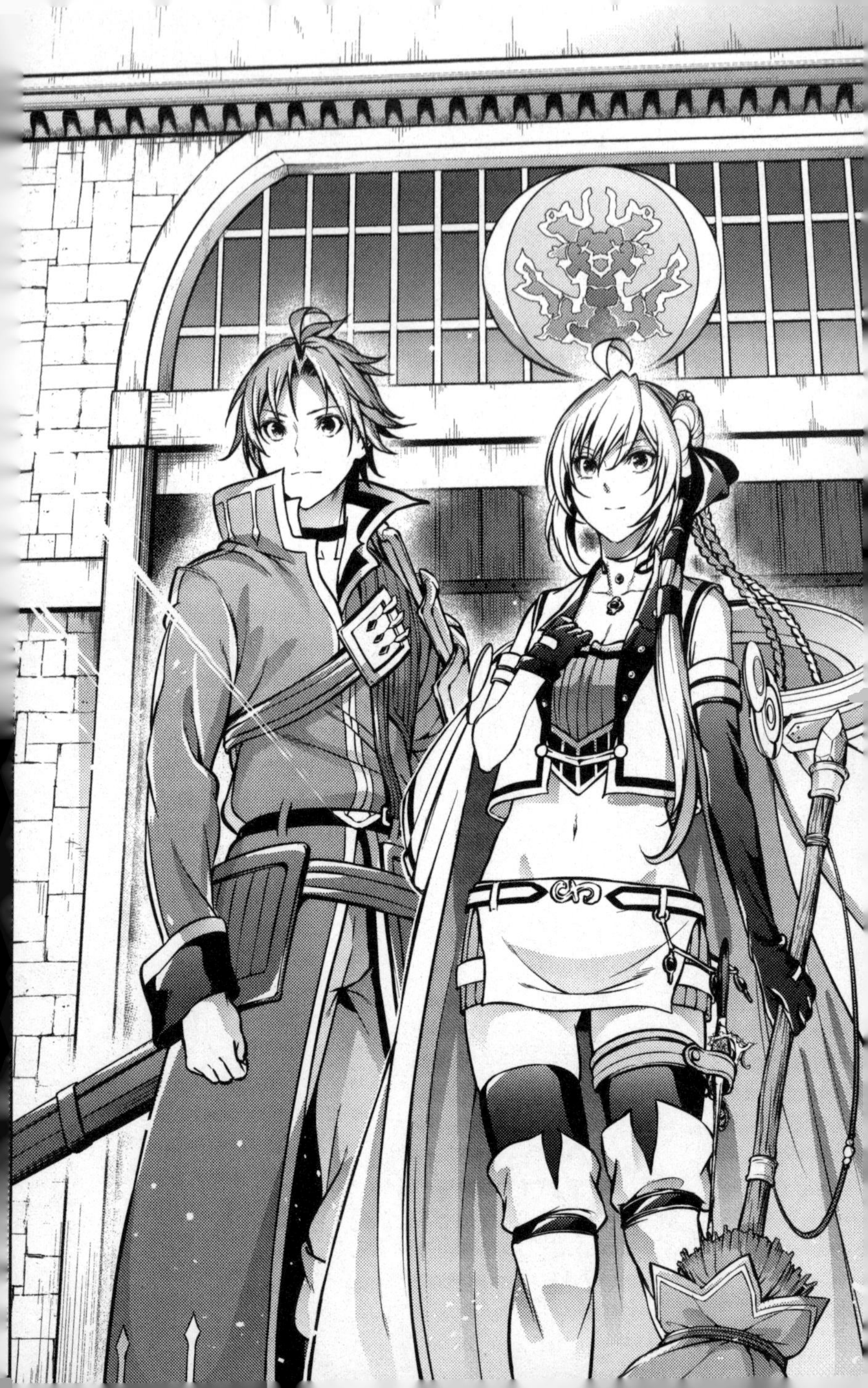

RECORD OF
GRANCREST
WAR

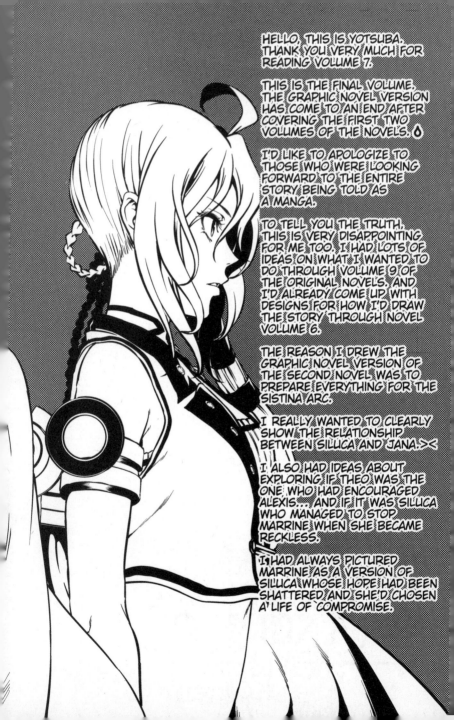

HELLO, THIS IS YOTSUBA. THANK YOU VERY MUCH FOR READING VOLUME 7.

THIS IS THE FINAL VOLUME. THE GRAPHIC NOVEL VERSION HAS COME TO AN END AFTER COVERING THE FIRST TWO VOLUMES OF THE NOVELS. ◊

I'D LIKE TO APOLOGIZE TO THOSE WHO WERE LOOKING FORWARD TO THE ENTIRE STORY BEING TOLD AS A MANGA.

TO TELL YOU THE TRUTH, THIS IS VERY DISAPPOINTING FOR ME TOO. I HAD LOTS OF IDEAS ON WHAT I WANTED TO DO THROUGH VOLUME 9 OF THE ORIGINAL NOVELS, AND I'D ALREADY COME UP WITH DESIGNS FOR HOW I'D DRAW THE STORY THROUGH NOVEL VOLUME 6.

THE REASON I DREW THE GRAPHIC NOVEL VERSION OF THE SECOND NOVEL WAS TO PREPARE EVERYTHING FOR THE SISTINA ARC.

I REALLY WANTED TO CLEARLY SHOW THE RELATIONSHIP BETWEEN SILUCA AND JANA. ><

I ALSO HAD IDEAS ABOUT EXPLORING IF THEO WAS THE ONE WHO HAD ENCOURAGED ALEXIS... AND IF IT WAS SILUCA WHO MANAGED TO STOP MARRINE WHEN SHE BECAME RECKLESS.

I HAD ALWAYS PICTURED MARRINE AS A VERSION OF SILUCA WHOSE HOPE HAD BEEN SHATTERED AND SHE'D CHOSEN A LIFE OF COMPROMISE.

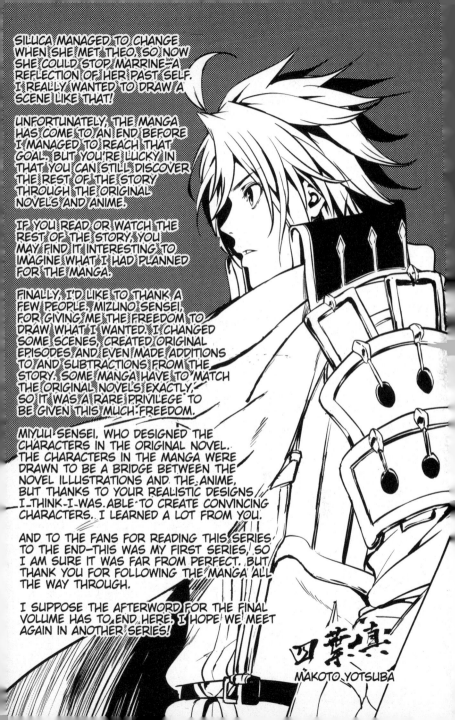

SILUCA MANAGED TO CHANGE WHEN SHE MET THEO, SO NOW SHE COULD STOP MARRINE—A REFLECTION OF HER PAST SELF. I REALLY WANTED TO DRAW A SCENE LIKE THAT!

UNFORTUNATELY, THE MANGA HAS COME TO AN END BEFORE I MANAGED TO REACH THAT GOAL... BUT YOU'RE LUCKY IN THAT YOU CAN STILL DISCOVER THE REST OF THE STORY THROUGH THE ORIGINAL NOVELS AND ANIME.

IF YOU READ OR WATCH THE REST OF THE STORY, YOU MAY FIND IT INTERESTING TO IMAGINE WHAT I HAD PLANNED FOR THE MANGA.

FINALLY, I'D LIKE TO THANK A FEW PEOPLE. MIZUNO SENSEI, FOR GIVING ME THE FREEDOM TO DRAW WHAT I WANTED. I CHANGED SOME SCENES, CREATED ORIGINAL EPISODES AND EVEN MADE ADDITIONS TO AND SUBTRACTIONS FROM THE STORY. SOME MANGA HAVE TO MATCH THE ORIGINAL NOVELS EXACTLY, SO IT WAS A RARE PRIVILEGE TO BE GIVEN THIS MUCH FREEDOM.

MIYUU SENSEI, WHO DESIGNED THE CHARACTERS IN THE ORIGINAL NOVEL. THE CHARACTERS IN THE MANGA WERE DRAWN TO BE A BRIDGE BETWEEN THE NOVEL ILLUSTRATIONS AND THE ANIME, BUT THANKS TO YOUR REALISTIC DESIGNS —I THINK I WAS ABLE TO CREATE CONVINCING CHARACTERS... I LEARNED A LOT FROM YOU.

AND TO THE FANS FOR READING THIS SERIES TO THE END—THIS WAS MY FIRST SERIES, SO I AM SURE IT WAS FAR FROM PERFECT. BUT THANK YOU FOR FOLLOWING THE MANGA ALL THE WAY THROUGH.

I SUPPOSE THE AFTERWORD FOR THE FINAL VOLUME HAS TO END HERE. I HOPE WE MEET AGAIN IN ANOTHER SERIES!

MAKOTO YOTSUBA

ORIGINAL AUTHOR: RYO MIZUNO

Hello, my name is Ryo Mizuno. I'm the author of the original novel series. I'm a light-novel creator who has been in this business for more than 30 years. I'd like to thank all of you for reading this *Record of Grancrest War* manga to the end. The original novel series is ten volumes long, and the first two volumes of that were adapted into this manga series—with numerous original episodes added to it. The climax was very exciting too, so I think it was a very satisfying manga to read. But if you are still interested in finding out what happens in the story, please take a look at the novels or the anime.

Since this is a war chronicle fantasy novel, it has many characters and countless details in the form of the weapons, armor, spells and background artwork. It must have been very challenging to draw it. But Makoto Yotsuba took on that difficult task and accomplished it successfully, and I'd like to take this opportunity to thank him for his long, hard work on this series. I look forward to his next work as a fellow fan.

I'd also like to thank the Young Animal editorial office for accepting the project to create a manga out of my novels. Reincarnation stories have been the latest fad, so stereotypical fantasy works like this aren't given a lot of attention nowadays. But I thought the readers of Young Animal would welcome this story since Kentaro Miura's *Berserk* was serialized in the magazine, so I was the one who approached them about this project. The result was a success and we managed to complete the manga series. This means Kentaro Miura was a great benefactor for this work. And on top of that, he was kind enough to write heartwarming words of recommendation for the original novels too. I am incredibly grateful. I believe that fantasy has infinite possibilities and intend to keep creating new pieces of work, so please keep an eye out for them.

水 野 良 • RYO MIZUNO

A novelist and game designer living in Kobe. Best known for works such as the *Record of Lodoss War* series and *Rune Soldier*.

ORIGINAL CHARACTER DESIGN: MIYUU

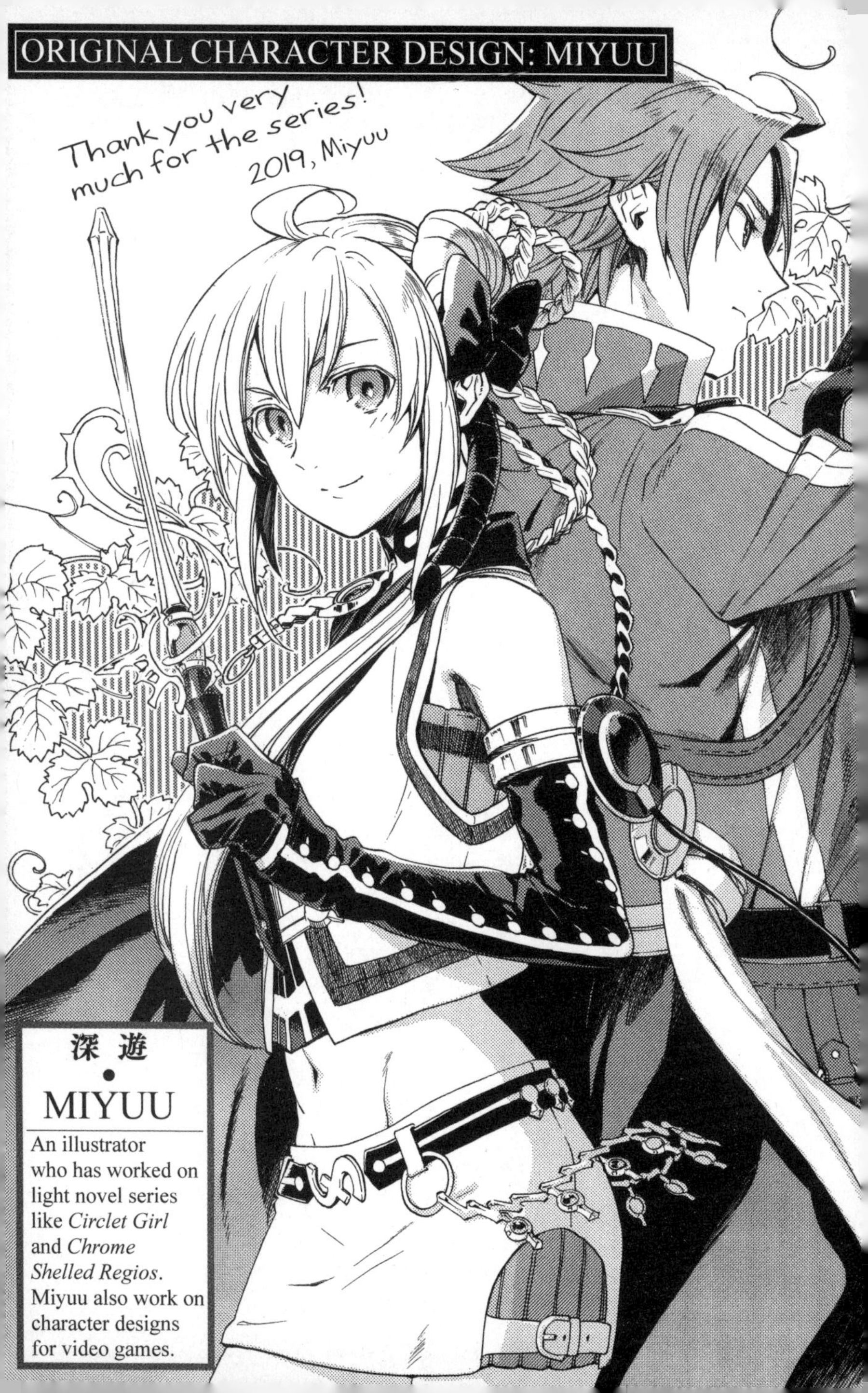
Thank you very much for the series!
2019, Miyuu

深遊
•
MIYUU

An illustrator who has worked on light novel series like *Circlet Girl* and *Chrome Shelled Regios*. Miyuu also work on character designs for video games.

RECORD OF GRANCREST WAR

VOLUME 7

Original Story by **Ryo Mizuno**
Story & Art by **Makoto Yotsuba**
Character Design by **Miyuu**

Translation: **Tetsu Miyaki**
Touch-Up Art & Lettering: **James Gaubatz**
English Adaptation: **Stan!**
Design: **Julian [JR] Robinson**
Editor: **David Brothers**

Printed in the U.S.A.

Published by VIZ Media, LLC
P.O. Box 77010
San Francisco, CA 94107

10 9 8 7 6 5 4 3 2 1
First printing, July 2020

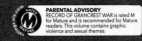

PARENTAL ADVISORY
RECORD OF GRANCREST WAR is rated M
for Mature and is recommended for Mature
readers. This volume contains graphic
violence and sexual themes.

VIZ MEDIA
viz.com

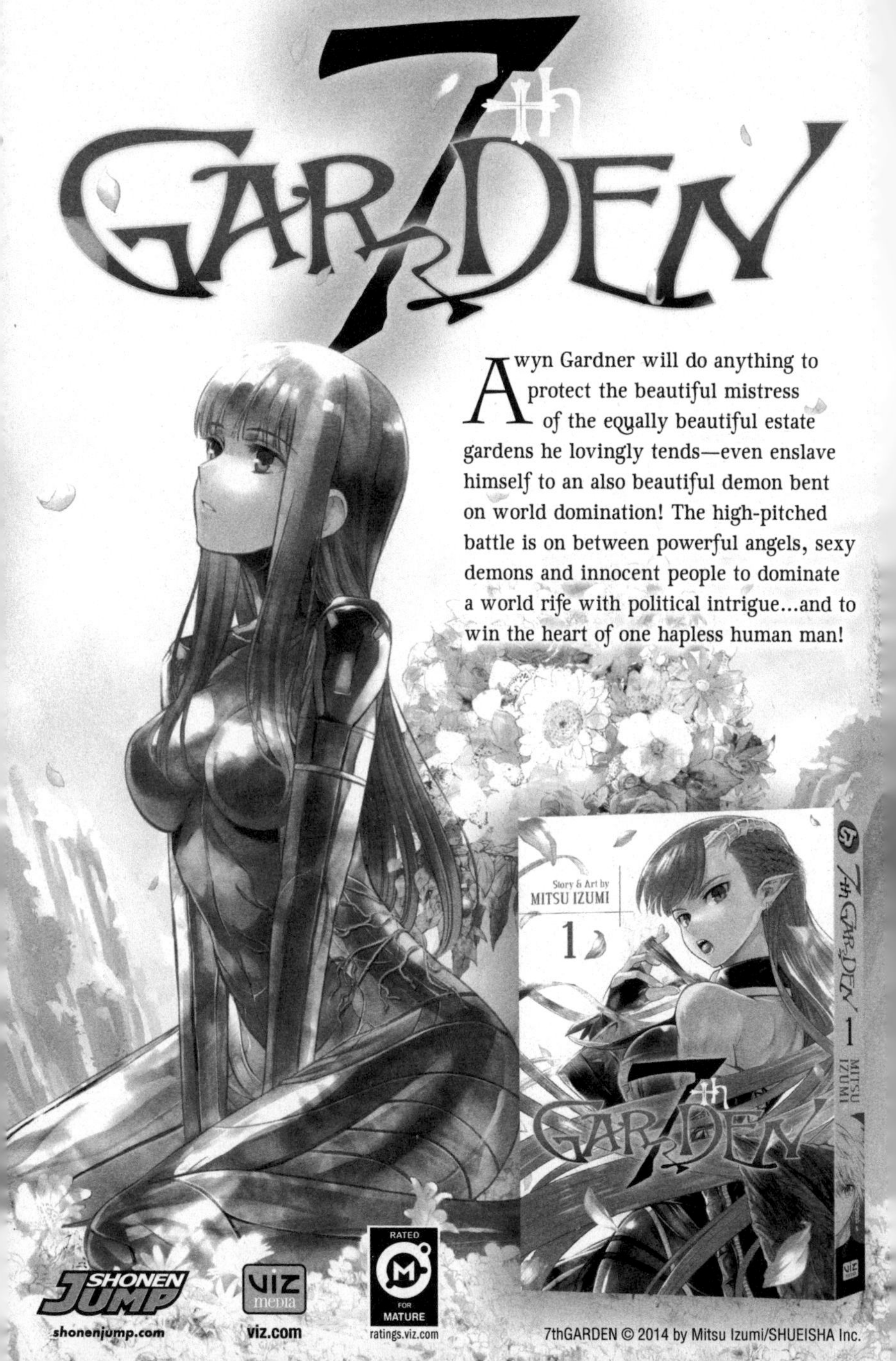
7th GARDEN
Awyn Gardner will do anything to protect the beautiful mistress of the equally beautiful estate gardens he lovingly tends—even enslave himself to an also beautiful demon bent on world domination! The high-pitched battle is on between powerful angels, sexy demons and innocent people to dominate a world rife with political intrigue...and to win the heart of one hapless human man!
Story & Art by
MITSU IZUMI
1
7th GARDEN
MITSU IZUMI
SHONEN JUMP
shonenjump.com
VIZ media
viz.com
RATED M FOR MATURE
ratings.viz.com
7thGARDEN © 2014 by Mitsu Izumi/SHUEISHA Inc.

ASSASSINATION CLASSROOM

COMPLETE BOX SET

STORY AND ART BY YUSEI MATSUI

The complete bestselling *Assassination Classroom* series is now available in a boldly designed, value-priced box set!

· Includes all 21 volumes of this unique tale of a mysterious, smiley-faced, tentacled, superpowered teacher who guides a group of misfit students to find themselves—while doing their best to assassinate him.

· Also includes an exclusive, full-color, mini "yearbook" filled with images of favorite characters in different art styles and contexts (previously unreleased in the English editions).

ANSATSU KYOSHITSU © 2012 by Yusei Matsui/SHUEISHA Inc.

BLACK TORCH

Ninja and animal lover Jiro Azuma's life is changed forever when he finds himself in the middle of a war of ninjas vs. demons.

Jiro Azuma is descended from a long line of ninja, and he can talk to animals. One day he rescues a unique black cat named Rago, a supernatural being, and is dragged into a mystical war.

VIZ

DEATH NOTE

ALL-IN-ONE EDITION

Story by **Tsugumi Ohba**   Art by **Takeshi Obata**

Light Yagami is an ace student with great prospects—
and he's bored out of his mind. But all that changes
when he finds the Death Note, a notebook dropped by
a rogue Shinigami death god. Any human whose name
is written in the notebook dies, and now Light has
vowed to use the power of the Death Note to rid the
world of evil. But when criminals begin dropping dead,
the authorities send the legendary detective L to track
down the killer. With L hot on his heels, will Light lose
sight of his noble goal...or his life?

*Includes a
NEW epilogue
chapter!*

All 12 volumes in ONE monstrously large edition!

VIZ

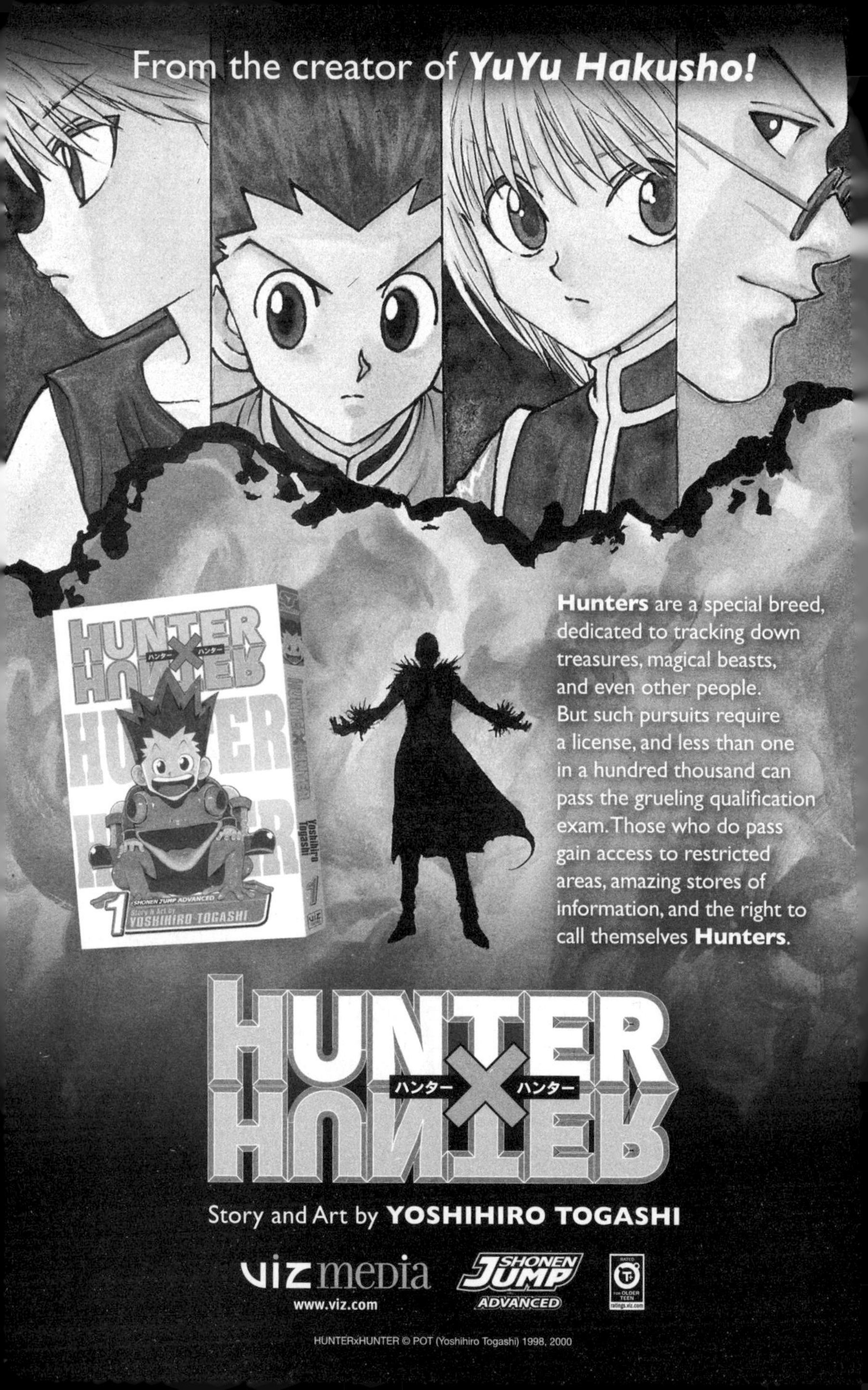
From the creator of YuYu Hakusho!
HUNTER × HUNTER
ハンター ハンター
1
YOSHIHIRO TOGASHI
Yoshihiro Togashi
Hunters are a special breed, dedicated to tracking down treasures, magical beasts, and even other people. But such pursuits require a license, and less than one in a hundred thousand can pass the grueling qualification exam. Those who do pass gain access to restricted areas, amazing stores of information, and the right to call themselves Hunters.
HUNTER × HUNTER
ハンター ハンター
Story and Art by YOSHIHIRO TOGASHI
viz media
www.viz.com
SHONEN JUMP ADVANCED
RATED T+ FOR OLDER TEEN
ratings.viz.com
HUNTERxHUNTER © POT (Yoshihiro Togashi) 1998, 2000

From the creators of

DEATH NOTE

PLATINVM END

STORY
TSUGUMI OHBA

ART
TAKESHI OBATA

As his classmates celebrate their
middle school graduation, troubled
Mirai is mired in darkness. But his
battle is just beginning when he receives
some salvation from above in the form
of an angel. Now Mirai is pitted against
12 other chosen humans in a battle in
which the winner becomes the next god
of the world. Mirai has an angel in his
corner, but he may need to become a
devil to survive.

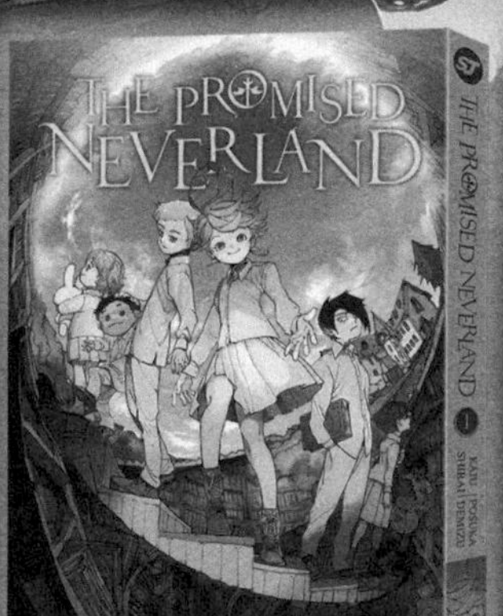

THE PROMISED NEVERLAND

STORY BY **KAIU SHIRAI**
ART BY **POSUKA DEMIZU**

Emma, Norman and Ray are the brightest kids
at the Grace Field House orphanage. And under
the care of the woman they refer to as "Mom,"
all the kids have enjoyed a comfortable life.
Good food, clean clothes and the perfect envi-
ronment to learn—what more could an orphan
ask for? One day, though, Emma and Norman
uncover the dark truth of the outside world
they are forbidden from seeing.

YOU'RE READING THE WRONG WAY

Record of Grancrest War reads from right to left, starting in the upper-right corner. Japanese is read from right to left, meaning that action, sound effects, and word-balloon order are completely reversed from English order.

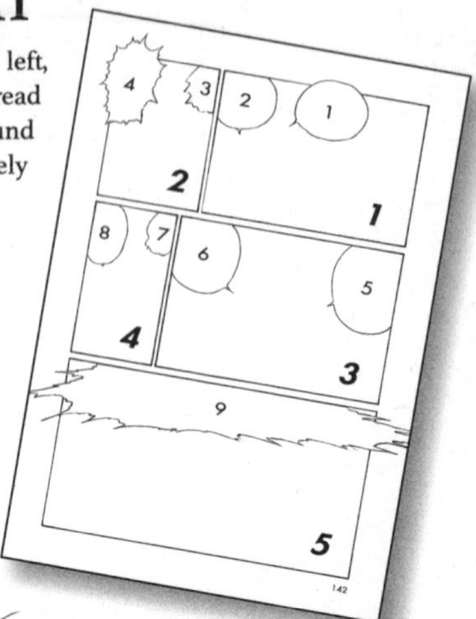

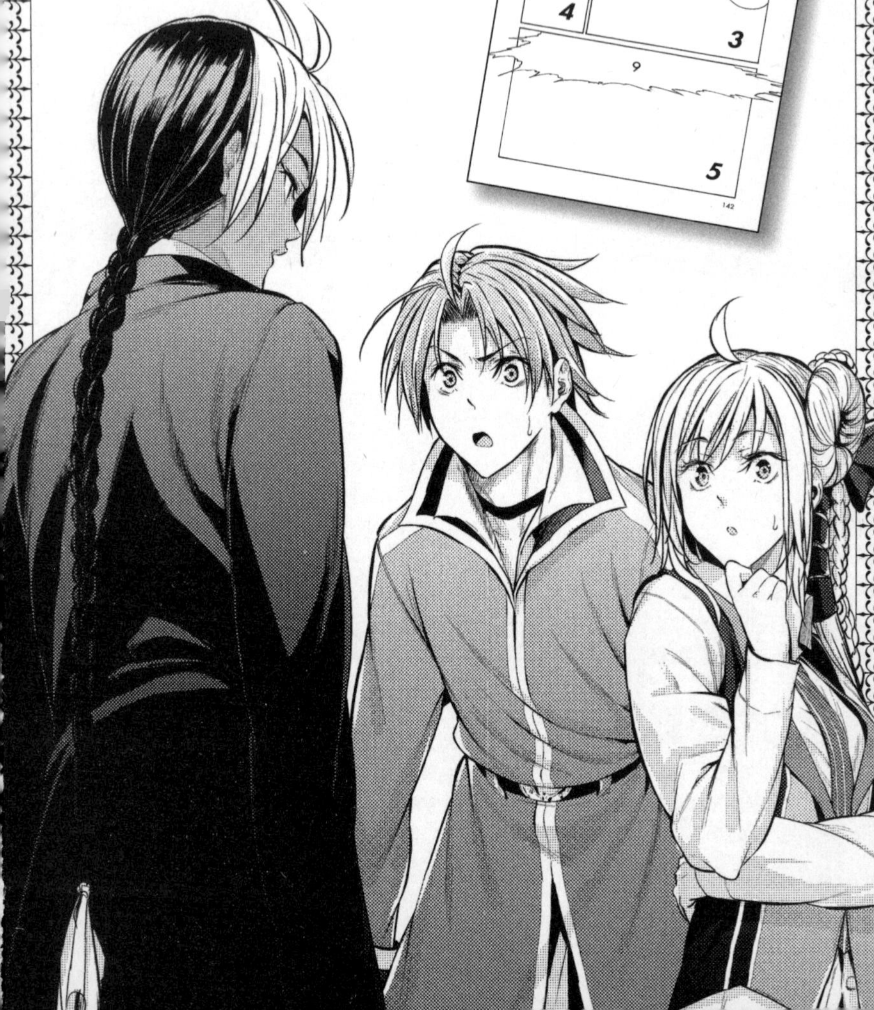